The Great Hangover

The
Great Hangover

—•—

21 TALES *of* THE NEW RECESSION

Edited by

GRAYDON CARTER

From the Pages of

VANITY FAIR

HARPER ● PERENNIAL

NEW YORK ● LONDON ● TORONTO ● SYDNEY ● NEW DELHI ● AUCKLAND

HARPER ● PERENNIAL

HarperCollins books may be purchased for educational, business, or
sales promotional use. For information, please write: Special Markets
Department, HarperCollins Publishers, 10 East 53rd Street, New
York, NY 10022.

FIRST EDITION

Library of Congress Cataloging-in-Publication data is available upon
request.

ISBN 978-0-06-196442-8

10 11 12 13 14   OV/RRD   10 9 8 7 6 5 4 3 2 1

Contents

Part Three: Beyond

Part Four: The Madoff Chronicles

Afterword: The Blame

The recent collapse of the stock market . . .

was a thoroughly democratic affair:

everybody was in it . . . Wall Street was

coincident with Main Street.

—David Cort, *VANITY FAIR*, January 1930

Where Did All the Billions Go?

By CULLEN MURPHY

There had been plenty of danger signs—there always are. Some lonely prophets, dismissed as Jeremiahs, had been pointing out for years that housing prices were preposterously inflated and inevitably unsustainable, and that America was again spiraling into "bubble" territory. Others had cast worried glances at a raft of new and risky Wall Street offerings—the securitized mortgage, the credit-default swap, the collateralized debt obligation. Their swift proliferation around the globe meant that trouble anywhere would spell trouble everywhere. Still others had pointed to a lack of regulation in the financial system. Existing rules had been eviscerated—the free market would regulate itself!—and no one had come up with new rules to govern the exotic new ways of doing business.

So there had been dark portents. But nothing prepared America or the world for the financial crisis that gathered momentum in the spring of 2008—symbolized by the sudden collapse of Bear Stearns—and that within a year saw the stock market plunge by 30 percent, home foreclosures rise to more than two million annually, and America and the entire global economy thrown into a tailspin from which it has yet to recover.

Economists and commentators nervously dusted off the word "depression," which for decades had been the province of psychiatry and pharmacology. Alan Greenspan, former chairman of the Federal Reserve Board and one of the pivotal contributors to the crisis, appeared before Congress and, with a lugubrious sheepishness that some interpreted as humility, admitted that there had been "a flaw" in his free-market worldview.

A character in Woody Allen's *Crimes and Misdemeanors* observes that "comedy is tragedy, plus time." The notion already feels antique. In a world of 24-7 news crawls and millions of frenetic bloggers, comedy and tragedy are now intermingled from the start. The human consequences of the financial crisis—the loss of homes and jobs, the disappearance of savings and pensions, the evaporation of trust in business and government, the disruption of countless lives—are beyond calculus. The elements of farce are no less real, as the machinations of Wall Street upend governments and turn the glitter of Greenwich and Southampton into dross.

This collection of articles from *Vanity Fair* is an attempt to capture the pitch and moment of the whole mess. Monthly-magazine journalism occupies a strategic middle ground between the headlong rush of headlines and the distant rumble of weighty scholarship. It can tell full, coherent stories in a way no newspaper can (and no expert will). It can also capture the immediacy of events while providing background context and considered judgment: history in the round—and on the fly.

The economic crisis—the Great Hangover—is the most important global story of recent times, and over the course of two years *Vanity Fair* has devoted an immense amount of reporting energy (and hundreds of pages) to covering it. It may be the most sustained journalistic endeavor in the magazine's history—and even the business press has taken note. As the Reuters financial blogger Felix Salmon recently observed, "*V.F.* has, improbably, become the home of the best financial journalism in the world of magazines."

Improbable, maybe—if you ignore the team of contributors that *V.F.* editor Graydon Carter has assigned to the task. It includes some of the most highly regarded writers about money and business in the country—people such as Michael Lewis, Bethany McLean, and Bryan Burrough. It includes renowned scholars, such as the historian Niall Ferguson and the

Nobel-laureate economist Joseph E. Stiglitz. It includes veteran political reporters (such as Todd S. Purdum), investigative sleuths (Donald L. Barlett
and James B. Steele), some *V.F.* newcomers (such as Mark Bowden), and a
cadre of longtime regulars (Bruce Feirstein, David Margolick, Nina Munk,
Mark Seal, Michael Shnayerson, and Vicky Ward).

The curtain rises in the spring of 2008. Gloom and anxiety grip Wall
Street, brought on by the collapse of the subprime-mortgage market
and the onset of a credit crisis. On an otherwise unremarkable Monday
morning in March a rumor begins to escalate on trading floors about a "liquidity problem" at a major investment bank. It is, writes Bryan Burrough
in his day-by-day (sometimes minute-by-minute) account of the sudden
disintegration of Bear Stearns, "the first tiny ripple in what within hours
would grow into a tidal wave of rumor and speculation" that within a week
will bring down the firm.

More implosions follow—first the mortgage financiers Fannie Mae
and Freddie Mac on September 7, then Lehman Brothers and the insurance giant A.I.G. a week later. The action shifts to Washington, where the
Treasury and the Federal Reserve (President Bush plays little apparent role)
scramble to stave off a meltdown, eventually provoking Congress to pass
a $700 billion bank-bailout bill. Don Barlett and Jim Steele describe the
scene in October when Treasury secretary Henry Paulson hands a single
sheet of paper to each of the "big nine" bankers and tells them to sign their
names and fill in the blank to indicate how many billions they want. That is
all it takes to start shoveling money out the door.

The crisis seeps everywhere—vertically, to the entire domestic economy, and horizontally, around the planet. Iceland, an economic mite, tries to
leverage itself into a muscle-flexing behemoth. Michael Lewis's case study
of the country's collapse—cash-strapped Icelanders begin torching their
Range Rovers for insurance money—is a tale that blends equal measures
of hubris and opéra bouffe. There's plenty of both to go around, surely. The
plunge in the stock market drags down even the mightiest endowments—
such as that of Harvard University, whose reversal of fortune is chronicled
by Nina Munk. Say what you will about Harvard, but its administrators
don't have to look up the word "Schadenfreude."

And then there is the Bernard Madoff scandal. It provides a narrative skein that epitomizes every aspect of the economic crisis: the sleepy regulators, the lubricious greed, and the mingled arrogance, idiocy, and criminality. Madoff remains in character all the way to the end, holding his annual holiday dinner for employees the night before admitting to F.B.I. agents that his business is "one big lie." *Vanity Fair*'s Mark Seal has the inside track from the start on Bernie Madoff and his manipulations, and Seal's stunning trifecta of articles serves as a self-contained play within a play—part Shakespeare, part Stoppard, part Miller.

The Great Hangover is the worst morning after we've endured in 70 years. We can be sure it won't be the last. In his now classic study, *Manias, Panics, and Crashes,* the economic historian Charles Kindleberger quotes a 19th-century British banker who described the economic history of mankind as an unhappy cycle: "quiescence, improvement, confidence, prosperity, excitement, overtrading, *CONVULSION,* pressure, stagnation, ending again in quiescence." As Kindleberger and others have observed, if one looks back over the long history of financial implosions—from the 17th-century Tulip Bubble to the 18th-century South Sea Bubble to the Crash of 1929—three constants stand out.

The first is the belief that good times will last forever and that speculative exuberance will never come to an end. Henry Paulson put it this way to *V.F.*'s Todd S. Purdum: "The investors all assume that prices will keep going up, and so they do things that don't seem foolish at the time, but in retrospect seem utterly ridiculous." (The problem with retrospect is that it never seems to arrive in time.) The second constant is fraud. Like a rapidly ebbing tide, the crisis swamps some vessels and strands others—and exposes rotting hulks to the light of day. The third constant is the onset of remorse: the public wailing, the donning of sackcloth, the fervent resolve to "go and sin no more"—something akin to that morning-after remorse following a night on the town.

As of this writing, there seem to be uncertain glimmers of recovery. The rate of job loss has slowed, the stock market is no longer plummeting, and some industries, such as construction, are showing signs of life. Meanwhile, voices in Washington, mindful that the U.S. taxpayer came to the rescue with a quarter-trillion-dollar bank bailout, are calling for a new round of regulation to curb Wall Street abuses and set the financial system on a sounder footing.

It remains to be seen whether those voices emanate from anyone with conviction or resolve. Already there are indications that the "go and sin no more" phase has come to an end. By the summer of 2009, the big financial institutions had put their hair shirts away. Goldman Sachs, suddenly flush with record profits, announced that in the first half of the year alone it had earmarked $11.4 billion for year-end bonuses. J. P. Morgan Chase announced that it would dispense even more—some $14.5 billion. Other institutions joined in. Then, in September, *The New York Times* reported that banks across the country were once again seeking inventive new products to bring to market—for instance, buying up life-insurance policies at a discount, from people needing cash *now,* and then securitizing those policies the way they did with those toxic subprime mortgages.

In 1720, as the dimensions of the South Sea Bubble were becoming clear, Lord Molesworth advanced the view in the British Parliament that the perpetrators should be treated the way the Romans treated a parricide: "They adjudged the guilty wretch to be sown in a sack, and thrown alive into the Tyber"—with a monkey and a snake sewn into the sack with him. That is barbaric, and hardly the American way. We'd have probably put the monkey and the snake in charge.

PART ONE

WALL STREET

· 1 ·

Bringing Down
Bear Stearns

By BRYAN BURROUGH

August 2008

O n Monday, March 10, Wall Street was tense, as it had been for
months. The mortgage market had crashed; major companies like
Citigroup and Merrill Lynch had written off billions of dollars in
bad loans. In what the economists called a "credit crisis," the big banks
were so spooked they had all but stopped lending money, a trend which, if it
continued, would spell disaster on 21st-century Wall Street, where trading
firms routinely borrow as much as 50 times the cash in their accounts to
trade complex financial instruments such as derivatives.

Still, as he drove in from his Connecticut home to the glass-sheathed
Midtown Manhattan headquarters of Bear Stearns, Sam Molinaro wasn't
expecting trouble. Molinaro, 50, Bear's popular chief financial officer,
thought he could spot the first rays of daylight at the end of nine solid
months of nonstop crisis. The nation's fifth-largest investment bank, known
for its notoriously freewheeling—some would say maverick—culture, Bear
had pledged to fork over more than $3 billion the previous summer to bail
out one of its two hedge funds that had bet heavily on subprime loans. At
the time, rumors flew it would go bankrupt. Bear's swashbuckling C.E.O.,

74-year-old Jimmy Cayne, pilloried as a detached figure who played bridge and rounds of golf while his firm was in crisis, had been ousted in January. His replacement, an easygoing 58-year-old investment banker named Alan Schwartz, was down at the Breakers resort in Palm Beach that morning, rubbing elbows with News Corp.'s Rupert Murdoch and Viacom's Sumner Redstone at Bear's annual media conference.

It was an uneventful morning—at first. Molinaro sat in his sixth-floor corner office, overlooking Madison Avenue, catching up on paperwork after a week-long trip visiting European investors. Then, around 11, something happened. Exactly what, no one knows to this day. But Bear's stock began to fall. It was then, questioning his trading desks downstairs, that Molinaro first heard the rumor: Bear was having liquidity troubles, Wall Street's way of saying the firm was running out of money. Molinaro made a face. This was crazy. There was no liquidity problem. Bear had about $18 billion in cash reserves.

Yet the whiff of gossip Molinaro heard that morning was the first tiny ripple in what within hours would grow into a tidal wave of rumor and speculation that would crash down upon Bear Stearns and, in the span of one fateful week, destroy a firm that had thrived on Wall Street since its founding, in 1923.

The fall of Bear Stearns wasn't just another financial collapse. There has never been anything on Wall Street to compare to it: a "run" on a major investment bank, caused in large part not by a criminal indictment or some mammoth quarterly loss but by rumor and innuendo that, as best one can tell, had little basis in fact. Bear had endured more than its share of self-inflicted wounds in the previous year, but there was no reason it had to die that week in March.

What happened? Was it death by natural causes, or was it, as some suspect, murder? More than a few veteran Wall Streeters believe an investigation by the Securities and Exchange Commission will uncover evidence that Bear was the victim of a gigantic "bear raid"—that is, a malicious attack brought by so-called short-sellers, the vultures of Wall Street, who make bets that a firm's stock will go down. It's a surprisingly difficult theory to prove, and nothing short of government subpoenas is likely to do it. Faced with a thicket of lawsuits and federal investigations, not a soul in Bear's boardroom will speak for the record, but on background, a few are finally ready to name names.

"I don't know of any firm, no matter the capital, that could have withstood that kind of bombardment by the shorts," says a vice-chairman of another major investment bank. "This was not about capital. It was about people losing confidence, spurred on by rumors fueled by people who had an interest in the fall of Bear Stearns."

He pauses to let the idea sink in. "If I had to pick the biggest financial crime ever perpetuated," he concludes, "I would say, 'Bear Stearns.'"

At Phi Kappa Wall Street, most of the frat boys are instantly recognizable. There's the big, backslapping Irishman, Merrill Lynch, the humorless grind, Goldman Sachs, and the straitlaced rich kid, Morgan Stanley. And then, off in the corner, wearing its beat-up leather jacket and nursing a cigarette, was the tough-guy loner, scrawny Bear Stearns, who disdained secret handshakes and towel snapping in favor of an extended middle finger toward pretty much everyone. Bear was bridge-and-tunnel and proud of it. Since the days when the Goldmans and Morgans cared mostly about hiring young men from the best families and schools, "the Bear," as old-timers still call it, cared about one thing and one thing only: making money. Brooklyn, Queens, or Poughkeepsie; City College, Hofstra, or Ohio State; Jew or Gentile—it didn't matter where you came from; if you could make money on the trading floor, Bear Stearns was the place for you. Its longtime chairman Alan "Ace" Greenberg even coined a name for his motley hires: P.S.D.'s, for poor, smart, and a deep desire to get rich.

Bear Stearns was an investment bank, but the traditional banking roles, such as advising on corporate mergers and trading stocks, were always an afterthought there. What the P.S.D.'s at Bear Stearns did best was trade bonds. The firm's executive history was the story of three bond traders, each with his own outsize personality. From the mid-1930s till the late 1970s, Bear was the province of Salim "Cy" Lewis, the cantankerous Wall Street legend who forged a cutthroat culture run less as a modern corporation than as a series of squabbling fiefdoms, each vying for his approval. Ace Greenberg, an avuncular sort who kept his desk on the trading floor and answered his own phone, took over after Lewis's death, in 1978, and while his edges were softer, Bear remained a Mametesque pressure cooker where top traders could pull down $10 million a year while runners-up were tossed into the alley.

The third man, the one who oversaw Bear's demise after nudging Greenberg aside in 1993, was his longtime protégé, Jimmy Cayne. Cayne was a cigar-chomping kid from Chicago's South Side, who in his early years sold scrap metal for his father-in-law. After a divorce, he found himself driving a New York taxi while pursuing his beloved pastime, playing bridge. It was at a bridge table, in fact, that Greenberg, himself an ardent player, met Cayne and lured him to Bear Stearns. "If you can sell scrap metal," Bear lore quotes Greenberg telling Cayne, "you can sell bonds." Cayne found his life's calling on the trading floor, earning his bones by moving huge numbers of New York municipal bonds during the city's financial crisis of the 1970s. He became the embodiment of Bear Stearns, a go-it-alone maverick who hunkered down in his smoke-filled sixth-floor office, not giving a rat's ass what Wall Street thought so long as Bear made money. When an early hedge fund, Long-Term Capital Management, collapsed in 1998, losing $4.6 billion and triggering fears of a global financial meltdown, Cayne famously refused to join the syndicate of Wall Street firms that bailed it out. Instead, while much of the Street reaped billions trading stocks during the booming 1990s, Cayne kept Bear focused on bonds and the grimier corners of Wall Street plumbing, clearing trades for just about anyone, however notorious their reputation.

Through it all, Bear remained proudly independent, refusing to sell out to larger firms. Cayne listened to lots of offers, especially after his pal Don Marron sold rival PaineWebber to U.B.S. for $12 billion, in 2000, but Cayne preferred life as it was. Senior managers had wide autonomy, and in good years Bear all but ran itself, allowing Cayne to spend weeks away from his desk at bridge tournaments or playing golf near his vacation home on the Jersey Shore. In recent years much of the oversight fell to Cayne's two co-presidents, Alan Schwartz, a onetime pitcher at Duke University who specialized in media mergers, and another bridge aficionado, a talented trader named Warren Spector. Bear continued to thrive, piling up record profits all through the 2000s, and Bear's stock price rose nearly 600 percent during Cayne's 14 years as C.E.O.

Eventually Bear, like most on Wall Street, branched into asset management, forming a series of large funds that put investor money to work in a variety of stocks, bonds, and derivatives. Unlike some firms, however, Bear promoted its own traders rather than outsiders to run these funds, and decided that each would specialize in a specific type of security, rather than a diversified mix. As co-president, Alan Schwartz, for one, questioned the move, thinking it was a bit risky, but deferred to the thinking of Spector and others.

Everything went swimmingly, in fact, until poor Ralph Cioffi ran into trouble.

Cioffi, 52, was a Bear lifer, a wisecracking salesman who commuted to Midtown from Tenafly, New Jersey, to oversee two hedge funds at Bear Stearns Asset Management, an affiliate known as B.S.A.M. His main fund, the High-Grade Structured Credit Strategies fund, plowed investor cash into complex derivatives backed by home mortgages. For years he was spectacularly profitable, posting average monthly gains of one percent or more. But as the housing market turned down in late 2006, his returns began to even out. Like many a Wall Street gambler before him, Cioffi decided to double-down, creating a second fund. Whereas the first borrowed, or "leveraged," as much as 35 times its available money to trade, the new fund would borrow an astounding 100 times its cash.

It blew up in his face. As the housing market worsened during the winter of 2006–7, Cioffi's returns for both funds plummeted. He urged investors to stay put, promising an imminent turnaround. (Cioffi and a colleague, Matthew Tannin, were indicted in June for misleading investors.) When the market downturn accelerated last spring, leaving Cioffi with billions of dollars in money-losing mortgage-backed securities no one would take off his hands, he concocted an audacious way to rescue himself, planning an initial offering for a new company called Everquest Financial that would sell its shares to the public. Everquest's main asset, it turned out, was billions of dollars of Cioffi's untradable securities, or, as Wall Street termed it, "toxic waste."

Foisting his garbage onto the public might have worked, but financial journalists at *BusinessWeek* and *The Wall Street Journal* discovered the scheme in early June. Once the truth was out, B.S.A.M. had no choice but to withdraw Everquest's offering, at which point Cioffi was all but doomed. Investors were beginning to flee. Worse, some of Cioffi's biggest lenders, firms like Merrill Lynch and J. P. Morgan Chase, were threatening to seize his collateral, which was about $1.2 billion. In a panic, Cioffi and his aides convened a meeting of creditors, where they asked for more time and more money. The gathering turned angry when several in the audience urged Bear to pony up its own money to save the funds, an alternative Bear executives dismissed out of hand.

Afterward, Warren Spector got on the phone with a series of Cioffi's lenders, including a group of J. P. Morgan executives. "I'll never forget this," one recalls. "Spector gets on and goes, 'You guys don't know what you're talking about—you don't understand the business; only [Cioffi and colleagues] understand the business; only we are standing in the way of them finishing this [rescue] deal.'" It was a classic display of Bear-style arrogance, and it incensed the Morgan men. Steve Black, Morgan's head of investment banking, telephoned Alan Schwartz and said, "This is bullshit. We're defaulting you."

Merrill Lynch, in fact, did confiscate Bear's collateral—an aggressive and highly unusual move that forced Cayne into the unthinkable: using Bear's own money, about $1.6 billion, to bail out one of Cioffi's two troubled funds, both of which ultimately filed for bankruptcy. It was a massive blow not only to Bear's capital base but to its reputation on Wall Street. Inside the firm, much of the blame fell squarely on Spector, who oversaw Cioffi and other B.S.A.M. managers. "Whenever someone raised a question, Warren would always say, 'Don't worry about Ralph—he'll be fine,'" one top Bear executive recalls. "Everybody assumed Warren knew what was going on. Well, later, after everything happened, Warren would say, 'Well, I never knew his actual positions.' It was one of those things where everyone thought someone else was paying attention."

As one of Bear's lenders told me, "The B.S.A.M. situation confirmed to me my impression, which was that [Bear's] subsidiary businesses were run in silos—basically the guys ran their sub-businesses as they saw fit. So long as they were hitting their P&L targets, no one asked any real questions. To my mind, that contributed in a very large part to what happened later."

For the rest of the summer of 2007, Bear was buffeted by rumors that the bailout might force it into bankruptcy, or worse. For the most part,

Cayne rode out the storm at the bridge table and his golf club, though by late July he began to sour on Spector. "Warren never showed any real remorse or contrition," says another Bear executive. "That just drove Jimmy mad." For three solid hours Alan Schwartz sat down with Cayne and argued against firing Spector, whom he genuinely liked, a conversation that ended when Cayne said of Spector, "Do you know he's never once said, 'I'm sorry'?" Schwartz replied, "That's kind of shocking."

Cayne forced Spector to resign on August 5. Bear Stearns had survived what many came to call a "near-death experience," but its troubles were only just beginning.

As summer turned to fall, mortgage-related losses hit scores of big banks just as they had Bear, yet Bear, for reasons that eluded Cayne and others, seemed to remain the poster boy for the credit crunch. Every story about other firms' losses seemed to carry a mention of Bear's, dredging up memories Bear executives would just as soon have buried. The perception of Bear's weakness put Cayne and Alan Schwartz in a bind. The bailout had blown a sizable hole in Bear's bottom line, and while the firm was in no immediate danger, everyone expected it would seek some kind of capital infusion.

Both Cayne and Schwartz, however, were deeply ambivalent about accepting a big chunk of money from another bank or private-equity fund. Cynics would later snipe that this was because Cayne didn't want to dilute his own substantial share of Bear's stock. In fact, it was more complicated. If they accepted outside help, Schwartz argued, they risked looking as if they needed it, which would only worsen the whispers about their financial health. In those early weeks of fall, Cayne and Schwartz engaged in a lengthy negotiation with private-equity veteran Henry Kravis in which he considered buying 20 percent of Bear's stock. The deal died, however, when Schwartz pointed out that Bear's own private-equity clients might not be thrilled to see Kravis on the board.

In the following months Cayne and Schwartz held a series of discussions with potential investors, at one point hiring a top investment banker, Gary Parr, of Lazard, to help out. There were discussions with private-equity investment company J. C. Flowers, a long set of talks with Jamie Dimon, J. P. Morgan Chase's C.E.O., who wasn't interested, and even a flirtation with legendary investor Warren Buffett that left Bear executives feeling Buffett was averse to risk. "Warren Buffett will only take nickels from dead people," one snipes. In the end, Cayne managed to arrange one deal: a strategic partnership with a leading Chinese securities firm, CITIC, which agreed to invest $1 billion in Bear in return for Bear's investing $1 billion with it. The market yawned.

Then, in November, came back-to-back body blows. On November 1, *The Wall Street Journal*, in a widely read front-page story, excoriated Cayne for his relaxed management style, portraying him as a bridge-crazy, pot-smoking Nero who fiddled while Bear burned. A few weeks later the firm was forced to disclose it would write down another $1.2 billion (which ended up being $1.9 billion) in mortgage-related securities and post the first quarterly loss in its history. The stock went into a prolonged dive—down 40 percent for the year. By January many executives were openly calling for Cayne's head. A few slipped into Schwartz's 42nd-floor office with an ultimatum: if Cayne wasn't gone by the time bonuses were paid in late January, they would leave. Schwartz was conflicted. He loved Cayne, but he couldn't afford to lose a group of top people, not at this point. He canvassed Bear's board, found them open to a change, then broke the news to Cayne himself. To Schwartz's surprise, Cayne took the news peacefully. He resigned as C.E.O. on January 8, but remained chairman of the board.

Schwartz was named the new C.E.O. His immediate priority was making sure Bear posted a profit in its current quarter, which ended February 29. There were still whispers out there about Bear's financial health, many fanned by rumors of federal investigations into the hedge-fund collapse, and Schwartz badly needed some good news to report. As mortgage-related losses struck firm after firm that winter, Schwartz kept his fingers crossed, watching the calendar tick off the days until February's end. He sweated out an entire extra day—leap day, February 29—but Bear made it. Preliminary figures showed they would report a quarterly profit of $1.10 or so a share. With luck, Schwartz said, that would end the whispers.

Nevertheless, by Wednesday, March 5, Schwartz wasn't breathing any easier. The rumors continued, faint but insistent, now fueled by the troubles at a trio of hedge funds, Carlyle Capital, Peloton Partners, and Thornburg Mortgage. At a weekly risk-assessment meeting that day, Schwartz queried his people about Bear's exposure to the three funds, all of which were thought near collapse. Bear had lent to all three. Still, Bear's risk, Schwartz was told, was believed to be minimal.

The next day, Thursday, Schwartz flew to Palm Beach, where the firm's annual media conference was poised to start the following Monday at the Breakers hotel. The conference, one of Bear's best-attended events, brought together a host of media titans, many of them Schwartz's longtime clients: Murdoch, Redstone, Viacom's Philippe Dauman, Time Warner's Jeff Bewkes, Disney's Robert Iger. On Friday, while checking in with head-quarters, Schwartz heard the rumors again, now a bit stronger: Bear was having liquidity problems. He trained his eye on a key auction of municipal bonds that Friday afternoon. Bear was providing $2 billion in liquidity to various buyers. "That was the trip wire," another Bear executive recalls. "If anyone refused to take our name there, we knew we were in real trouble." All through the afternoon and into the evening, Schwartz monitored the note sales. To his relief, they went off without a hitch.

The storm struck full force without warning on Monday. That morning, when Sam Molinaro returned to his sixth-floor corner office from a week-long trip in Europe, he expected a normal day, nothing special; they would release the new, positive earnings the following week. After the trading day opened, at 9:30, one of the rating agencies, Moody's, downgraded another grouping of Bear's bonds. It was to be expected; the agency had been downgrading most of its offerings. Then, around 11, Bear's stock suddenly began to fall, gradually at first, then sharply. All the "financials"—Lehman, Merrill, Citi—were falling. Molinaro shrugged. But as he checked with the trading floor, he heard the rumors: Bear was having liquidity problems. Molinaro rolled his eyes. Not again.

Bear's P.R. man, Russell Sherman, heard the rumors, too. As the stock continued to slide, Sherman began calling reporters, trying in vain to pin down their source. As he did, Molinaro checked to see what could be fueling the rumor. Bear itself had no liquidity problem—he knew that. That morning the firm sat atop $18 billion in cash reserves. Molinaro checked with his finance desk, the repo desk, his treasurer. Had anyone heard of anything like a margin call (in which a lender was demanding a huge chunk of cash back)? A trade gone bad? Was anything out of the ordinary? "Across the board, it was 'No, no, no, no—no problems,' " a Bear executive says.

At one point, Schwartz called in from Palm Beach to assess the situation. "I'm getting a little nervous," he said. Molinaro assured him there was no substance to the rumor.

At that point the rumor went public—on CNBC, the cable network that serves as Wall Street's daily backdrop. On every trading floor dozens of TV sets, mounted high on the walls, are perpetually tuned to the network, which runs nothing but shows about finance and money—from *Squawk Box* to *Closing Bell* to Jim Cramer's *Mad Money*.

By noon, when CNBC anchor Bill Griffeth opened *Power Lunch*, Bear's stock was down more than $7, to $63. "There are rumors out there that some unnamed Wall Street firm might be having liquidity problems," Griffeth noted. A correspondent on the show, Dennis Kneale, a veteran of *The Wall Street Journal*, said, "The speculation at this point is that it's Bear Stearns. They're down the most in the market today. Supposedly, a couple of weeks ago, they started looking at a way to try to shop their clearing operations. . . . [They] couldn't find a buyer. At least that's what one guy says."

At Bear Stearns, 80-year-old Ace Greenberg was already pelting senior officials with phone calls, demanding that someone go public to rebut the rumor. "Ace was kind of freaking out that morning," one senior Bear executive says with a sigh. "He just couldn't contain himself."

A few minutes past 12, another CNBC correspondent, Michelle Caruso-Cabrera, reached Greenberg at Bear. He told her the rumor was "totally ridiculous." CNBC reported his comments within minutes, then incorporated them into a running headline—BEAR STEARNS' ACE GREENBERG TELLS CNBC LIQUIDITY RUMORS ARE "TOTALLY RIDICULOUS"—the rest of the hour. In his office, Molinaro saw the headline and fumed. Addressing the rumor at this stage, he and others felt, merely appeared to legitimize it.

From Palm Beach, Schwartz telephoned Greenberg in frustration. "Ace, you can't just do that!" he said.

"Well, I had to!" Greenberg replied.

Once the CNBC headline began running, reporters began calling Russell Sherman's office. Sherman told the Bloomberg reporter the rumor was untrue, but Bear's stock was going crazy. The total volume was over 50 million shares; on a normal day it might trade 7 million.

At a little after one CNBC correspondent Charlie Gasparino, an especially aggressive reporter who for months had been suggesting Bear's possible indictment on criminal charges in the hedge-fund collapse, joined an on-air roundtable to discuss the rumor. Gasparino was the bane of Bear Stearns; more than once he had predicted that the firm would go under. "I don't believe there is a liquidity problem at Bear Stearns," Gasparino said on-air. "Bear Stearns has a problem with whether they should exist or not in the future in this sense. . . . What do they have left? A clearing business, a second-rate investment bank?" If the credit crisis continued, Gasparino said a few moments later, "I don't see how they could survive independently. They don't have enough horses out there."

Sitting on a stool beside him, Bill Griffeth appeared startled at the strength of the statement.

"You're on record, then," he remarked.

Gasparino laughed. "Wouldn't be the first time I was wrong," he said.

At Bear Stearns, no one was laughing. Publicly speculating on a firm's liquidity is akin to shouting "Fire!!!" in a crowded theater; in catastrophic cases it can trigger panic selling. It risks, in other words, becoming a self-fulfilling prophecy.

For the next hour the Bear Stearns rumor became a topic of conversation between CNBC correspondents and various market traders and analysts. At 1:50, Matthew Cheslock remarked, "The sentiment [on Bear] is pretty negative. The general consensus is 'Where there's smoke, there's fire.'"

A few minutes later, Griffeth, perhaps sensing the network might have gone a bit too far, asked Dennis Kneale, "What about the jittery nature of this market right now? Are we starting to believe some rumors that may or may not be true?" Kneale agreed. "Someone," he observed, "is always making money on the other side of that bad news or that rumor."

Yet CNBC's coverage remained anything but skeptical of the rumor. At two the network's new "money honey," Erin Burnett, headlined the hour by announcing "credit issues at Bear," never mind that there was no such thing. She turned to correspondent David Faber, who observed, "Of course, no firm's ever going to say that they are having trouble with liquidity, and, in fact, you've either got liquidity or you don't. So if you don't have it, you're done. Those are the kinds of concerns in this market, concerns of confidence. . . . You can have crises of confidence, causing meltdowns."

At 2:07 came shocking news: the first mention that New York governor Eliot Spitzer had had dealings with a prostitution ring. That news shoved Bear Stearns out of CNBC's headlines, much to the relief of the firm's executives. At day's end, Sherman issued a formal statement denying any liquidity problems. On Monday night, Schwartz and Molinaro held their breaths, hoping the worst was over.

In fact, it had just started.

Tuesday morning the Federal Reserve announced a novel new securities lending program for major Wall Street firms to help them weather the credit crisis. Most financial stocks rebounded, but not Bear. After lunch, Gasparino went on-air and said the Fed initiative was being interpreted as an effort to save one firm—Bear. By early afternoon the rumors were once again flying, now stronger than ever.

The first to pull their money from Bear were several major hedge funds. So Molinaro and his men canvassed the repo lenders, which give banks billions of dollars in overnight loans that have to be renewed each day. However, Molinaro found that all planned to "roll over" Bear's loans the next morning. "Nobody was cutting us off," says a Bear executive involved in the events. "There was a lot of chatter, though. The hedge funds were agitated. That was concerning, because they could influence the outcome by pulling out cash balances."

That same day Bear executives noticed a worrisome development whose potential significance they would not appreciate for weeks. It involved an avalanche of what are called "novation" requests. When a firm wants to rid itself of a contract that carries credit risk with another firm, in this case Bear Stearns, it can either sell the contract back to Bear or, in a novation request, to a third firm for a fee. By Tuesday afternoon, three big Wall Street companies—Goldman Sachs, Credit Suisse, and Deutsche Bank—were experiencing a torrent of novation requests for Bear instruments. Alan Schwartz thought it strange that so many requests were being channeled to the same three firms, but did his best to assure them all that Bear remained on sound footing. "Deutsche Bank we talked to, and they said, 'We're getting killed!' " says a Bear executive. "We said, 'We'll take you out of your positions,' and we did. But it was too late."

Too late—because, before Bear could calm the waters, executives at both Goldman and Credit Suisse told their traders to hold up all novation requests dealing with Bear Stearns, pending approval by their credit departments. The Credit Suisse memo, a "blast" e-mail to much of its trading staff, quickly became the subject of widespread rumor and gossip. Both memos were essentially routine, a way to handle the deluge of novation requests rather than comments on Bear's viability, but they nevertheless served as the first concrete sign that some of Wall Street's biggest firms were having concerns about doing business with Bear.

S am Molinaro felt it was time for another public assurance. CNBC's Charlie Gasparino had been peppering him with phone calls seeking comment. Molinaro talked to Russell Sherman, who felt Gasparino could be played. "He'll say something negative if you shut him out. But if you talk to him, he'll go positive," one Bear executive told me.

Around three, Molinaro spoke to Gasparino, telling him, "I've spent all day trying to track down the source of the rumors, but they are false. There is no liquidity crisis. No margin calls. It's all nonsense." Gasparino's on-air comments were mild, but for the first time he raised the specter of a nightmare scenario: "They are really worried about this inside [Bear], that these rumors are taking a very nasty turn, and they might cause a run on the bank."

Still, by day's end, there was no rush among Bear's lenders to withdraw cash from the firm. At that point, this executive says, "the notion of a liquidity crisis seemed silly."

That night Schwartz, Molinaro, and others discussed what to do. The talks centered on whether Schwartz should go public in an interview with CNBC. "We debated putting Alan on the air a long time," says one board member. "Yes, it might draw attention to the rumors. But it would definitely answer the questions. Our view was: we had to get him out."

Schwartz, though, wanted some assurances first. From experience, he knew he faced a risk in picking the wrong CNBC correspondent for the interview. All the network's talent—Gasparino, Maria Bartiromo,

Faber, Larry Kudlow—had requested the interview, and whoever didn't get it, Schwartz feared, might retaliate on the air. "Each of these correspondents has his own producer, and they all seem to hate each other," one Bear executive told me. "If you choose Faber, you know Bartiromo will bash you the next day." Schwartz directed Russell Sherman to identify the CNBC executive who supervised the correspondents, explain the situation, and ask that the correspondents who didn't get the interview refrain from attacks. Sherman, however, couldn't identify a single CNBC executive who seemed to have control over the correspondents. "Everyone on Wall Street knows the joke," says another Bear executive involved in the discussions. "At CNBC, there is simply no adult supervision."

In the end they chose the safest of the lot, Faber. Wednesday morning, all across Manhattan, Wall Street traders crowded around their monitors to see what Schwartz had to say. More than a few shook their heads that the Bear C.E.O. was not in his office, grappling with the emerging crisis, but in, of all places, Palm Beach! As a senior executive of one competing firm put it, "To come on CNBC from Palm Beach and, you know, tell everyone everything was going to be O.K., they had to be crazy." (Schwartz was worried that an abrupt departure from his conference might raise even more questions.)

Faber's first question was a bombshell. He told Schwartz he had direct knowledge of a trader—a single trader—whose credit department had held up a trade with Bear Stearns, citing concerns about its health. At Bear, many executives gasped. It was a killer statement: Faber was saying, in essence, that Bear's status as a trader, the basis of its business, was in question. Schwartz answered as best he could, saying everything was fine; only later did Faber say on-air the trade in question had finally gone through. But the damage had been done.

"You knew right at that moment that Bear Stearns was dead, right at the moment he asked that question," a Wall Street trader of 40 years told me. "Once you raise that idea, that the firm can't follow through on a trade, it's over. Faber killed him. He just killed him."

At Bear Stearns, however, the sentiment on the sixth floor was that Schwartz had done a good job. The interview did nothing, however, to stop the rumors. When Schwartz returned to his office that afternoon, he tried calling customers, but nothing he did could stem the tide. By the end of the trading day, the first repo lenders had warned Molinaro they would not renew their loans the next morning.

"The tone of Wednesday afternoon was not positive—three days of rumors were starting to take their toll," says a senior Bear executive. Mostly because of hedge-fund withdrawals, the firm's reserves had shrunk to less than $15 billion. That evening, meeting in Molinaro's conference room, the chief financial officer told Schwartz they could probably replace those reserves the following day. If the repo lenders began backing out, though, they were in serious trouble. Schwartz had a longstanding emergency plan in place, involving the sale of Bear assets, and for the first time Molinaro pulled it out and began studying it in earnest. Schwartz, meanwhile, got on the phone to Gary Parr at Lazard. They agreed to meet the next day. Late that night a Bear lawyer telephoned Tim Geithner, president of the New York Federal Reserve. He briefed him on Bear's plight and urged him to have the Fed accelerate its plan to provide liquidity to the market.

The next morning, on his drive in from Connecticut, Molinaro began calling the repo and finance desks to check the tone of their early calls. The *Journal* had a story suggesting that any number of Bear's lenders, including the all-important repo lenders, were growing nervous. Still, those first calls went as well as could be hoped. Other firms were still trading with Bear. Few of the repo lenders were talking about refusing to roll over their daily loans. "Thursday morning, things looked good," says one Bear executive.

Then, just as they had the day before, the rumors began to multiply— and with them the withdrawals. One by one, repo lenders began to warn Molinaro and his people they would not renew Bear's overnight loans the next morning. By midafternoon the dam was breaking. As word spread of the repo withdrawals, still more repo lenders turned tail. The hedge-fund cash was almost all gone. "A lot of people were pulling out," one Bear executive remembers. "The nail in the coffin was the repo capacity."

Molinaro and Robert Upton, Bear's treasurer, ended the day toting up the withdrawals. By five, Molinaro could see his worst fears had been realized. He picked up the phone and called Schwartz in his 42nd-floor office. "You need to get down here," he said.

The numbers, scribbled out on a yellow legal pad, told the story. Standing in Molinaro's conference room, Schwartz listened as Robert Upton guided them through the wreckage. A full $30 billion or so of repo loans would not be rolled over the next morning. They might be able to replace maybe half that in the next day's market, but that would still leave Bear $15 billion short of what it needed to make it through the day. By seven it was obvious they had only two options: an emergency cash infusion or a bankruptcy filing the next day. The one thing everyone agreed upon was the need for secrecy. "If word gets out, it might be the end," one participant recalls saying.

Schwartz was stricken. He had genuinely thought they would make it. By early evening, realizing that Bear's life expectancy might now be numbered not in days but hours, he hit the phones. The regulators—the S.E.C., Treasury, the Fed—had been watching the situation all day and were waiting when he called to brief them. Gary Parr, the Lazard banker, had already touched base with J. P. Morgan's C.E.O., Jamie Dimon, that afternoon, letting him know where Bear stood. J. P. Morgan was the obvious candidate for overnight cash. The two firms had long-standing ties. Their headquarters faced each other across 47th Street.

That day was Dimon's 52nd birthday, and he was celebrating with a quiet family dinner at Avra, a Greek restaurant on East 48th Street. He was irked when his private cell phone rang; it was to be used only in emergencies. On the line was Parr, who put Schwartz on as Dimon stepped outside onto the sidewalk. Schwartz quickly explained the depth of Bear's plight and said, "We really need help."

Still irked, Dimon said, "How much?"

"As much as 30 billion," Schwartz said.

"Alan, I can't do that," Dimon said. "It's too much."

"Well, could you guys buy us overnight?"

"I can't—that's impossible," Dimon replied. "There's no time to do the homework. We don't know the issues. I've got a board."

The people he should call, Dimon said, were at the Fed and the

Treasury—the only place Bear could get $30 billion overnight. Still, Dimon promised to see what he could do to help. He hung up and dialed Tim Geithner at the New York Fed downtown.

Twenty-first-century Wall Street is a highly interconnected world, with just about everyone lending billions of dollars to everyone else, and Geithner worried that Bear's collapse might trigger a domino effect, taking down scores of other firms around the world; he urged Dimon in the strongest terms to think about somehow helping Bear. "Tim, look, we can't do it alone," Dimon said. "Just do something to get them to the weekend. Then you'll have some time."

Dimon hung up, reluctantly realizing Morgan was in this, like it or not. He knew everyone involved would push Morgan to consider buying Bear, but while there were certain of its businesses he coveted—prime brokerage, energy, correspondent banking—he wasn't thrilled at the prospect of taking aboard its massive mortgage-related problems. Still, in short order, he dispatched a credit team of a half-dozen traders to Bear to begin looking at its books. Then he realized he had a problem.

I t was Steve Black, his investment-banking chief. The Morgan man who probably knew Bear best, Black was on a family vacation on the Caribbean island of Anguilla. That evening, in fact, Black was looking forward to three days of peace and quiet with his wife, Debbie. At her insistence, he had left his cell phone at the hotel when they went for a late dinner at a beachside restaurant. Midway through their meal, Black looked up and saw a man marching toward the table.

"Oh, shit," Black said under his breath.

"Are you Mr. Black?" the man asked. When Black nodded, the man said, "I have an emergency call from your hotel."

Black told the hotel to have Dimon call him at the restaurant. He was waiting in its bustling kitchen when the phone rang. "It's for me," he told a cook. By nine Black was back in his hotel, orchestrating the teams beginning to study Bear's situation. A Morgan jet would arrive in the morning to ferry him back to New York.

The first team of Morgan executives reached Bear's sixth-floor executive suite around 11 that night. It didn't take long for them to realize the danger in what they were being asked to do. If Dimon lent Bear $15 billion or so and the firm imploded the next day, they could lose it all. A little after midnight Dimon told Schwartz in a phone call, "We've got to get the Fed in on this."

Downtown, Tim Geithner was waiting when Dimon telephoned. Any bailout, Dimon reiterated, was too big, too risky, for Morgan to handle alone. Both men knew that meant only one thing: somehow Bear had to be given access to the Fed "window," that is, the spigot of cash that was available to the nation's commercial banks, but not its investment banks. The only way for the Fed to help, to give Bear access to the "window," was to lend Morgan the money, allowing the bank to act as a bridge across which the Fed cash could stream into Bear's vaults.

Geithner, quickly grasping the wisdom of the move, got on the phone with Washington, going through the details with the Fed's chairman, Ben Bernanke, and the Treasury secretary, Hank Paulson, and his counterparts at the S.E.C. If they could just get Bear through the next day, perhaps a bigger and better deal could be forged over the weekend. By two A.M. teams from the Fed and the S.E.C. had joined the Morgan bankers at Bear, poring over the numbers. In Molinaro's conference room, Schwartz and Molinaro paced, occasionally taking bites of cold pizza; their fate, they now realized, was largely out of their hands.

By four A.M. the outlines of a deal were taking shape. Morgan would give Bear a credit line; the money would come from the Fed. It took three more hours for the details to be pounded out. At the last minute Morgan's general counsel, Stephen Cutler, inserted a line into the press release stating the credit line would be good for up to 28 days.

At Bear, Schwartz and Molinaro allowed themselves a few nervous smiles. They were saved—for 28 days. "We all thought this was a huge win," remembers one Bear executive. "We were all pretty pleased, thinking we had averted our potential deaths."

They wouldn't be so sanguine for long.

When the markets opened Friday morning, traders greeted the news from Bear with surprise but not, at least initially, with panic. For the first hour or so of trading, the stock remained where it had been the day before, in the low 60s. In Anguilla, Steve Black furrowed his brow. "This is nuts," he remarked to his wife as they headed for the airport. "No one understands what happened here. This stock should be half that." By the time the Blacks arrived at the airport, it was.

By four o'clock the firm's capital reserves, which had been $17 billion that Monday, had dwindled to almost nothing. "The balances leaving was a flood," remembers one Bear executive. "By Friday afternoon we couldn't even keep track of the money going out. Friday afternoon, I have to say, caught everyone by surprise. Because Friday morning we thought we had bought some 'stop, look, and listen' time."

Gary Parr, meanwhile, was already on the phones, canvassing every prospective rescuer he could think of. Just about anything was on the table: a merger, a sale of prime brokerage or other valuable assets, even an outright sale of Bear itself. The only way to stop the run, everyone knew, was to find what Parr kept calling a "validating investor"—a big name, hopefully with big money, who would send a message that Bear was still solid. Warren Buffett, with his unmatched reputation for identifying value, was the ideal solution. "If Buffett had put in a hundred dollars, that would've been enough," says one person involved that day. "That would have sent the message." But there was no rush, at least not at first.

Around six Schwartz slipped into the back of a black town car for the drive home to Greenwich. Somehow Bear was still alive, if barely. Thanks to the Morgan credit line, they could probably open on Monday. Now he had 28 days—28 days to raise new capital, find a merger partner, or sell Bear outright. It wouldn't be easy, he knew, but it was doable. Then, as the car cruised northeast, Schwartz's phone rang. It was Tim Geithner of the Fed, with the Treasury secretary, Hank Paulson.

Paulson came right to the point. "You'll recall I told you when we cut this facility [that] your fate was no longer in your hands," he told Schwartz. "Well, we don't plan on being here on Sunday night like we were last night. You've got the weekend to do a deal with J. P. Morgan or anyone else you can find. But if you're not done by Monday, we're pulling the plug." And, like that, Bear's 28-day cushion evaporated. The Fed's credit line was good only till Sunday night.

Schwartz hung up the phone, stunned. He telephoned Molinaro, who was also on his way home, at that moment buying a cup of coffee at a rest stop on the Merritt Parkway. "You've got to be kidding me," Molinaro said.

To this day, top Bear officials aren't sure whether they misread the "28-day" language or whether Paulson simply had a change of heart after the events of Friday afternoon. "Everyone thought we had 28 days," says one senior Bear executive. "Do we think they thought that? We think so. But, look, when this was done, we just got a piece of paper that said, 'If you agree to this, you'll be O.K.' We signed. No one spent a lot of time going over all the little details."

In fact, no one—not even Federal Reserve officials—had been sure what the credit line or the "28-day" mention actually meant. "They took hope in that language," says a Fed official. "I don't know why they did. We made it very clear at the time, 'This is not the be-all end-all.' Then again, this whole thing was done so fast. We didn't think through all the details of what would happen next."

When Schwartz returned to his office Saturday morning, one of his first calls was to Geithner. He appealed for more time, explaining that Bear thought it had 28 days. Geithner held firm. Sunday night, he repeated. By that point, representatives of prospective suitors were already streaming through Bear's hallways, poring over financial documents. Their efforts switched into overdrive as word spread of the Sunday deadline. A team from Flowers was there, a team representing Henry Kravis, plus another half-dozen or so groups from major banks. J. P. Morgan alone had 16 different teams meeting with all of Schwartz's top people.

It was a sobering process: as the day wore on, the bidders began dropping out, one by one. Everyone had an excuse: they didn't have the time or the money or the balls to do such a risky deal in so short a time. The two best possibilities, it appeared, were Morgan and Flowers. The latter told Parr on Saturday afternoon it was prepared to buy 90 percent of Bear for about $30 billion, or $28 a share—that is, if it could scrape up $20 billion from a bank consortium by the next day. No one thought Flowers could possibly get such a deal done in time.

From the outset, Schwartz assumed Morgan was the bridegroom. Across the street, in Morgan's eighth-floor executive suite, Jamie Dimon and Steve Black fielded nonstop reports from their due-diligence teams, now numbering more than 300 people. The key, everyone knew, was Bear's mortgage "book," that is, its inventory of mortgage-backed securities. Much of it was illiquid—it couldn't be sold. How to value these Rube Goldberg devices was anyone's guess. The more Black studied Bear's book, the more worried he grew. He and another Morgan executive, Doug Braunstein, got on the phone with Schwartz and Parr that night and told them that, if Morgan did bid, it wouldn't be much.

Bear's stock had closed Friday at $32. "The fact you're at 32 doesn't mean much at this point," Black said. He suggested that a Morgan bid might be in the range of $8 to $12 a share. "We said, 'That's all there is, and that's with a lack of due diligence and a lot of other issues,'" says a person involved in the call. "Alan asked, 'Will you do it come hell or high water?' That was their key issue."

At nightfall everyone hunkered down for long hours studying Bear's numbers, especially its mortgage book. By dawn, however, many Morgan executives were having second thoughts. The more they studied the securities Bear owned, the worse it looked. Bear, for instance, had initially estimated it had $120 billion in so-called risk-weighted assets, those that might go bad. By Sunday morning, Morgan executives felt the actual number was closer to $220 billion.

"We all kind of slept on it," says one executive involved in the talks, "or not slept on it, kind of closed our eyes for a half-hour, and realized that if you take a step back and remove yourself from the enormity of it, what we were being asked to take over, from a risk factor, was gargantuan." And it wasn't just the financial risk. The morning's *New York Times* carried a piece on Bear, by veteran reporter Gretchen Morgenson, that dredged through all the seamiest aspects of Bear's recent history. Steve Black walked around the eighth floor making sure everyone read it. "That article certainly had an impact on my thinking," remembers one Morgan executive. "Just the reputational aspects of it, getting into bed with these people." He shudders.

Dimon had to agree. It was just too much. Steve Black broke the news to Schwartz. "Whatever other things you are working on, you should actively pursue them," he said. Downtown, at the Fed, Tim Geithner stepped out of his conference room to hear the news from Dimon. "I remember he came back in a minute later, with this look on his face that said, 'Huh?'" recalls a member of the Fed team.

"They're not going to do it," Geithner said.

Geithner believed he couldn't let Bear die. The repercussions were unthinkable. "For the first time in history the entire world was looking at the failure of a major financial institution that could lead to a run on the entire world financial system," a Fed official recalls. "It was clear we couldn't let that happen."

Within minutes Geithner was back on the phone with Dimon. There ensued a series of conversations where, in one Fed official's words, "they kept saying, 'We're not going to do it,' and we kept saying, 'We really think you should do it.' This went on for hours. Finally, [the conversation] shifted to 'Well, maybe if.' They kept saying, 'We can't do this on our own.'" All through these talks, Geithner kept a nervous eye on the clock. The Australian markets opened at six on Sunday evening, New York time. They had to have some kind of deal by then or risk chaos.

Geithner had several long conversations with Ben Bernanke and Hank Paulson. There was never any serious question whether the Fed would help out. Even though it had never attempted anything like this before, there was ample precedent for the move; both the German and British central banks had stepped up to rescue institutions laid low by the mortgage crisis in just the last year. Still, the details took hours to unspool. At one point, Paulson had to sign a document confirming that, yes, in the event Bear defaulted on its securities, the American taxpayer would pay the tab.

Meanwhile, at Bear, Alan Schwartz, now merely a spectator at his firm's funeral, watched the clock. By one, Bear's board was in session, many of its members, including Jimmy Cayne, present by phone; Cayne was in Detroit at a bridge tournament. At one point, Schwartz took a call from Morgan executives, who told him that any bid was likely to be less than the $8-to-$12 range mentioned the night before. In fact, they suggested the likely number was $4.

When Schwartz relayed the $4 idea to his board, several, including Cayne, grew apoplectic. Cayne argued strenuously that Bear simply file for bankruptcy. "There were a lot of people at that point who were just saying, 'Fuck 'em—let's go 11,'" remembers one person in the boardroom. It was then that Gary Parr and the bankruptcy attorneys patiently explained that bankruptcy was actually not an option, not for a major securities firm.

Changes to the bankruptcy code in 2005 would force federal regulators to take over customer accounts. All its securities would be subject to immediate seizure by creditors.

Slowly, the humiliating inevitability of a $4-a-share buyout—for a firm whose shares had traded as high as $170 the year before—sank in. It was at that point, midafternoon, that Treasury secretary Paulson twisted the knife. As the ranking politician involved in the deal, he was concerned with appearances—both how it would look that the federal government was bailing out a well-heeled investment bank at a time when normal Americans were losing their homes, and the appearance of something lawyers call "moral hazard," that is, the idea that a Bear deal, by appearing to "save" a bank whose poor judgment had pushed it to the brink of bankruptcy, might actually encourage risky behavior by other financial institutions. This deal, Paulson judged, had to hurt Bear. And it had to hurt badly.

Paulson and Tim Geithner telephoned Dimon at Morgan. He put them on speaker. Dimon said he was considering a price in the $4-to-$5 range. "That sounds high to me," Paulson said. "I think this should be done at a very low price." A little later, Morgan's Doug Braunstein reached Gary Parr at Bear. A formal offer would be forthcoming, Braunstein said. "The number's $2," he said.

Parr nearly choked. "You can't mean that," he said.

He did. Schwartz took the news quietly, which was more than one could say about some of his board members. Jimmy Cayne—whose 5.66 million shares, once worth more than a billion, would now be worth less than $12 million—swore he would never accept such a humiliating offer. "The people around the table, some of them, their net worth was being wiped out," says one person who was in the room. "There was every emotion you can think of: sadness, anger. They saw the tragedy. But the bottom line was, you know, when they got in a pickle, Bear Stearns didn't have many friends."

Schwartz took a half-hour explaining that the board really had no choice. It was Morgan or bankruptcy, which would mean liquidation, putting 14,000 employees out of work by noon the next day. "What can I say?" he said at one point. "It's better than nothing."

And like that, with the signatures on an unprecedented merger agreement, a major American investment bank vanished, along with $29 billion in shareholder value and the secure futures of 14,000 employees. In the following days the hallways of Bear Stearns & Co. erupted in rage. Longtime friends fumed and even screamed in Schwartz's face; at a town-hall meeting he chaired, where one man hollered, "This is rape!"; in the hallway outside his office; even in the Bear gym. Shareholders were so angry that everyone was forced back to the negotiating table the next weekend, when Morgan and the Fed, in a second set of manic around-the-clock meetings, agreed to boost the price to $10 a share. Yet, for all the anger, all the frustration, no one could answer the one question on everyone's mind: How on earth had this happened?

Even among the circle of top executives who lived through that frantic week, no two people see the crisis at Bear the same way. Many, though, agree with some version of the scenario Alan Schwartz has come to believe. Yes, Schwartz tells friends, mistakes were made. Yes, the firm was financially weakened. But the more he learned about what had happened behind the scenes that week, the more Schwartz came to believe that Bear's collapse was a pre-meditated attack orchestrated by market speculators who stood to profit from its demise. According to those Schwartz has briefed, these unnamed speculators—several now being investigated by the S.E.C.—employed a complex scheme to force a handful of major Wall Street firms to hold up trades with Bear, then leaked the news to the media, creating an artificial panic.

"Something happened Monday that triggered this mess," says one Bear executive who has spoken to the S.E.C. "It was as though a computer virus had been launched. Where the hell was this coming from? Who started it? We tried, believe me, but we could not track it down. We know lots of big hedge funds were spreading rumors, but how can you pursue that? Only the S.E.C. can, and they're all over this."

At the heart of this theory are the "novation" requests that began to pick up steam that Tuesday and Wednesday. As Bear executives later analyzed these trades, they discovered the overwhelming majority had been made with just three firms: Goldman Sachs, Credit Suisse, and Deutsche Bank. Schwartz came to believe this was no accident. In his mind, the flood of novation requests was designed to force at least one of the three firms to put a temporary halt to accepting them, which is what happened: Goldman and Credit Suisse did. News of that halt not only swept Wall Street trading floors, it appeared to gain credence the next day when David Faber asked Schwartz about it on CNBC. "I like Faber, he's a good guy, but I wonder if he ever asked himself, 'Why is someone telling me this?'" a top Bear executive asks. "There was a reason this was leaked, and the reason is simple: someone wanted us to go down, and go down hard." (Faber says his reporting was accurate, and arose from talks with a source he has known for 20 years.)

B ut who? According to one vague tale, initially picked up at Lehman Brothers, a group of hedge-fund managers actually celebrated Bear's collapse at a breakfast that following Sunday morning and planned a similar assault on Lehman the next week. True or not, Bear executives repeated the story to the S.E.C., along with the names of the three firms it suspects were behind its demise. Two are hedge funds, Chicago-based Citadel, run by a trader named Ken Griffin, and SAC Capital Partners of Stamford, Connecticut, run by Steven Cohen. (A spokesman for SAC Capital said the firm "vehemently denies" any suggestion that it played a role in Bear's demise. A Citadel spokeswoman said, "These claims have no merit.") The third suspect, at least in Bear executives' minds, is one of its main competitors, Goldman Sachs. ("Goldman Sachs was supportive of Bear Stearns," says a Goldman Sachs spokeswoman. "There is no foundation to rumors that we behaved otherwise.")

Several Bear executives also named an individual they believed was spreading rumors about them that week, Jeff Dorman, who briefly served as global co-head of Bear's prime brokerage business until resigning to take a similar position at Deutsche Bank last summer. "We heard Dorman was saying things last summer," says a Bear executive. "At the time we reached out to Deutsche Bank and told them he better stop it." (Asked about the allegation, a Deutsche Bank spokeswoman acknowledged that Bear had sent its executives a letter last August asking Dorman not to solicit its clients, as he had agreed upon leaving Bear. Deutsche Bank replied that he wasn't. The exchange didn't explicitly address what Dorman might have been saying about the firm, nor would the spokeswoman.)

Today, many of Bear Stearns's former employees are out of work. The firm has effectively disappeared into the maw of J. P. Morgan along with a number of key executives, including Ace Greenberg, who became a Morgan vice-chairman, and Alan Schwartz, who will probably take a position in the investment-banking department.

Maybe the S.E.C. will figure out whether Bear was murdered. But maybe it won't. Even those who believe the firm was the victim of a predatory raid have their doubts it can ever be proved.

"Even with subpoena power, I'm not sure the S.E.C. will get to the bottom of this, because the standard of proof is just so difficult," says an executive at Lehman Brothers. "But I hope they do. Because you can look at this as just another run on a bank or as a seminal point in the financial history of this country that could bring about a change, perhaps a drastic change, in the way we govern financial markets. If there is a solution to this kind of thing, it must be found in the roots of what happened at Bear Stearns. Because otherwise, I can guarantee you, it will happen again somewhere else."

· 2 ·

Profiles in Panic

Wall Street High Society in Free Fall

By *MICHAEL SHNAYERSON*

January 2009

A snapshot: East Hampton, late summer, a lawn party at a house on the ocean overlooking the dunes. The host is a prince of private equity known for dressing well. One of his guests is Steven Cohen, the publicity-shy billionaire whose SAC Capital, with $16 billion under management, is perhaps the most revered of the 10,000 or so hedge funds spawned by this giddily rich time. Nearby is Daniel Loeb, of Third Point, one of the better-known "activist" hedge funds, who hopes to move soon into a 10,700-square-foot, $45 million penthouse at 15 Central Park West, a Manhattan monument to the new gilded age. Gliding easily between them is art dealer Larry Gagosian, so successful at selling Bacons and Serras to Wall Street's new titans—including to Cohen—that he now travels in his own private jet and has his own helicopter to take him to it.

But here's the odd thing: despite the beauty of the ocean view, nearly all the guests have their backs to it. Cohen is deep in conversation with a colleague who seems to be pitching him a deal. Loeb hovers close to his wife, a former yoga teacher. Gagosian is near his stunning young girlfriend. No one notices the clouds that are, quite literally, on the horizon. Snap.

Six weeks later, the photograph is cracked and sepia-toned, curling at the edges, a historic print. In just that short time, the storm has hit and nothing looks the same.

I t may be premature to say our gilded age has ended. Third Point dropped 10 percent in October, bringing it down 27 percent for the year, but Daniel Loeb is still moving into his extravagant new apartment. Steven Cohen's SAC was down 11 percent in October and 18 percent for the year to date, but that still leaves him plenty of money to add a second ice-skating rink to his Greenwich, Connecticut, estate. And Larry Gagosian is still selling plenty of art.

What's definitely gone—along with Lehman Brothers and Bear Stearns—is leverage, at least to the dizzying degree it was recently used by Wall Street's investment banks, hedge funds, and private-equity firms to parlay each dollar of their assets into $10, $20, even $30 or more of credit to make gargantuan deals and profits. The credit crunch has made such leverage as quaint as the market in Dutch tulips. Without it, Wall Street salaries have already started drifting gently back to earth like so many limp balloons.

Gone, too, are jobs—lots and lots of them. Along with a sizable portion of Lehman's 26,000 worldwide, and Bear Stearns's 14,000, Wall Street firms across the board—even Goldman Sachs—are cutting back, and that pain radiates out to the limousine drivers and caterers and lawyers and personal trainers and restaurant owners and real-estate brokers who rely on Wall Street clients, not to mention to the many nonprofits and charities that have grown accustomed to Wall Street money. The latest estimate of jobs New York will lose, both on and off Wall Street, is 160,000. Governor David Paterson says the state's budget deficit has already reached $12.5 billion. In New York City, where Wall Street accounts for more than a quarter of the tax revenues, Mayor Michael Bloomberg thinks the financial-sector crisis will leave a $2 billion hole in the next fiscal year's budget.

Almost everyone has lost something—if not their jobs, then 25 to 50 percent of their retirement savings—and nearly everyone is glum, anxious, hung over. Prudence is the watchword now: sackcloth after the brilliant silks and brocades of the gilded age. The day after Lehman Brothers went down, a high-end Manhattan department store reportedly had the biggest day of returns in its history. "Because the wives didn't want the husbands to get the credit-card bills," says a fashion-world insider. A prominent designer says ruefully, "People really aren't shopping at all unless there's a deal or sale. It's pretty dramatic—they have the stores at their mercy."

Even those who have plenty left to spend aren't spending it. "I ran into a couple I always see at the antiques show," one Upper East Side woman recounts of her visit to the Armory show on Park Avenue. "They always buy something fairly grand. 'What have you bought this time?' I asked. 'Oh, nothing!' they said. 'We'd feel . . . ashamed.' " Another Upper East Side woman often goes from lunch at Michael's restaurant on West 55th Street to Manolo Blahnik a block away to pick up a $600 or $700 pair of shoes as "retail therapy." No more. "I was at Michael's yesterday and was thinking, Oh, Manolo's . . . But then I thought, Why? Why do that? It just doesn't feel good."

Only months ago, ordering that $1,950 bottle of 2003 Screaming Eagle Cabernet Sauvignon at Craft restaurant or the $26-per-ounce Wagyu beef at Nobu, or sliding into Masa for the $600 prix fixe dinner (not including tax, tip, or drinks), was a way of life for many Wall Street investment bankers. "The culture was that if you didn't spend extravagantly you'd be ridiculed at work," says a former Lehmanite. But that was when there *were* investment banks. Now many bankers, along with discovering $15 bottles of wine, are finding other ways to cut back—if not out of necessity, then from collective guilt and fear: the fitness trainer from three times a week to once a week; the haircut and highlights every eight weeks instead of every five. One prominent "hedgie" recently flew to China for business—but not on a private plane, as before. "Why should I pay $250,000 for a private plane," he said to a friend, "when I can pay $20,000 to fly commercial first class?"

The new thriftiness takes a bit of getting used to. "I was at the Food Emporium in Bedford [in Westchester County] yesterday, using my Food Emporium discount card," recounts one Greenwich woman. "The well-dressed wife of a Wall Street guy was standing behind me. She asked me how to get one. Then she said, 'Have you ever used coupons?' I said, 'Sure, maybe not lately, but sure.' She said, 'It's all the rage now—where do you get them?' "

One former Lehman executive in her 40s stood in her vast clothes closet not long ago, talking to her personal stylist. On shelves around her were at least 10 designer handbags that had cost her anywhere from $6,000 to $10,000 each.

"I don't know what to do," she said. "I guess I'll have to get rid of the maid."

Why not sell a few of those bags?, the stylist thought, but didn't say so.

"Well," the executive said after a moment, "I guess I'll cut her from five days a week to four."

There were, to be sure, some big-name "blowups" as the market began to implode. Here was Sumner Redstone, chairman of Viacom and CBS, who had to sell $233 million worth of Viacom and CBS stock in order to pay down part of an $800 million loan. T. Boone Pickens, legendary Texas oilman, was another blowup, and so was Chesapeake Energy's Aubrey McClendon, forced by a margin call to sell 94 percent of his 32 million company shares into the bear market. (Worth $2.2 billion last July, the shares were sold in October for $569 million.) Kirk Kerkorian, 91, has lost about $12 billion on his 54 percent ownership stake in MGM Mirage, the casino and hotel operator that owns almost half the hotel rooms on the Las Vegas Strip, including those in the Bellagio, the MGM Grand, the Mirage, and Mandalay Bay. The company's stock is down 86 percent this year, and its bonds were downgraded deeper into junk status in October. Kerkorian has reportedly told friends that he "lived one year too long." (He now claims he never said it.) Nevertheless, he and the other three men are all still billionaires.

These were the stories known because they involved large chunks of publicly traded stock. But as October turned into one of the worst market months since October 1929, rumors ran rampant about which high-flying hedge funds would crash as they tried in vain to unwind their investments in derivatives and other unregulated securities, many of them entwined with subprime mortgages. With their lenders forcing them to sell assets at new lows, and their investors trying to pull their money out, the hedge funds were caught in the middle: the gilded age's biggest winners were now among its biggest losers. Would Ken Griffin's Citadel be the first big hedge fund to go? Or Fortress—whose clients are trying to redeem $4.5 billion? In fact, the first big tree down following that dreadful month was Tontine Associates, which managed $11 billion through its four hedge funds and whose activist founder, Jeffrey Gendell, had become a billionaire by generating more than 100 percent returns in 2003 and 2005. After two of his funds had lost two-thirds of their value, Gendell bowed to the inevitable and is expected to close them. Days later came word that Steven Rattner was closing his small but high-profile media hedge fund, Quadrangle Equity Investors, after approximately 25 percent year-to-date losses.

Of those 10,000 hedge funds, as many as half may join the casualty list in the next few years. Not that many hedge-fund managers, though, will be reduced to selling apples. Take Remy Trafelet, 38, a handsome, smooth-faced preppy whose fund faces steep year-end losses and dwindling capital—from $6 billion to $3 billion—as investors depart. In a good year, such as 2005, when Trafelet racked up 42 percent returns, he and his partners pocketed hundreds of millions of dollars.

Still, he may have to trim his lifestyle a bit.

Tellingly, no fewer than 50 high-end New York apartments have been put on the market since late September, most by Wall Streeters. Usually, the fall listings for apartments between $10 and $20 million are all teed up by Labor Day. Not this year, as *The New York Times*'s Josh Barbanel notes. At the Majestic, on Central Park West, two Wall Streeters listed their three-bedroom units within hours of each other. Robert Long, a managing director of hard-hit Allied Capital, listed 8C for $13.8 million as "the most magnificently renovated grand apartment to become available on Central Park West in years." James Kern, a former senior managing director of Bear Stearns, listed 17D—the "ultimate renovation"—for $12 million.

Ten blocks away, at the Park Laurel tower, on 63rd Street, Charles Michaels, of the hedge fund Sierra Global Management, listed his 2,800-square-foot, four-bedroom apartment with terrace for $14.9 million. In early October, Steven F. Stuart, of the Garrison Investment hedge fund, listed the apartment directly above Michaels's—no terrace—for $10.8 million. Ten days later, real-estate developer Ira Resnick put his own, similar apartment at the Park Laurel up for sale—for $10 million.

Nowhere is the downturn more dramatic, though, than downtown, where new condominium towers by cutting-edge architects vie for a market that's almost vanished overnight: young Wall Streeters with bonuses to throw at sleek, overpriced apartments in Richard Meier–knockoff buildings. For the developers, it's proved a game of high-stakes musical chairs. Those who got their buildings up by early 2007 have sold many of their units by now. Those who started selling after Bear Stearns's collapse, last March, are struggling, as the Web site StreetEasy confirms. And for those just getting started, good luck.

In the financial district itself, hotel impresario André Balazs embarked on the 47-story William Beaver House in 2006. StreetEasy's Sofia Kim suggests the name was meant—or at least interpreted—as a naughty wink to hard-partying bachelor traders. With the Tsao & McKown–designed building due to open this month, 209 of its 320 mostly one- and two-bedroom units have sold at top-of-the-market prices—from $900,000 to $6 million. But the rest are either for sale or being held in reserve. That's a lot of unsold units.

Still, Balazs has done better with the Beaver House than Kent Swig has with his condominium tower at 25 Broad Street, designed by Cetra/Ruddy. Swig closed its sales office until further notice, citing liquidity problems due to Lehman Brothers' demise. At One York Street, the soaring glass tower designed by Enrique Norten overlooking busy Canal Street, developer Stan Perelman says 28 of his 40 units have closed, though he admits that his 6,096-square-foot penthouse, with an asking price of $34 million, has yet to find a taker. The raw space, entirely glass-walled, is both exhilarating and somewhat vertiginous; as for the small ventilation windows at ankle height, they're probably not a good idea for an owner with cats. "When the hardwood floors are in, the slabs, the home theater—press a remote and all the shades go up automatically and the music begins—someone will say, 'Where do I sign?,'" Perelman suggests. Next month, that is, or the month or the year after . . .

River views—and the cachet of a world-class architect—do help. The Superior Ink building, a former factory on West 12th Street overlooking the Hudson, was given a Robert A. M. Stern makeover, and most of its 68 apartments and seven adjoining town houses have sold. So, then, how about partial river views and a famous artist, just one block away?

On West 11th Street, painter and filmmaker Julian Schnabel has lived for years in a wide former stable he calls Palazzo Chupi. In keeping with the gilded age, he added nine lavish floors of his own design. Richard Gere bought the fourth floor, but now it's back on the market. A "private individual" took the fifth, and Schnabel himself lives on the sixth and seventh. Still for sale above are a duplex and a triplex penthouse.

From across the street, the addition's dusty-rose stucco and Italianate arches look striking enough. Inside, Palazzo Chupi is nothing less than a brilliant artist's interpretation of a gilded age—only not this one. More like the Italian Renaissance.

A bronze-domed elevator with Italian-tile floor opens into the penthouse's furnished living room, with nearly 15-foot ceilings of hand-hewn wood beams, a colorful Venetian-glass chandelier, and a massive, 8-foot-high fireplace. Giant Schnabel canvases fill the walls. They aren't included in the $24 million price, but as Corcoran broker James Lansill puts it, "You could try . . ." Schnabel is, he says, a seller. In fact, the triplex started at $32 million—before the market meltdown.

The triplex has 3,713 square feet of interior space, but also 2,304 square feet of balconies and terraces (seven in all). It has arched windows throughout, baronial bathrooms with vintage fixtures, and the most romantic master bedroom in New York. The interior of the duplex is even larger, and features a living room—25 feet by 41.6 feet—with wood-beamed ceilings nearly 20 feet high. Only three terraces, though, hence the bargain price of $23 million. Among its many splendors is a huge square bathroom with a sunken tub in the middle, a fireplace, and French doors that open out through red velvet drapes to an Italian-tiled balcony. "His idea is for you to be able to sit in the bath with a roaring fire, the doors wide open, and snow on the balcony," Lansill says.

Either of Schnabel's gilded-age fantasies is well worth the price for anyone with $20 to $30 million to spare. The question is: Does anyone have $20 to $30 million to spare on a gilded-age fantasy these days? Perhaps. In the black-and-white-tiled lobby as Lansill leads the way out, a trim, elegantly dressed Russian fellow with blond hair and wraparound sunglasses sweeps in. "I have an appointment," he says to the guard in a thick Russian accent, "with Mr. Schnabel."

Fall's auctions, in both London and New York, have tracked the deepening gloom as surely as real estate and stocks have. Literally on the heels of Lehman's bankruptcy, in mid-September, Damien Hirst held a two-day sale of animals in formaldehyde and other nature-based art at Sotheby's in London and raised $200 million, apparently from Russian, Middle Eastern, and Asian buyers for the most part, thus panicking the private-art-dealer world, which he'd circumvented by using the auction house. For perfect end-of-an-age timing, his "Beautiful Inside My Head Forever" auction ranked right up there with Blackstone's June 2007 I.P.O., at private equity's high-water mark. Then came the sickening slide in the stock market. By early November London's *Evening Standard* was reporting rumors that some buyers had reneged on their bids and that a lot that had purportedly sold was being offered to a collector. (A Sotheby's spokesman denied the rumors.)

By mid-November, Sotheby's was reporting a $52 million loss in guarantees from the season's first auctions—sums the auction house had guaranteed sellers before the market meltdown and had to make good on when their art fetched prices below those figures. That included the $40-million-plus guarantee reportedly promised to private-equity titan Henry Kravis and his wife, Marie-Josée, for Edgar Degas's *Dancer in Repose*. On November 3, the circa-1879 pastel and gouache sold over the phone, with a bid placed in Tokyo for only $33 million, leaving Sotheby's on the hook for millions. William Ruprecht, Sotheby's chief executive, later announced, "We're out of the guarantee business, at least for a while."

Christie's had its own problems. One in particular involved auctioning 16 postwar drawings owned by former Lehman chairman Richard Fuld and his wife, Kathy, in New York on November 12. Christie's had given them a $20 million guarantee, but the group fetched only $13.5 million. The entire auction, of contemporary works by such noted artists as Barnett Newman, Willem de Kooning, and Roy Lichtenstein, achieved only half its pre-sale low estimate.

As auctions go, so, soon enough, will museums, accustomed to Wall Street largesse. People are wondering: Will Kathy Fuld, who has donated or helped acquire 42 artworks for the Museum of Modern Art, stay on the board as a vice-chairman? For that matter, will private-equity billionaire Leon Black, another MoMA vice-chairman? In early October a company owned by Black's Apollo Management lost a legal battle in Delaware chancery court over its efforts to back out of a $6.5 billion deal. The judge ruled that a deal was a deal and must go forward, but Apollo's lenders, Credit Suisse and Deutsche Bank, now seem unlikely to participate, and Black and his Apollo co-founder, Joshua Harris, may face having to pay billions in damages. That may not put Black in a mood to buy art for MoMA.

Other museums face similar funding threats, as do all philanthropies. When the meltdown deepened, talk inevitably turned to the Robin Hood Foundation, started by hedge-fund legend Paul Tudor Jones II and under-written largely by hedge-fund money. Citadel Investment's Ken Griffin has been a generous donor, but with his largest fund down nearly 40 percent for the year, how likely is Citadel to pony up a major gift in 2009? Or Glenn Dubin, of Highbridge Capital Management? (Two of its funds are down 32 and 37 percent for the year.) Or Alan D. Schwartz, on whose watch as C.E.O. Bear Stearns went down? In the case of Richard Fuld, the answer seems already clear: as of late October, his name was no longer listed on Robin Hood's board of directors.

The fate of the Lehman Brothers Foundation tells the larger story of post-meltdown Wall Street philanthropy all too well. In the halcyon days, before the downturn, when one year Lehman Brothers was racking up a record $4 billion net income, its employee-funded foundation pledged $3 million to Lincoln Center's redevelopment campaign, $1 million to the Apollo Theater's education and outreach programs, and $50,000 to the Orchestra of St. Luke's, among other New York causes. The good news is that the foundation, as a non-profit entity, wasn't linked to Lehman's bank-ruptcy filing. The bad news is that Lehman's ex-employees, their jobs gone and their stock all but worthless, probably won't be kicking in any more money to the foundation. (A spokesman for the Lehman foundation did not respond to a call from *Vanity Fair.*)

If the gilded age has come to an end this fall, surely Lehman's demise—with its bankruptcy filing on that Monday morning of September 15, 2008—was the tipping point. It panicked the money markets, froze global credit, and sent stock prices spiraling down.

Lehman's 31st floor—where Fuld and his top executives worked—was by all accounts a quiet place, especially by midafternoon, one managing di-rector recalls dryly. Among Fuld's loyalists, no one was more loyal than his number two, chief operating officer Joe Gregory, whose story, even more than Fuld's, seems emblematic of the age now past. If Tom Wolfe were writ-ing a sequel to *The Bonfire of the Vanities,* Gregory would be his man.

Gregory, 56, was a legend at Lehman—less for his business exploits than for his lifestyle. He had several homes: a principal residence in Lloyd Harbor, on Long Island's North Shore; an oceanfront McMansion in Bridgehampton; a ski home in Manchester, Vermont; an apartment at 610 Park Avenue; and reportedly a house in Pennsylvania. "He had a kid who went to a small school in Pennsylvania," a former senior colleague recalls. "Joe didn't like the hotel, so he bought [a] house in town. It was probably only $500,000, but he paid for it so that, on the maybe two trips a year he took there, he'd have a nice place to stay. And then he had it re-decorated!" The colleague says he heard it on good authority that Gregory's after-tax expenses approached $15 million per year. That, he heard, was ex-clusive of mortgages. (Gregory's lawyer declined to comment on e-mails from *Vanity Fair*.)

Gregory came from a modest background, an ex-colleague recalls; at one time he had aspired to be a high-school history teacher. One summer while attending Long Island's Hofstra University, though, he worked as an intern at Lehman and got hooked. Both he and Fuld joined the firm soon after college; as the two men rose in the ranks, they became close friends.

Like Fuld, Gregory started on the commercial-paper trading desk. By the 1980s he'd become a top executive in fixed income and was known as one of Lehman's Huntington Mafia, because all four executives in it lived in or near that North Shore town and often commuted together. "It was said that the four of them decided the fate of the floor every day on their drives back and forth," recalls one ex-colleague. "And you had to be in their good graces to survive on the fixed-income floor."

Gregory's rise was strongly linked to Fuld's: loyalty was his strong suit. "Joe never had clients," says a lawyer who worked with the firm. "So he wasn't on 31 because he was a rainmaker. And he never really had a business he was responsible for. He was Fuld's full-time loyal lieutenant. And Fuld did have a yes-man mentality, where if people didn't agree with him they'd get shot. And Gregory was sort of the hatchet man, who fired them or tried to enforce rules."

Gregory played the sidekick role well, two ex-colleagues suggest. The problem, says one, is that as president and chief operating officer, begin-ning in 2004, he came to oversee all departments, including the derivatives that would get so tricky. The commercial paper (i.e., short-term loans solicited by creditworthy companies and banks) he'd traded in his early days was lower-risk. "If you bought it wrong, you could hold the position," one ex-colleague explains, "till it rolled off—30 or 60 days. So it would cost you a few basis points, that's all." The longer end of the market involved bonds you might get stuck with if the market changed. "I don't know if Gregory knew how much risk he was taking," the ex-colleague says. "The other thing, which Joe had never seen, was how a market could go highly illiquid. Joe had observed this but not lived it."

As the real-estate bubble swelled, and with it the $55 trillion market in unregulated, collateralized debt obligations and credit-default swaps, so did Gregory's compensation—and lifestyle. He and his current wife, Niki, provided generously for their five children—three of them hers, two his. They gave to medical charities—Huntington Hospital, Weill Cornell Medical Center, and the Maurer Foundation for Breast Health Education, among others. When their daughter became a serious soccer player, the Gregorys underwrote a new local soccer field. "Joe had a huge heart—he gave a ton of money away," says one ex-colleague. At Lehman, the ex-colleague adds, "he drove all the diversity and philanthropic initiatives."

But the Gregorys rewarded themselves too. Tired of the 90-minute commute, Joe bought a helicopter for the ride. When he realized the chopper couldn't fly to Manhattan in inclement weather, he got a seaplane. Niki was known as the best customer at the high-end boutique where all the wealthy North Shore wives shopped; the store's personal buyers came to the house, their arms filled with couture and cashmere. The Gregorys undertook a renovation of the Lloyd Harbor home that would cost, by one report, $3.5 million. They bought the Bridgehampton home for about $19 million in 2006 and hired a top local designer to do it up. One day Gregory called his staff out to admire the new Bentley he'd just bought for his wife. "Look at the dashboard," he allegedly said. "It's one piece of burled wood."

"They weren't society people," says an acquaintance of the Gregorys. "They didn't buy art the way the Fulds did; they didn't really entertain." The Lloyd Harbor renovation included a new state-of-the-art kitchen, but the Gregorys ate cold cuts on their fine china. (One guest espied a $4,600 price sticker on one of the plates. She chose not to ask whether the price was for one plate or the set.) At a local restaurant he frequented, Gregory once left an $1,800 tip for a $200 tab, says a Lehman colleague.

The problem was that roughly 75 percent of Gregory's compensation—which reached $26 million in 2007—was in Lehman stock. Some of the stock could be sold only after a five-year waiting period, but most Lehman employees kept the bulk of their holdings long after that—not only out of loyalty but because its rise from $6 a share in 1998 to $85 in early 2007 had made them very, very rich. At least on paper. Fuld had by far the largest in-house holding: at the high-water mark, he owned stock worth almost $1 billion—not counting his stock options. Gregory had the second-largest stake: an estimated $574 million.

Most Lehman bankers saw little risk in borrowing against their stock to fund the lifestyle to which they were, on paper, entitled. "Say you have $8 million of Lehman stock," suggests a senior investment adviser, using hypothetical numbers but a true-life case about a good friend who worked at Lehman. "You want to build a $2 million house. You pledge your stock and you borrow the money and you say to yourself, 'Let's say the worst happens: we have a terrible drop in the market. My $8 million will still be worth $4 million, and I've only borrowed half of that. So I'm being very conservative.' But that doesn't allow for $8 million down to zero."

At Lehman, Gregory set a new goal in 2007, according to a former colleague: he wanted Lehman to overtake Goldman Sachs, which was raking in huge profits by leveraging as much as 40 to 1. And he wanted Lehman's share price to reach $100. He imposed ambitious targets on all of Lehman's capital departments, targets that required taking big risks on deals that would become increasingly shaky.

As the real-estate market collapsed, so did those investments. For Gregory, the end came in June 2008, with the release of Lehman's shockingly bad second-quarter numbers: $2.8 billion in losses, after months of confident pronouncements from the firm.

When the numbers came out, the outcry was fierce. Lehman was accused of misleading the market by attaching wildly over-optimistic values to its portfolio of commercial real estate and mortgage-backed securities. Class-action suits by pension funds hard-hit by Lehman's losses were filed. Groups like the Operative Plasterers and Cement Masons International Association Local 262 and the Fire & Police Pension Association of Colorado—these were among the plaintiffs who hadn't even known they were part of the gilded age. Only they were: Lehman's bankers had used their retirement money to make those 40-to-1 bets and live like princes. Now that money was gone.

Fuld seemed reluctant to fire his old friend, so Gregory made the decision for him. "Wall Street wants a head," he said sadly, *The Wall Street Journal* reported. At some point, Gregory apparently turned to Lehman for a loan, according to *New York* magazine, borrowing money against his stock.

He did not sell any of his Lehman stock in the first half of 2008, company records show. How much of it he was able to sell over the summer—if any—remains an open question, since upon his departure from the firm his transactions were no longer publicly posted. Ben Silverman, of InsiderScore.com, which tracks corporate compensation and insiders' transactions, says that regulatory filings indicate that Gregory was bound by a lockup agreement preventing him from selling his stock for 90 days. By the time that period was up, it was Friday, September 12; the following Monday, Lehman announced its bankruptcy and the stock closed at 15 cents a share. Unless Lehman had agreed to release Gregory from the lockup after he resigned, he would barely have had a chance to act before his paper millions vanished into thin air.

What Gregory could do—and did—was put property up for sale. The apartment at 610 Park Avenue found a buyer in October for $4.4 million. The Bridgehampton house is still on the market for what local brokers diplomatically call an "aggressive" price: $32.5 million.

Outside, the Gregory house on Surfside Drive looks like a thousand other Hamptons McMansions—an architectural hodgepodge built on spec—though it sits somewhat oddly next to a public parking lot, separated only by a hedge of tall firs.

Inside, the house is decorated not just exquisitely but relentlessly. The long foyer has a high, arched ceiling, raised-panel walls, and a curved papal balcony from which the owners might look down from the second floor to greet arriving guests. One guest recalls that when the Gregorys bought the house it was already fully decorated, but the couple hired Winn Cullen, a decorator based in nearby Locust Valley, to rip everything out and make it perfect again—in an entirely new way. No expense was spared.

In the main living room—all creams and beiges—the built-in book-cases hold not one but two large flat-screen TVs: one on either side of the fireplace, like big black bookends. Why two? The broker is stumped. Perhaps because the bookcases would be almost empty without them. Or perhaps it's a theme: in the kitchen are two Sub-Zero refrigerators flanking the large butcher-block island. And upstairs are two master bedrooms, each with a grand view of the Atlantic.

Sometime over the summer, before the market meltdown, the house on Surfside was nearly sold. Unfortunately, the would-be buyer was perturbed to learn that the large back lawn, with its gunite pool and walkway over the dunes to the beach, would have to be drastically reduced before the house could be sold. That's because Gregory's property is in violation of a South-ampton town ordinance requiring preservation of natural beachfront vegeta-tion. Before a sale can close, the broker explains, a broad swath of the lawn will need to be ripped up and the natural flora restored. The potential buyer may also have balked at the carrying costs: $66,000 annually for full insur-ance, including extra flood coverage for hurricane damage, and $34,000 in taxes—$100,000 a year before walking in the door. Plus the grounds crew.

Gregory never used the Bridgehampton house much; these days, he spends his time dealing with his lawyers. He's one of a dozen top Lehman officers federal prosecutors have subpoenaed for one of three grand-jury investigations probing whether Lehman painted too rosy a picture of its finances—including that portfolio of commercial real estate. If they know-ingly misled investors, some of those officers may go to jail.

Most 60-year-old ex–Lehman Brothers bankers likely squirreled away enough to at least scrape by on a couple of million a year. As for the 25-year-olds, they never earned enough to have much to lose. But the mid-30s or mid-40s Lehman banker who lived up to his high compensation—or beyond it—is reeling, hurting, and possibly bankrupt.

One Sunday evening in October, a former Lehmanite in his mid-30s settles into a velvet banquette at the Gramercy Park Hotel's elegant Rose Bar. At first he's circumspect. But after a couple of Johnnie Walker Blacks on the rocks, he opens up.

"Let's take a guy who makes $5 million a year," the banker suggests. "He's paid two and a half million dollars of that in equity compensation"—

Lehman Brothers stock. Plus he gets to buy that stock at a 30 percent discount, so he's really getting $3.25 million in stock. "Plus appreciation? Over five years? That's $25 to $30 million!

"Then let's say a guy in that position borrowed $5 million against the $30 million in stock. It would seem a very conservative loan, right? Until the $30 million goes down to zero, which is what happened. So now he's negative $5 million."

True, that same Lehman banker got the other half of his compensation in cash. The banker nods. "For five years, he made two and a half million dollars a year in cash. So that's twelve and a half million dollars. But of course he's had to pay more or less 50 percent in taxes, so divide that and he's got six and a quarter million. He's probably spent that money over those five years—$1 million a year, it's not so hard to do, right? So he has nothing—and he has to repay that $5 million loan."

A month before the bankruptcy, the banker muses, his peers were complaining about the $10,000 or $20,000 they had to pay for lifetime dibs on the best season tickets in the New York Giants' new stadium. But they were paying. They were complaining about private-school tuitions. "But it was actually a way of saying, 'I'm rich—rich enough to afford it.'

"The day Lehman went bankrupt, people realized they were going to get no bonuses, no severance, and no equity. Oh—and no health care. And no salary."

So far, many seem more stunned than angry, or even timidly hopeful now that Barclays, the English bank, has bought much of the firm and offered shell-shocked Lehmanites their jobs—for now. Peter J. Solomon, 70, a former vice-chairman of Lehman Brothers who runs his own investment-banking firm, says, "What I see in the Lehman people is not enough bitterness. They're still there, they have three months, Barclays is offering them jobs for a while. But that won't last for most of them. You're going to see the biggest impact in the first quarter of next year."

At least the thirtysomething banker in the Rose Bar isn't married with kids.

Alexandra Lebenthal, a New York–based wealth manager for investors with between $2 million and $20 million in assets—the modest to mid-level rich—offers a keenly authoritative portrait of a thirtysomething

Lehman banker, married with kids, in a guest column called "What It Costs" on the Web site NewYorkSocialDiary. Blake and Grigsby Somerset are fictional, their finances all too plausible.

Before Lehman's stock began to plummet, Lebenthal suggests, Blake's annual compensation was $9.5 million—much of that in company stock. He was carrying a $2 million loan used for a house in the Hamptons, but felt perfectly able to afford his annual expenses: the Park Avenue apartment maintenance ($120,000); the Hamptons house mortgage ($75,000); the nanny and driver ($100,000); his wife's clothing ($100,000); the personal trainer three times a week ($18,000); food, including restaurants ($30,000); charitable benefits and other nonprofit causes ($200,000); private school for three children ($78,000); Christmas in Palm Beach ($15,000); spring in Aspen ($15,000); and a wedding-anniversary diamond necklace for Grigsby ($50,000).

At least Blake has been hired on by Barclays. But his Lehman stock portfolio is now worthless. He and Grigsby have to cut their annual living expenses from about $1 million to a fraction of that, and do it in ways that don't show, for the worst—*the worst*—would be the public disgrace of falling out of their social class.

First to go: vacations, the trainer, the driver, and entertaining. No restaurants, no shopping excursions, no new ball clothes for Grigsby (last year's will have to do). But, for now—for appearances—the Somersets will scrimp to keep the kids in their schools, and the nanny, and the Hamptons house. For now.

What, indeed, of the Hamptons, where the Somersets still go, though they can't afford to anymore? On high-hedged roads everywhere, for-sale signs are nearly as prevalent as in southern Florida. A broker in Bridgehampton says she's often the only one in her storefront office, the neat rows of little white desks as desolate as tombstones. Some brokers are rumored to have even taken jobs in East Hampton Main Street stores.

All over the Hamptons, overstretched owners hope to rent next summer to cover the bills. But even if supply doesn't overwhelm demand, fear and greed may roil the market. One East Hampton broker tells a story of clients who wanted to renovate their house and asked her—before the meltdown—to find them a rental to live in for a year while the work was being done. The broker called an owner on Further Lane, who agreed to rent for $425,000. Then came Lehman's demise. The owner decided she'd need more money: $500,000. One week later, the market had fallen again. Now the owner panicked: "I'll take $400,000," she declared. Six days later, she was down to $300,000. Then . . . $250,000. "The $500,000 was all about greed," says the broker, "and the $250,000 was all about fear."

At East Hampton airport, so recently the scene of Gulfstream gridlock, an eerie silence has settled in. The private-jet parade diminishes, of course, right after Labor Day, but this fall, says one airport employee, "it was like turning off a light." September traffic was down 35 percent from the previous year. The stalwarts still come, sources say: Revlon's Ronald Perelman, industrialist Ira Rennert, Michael Bloomberg, and Starbucks chairman Howard Schultz. But there's a lot of time for staff to read.

Up in Greenwich, Connecticut, unofficial hedge-fund capital of the world, the real-estate market is, if anything, worse. Jean Ruggiero, one of the town's leading brokers, at William Raveis, still sells houses—the good brokers know how to play a down market—but currently there are 55 available for $9 million and up. That's a lot for Greenwich. "The owners are having a hard time just getting the brokers to come," says Ruggiero. "The broker thinks, Why bother? I don't have any clients—why waste the gas?"

Ruggiero offers a white-elephant tour. Here's a Georgian mansion that sold not long ago, she says, to a Russian oligarch for more than $10 million, with a 10 percent down payment. Unfortunately, says Ruggiero, the Russian was unable to close on the deal. "So he lost the deposit, and the house is still on the market."

Here's the infamous "Lake Carrington Estate," an unfinished stone mansion of 35,000 square feet that sits seemingly abandoned in an overgrown field surrounded by a chain-link fence. When the spec mansion was listed at $28 million in mid-2007, it was declared "couture-ready." Ready, that is, for a proud hedge-fund buyer to make his own design decisions about the interior, since the house was raw inside, with unfinished floors and no kitchen or bathroom fixtures. Those flourishes would probably cost another $10 million, not counting the grounds, which are couture-ready too. Is its recent sale for $13.7 million to an unnamed buyer a good market sign . . . or a bad one?

Here's one more: a $19.9 million mansion that just sold—after 763 days on the market—for $11 million. Good or bad? "Oh, that's a good one," Ruggiero says.

Greenwich estate manager Jacqueline de Bar describes how wealthy locals are cutting back: letting the pastures grow, canceling the leaf blowers, doing the storm windows themselves. At Betteridge Jewelers—known as Wall Street's jeweler—third-generation owner Terry Betteridge says a lot more customers are coming in since the meltdown, to sell, not buy. "I've seen some bad ones in the last two months," he says. "I know a Wall Street guy who's literally been selling jewelry to make the mortgage payments. He and his wife came in together, bringing things to sell. . . . Just this morning, we took in a $2.7 million lot. An amazing collection, some of the best jewelry in the world, everything signed—extraordinary things I couldn't buy before. No matter what I bid wasn't enough. Now I can."

Down the street is Consigned Couture, where Wall Street wives come to unload last year's designer clothes and accessories. Some send their housekeepers, others their daughters. "My calendar is booked a month ahead, up to eight appointments a day," says owner Dolly Ledingham. That's sellers. Buyers? Not so much. "They used to come in to spend $1,000. Now they spend $100."

In this global economy, the age's excesses and aftermath are spread wide, nowhere as vividly as in London. Notting Hill was the epicenter of London's gilded age, where every driveway, it seemed, had a Maserati, every mansion a makeover, often including an underground pool. Now, says *Sunday Times* columnist Rachel Johnson, who chronicled the invasion of the financiers in her 2006 novel, *Notting Hell*, bankers are staggering around like lost souls, while their wives gather at 202, the stylish Westbourne Grove restaurant in Nicole Farhi's boutique, to share their fears. "What they're crying about is they've lost all their stock, and their houses are worth less than they were," says Johnson of the wives, "but they're really upset that on January 31 they have to pay huge tax bills. Even though they don't have the cash anymore, the liability remains on what they earned before."

In London as in New York, Lehman bankers are among those hardest hit. One in his mid-30s says that for two weeks after the bankruptcy the New York office was cloaked in ominous silence—no communication from the 31st floor to London's Canary Wharf. After the filing, the banker and his colleagues were all told to keep coming to work, or else possibly not get paid. So they came in and played Pac-Man and Tetris. Finally, he says, the whole London-based fixed-income group was called into an auditorium and "made redundant" by a representative from the accounting firm PricewaterhouseCoopers. That was it for the banker's Lehman career—and the $1 million in company stock that a friend says he lost.

On a higher level, major figures on the London financial scene have lost billions—tens of billions, in some cases. Only last May, Indian tycoon Lakshmi Mittal, who owns the world's largest steel company, paid $230 million for Israeli-American hedge-fund tycoon Noam Gottesman's Georgian mansion, in Kensington Palace Gardens—a London record. Now, amid the commodities plunge, Mittal is said to have lost some $50 billion, and to be down to his last $16 billion. Michael Spencer, founder of ICAP, the inter-dealer broker, watched roughly $700 million of his stake in the firm go up in smoke as the market came down.

Another name bandied about is that of Nat Rothschild. The 37-year-old son of Lord (Jacob) Rothschild, he some years ago weaned himself from a dissolute life, gave up alcohol (even his family's Château Lafite Rothschild wine), and turned to the serious work of making money, eventually becoming co-chairman and rainmaker of the New York–based hedge fund Atticus Capital. Rothschild continued to live well—very well, with homes in London, Manhattan, Moscow, Greece, and Klosters, Switzerland, where he established his principal residence, where there are no English taxes. He went from home to home, the London *Daily Mail* reports, in an elaborately equipped Gulfstream jet, supposedly always with two uniformed butlers, rarely staying more than four days in any locale. But the rainmaking worked: Atticus pulled in eye-popping returns, and Rothschild probably made more than $800 million—all in advance of the $750 million or so he'd one day inherit. "He has a very difficult relationship with his father," suggests London-based columnist Taki Theodoracopulos. "I think his father would have liked him to be more interested in houses and furniture. This guy just cares about making money."

Now Atticus has racked up staggering losses of $7.5 billion. Its Atticus European fund, once worth $8 billion alone, was down 43 percent by early October.

Usually, December is the year's most festive time in New York. Wall Street bankers either have their bonuses or know what they will be. Their wives have bought new gowns for the season's charity balls—the Metropolitan Museum's acquisition-fund benefit and the New York Botanical Garden's Winter Wonderland Ball, and more, at ticket prices ranging from $400 to $15,000. Then it's off to St. Barth's for sun worshippers, Aspen for skiers.

But not this year.

Privately, some New York benefit organizers wonder if even half the stalwarts will show up. On St. Barth's, rental villas are usually booked by early fall; this year, many were available as of early November. At Aspen's St. Regis hotel, Christmas week was still available, at $13,920 for two.

For bankers and hedgies, the fear this holiday season is not of bonuses reduced or denied—that's expected. The real fear is of massive layoffs and massive redemptions by hedge-fund investors, of another Wall Street bloodbath in early '09.

Soon, says wealth manager Alexandra Lebenthal, the Blake and Grigsby Somersets will find out what they're really made of. "Were their lifestyle, friends, and even marriage based on living a certain way, without limits, or do they have the values to make it through the tough times?"

Philip K. Howard, a New York lawyer and social critic whose new book is *Life Without Lawyers,* sees a sea change which was overdue. Every 30 years or so, he notes, the country has to redefine its social values. We've just reached the next time. "So this end of the new gilded era—it's like a bucket that spilled, and finally the money spilled out, and we were left with a culture whose sense of purpose and responsibility were lacking. And now there's a real need for people, and society as a whole, to rethink and restructure their values."

"I may be the only one who's thrilled by this recession," says the wife of one London private-equity manager who took his lumps this fall. "It just means we'll have to get possibly another job. But the bottom line is that it is just money. When you realize that you have enough—your health and a roof and good food and your family—you have to just feel lucky."

Happy New Year.

·3·

Wall Street Lays Another Egg

Derivatives and Mathematical Models

By *Niall Ferguson*

December 2008

This year we have lived through something more than a financial crisis. We have witnessed the death of a planet. Call it Planet Finance. Two years ago, in 2006, the measured economic output of the entire world was worth around $48.6 trillion. The total market capitalization of the world's stock markets was $50.6 trillion, 4 percent larger. The total value of domestic and international bonds was $67.9 trillion, 40 percent larger. Planet Finance was beginning to dwarf Planet Earth.

Planet Finance seemed to spin faster, too. Every day $3.1 trillion changed hands on foreign-exchange markets. Every month $5.8 trillion changed hands on global stock markets. And all the time new financial life-forms were evolving. The total annual issuance of mortgage-backed securities, including fancy new "collateralized debt obligations" (C.D.O.'s), rose to more than $1 trillion. The volume of "derivatives"—contracts such as options and swaps—grew even faster, so that by the end of 2006 their notional value was just over $400 trillion. Before the 1980s, such things were virtually unknown. In the space of a few years their populations exploded.

On Planet Finance, the securities outnumbered the people; the transactions outnumbered the relationships.

New institutions also proliferated. In 1990 there were just 610 hedge funds, with $38.9 billion under management. At the end of 2006 there were 9,462, with $1.5 trillion under management. Private-equity partnerships also went forth and multiplied. Banks, meanwhile, set up a host of "conduits" and "structured investment vehicles" (SIVs—surely the most apt acronym in financial history) to keep potentially risky assets off their balance sheets. It was as if an entire shadow banking system had come into being.

Then, beginning in the summer of 2007, Planet Finance began to self-destruct in what the International Monetary Fund soon acknowledged to be "the largest financial shock since the Great Depression." Did the crisis of 2007–8 happen because American companies had gotten worse at designing new products? Had the pace of technological innovation or productivity growth suddenly slackened? No. The proximate cause of the economic uncertainty of 2008 was financial: to be precise, a crunch in the credit markets triggered by mounting defaults on a hitherto obscure species of housing loan known euphemistically as "subprime mortgages."

Central banks in the United States and Europe sought to alleviate the pressure on the banks with interest-rate cuts and offers of funds through special "term auction facilities." Yet the market rates at which banks could borrow money, whether by issuing commercial paper, selling bonds, or borrowing from one another, failed to follow the lead of the official federal-funds rate. The banks had to turn not only to Western central banks for short-term assistance to rebuild their reserves but also to Asian and Middle Eastern sovereign-wealth funds for equity injections. When these sources proved insufficient, investors—and speculative short-sellers—began to lose faith.

Beginning with Bear Stearns, Wall Street's investment banks entered a death spiral that ended with their being either taken over by a commercial bank (as Bear was, followed by Merrill Lynch) or driven into bankruptcy (as Lehman Brothers was). In September the two survivors—Goldman Sachs and Morgan Stanley—formally ceased to be investment banks, signaling the death of a business model that dated back to the Depression. Other institutions deemed "too big to fail" by the U.S. Treasury were effectively taken over by the government, including the mortgage lenders and guarantors Fannie Mae and Freddie Mac and the insurance giant American International Group (A.I.G.).

By September 18 the U.S. financial system was gripped by such panic that the Treasury had to abandon this ad hoc policy. Treasury Secretary Henry Paulson hastily devised a plan whereby the government would be authorized to buy "troubled" securities with up to $700 billion of taxpayers' money—a figure apparently plucked from the air. When a modified version of the measure was rejected by Congress 11 days later, there was panic. When it was passed four days after that, there was more panic. Now it wasn't just bank stocks that were tanking. The entire stock market seemed to be in free fall as fears mounted that the credit crunch was going to trigger a recession. Moreover, the crisis was now clearly global in scale. European banks were in much the same trouble as their American counterparts, while emerging-market stock markets were crashing. A week of frenetic improvisation by national governments culminated on the weekend of October 11–12, when the United States reluctantly followed the British government's lead, buying equity stakes in banks rather than just their dodgy assets and offering unprecedented guarantees of banks' debt and deposits.

Since these events coincided with the final phase of a U.S. presidential-election campaign, it was not surprising that some rather simplistic lessons were soon being touted by candidates and commentators. The crisis, some said, was the result of excessive deregulation of financial markets. Others sought to lay the blame on unscrupulous speculators: short-sellers, who borrowed the stocks of vulnerable banks and sold them in the expectation of further price declines. Still other suspects in the frame were negligent regulators and corrupt congressmen.

This hunt for scapegoats is futile. To understand the downfall of Planet Finance, you need to take several steps back and locate this crisis in the long run of financial history. Only then will you see that we have all played a part in this latest sorry example of what the Victorian journalist Charles Mackay described in his 1841 book, *Extraordinary Popular Delusions and the Madness of Crowds.*

As long as there have been banks, bond markets, and stock markets, there have been financial crises. Banks went bust in the days of the Medici. There were bond-market panics in the Venice of Shylock's day.

And the world's first stock-market crash happened in 1720, when the Mississippi Company—the Enron of its day—blew up. According to economists Carmen Reinhart and Kenneth Rogoff, the financial history of the past 800 years is a litany of debt defaults, banking crises, currency crises, and inflationary spikes. Moreover, financial crises seldom happen without inflicting pain on the wider economy. Another recent paper, co-authored by Rogoff's Harvard colleague Robert Barro, has identified 148 crises since 1870 in which a country experienced a cumulative decline in gross domestic product (G.D.P.) of at least 10 percent, implying a probability of financial disaster of around 3.6 percent per year.

If stock-market movements followed the normal-distribution, or bell, curve, like human heights, an annual drop of 10 percent or more would happen only once every 500 years, whereas in the case of the Dow Jones Industrial Average it has happened in 20 of the last 100 years. And stock-market plunges of 20 percent or more would be unheard of—rather like people a foot and a half tall—whereas in fact there have been eight such crashes in the past century.

The most famous financial crisis—the Wall Street Crash—is conventionally said to have begun on "Black Thursday," October 24, 1929, when the Dow declined by 2 percent, though in fact the market had been slipping since early September and had suffered a sharp, 6 percent drop on October 23. On "Black Monday," October 28, it plunged by 13 percent, and the next day by a further 12 percent. In the course of the next three years the U.S. stock market declined by a staggering 89 percent, reaching its nadir in July 1932. The index did not regain its 1929 peak until November 1954.

That helps put our current troubles into perspective. From its peak of 14,164, on October 9, 2007, to a dismal level of 8,579, exactly a year later, the Dow declined by 39 percent. By contrast, on a single day just over two decades ago—October 19, 1987—the index fell by 23 percent, one of only four days in history when the index has fallen by more than 10 percent in a single trading session.

This crisis, however, is about much more than just the stock market. It needs to be understood as a fundamental breakdown of the entire financial system, extending from the monetary-and-banking system through the bond market, the stock market, the insurance market, and the real-estate market. It affects not only established financial institutions such as investment banks but also relatively novel ones such as hedge funds. It is global in scope and unfathomable in scale.

Had it not been for the frantic efforts of the Federal Reserve and the Treasury, to say nothing of their counterparts in almost equally afflicted Europe, there would by now have been a repeat of that "great contraction" of credit and economic activity that was the prime mover of the Depression. Back then, the Fed and the Treasury did next to nothing to prevent bank failures from translating into a drastic contraction of credit and hence of business activity and employment. If the more openhanded monetary and fiscal authorities of today are ultimately successful in preventing a comparable slump of output, future historians may end up calling this "the Great Repression." This is the Depression they are hoping to bottle up—a Depression in denial.

To understand why we have come so close to a rerun of the 1930s, we need to begin at the beginning, with banks and the money they make. From the Middle Ages until the mid-20th century, most banks made their money by maximizing the difference between the costs of their liabilities (payments to depositors) and the earnings on their assets (interest and commissions on loans). Some banks also made money by financing trade, discounting the commercial bills issued by merchants. Others issued and traded bonds and stocks, or dealt in commodities (especially precious metals). But the core business of banking was simple. It consisted, as the third Lord Rothschild pithily put it, "essentially of facilitating the movement of money from Point A, where it is, to Point B, where it is needed."

The system evolved gradually. First came the invention of cashless intra-bank and inter-bank transactions, which allowed debts to be settled between account holders without having money physically change hands. Then came the idea of fractional-reserve banking, whereby banks kept only a small proportion of their existing deposits on hand to satisfy the needs of depositors (who seldom wanted all their money simultaneously), allowing the rest to be lent out profitably. That was followed by the rise of special public banks with monopolies on the issuing of banknotes and other powers and privileges: the first central banks.

With these innovations, money ceased to be understood as precious metal minted into coins. Now it was the sum total of specific liabilities (deposits and reserves) incurred by banks. Credit was the other side of banks' balance sheets: the total of their assets; in other words, the loans they made. Some of this money might still consist of precious metal, though a rising proportion of that would be held in the central bank's vault. Most would be made up of banknotes and coins recognized as "legal tender," along with money that was visible only in current- and deposit-account statements.

Until the late 20th century, the system of bank money retained an anchor in the pre-modern conception of money in the form of the gold standard: fixed ratios between units of account and quantities of precious metal. As early as 1924, the English economist John Maynard Keynes dismissed the gold standard as a "barbarous relic," but the last vestige of the system did not disappear until August 15, 1971—the day President Richard Nixon closed the so-called gold window, through which foreign central banks could still exchange dollars for gold. With that, the centuries-old link between money and precious metal was broken.

Though we tend to think of money today as being made of paper, in reality most of it now consists of bank deposits. If we measure the ratio of actual money to output in developed economies, it becomes clear that the trend since the 1970s has been for that ratio to rise from around 70 percent, before the closing of the gold window, to more than 100 percent by 2005. The corollary has been a parallel growth of credit on the other side of bank balance sheets. A significant component of that credit growth has been a surge of lending to consumers. Back in 1952, the ratio of household debt to disposable income was less than 40 percent in the United States. At its peak in 2007, it reached 133 percent, up from 90 percent a decade before. Today Americans carry a total of $2.56 trillion in consumer debt, up by more than a fifth since 2000.

Even more spectacular, however, has been the rising indebtedness of banks themselves. In 1980, bank indebtedness was equivalent to 21 percent of U.S. gross domestic product. In 2007 the figure was 116 percent. Another measure of this was the declining capital adequacy of banks. On the eve of "the Great Repression," average bank capital in Europe was equivalent to less than 10 percent of assets; at the beginning of the 20th century, it was around 25 percent. It was not unusual for investment banks' balance sheets to be as much as 20 or 30 times larger than their capital, thanks in large part to a 2004 rule change by the Securities and Exchange Commission that exempted the five largest of those banks from the regulation that had capped their debt-to-capital ratio at 12 to 1. The Age of Leverage had truly arrived for Planet Finance.

Credit and money, in other words, have for decades been growing more rapidly than underlying economic activity. Is it any wonder, then, that money has ceased to hold its value the way it did in the era of the gold standard? The motto "In God we trust" was added to the dollar bill in 1957. Since then its purchasing power, relative to the consumer price index, has declined by a staggering 87 percent. Average annual inflation during that period has been more than 4 percent. A man who decided to put his savings into gold in 1970 could have bought just over 27.8 ounces of the precious metal for $1,000. At the time of writing, with gold trading at $900 an ounce, he could have sold it for around $25,000.

Those few goldbugs who always doubted the soundness of fiat money—paper currency without a metal anchor—have in large measure been vindicated. But why were the rest of us so blinded by money illusion?

In the immediate aftermath of the death of gold as the anchor of the monetary system, the problem of inflation affected mainly retail prices and wages. Today, only around one out of seven countries has an inflation rate above 10 percent, and only one, Zimbabwe, is afflicted with hyperinflation. But back in 1979 at least 7 countries had an annual inflation rate above 50 percent, and more than 60 countries—including Britain and the United States—had inflation in double digits.

Inflation has come down since then, partly because many of the items we buy—from clothes to computers—have gotten cheaper as a result of technological innovation and the relocation of production to low-wage economies in Asia. It has also been reduced because of a worldwide transformation in monetary policy, which began with the monetarist-inspired increases in short-term rates implemented by the Federal Reserve in 1979. Just as important, some of the structural drivers of inflation, such as powerful trade unions, have also been weakened.

By the 1980s, in any case, more and more people had grasped how to protect their wealth from inflation: by investing it in assets they expected to appreciate in line with, or ahead of, the cost of living. These assets could take multiple forms, from modern art to vintage wine, but the most popular proved to be stocks and real estate. Once it became clear that this formula worked, the Age of Leverage could begin. For it clearly made sense to borrow to the hilt to maximize your holdings of stocks and real estate if these promised to generate higher rates of return than the interest payments on your borrowings. Between 1990 and 2004, most American households did not see an appreciable improvement in their incomes. Adjusted for inflation, the median household income rose by about 6 percent. But people could raise their living standards by borrowing and investing in stocks and housing.

Nearly all of us did it. And the bankers were there to help. Not only could they borrow more cheaply from one another than we could borrow from them; increasingly they devised all kinds of new mortgages that looked more attractive to us (and promised to be more lucrative to them) than boring old 30-year fixed-rate deals. Moreover, the banks were just as ready to play the asset markets as we were. Proprietary trading soon became the most profitable arm of investment banking: buying and selling assets on the bank's own account.

There was, however, a catch. The Age of Leverage was also an age of bubbles, beginning with the dot-com bubble of the irrationally exuberant 1990s and ending with the real-estate mania of the exuberantly irrational 2000s. Why was this?

The future is in large measure uncertain, so our assessments of future asset prices are bound to vary. If we were all calculating machines, we would simultaneously process all the available information and come to the same conclusion. But we are human beings, and as such are prone to myopia and mood swings. When asset prices surge upward in sync, it is as if investors are gripped by a kind of collective euphoria. Conversely, when their "animal spirits" flip from greed to fear, the bubble that their earlier euphoria inflated can burst with amazing suddenness. Zoological imagery is an integral part of the culture of Planet Finance. Optimistic buyers are "bulls," pessimistic sellers are "bears." The real point, however, is that stock markets are mirrors of the *human* psyche. Like *Homo sapiens*, they can become depressed. They can even suffer complete breakdowns.

This is no new insight. In the 400 years since the first shares were bought and sold on the Amsterdam Beurs, there has been a long succession of financial bubbles. Time and again, asset prices have soared to unsustainable heights only to crash downward again. So familiar is this pattern—described by the economic historian Charles Kindleberger—that it is possible to distill it into five stages:

(1) *Displacement:* Some change in economic circumstances creates new and profitable opportunities. (2) *Euphoria,* or overtrading: A feedback process sets in whereby expectation of rising profits leads to rapid growth in asset prices. (3) *Mania,* or bubble: The prospect of easy capital gains attracts first-time investors and swindlers eager to mulct them of their money. (4) *Distress:* The insiders discern that profits cannot possibly justify the now exorbitant price of the assets and begin to take profits by selling. (5) *Revulsion,* or discredit: As asset prices fall, the outsiders stampede for the exits, causing the bubble to burst.

The key point is that without easy credit creation a true bubble cannot occur. That is why so many bubbles have their origins in the sins of omission and commission of central banks.

The bubbles of our time had their origins in the aftermath of the 1987 stock-market crash, when then novice Federal Reserve chairman Alan Greenspan boldly affirmed the Fed's "readiness to serve as a source of liquidity to support the economic and financial system." This sent a signal to the markets, particularly the New York banks: if things got really bad, he stood ready to bail them out. Thus was born the "Greenspan put"—the implicit option the Fed gave traders to be able to sell their stocks at today's prices even in the event of a meltdown tomorrow.

Having contained a panic once, Greenspan thereafter had a dilemma lurking in the back of his mind: whether or not to act pre-emptively the next time—to prevent a panic altogether. This dilemma came to the fore as a classic stock-market bubble took shape in the mid-90s. The displacement in this case was the explosion of innovation by the technology and software industry as personal computers met the Internet. But, as in all of history's bubbles, an accommodative monetary policy also played a role. From a peak of 6 percent in February 1995, the federal-funds target rate had been reduced to 5.25 percent by January 1996. It was then cut in steps, in the fall of 1998, down to 4.75 percent, and it remained at that level until June 1999, by which time the Dow had passed the 10,000 mark.

Why did the Fed allow euphoria to run loose in the 1990s? Partly because Greenspan and his colleagues underestimated the momentum of the technology bubble; as early as December 1995, with the Dow just past the 5,000 mark, members of the Fed's Open Market Committee speculated that the market might be approaching its peak. Partly, also, because Greenspan came to the conclusion that it was not the Fed's responsibility to worry about asset-price inflation, only consumer-price inflation, and this, he believed, was being reduced by a major improvement in productivity due precisely to the tech boom.

Greenspan could not postpone a stock-exchange crash indefinitely. After Silicon Valley's dot-com bubble peaked, in March 2000, the U.S. stock market fell by almost half over the next two and a half years. It was not until May 2007 that investors in the Standard & Poor's 500 had recouped their losses. But the Fed's response to the sell-off—and the massive shot of liquidity it injected into the financial markets after the 9/11 terrorist attacks—prevented the "correction" from precipitating a depression. Not only were the 1930s averted; so too, it seemed, was a repeat of the Japanese experience after 1989, when a conscious effort by the central bank to prick an asset bubble had ended up triggering an 80 percent stock-market sell-off, a real-estate collapse, and a decade of economic stagnation.

What was not immediately obvious was that Greenspan's easy-money policy was already generating another bubble—this time in the financial market that a majority of Americans have been encouraged for generations to play: the real-estate market.

Real estate is the English-speaking world's favorite economic game. No other facet of financial life has such a hold on the popular imagination. The real-estate market is unique. Every adult, no matter how economically illiterate, has a view on its future prospects. Through the evergreen board game Monopoly, even children are taught how to climb the property ladder.

Once upon a time, people saved a portion of their earnings for the proverbial rainy day, stowing the cash in a mattress or a bank safe. The Age of Leverage, as we have seen, brought a growing reliance on borrowing to buy assets in the expectation of their future appreciation in value. For a majority of families, this meant a leveraged investment in a house. That strategy had one very obvious flaw. It represented a one-way, totally unhedged bet on a single asset.

To be sure, investing in housing paid off handsomely for more than half a century, up until 2006. Suppose you had put $100,000 into the U.S. property market back in the first quarter of 1987. According to the Case-Shiller national home-price index, you would have nearly tripled your money by the first quarter of 2007, to $299,000. On the other hand, if you had put the same money into the S&P 500, and had continued to reinvest the dividend income in that index, you would have ended up with $772,000 to play with—more than double what you would have made on bricks and mortar.

There is, obviously, an important difference between a house and a stock-market index. You cannot live in a stock-market index. For the sake of a fair comparison, allowance must therefore be made for the rent you save by owning your house (or the rent you can collect if you own a second property). A simple way to proceed is just to leave out both dividends and rents. In that case the difference is somewhat reduced. In the two decades after 1987, the S&P 500, excluding dividends, rose by a factor of just over six, meaning that an investment of $100,000 would be worth some $600,000. But that still comfortably beat housing.

There are three other considerations to bear in mind when trying to compare housing with other forms of assets. The first is depreciation. Stocks do not wear out and require new roofs; houses do. The second is liquidity. As assets, houses are a great deal more expensive to convert into cash than stocks. The third is volatility. Housing markets since World War II have been far less volatile than stock markets. Yet that is not to say that house prices have never deviated from a steady upward path. In Britain between 1989 and 1995, for example, the average house price fell by 18 percent, or, in inflation-adjusted terms, by more than a third—37 percent. In London, the real decline was closer to 47 percent. In Japan between 1990 and 2000, property prices fell by more than 60 percent.

The recent decline of property prices in the United States should therefore have come as less of a shock than it did. Between July 2006 and June 2008, the Case-Shiller index of home prices in 20 big American cities declined on average by 19 percent. In some of these cities—Phoenix, San Diego, Los Angeles, and Miami—the total decline was as much as a third. Seen in international perspective, those are not unprecedented figures. Seen in the context of the post-2000 bubble, prices have yet to return to their starting point. On average, house prices are still 50 percent higher than they were at the beginning of this process.

So why were we oblivious to the likely bursting of the real-estate bubble? The answer is that for generations we have been brainwashed into thinking that borrowing to buy a house is the only rational financial strategy to pursue. Think of Frank Capra's classic 1946 movie, *It's a Wonderful Life*, which tells the story of the family-owned Bailey Building & Loan, a small-town mortgage firm that George Bailey (played by James Stewart) struggles to keep afloat in the teeth of the Depression. "You know, George," his father tells him, "I feel that in a small way we are doing something important. It's satisfying a fundamental urge. It's deep in the race for a man to want his own roof and walls and fireplace, and we're helping him get those things in our shabby little office." George gets the message, as he passionately explains to the villainous slumlord Potter after Bailey Sr.'s death: "[My father] never once thought of himself. . . . But he did help a few people get out of your slums, Mr. Potter. And what's wrong with that? . . . Doesn't it make them better citizens? Doesn't it make them better customers?"

There, in a nutshell, is one of the key concepts of the 20th century: the notion that property ownership enhances citizenship, and that therefore a property-owning democracy is more socially and politically stable than a democracy divided into an elite of landlords and a majority of property-less tenants. So deeply rooted is this idea in our political culture that it comes as a surprise to learn that it was invented just 70 years ago.

Prior to the 1930s, only a minority of Americans owned their homes. During the Depression, however, the Roosevelt administration created a whole complex of institutions to change that. A Federal Home Loan Bank Board was set up in 1932 to encourage and oversee local mortgage lenders known as savings-and-loans (S&Ls)—mutual associations that took in deposits and lent to homebuyers. Under the New Deal, the Home Owners' Loan Corporation stepped in to refinance mortgages on longer terms, up to 15 years. To reassure depositors, who had been traumatized by the thousands of bank failures of the previous three years, Roosevelt introduced federal deposit insurance. And by providing federally backed insurance for mortgage lenders, the Federal Housing Administration (F.H.A.) sought to encourage large (up to 80 percent of the purchase price), long (20- to 25-year), fully amortized, low-interest loans.

By standardizing the long-term mortgage and creating a national system of official inspection and valuation, the F.H.A. laid the foundation for a secondary market in mortgages. This market came to life in 1938, when a new Federal National Mortgage Association—nicknamed Fannie Mae— was authorized to issue bonds and use the proceeds to buy mortgages from the local S&Ls, which were restricted by regulation both in terms of geography (they could not lend to borrowers more than 50 miles from their offices) and in terms of the rates they could offer (the so-called Regulation Q, which imposed a low ceiling on interest paid on deposits). Because these changes tended to reduce the average monthly payment on a mortgage, the F.H.A. made home ownership viable for many more Americans than ever before. Indeed, it is not too much to say that the modern United States, with its seductively samey suburbs, was born with Fannie Mae. Between 1940 and 1960, the home-ownership rate soared from 43 to 62 percent.

These were not the only ways in which the federal government sought to encourage Americans to own their own homes. Mortgage-interest payments were always tax-deductible, from the inception of the federal income tax in 1913. As Ronald Reagan said when the rationality of this tax break was challenged, mortgage-interest relief was "part of the American dream."

In 1968, to broaden the secondary mortgage market still further, Fannie Mae was split in two—the Government National Mortgage Association (Ginnie Mae), which was to cater to poor borrowers, and a rechartered Fannie Mae, now a privately owned government-sponsored enterprise (G.S.E.). Two years later, to provide competition for Fannie Mae, the Federal Home Loan Mortgage Corporation (Freddie Mac) was set up. In addition, Fannie Mae was permitted to buy conventional as well as government-guaranteed mortgages. Later, with the Community Reinvestment Act of 1977, American banks found themselves under pressure for the first time to lend to poor, minority communities.

These changes presaged a more radical modification to the New Deal system. In the late 1970s, the savings-and-loan industry was hit first by double-digit inflation and then by sharply rising interest rates. This double punch was potentially lethal. The S&Ls were simultaneously losing money on long-term, fixed-rate mortgages, due to inflation, and hemorrhaging deposits to higher-interest money-market funds. The response in Washington from both the Carter and Reagan administrations was to try to salvage the S&Ls with tax breaks and deregulation. When the new legislation was passed, President Reagan declared, "All in all, I think we hit the jackpot." Some people certainly did.

On the one hand, S&Ls could now invest in whatever they liked, not just local long-term mortgages. Commercial property, stocks, junk bonds—anything was allowed. They could even issue credit cards. On the other, they could now pay whatever interest rate they liked to depositors. Yet all their deposits were still effectively insured, with the maximum covered amount raised from $40,000 to $100,000, thanks to a government regulation two years earlier. And if ordinary deposits did not suffice, the S&Ls could raise money in the form of brokered deposits from middlemen. What happened next perfectly illustrated the great financial precept first enunciated by William Crawford, the commissioner of the California Department of Savings and Loan: "The best way to rob a bank is to own one." Some S&Ls bet their depositors' money on highly dubious real-estate developments. Many simply stole the money, as if deregulation meant that the law no longer applied to them at all.

When the ensuing bubble burst, nearly 300 S&Ls collapsed, while another 747 were closed or reorganized under the auspices of the Resolution Trust Corporation, established by Congress in 1989 to clear up the mess. The final cost of the crisis was $153 billion (around 3 percent of the 1989 G.D.P.), of which taxpayers had to pay $124 billion.

But even as the S&Ls were going belly-up, they offered another, very different group of American financial institutions a fast track to megabucks. To the bond traders at Salomon Brothers, the New York investment bank, the breakdown of the New Deal mortgage system was not a crisis but a wonderful opportunity. As profit-hungry as their language was profane, the self-styled "Big Swinging Dicks" at Salomon saw a way of exploiting the gyrating interest rates of the early 1980s.

The idea was to re-invent mortgages by bundling thousands of them together as the backing for new and alluring securities that could be sold as alternatives to traditional government and corporate bonds—in short, to convert mortgages into bonds. Once lumped together, the interest payments due on the mortgages could be subdivided into strips with different maturities and credit risks. The first issue of this new kind of mortgage-backed security (known as a "collateralized mortgage obligation") occurred in June 1983. The dawn of securitization was a necessary prelude to the Age of Leverage.

Once again, however, it was the federal government that stood ready to pick up the tab in a crisis. For the majority of mortgages continued to enjoy an implicit guarantee from the government-sponsored trio of Fannie, Freddie, and Ginnie, meaning that bonds which used those mortgages as collateral could be represented as virtual government bonds and considered "investment grade." Between 1980 and 2007, the volume of such G.S.E.-backed mortgage-backed securities grew from less than $200 billion to more than $4 trillion. In 1980 only 10 percent of the home-mortgage market was securitized; by 2007, 56 percent of it was.

These changes swept away the last vestiges of the business model depicted in *It's a Wonderful Life*. Once, there had been meaningful social ties between mortgage lenders and borrowers. James Stewart's character knew both the depositors and the debtors. By contrast, in a securitized market the interest you paid on your mortgage ultimately went to someone who had no idea you existed. The full implications of this transition for ordinary homeowners would become apparent only 25 years later.

In July 2007, I paid a visit to Detroit, because I had the feeling that what was happening there was the shape of things to come in the United States as a whole. In the space of 10 years, house prices in Detroit, which probably possesses the worst housing stock of any American city other than New Orleans, had risen by more than a third—not much compared with the nationwide bubble, but still hard to explain, given the city's chronically depressed economic state. As I discovered, the explanation lay in fundamental changes in the rules of the housing game.

I arrived at the end of a borrowing spree. For several years agents and brokers selling subprime mortgages had been flooding Detroit with radio, television, and direct-mail advertisements, offering what sounded like attractive deals. In 2006, for example, subprime lenders pumped more than a billion dollars into 22 Detroit Zip Codes.

These were not the old 30-year fixed-rate mortgages invented in the New Deal. On the contrary, a high proportion were adjustable-rate mortgages—in other words, the interest rate could vary according to changes in short-term lending rates. Many were also interest-only mortgages, without amortization (repayment of principal), even when the principal represented 100 percent of the assessed value of the mortgaged property. And most had introductory "teaser" periods, whereby the initial interest payments—usually for the first two years—were kept artificially low, with the cost of the loan backloaded. All of these devices were intended to allow an immediate reduction in the debt-servicing costs of the borrower.

· In Detroit only a minority of these loans were going to first-time buyers. They were nearly all refinancing deals, which allowed borrowers to treat their homes as cash machines, converting their existing equity into cash and using the proceeds to pay off credit-card debts, carry out renovations, or buy new consumer durables. However, the combination of declining long-term interest rates and ever more alluring mortgage deals did attract new buyers into the housing market. By 2005, 69 percent of all U.S. householders were homeowners; 10 years earlier it had been 64 percent. About half of that increase could be attributed to the subprime-lending boom.

Significantly, a disproportionate number of subprime borrowers belonged to ethnic minorities. Indeed, I found myself wondering, as I drove around Detroit, if "subprime" was in fact a new financial euphemism for "black.". This was no idle supposition. According to a joint study by, among others, the Massachusetts Affordable Housing Alliance, 55 percent of black and Latino borrowers in Boston who had obtained loans for single-family homes in 2005 had been given subprime mortgages; the figure for white borrowers was just 13 percent. More than three-quarters of black and Latino borrowers from Washington Mutual were classed as subprime, whereas only 17 percent of white borrowers were. According to a report in *The Wall Street Journal*, minority ownership increased by 3.1 million between 2002 and 2007.

H ere, surely, was the zenith of the property-owning democracy. It was an achievement that the Bush administration was proud of. "We want everybody in America to own their own home," President George W.

Bush had said in October 2002. Having challenged lenders to create 5.5 million new minority homeowners by the end of the decade, Bush signed the American Dream Downpayment Act in 2003, a measure designed to subsidize first-time house purchases in low-income groups. Between 2000 and 2006, the share of undocumented subprime contracts rose from 17 to 44 percent. Fannie Mae and Freddie Mac also came under pressure from the Department of Housing and Urban Development to support the sub-prime market. As Bush put it in December 2003, "It is in our national inter-est that more people own their own home." Few people dissented.

As a business model, subprime lending worked beautifully—as long, that is, as interest rates stayed low, people kept their jobs, and real-estate prices continued to rise. Such conditions could not be relied upon to last, however, least of all in a city like Detroit. But that did not worry the sub-prime lenders. They simply followed the trail blazed by mainstream mort-gage lenders in the 1980s. Having pocketed fat commissions on the signing of the original loan contracts, they hastily resold their loans in bulk to Wall Street banks. The banks, in turn, bundled the loans into high-yielding mortgage-backed securities and sold them to investors around the world, all eager for a few hundredths of a percentage point more of return on their capital. Repackaged as C.D.O.'s, these subprime securities could be trans-formed from risky loans to flaky borrowers into triple-A-rated investment-grade securities. All that was required was certification from one of the rating agencies that at least the top tier of these securities was unlikely to go into default.

The risk was spread across the globe, from American state pension funds to public-hospital networks in Australia, to town councils near the Arctic Circle. In Norway, for example, eight municipalities, including Rana and Hemnes, invested some $120 million of their taxpayers' money in C.D.O.'s secured on American subprime mortgages.

In Detroit the rise of subprime mortgages had in fact coincided with a new slump in the inexorably declining automobile industry. That antici-pated a wider American slowdown, an almost inevitable consequence of a tightening of monetary policy as the Federal Reserve belatedly raised short-term interest rates from 1 percent to 5.25 percent. As soon as the teaser rates expired and mortgages were reset at new and much higher interest rates, hundreds of Detroit households swiftly fell behind in their mortgage payments. The effect was to burst the real-estate bubble, causing house prices to start falling significantly for the first time since the early 1990s. And the further house prices fell, the more homeowners found themselves with "negative equity"—in other words, owing more money than their homes were worth.

The rest—the chain reaction as defaults in Detroit and elsewhere unleashed huge losses on C.D.O.'s in financial institutions all around the world—you know.

Do you, however, know about the second-order effects of this crisis in the markets for derivatives? Do you in fact know what a derivative is? Once excoriated by Warren Buffett as "financial weapons of mass destruction," derivatives are what make this crisis both unique and unfathomable in its ramifications. To understand what they are, you need, literally, to go back to the future.

For a farmer planting a crop, nothing is more crucial than the future price it will fetch after it has been harvested and taken to market. A futures contract allows him to protect himself by committing a merchant to buy his crop when it comes to market at a price agreed upon when the seeds are being planted. If the market price on the day of delivery is lower than expected, the farmer is protected.

The earliest forms of protection for farmers were known as forward contracts, which were simply bilateral agreements between seller and buyer. A true futures contract, however, is a standardized instrument issued by a futures exchange and hence tradable. With the development of a standard "to arrive" futures contract, along with a set of rules to enforce settlement and, finally, an effective clearinghouse, the first true futures market was born.

Because they are derived from the value of underlying assets, all futures contracts are forms of derivatives. Closely related, though distinct from futures, are the contracts known as options. In essence, the buyer of a "call" option has the right, but not the obligation, to buy an agreed-upon quantity of a particular commodity or financial asset from the seller ("writer") of the option at a certain time (the expiration date) for a certain price (known as the "strike price"). Clearly, the buyer of a call option expects the price of the underlying instrument to rise in the future. When the price passes the agreed-upon strike price, the option is "in the money"—and so is the smart guy who bought it. A "put" option is just the opposite: the buyer has the right but not the obligation to sell an agreed-upon quantity of something to the seller of the option at an agreed-upon price.

A third kind of derivative is the interest-rate "swap," which is effectively a bet between two parties on the future path of interest rates. A pure interest-rate swap allows two parties already receiving interest payments literally to swap them, allowing someone receiving a variable rate of interest to exchange it for a fixed rate, in case interest rates decline. A credit-default swap (C.D.S.), meanwhile, offers protection against a company's defaulting on its bonds.

There was a time when derivatives were standardized instruments traded on exchanges such as the Chicago Board of Trade. Now, however, the vast proportion are custom-made and sold "over the counter" (O.T.C.), often by banks, which charge attractive commissions for their services, but also by insurance companies (notably A.I.G.). According to the Bank for International Settlements, the total notional amounts outstanding of O.T.C. derivative contracts—arranged on an ad hoc basis between two parties—reached a staggering $596 trillion in December 2007, with a gross market value of just over $14.5 trillion.

But how exactly do you price a derivative? What precisely is an option worth? The answers to those questions required a revolution in financial theory. From an academic point of view, what this revolution achieved was highly impressive. But the events of the 1990s, as the rise of quantitative finance replaced preppies with quants (quantitative analysts) all along Wall Street, revealed a new truth: those whom the gods want to destroy they first teach math.

Working closely with Fischer Black, of the consulting firm Arthur D. Little, M.I.T.'s Myron Scholes invented a groundbreaking new theory of pricing options, to which his colleague Robert Merton also contributed. (Scholes and Merton would share the 1997 Nobel Prize in economics.) They reasoned that a call option's value depended on six variables: the current market price of the stock (S), the agreed future price at which the stock could be bought (L), the time until the expiration date of the option (t), the risk-free rate of return in the economy as a whole (r), the probability that the option will be exercised (N), and—the crucial variable—the expected volatility of the stock, i.e., the likely fluctuations of its price between the time of purchase and the expiration date (σ). With wonderful mathematical wizardry, the quants reduced the price of a call option to this formula (the Black-Scholes formula):

$$C = SN(d) - Le^{-rt}N(d - \sigma\sqrt{t})$$

in which:

$$d = \frac{\ln(\frac{S}{L}) + (r + \frac{\sigma^2}{2})t}{\sigma\sqrt{t}}$$

Feeling a bit baffled? Can't follow the algebra? That was just fine by the quants. To make money from this magic formula, they needed markets to be full of people who didn't have a clue about how to price options but relied instead on their (seldom accurate) gut instincts. They also needed a great deal of computing power, a force which had been transforming the financial markets since the early 1980s. Their final requirement was a partner with some market savvy in order to make the leap from the faculty club to the trading floor. Black, who would soon be struck down by cancer, could not be that partner. But John Meriwether could. The former head of the bond-arbitrage group at Salomon Brothers, Meriwether had made his first fortune in the wake of the S&L meltdown of the late 1980s. The hedge fund he created with Scholes and Merton in 1994 was called Long-Term Capital Management.

In its brief, four-year life, Long-Term was the brightest star in the hedge-fund firmament, generating mind-blowing returns for its elite club of investors and even more money for its founders. Needless to say, the firm did more than just trade options, though selling puts on the stock market became such a big part of its business that it was nicknamed "the central bank of volatility" by banks buying insurance against a big stock-market sell-off. In fact, the partners were simultaneously pursuing multiple trading strategies, about 100 of them, with a total of 7,600 positions. This conformed to a second key rule of the new mathematical finance: the virtue of diversification, a principle that had been formalized by Harry M. Markowitz, of the Rand Corporation. Diversification was all about having a multitude of uncorrelated positions. One might go wrong, or even two. But thousands just could not go wrong simultaneously.

The mathematics were reassuring. According to the firm's "Value at Risk" models, it would take a 10-σ (in other words, 10-standard-deviation) event to cause the firm to lose all its capital in a single year. But the probability of such an event, according to the quants, was 1 in 10^{24}—or effectively zero. Indeed, the models said the most Long-Term was likely to lose in a single day was $45 million. For that reason, the partners felt no compunction about leveraging their trades. At the end of August 1997, the fund's capital was $6.7 billion, but the debt-financed assets on its balance sheet amounted to $126 billion, a ratio of assets to capital of 19 to 1.

There is no need to rehearse here the story of Long-Term's downfall, which was precipitated by a Russian debt default. Suffice it to say that on Friday, August 21, 1998, the firm lost $550 million—15 percent of its entire capital, and vastly more than its mathematical models had said was possible. The key point is to appreciate why the quants were so wrong.

The problem lay with the assumptions that underlie so much of mathematical finance. In order to construct their models, the quants had to postulate a planet where the inhabitants were omniscient and perfectly rational; where they instantly absorbed all new information and used it to maximize profits; where they never stopped trading; where markets were continuous, frictionless, and completely liquid. Financial markets on this planet followed a "random walk," meaning that each day's prices were quite unrelated to the previous day's, but reflected no more and no less than all the relevant information currently available. The returns on this planet's stock market were normally distributed along the bell curve, with most years clustered closely around the mean, and two-thirds of them within one standard deviation of the mean. On such a planet, a "six standard deviation" sell-off would be about as common as a person shorter than one foot in our world. It would happen only once in four million years of trading.

But Long-Term was not located on Planet Finance. It was based in Greenwich, Connecticut, on Planet Earth, a place inhabited by emotional human beings, always capable of flipping suddenly and en masse from greed to fear. In the case of Long-Term, the herding problem was acute, because many other firms had begun trying to copy Long-Term's strategies in the hope of replicating its stellar performance. When things began to go wrong, there was a truly bovine stampede for the exits. The result was a massive, synchronized downturn in virtually all asset markets. Diversification was no defense in such a crisis. As one leading London hedge-fund manager later put it to Meriwether, "John, you were the correlation."

There was, however, another reason why Long-Term failed. The quants' Value at Risk models had implied that the loss the firm suffered in August 1998 was so unlikely that it ought never to have happened in the entire life of the universe. But that was because the models were working with just five years of data. If they had gone back even 11 years, they would have captured the 1987 stock-market crash. If they had gone back 80 years they would have captured the last great Russian default, after the 1917 revolution. Meriwether himself, born in 1947, ruefully observed, "If I had lived through the Depression, I would have been in a better position to understand events." To put it bluntly, the Nobel Prize winners knew plenty of mathematics but not enough history.

One might assume that, after the catastrophic failure of L.T.C.M., quantitative hedge funds would have vanished from the financial scene, and derivatives such as options would be sold a good deal more circumspectly. Yet the very reverse happened. Far from declining, in the past 10 years hedge funds of every type have exploded in number and in the volume of assets they manage, with quantitative hedge funds such as Renaissance, Citadel, and D. E. Shaw emerging as leading players. The growth of derivatives has also been spectacular—and it has continued despite the onset of the credit crunch. Between December 2005 and December 2007, the notional amounts outstanding for all derivatives increased from $298 trillion to $596 trillion. Credit-default swaps quadrupled, from $14 trillion to $58 trillion.

An intimation of the problems likely to arise came in September 2008, when the government takeover of Fannie and Freddie cast doubt on the status of derivative contracts protecting the holders of more than $1.4 trillion of their bonds against default. The consequences of the failure of Lehman Brothers were substantially greater, because the firm was the counter-party in so many derivative contracts.

The big question is whether those active in the market waited too long to set up some kind of clearing mechanism. If, as seems inevitable, there is an upsurge in corporate defaults as the U.S. slides into recession, the whole system could completely seize up.

Just 10 years ago, during the Asian crisis of 1997–98, it was conventional wisdom that financial crises were more likely to happen on the periphery of the world economy—in the so-called emerging markets of East Asia and Latin America. Yet the biggest threats to the global financial system in this new century have come not from the periphery but from the core. The explanation for this strange role reversal may in fact lie in the way emerging markets changed their behavior after 1998.

For many decades it was assumed that poor countries could become rich only by borrowing capital from wealthy countries. Recurrent debt crises and currency crises associated with sudden withdrawals of Western money led to a rethinking, inspired largely by the Chinese example.

When the Chinese wanted to attract foreign capital, they insisted that it take the form of direct investment. That meant that instead of borrowing from Western banks to finance its industrial development, as many emerging markets did, China got foreigners to build factories in Chinese enterprise zones—large, lumpy assets that could not easily be withdrawn in a crisis.

The crucial point, though, is that the bulk of Chinese investment has been financed from China's own savings. Cautious after years of instability and unused to the panoply of credit facilities we have in the West, Chinese households save a high proportion of their rising incomes, in marked contrast to Americans, who in recent years have saved almost none at all. Chinese corporations save an even larger proportion of their soaring profits. The remarkable thing is that a growing share of that savings surplus has ended up being lent to the United States. In effect, the People's Republic of China has become banker to the United States of America.

The Chinese have not been acting out of altruism. Until very recently, the best way for China to employ its vast population was by exporting manufactured goods to the spendthrift U.S. consumer. To ensure that those exports were irresistibly cheap, China had to fight the tendency for its currency to strengthen against the dollar by buying literally billions of dollars on world markets. In 2006, Chinese holdings of dollars reached 700 billion. Other Asian and Middle Eastern economies adopted much the same strategy.

The benefits for the United States were manifold. Asian imports kept down U.S. inflation. Asian labor kept down U.S. wage costs. Above all, Asian savings kept down U.S. interest rates. But there was a catch. The more Asia was willing to lend to the United States, the more Americans were willing to borrow. The Asian savings glut was thus the underlying cause of the surge in bank lending, bond issuance, and new derivative contracts that Planet Finance witnessed after 2000. It was the underlying cause of the hedge-fund population explosion. It was the underlying reason why private-equity partnerships were able to borrow money left, right, and center to finance leveraged buyouts. And it was the underlying reason why the U.S. mortgage market was so awash with cash by 2006 that you could get a 100 percent mortgage with no income, no job, and no assets.

Whether or not China is now sufficiently "decoupled" from the United States that it can insulate itself from our credit crunch remains to be seen. At the time of writing, however, it looks very doubtful.

The modern financial system is the product of centuries of economic evolution. Banks transformed money from metal coins into accounts, allowing ever larger aggregations of borrowing and lending. From the Renaissance on, government bonds introduced the securitization of streams of interest payments. From the 17th century on, equity in corporations could be bought and sold in public stock markets. From the 18th century on, central banks slowly learned how to moderate or exacerbate the business cycle. From the 19th century on, insurance was supplemented by futures, the first derivatives. And from the 20th century on, households were encouraged by government to skew their portfolios in favor of real estate.

Economies that combined all these institutional innovations performed better over the long run than those that did not, because financial intermediation generally permits a more efficient allocation of resources than, say, feudalism or central planning. For this reason, it is not wholly surprising that the Western financial model tended to spread around the world, first in the guise of imperialism, then in the guise of globalization.

Yet money's ascent has not been, and can never be, a smooth one. On the contrary, financial history is a roller-coaster ride of ups and downs, bubbles and busts, manias and panics, shocks and crashes. The excesses of the Age of Leverage—the deluge of paper money, the asset-price inflation, the explosion of consumer and bank debt, and the hypertrophic growth of derivatives—were bound sooner or later to produce a really big crisis.

It remains unclear whether this crisis will have economic and social effects as disastrous as those of the Great Depression, or whether the monetary and fiscal authorities will succeed in achieving a Great Repression, averting a 1930s-style "great contraction" of credit and output by transferring the as yet unquantifiable losses from banks to taxpayers.

Either way, Planet Finance has now returned to Planet Earth with a bang. The key figures of the Age of Leverage—the lax central bankers, the reckless investment bankers, the hubristic quants—are now feeling the full force of this planet's gravity.

But what about the rest of us, the rank-and-file members of the deluded crowd? Well, we shall now have to question some of our most deeply rooted assumptions—not only about the benefits of paper money but also about the rationale of the property-owning democracy itself.

On Planet Finance it may have made sense to borrow billions of dollars to finance a massive speculation on the future prices of American houses, and then to erect on the back of this trade a vast inverted pyramid of incomprehensible securities and derivatives.

But back here on Planet Earth it suddenly seems like an extraordinary popular delusion.

·4·

Over the Hedge

By BETHANY MCLEAN

April 2009

It used to be that to become a billionaire, rather than a mere millionaire, you had to inherit money, or build an empire that would last for a long, long time. But in the era that has just ended, you could become a billionaire just by managing other people's money. You didn't have to do so for very long—and, maybe, you didn't even have to do so very well.

On February 9, 2007, a company called Fortress Investment Group began trading on the New York Stock Exchange. Fortress, which both runs hedge funds and makes private-equity investments, was part of the seemingly miraculous wave of money begetting more money, in which people who managed others' fortunes made even greater fortunes for themselves. Those who thought they'd found a way to get in on the miracle snapped up Fortress's shares. The stock had been priced at $18.50 the day before and promptly shot up to $35 when trading began in the morning. By the end of the day the five principals of Fortress—all youngish men who were present on that winter morning to ring the bell at the N.Y.S.E.—were worth a combined $10.7 billion.

The five Fortress guys hadn't spent years toiling in obscurity to build their business. Fortress was founded as a private partnership only a decade ago by Wesley Edens, now 47, Randal Nardone, 51, and Robert Kauffman, 45. Edens, the C.E.O., is a cerebral, intense, very private wunderkind who made his reputation at Lehman Brothers—and a fortune for his firm—buying assets from the Resolution Trust Corporation. He made partner at Lehman when he was barely past 30. In 1993, he left "abruptly," as the press described it, due to "philosophical differences with management." He joined a prestigious money-management firm called BlackRock, split to spend a short year at the Swiss bank UBS, and then set up his own shop—Fortress.

In 2002, Edens, Nardone, and Kauffman were joined by Peter Briger Jr., 44, and Michael "Novo" Novogratz, 43. Both are Princetonians who became Goldman Sachs partners. Of Briger, someone who knows him says, "He could take a pile of napkins and figure out how to make money." He is seen as a scrappy, tough trader type who knows how to play hardball in the often brutal world of distressed debt. His high-profile deals have included loans to both fallen New York real-estate mogul Harry Macklowe and Donald Trump's struggling Chicago hotel project. As for Novogratz, a former college wrestler and army helicopter pilot, he's the kind of guy who makes other guys "starry-eyed," as a friend puts it. This is due to his great charm and his embrace of a lifestyle that more than one person calls "lunatic"—they mean it as a compliment—due to his love of partying. Indeed, sources say that, while Goldman Sachs wanted Novo's considerable skills, the firm was nervous about his lifestyle issues, and the two parted ways.

Making money seemed to be simple for Fortress. And no wonder. While the five principals are seen by their colleagues as extremely smart—"these are not B-team guys," says one—in recent years it was hard to lose, and Fortress, like its peers, charged rich fees. For instance, its hedge funds, which were run by Novogratz and Briger, cost investors a management fee of between 1 and 3 percent of the total assets under management, as well as "incentive fees"—20 to 25 percent of any profits. At Fortress, such fees for all of its businesses totaled over $1 billion in 2007, more than double those in 2005.

While the $10.7 billion the five principals made with the I.P.O. was only paper wealth, that didn't really matter, because they'd already made fortunes from the business before they sold it to the public. They did so in three ways. First, they borrowed money, used $250 million of it to pay themselves a dividend, and used part of the I.P.O. proceeds to pay back the loan. Second, they sold a 15 percent stake to the Japanese bank Nomura for $888 million right before the I.P.O. Last, from 2005 until the date of the I.P.O., they distributed to themselves hundreds of millions from the accumulated fees that investors had paid. In other words, each man got an average of $400 million in cash even before the I.P.O. But the Fortress men are big believers in their own prowess. They say they took all that money—and more—and put it into the funds and investments they managed. And they still own 77 percent of the company's stock. "We have invested more than we have taken out," says Edens, in a rare interview. "We have bet on ourselves more than anyone else has."

To go with their bravado, they lived a normal lifestyle—that is, "normal" by the rarefied standards of those who made their fortunes in finance. Edens has had an apartment on Manhattan's Central Park West since his Lehman days, owns land in Montana, and bought an $18 million house on Martha's Vineyard from J. Crew C.E.O. Mickey Drexler. Kauffman, who runs Fortress's European business, bought into Michael Waltrip's NASCAR team, valued recently at $86 million. Novogratz purchased Robert De Niro's Tribeca duplex for $12.25 million—and then bought the apartment underneath to make a triplex. Briger built a 12,000-square-foot home in East Hampton in 2007 to add to his residence in Manhattan. A helicopter that is partially owned by Fortress, purchased before the company went public, sometimes shuttles Novogratz and Briger to and from the firm's Manhattan offices. (The men say they reimburse Fortress for the expense.)

There are few better measures of the end of the era of easy money than the chart of Fortress's stock, which went almost straight down after the I.P.O. On Wednesday, December 3, 2008, it plummeted 25 percent, to $1.87—a 95 percent drop from its opening-day high—after Fortress told investors that they would not be allowed to withdraw the $3.5 billion they had invested in Fortress's Drawbridge Global Macro fund, which is run by Novogratz. By the end of October, the fund was 26 percent below its high-water mark; Briger's fund had also suffered double-digit losses. The redemption requests, combined with the investment losses, would have brought down Novogratz's fund, which had $8 billion in assets on September 30, to just $3.65 billion. The firm also canceled its dividend for the last two quarters of 2008. Bad jokes about "cracks in the Fortress" and "pulling up the Drawbridge" are now making the rounds on the Street.

Truth be told, in the hedge-fund universe, about the only thing that makes Fortress unusual is its publicly traded stock. The entire industry is reeling as investors pull billions from funds that have lost billions. (While private equity has its own severe problems—maybe more severe—investors don't expect to get their money back for years, thereby delaying the day of reckoning.) According to the Chicago-based firm Hedge Fund Research, 2008 was by far the worst year for hedge funds since it began tracking the industry, in 1990. The average fund fell 18 percent—and for many top names, the numbers are even worse. The flagship hedge fund run by Steve Mandel of Lone Pine Capital, one of the most respected managers, was down 32 percent last year. "So many 'smart' guys had their heads handed to them," comments one knowledgeable observer. Or as famous hedge-fund manager George Soros told Congress in testimony last fall, "Many hedge-fund managers forgot the cardinal rule of hedge-fund investing, which is to protect investor capital during down markets."

Today, the burning question for most hedge-fund managers isn't whether their industry will contract but, rather, by how much. Soros told Congress that the amount of money hedge funds manage would shrink by 50 to 75 percent.

The industry's problem isn't just bad performance. Regulators in both the U.S. and the U.K. made headlines by charging that short-selling by hedge funds—in which a manager bets that a stock will decline in value—helped cause the market's crash. There's also outright fraud, for which the poster boy is Bernie Madoff. While his operation wasn't actually a hedge fund, the scandal has infused another dose of what-are-they-actually-doing-with-my-money fear into investors. Add to that Arthur Nadel, the Florida hedge-fund manager who allegedly bilked investors out of $300 million before fleeing. (The not-so-reassuring headline in *Forbes*: POOF! ANOTHER FUND MANAGER DISAPPEARS.) While fraud may not be exactly the norm, the underlying paranoia is this: Are hedge funds just a legal scam, in which investors pay through the nose for something that isn't what it's cracked up to be?

There are many managers who argue that the industry's problems are at least in part of its own making. Says Leon Cooperman, who founded the $3 billion hedge fund Omega Advisors in 1991, after a 25-year career at Goldman Sachs, "Hedge funds have shot themselves in the foot. They have not treated investors correctly." Atop his list of sins: refusing to allow investors to take their money out, which is known in the industry as "gating" investors. Cooperman is not alone. Says Brooke Parish, senior managing director at the $9 billion hedge fund York Capital Management, "Someone worked hard for that money, and it's someone else's money. You give their money back when you promised it. I'm upset with the hubris, the lack of humility, the arrogance. It gives this industry a black eye, and it will take a long period of time to work through."

Another manager tells me a story about Morgan Stanley's annual hedge-fund conference at the Breakers, in Palm Beach, which was held the last week of January. In years past, every hedge-fund manager wanted a plum spot on a panel, so they could present themselves to prospective investors. This year, Morgan had to beg its clients to participate. Managers were reluctant not because they didn't want—or need—the money, but because "no one wanted to be subject to a Q&A from strangers about why we all suck so bad," as this manager put it. And those who worried were right to do so. "It was open warfare," he says. He adds that the attitude from wealthy families was "Who are these bourgeois pigs who ripped us off?"

Another manager describes the mood at the Breakers as "pure, unbridled anger." A source says one foreign investor at the conference declared, "These hedge-fund managers are like the Somali pirates!"—and he wasn't kidding.

Contrast the Breakers with a scene from just a few years ago, when Goldman Sachs held its annual conference, this one aimed at so-called emerging managers—those who were supposed to be the industry's new rock stars—in Miami, Florida. Over cocktails at the pool, there was chatter by those who had never run hedge funds of raising billions for their start-ups. After all, Eric Mindich, who made partner at Goldman Sachs at

27 before quitting that plum perch to start a hedge fund called Eton Park, had begun with $3.5 billion. The air at the conference, says one attendee, was a mixture of "money lust, arrogance, and am-I-going-to-get-mine anxiety." (This year, Goldman Sachs canceled its conference.)

While hedge funds all manage money, they do so in very different ways. Some may invest solely in stocks, while others make bets on the direction of currencies around the globe. Many don't actually "hedge" at all. What unites them is the way that managers are paid. Like Fortress, all hedge funds charge investors a certain percentage of assets under management, plus a cut of the net profits. The standard is "2 and 20," or 2 percent of assets annually plus 20 percent of any profits. (As recently as five years ago, the standard was 1 and 20.) Some charge much more. Citadel, a well-known Chicago-based hedge fund, used to charge not 2 percent but whatever its expenses were, which could be as high as 8 or 9 percent of assets, plus 20 percent of profits. (Even after these fees, however, investors got an annualized return of 22 percent from 1998 through the end of 2007.)

For investors, it was supposed to make sense to pay so much more than the 1 percent of assets that a mutual fund might charge, because hedge funds were supposed to offer something that a mutual fund couldn't. The macho hedge-fund men scorned the mutual-fund boys, who measured themselves by the wimpy "relative return"—how their numbers stacked up against the S&P 500. In contrast, hedge funds, including Fortress, aimed for "absolute return"—positive numbers no matter what the S&P 500 did. The idea was that a hedge fund limited your "exposure to market risks," as Fortress puts it in financial filings. The setup was supposed to make so much sense that another industry—"fund of funds"—sprang up. Funds of funds sold investors a collection of hedge funds, and charged another layer of fees—usually 1 and 10—on top of the manager's fees.

S ome hedge-fund managers defend the loss of 18 percent of investors' money as trouncing the S&P 500, which lost 37 percent in 2008. True, but that wasn't supposed to be the goal. Cooperman calls hedge-fund compensation an "asymmetric fee structure": "If I make a lot, you pay me. If I lose a lot, I don't give anything back."

"Do the math," says another veteran Wall Streeter. What he means is this: Assume you give a manager $100 million and he doubles it. The manager gets $20 million. The next year, he's down 50 percent. Your $100 million is now $90 million, but the manager has $20 million.

Unfortunately, in flush times few did that particular math, and so, for wealthy investors, endowments, and pension funds, hedge funds became the new luxury must-have. And for smart youngsters—or those who thought they were smart—coming out of Harvard Business School, or with a few years on Wall Street, well, how else could you get rich so quickly? "The shocking thing was how easy it was to get in from 2002 to 2006," says one longtime manager. "All you had to do was raise your hand and say I'll take 2 and 20. That was the barrier to entry. It boggled my mind."

I n mid-2008, there were some 10,000 hedge funds, according to Hedge Fund Research—more than five times the number of companies listed on the New York Stock Exchange, and up from just 3,000 funds a decade earlier. Assets mushroomed from around $400 billion to about $2 trillion. Everyone wanted to be the next Eric Mindich—or the next Kenneth Griffin, who started trading when he was a sophomore at Harvard, and after graduation founded Citadel with $1 million of backing from a wealthy investor. At its peak, Citadel had some $20 billion in assets; Griffin's estimated net worth of $3 billion made him 117th on the 2007 *Forbes* Four Hundred.

Such wealth didn't make Griffin unique—on the contrary. By 2006 you needed to make at least $50 million to make *Trader Monthly*'s list of the top 100 traders, ranked by pay, on the Street. You needed $1 billion in annual earnings to crack the top five—and the top five were all hedge-fund managers. That year, the magazine—which suspended operations this February—gave up capping the number of hedge-fund managers who could make the list, because, the editors wrote, "we could no longer ignore the ever-widening chasm between hedge fund traders and the rest of the pack." By the following year, the bottom-of-the-list haul had risen to $75 million. "The size of paychecks as they relate to performance got out of control, particularly in the last few years," says Brad Balter, who runs a hedge-fund advisory firm called Balter Capital Management. "The numbers in many cases were staggering, and this is particularly frustrating in cases where performance ceased to matter." As Balter points out, if a fund with billions under management took the standard 2 percent fee on those dollars, managers could earn fortunes regardless of their returns.

Ound requisite toy of the newly rich hedge-fund managers was ex-
pensive art. Steven Cohen, who runs the multi-billion-dollar fund
SAC Capital, became the trendsetter when he paid $8 million in 2004 for
British artist Damien Hirst's shark in formaldehyde. He also owns two de
Koonings that he bought from DreamWorks co-founder David Geffen for
$63 million and $137.5 million, respectively, as well as works by Picasso,
Warhol, Pollock, and Munch.

The other was expensive offices. In New York, the place to be was "the
Plaza District"—the area stretching from Park Avenue to Sixth Avenue,
just south of Central Park. A view of the park was coveted: "The park
means power," says Ben Friedland, a senior vice president at the real-estate
company CB Richard Ellis, who does most of his business with financial-
services firms. And the higher the floor the better. Evan Margolin, a managing director at Studley, another real-estate firm, which helps tenants with
their commercial-real-estate requirements, says that over the last four or
five years rents increased between 50 and 100 percent or even more in the
Plaza District, depending on the building. At the peak, the most coveted
space rented for more than $200 per square foot. (By this measure, Fortress
was relatively conservative. Its offices on the 46th floor of 1345 Avenue of
the Americas, four blocks from the park, cost some $8.4 million in rent in
2007, but the building is considered more corporate than high hedge-fund
style.) After the crash of last fall, however, the Manhattan rent increases of
the last few years have been all but erased, says Friedland.

Bankers once lined up to pitch hedge funds on selling shares to the
public. One successful manager says he had no fewer than nine investment
banks urging him to do an I.P.O. Cooperman, for his part, says he gave
some advice for those funds that did go public: "I said to all of them, within
five years you will buy yourself back at 20 cents on the dollar." Indeed,
while the few other funds that followed in Fortress's footsteps have fared a
tiny bit better, they certainly haven't fared well. Both the Blackstone Group,
a private-equity firm, and the hedge fund Och-Ziff Capital Management
have seen their stocks fall more than 80 percent from their highs.

For old-timers, it was all a shock. "When I started a hedge fund, people
asked me what I did. I said, 'I run a hedge fund,' and they said, 'What's
that?' This included people on Wall Street," says one manager, who started

his now multi-billion-dollar fund over a decade ago. "We got to a period in the late 1990s where if someone said to me, 'Do you work at a hedge fund?' I would have said, 'Not as you know it. We hedge.'"

Jamie Dinan, C.E.O. of York Capital Management, says that, when he started, most of his friends thought he was nuts. If you graduated from Harvard Business School, as he did, you worked as a banker, not as a low-class trader. Initially, he operated out of a windowless office and figured that if things went well he might one day net some $200,000 annually from his management and performance fees. "I never dreamed this," he says.

I t all begs a fairly simple question, which is: How could there have been as many great investors as there were hedge funds being started?

The short answer is there weren't.

In the later years of the hedge-fund explosion, there weren't any serious tests of a manager's prowess, because it was so easy to make money. In addition, David Kabiller, a principal at AQR Capital Management—a roughly $20 billion hedge fund founded by Goldman Sachs alums Kabiller, Cliff Asness, John Liew, and Robert Krail—points out that there isn't any way to measure most hedge funds. While any investor in a mutual fund can glance at the S&P 500 to get a yardstick of how well his fund manager is doing, a hedge fund with a more esoteric strategy is harder to measure. "If there aren't any benchmarks, then you can't be discovered," says Kabiller.

As money flooded in, even those managers who did something unique soon found billions of dollars copying them. That reduced the available returns. In response, some managers began to hunt off the beaten paths and buy more exotic stuff—stakes in private Chinese companies, or securities based on mortgages, for instance—that wasn't as "liquid" (meaning it couldn't be sold as easily) as a stock.

And there was a secret sauce that washed away all sins: debt. The cost of borrowing money was so insanely low that a hedge-fund manager could make a trade that would earn only a sliver of a return, and then juice that return by using a truckload of borrowed money. As the money rolled in, many young managers thought they were geniuses. Or as Keith Mc-Cullough, who sold a hedge fund he founded and then started a research site for investors called Research Edge, says, "Some of them actually thought it was due to their intelligence, and not just the cycle."

While some funds resisted the siren call of debt, Fortress, for the most part, wasn't one of them. Its financial filings note that "the funds we manage may operate with a substantial degree of leverage. . . . This leverage creates the potential for higher returns, but also increases the volatility."

As another hedge-fund manager tells me, Warren Buffett brilliantly predicted that there would be a day of reckoning: "You only learn who has been swimming naked when the tide goes out."

Fortress's stock, which had sunk to $10 by August 2008, should have been a sign that the tide was going out. But few hedge-fund managers were adroit enough to head for shore.

"You know the children's books 'A Series of Unfortunate Events'?" Jamie Dinan asks me. "Horrible, horrible things happen in those books. That's how I feel about last fall."

Another manager tells me that his fund was down 2 percent at the end of August. By October, he was down 26 percent. "We have great confidence in our analytical ability, and when the world is panicking, we stand up," he says. "In retrospect, I should have panicked."

As the investment banks that provided the debt began to fight for their own survival, those hedge funds that depended on it were faced with margin calls. But even funds that weren't debt-laden were hit with problems from the banking panic. To reduce their risk, many funds began to sell their positions and move to cash. For example, the stock holdings of Atticus Capital, whose co-chairman is Nathaniel Rothschild, fell from $8.1 billion at the end of June to just $510 million by the end of September. In addition, just as you wouldn't want your money at a bank that goes under, hedge funds didn't want to be trapped at a firm that went under, so they moved their money to banks they thought were safer. In order to do so, they had to sell their long positions and get out of the short positions, driving down the price of the former and driving up the price of the latter—thereby exacerbating the selling pressure.

In a way, hedge funds were eating one another alive. As managers sold their positions, some discovered, as one manager puts it, that "all our names were owned by the same guys. We had become the market. When I ran for the exits, all the buyers who should have been there were doing the same." During the third quarter, a Goldman Sachs index which tracks stocks that are heavily owned by hedge funds lost 19 percent, more than twice the decline of the S&P 500, while another Goldman Sachs index that tracks stocks which hedge funds were likely to sell short actually gained 2.4 percent, according to a Cambridge Associates LLC report. "Hedge funds were shooting at each other," says one manager, meaning that some funds would make bets against stocks that were heavily owned by other managers.

And then there was the September 2008 bankruptcy of Lehman Brothers. Not only did that roil the market further—it caused a particular problem for hedge funds. Because the U.S. actually has fairly strict rules about the amount of debt you can use, many funds had set up offshore accounts—sometimes with Lehman London—where the rules were far laxer. What they failed to understand was that bankruptcy rules are also different in London, and that they wouldn't be able to get their money out. One manager estimates that roughly half of the hedge funds in existence had at least some exposure to Lehman London.

At the same time, hedge funds found themselves becoming a scapegoat for the problems in the market. "We are the whipping boys," says one executive. The C.E.O.'s of investment banks including Bear Stearns, Lehman, and Morgan Stanley blamed short-selling by hedge funds for the declines in their stock—no matter that these banks had previously made a lot of money from the industry, and that Morgan Stanley's C.E.O., John Mack, had once worked as the chairman of a hedge fund—Pequot Capital. On September 18, New York attorney general Andrew Cuomo announced an investigation into whether traders illegally spread rumors to drive down the stock prices of financial firms, and likened the activity to "looters after a hurricane." On September 19, the S.E.C. temporarily banned short-selling in a list of almost 1,000 finance-related stocks. A few days later, the agency ordered more than two dozen hedge funds to turn over records as part of an investigation into whether traders were spreading rumors to manipulate share prices downward.

Although Cuomo was careful to single out illegal short-selling, some managers took it as a criticism of the industry. So one manager was surprised to get a call from Cuomo's office, shortly after the announcement, inviting him to lunch at the Core Club (a Manhattan venue opened three years ago for "leaders" willing to part with a $50,000 initiation fee). The suggested campaign donation: $1,000. When he arrived, he battled for elevator space with other hedge-fund managers. "It was the hedge-fund community of New York," he recalls. Cuomo told the assembled managers that, if he were an investor, he would have sold housing-related stocks short as well. He also told them that they needed a Washington lobbyist because the industry lacked a voice. (One manager who was at the event emphasizes that Cuomo had targeted only illegal short-selling, and was right to launch an investigation into that.)

B y mid-October, rumors that Citadel—which also depended on debt— was in trouble began to sweep through the market. On October 24, more than 1,000 listeners crowded onto a conference call in which Citadel said that its two largest funds were down 35 percent due to the "unprecedented de-leveraging that took place around the world," as C.F.O. Gerald Beeson described it. Citadel finished the year with its two main funds down over 50 percent (although smaller funds were up more than 40 percent), and it told investors it would suspend redemptions in them until the end of March, at which time it would re-evaluate market conditions. (Citadel did reimburse investors for most of the fees they paid in 2008.) Other big-name funds, including Thomas Steyer's Farallon and Paul Tudor Jones's BVI Global, also limited redemptions. Even *Über*-trader Steve Cohen's SAC Capital put a chunk of investors' money in a "side pocket," meaning that they can't take it out, although SAC did say it would try to get people their money in 2009.

Managers who employ gates defend the practice on the grounds that it's within their legal rights, and that selling their positions to meet redemption requests would be unfair to those investors who wanted to stay. But the widespread impression among investors is that managers broke a social contract and are doing it to save their own skins. And there may be another reason for the gates. Fortress's documents, for instance, disclose that "our funds have various agreements that create debt or debt-like obligations . . . with a material number of counterparties. Such agreements in many instances contain covenants or 'triggers' that require our funds to maintain specified amounts of assets under management." (The firm says it renegotiated those deals, and has already returned 70 percent of investors' money. The rest of it will be paid out over the next 18 months.)

Other hedge-fund managers who do not employ gating are outraged, in part because the practice has hurt them. "It is the stupidest thing I have ever seen my industry do," says Jim Chanos, who runs a well-known hedge-fund firm called Kynikos Associates, which specializes in short-selling. "It's given rise to the worst fears—that hedge funds are a roach motel." He also says that, while his fund was up more than 50 percent last year, he has gotten redemption requests for 20 percent of his assets—not because investors want to cash out, but because they can't get money anywhere else. "I am an A.T.M. machine," he says, in a comment that was repeated to me by many other managers.

Others in the industry also say that preventing investors from taking their money out is nothing short of an admission that the assets in the fund can't be sold as they are currently valued. One manager tells me that he has a debt security that he is valuing at 50 cents on the dollar. He knows another fund that is marking the identical security at 90 cents on the dollar.

This means that the headline number for the industry—down 18 percent—may not be an accurate read. (In fairness, this is probably not an issue for hedge funds that deal mostly in actively traded securities.) One manager laughs when I ask him if 18 percent is really the right number. "It's way worse," he says. "Way worse."

Whether they're down 18 percent or more, many managers are subject to so-called high-water marks, according to which they agree to waive performance fees until they have made back investors' money. This can make it hard for a fund to stay in business, because there's no money coming in to pay employees. As Fortress's filings note, some of its funds "face particular retention issues with respect to investment professionals whose compensation is tied, often in large part, to performance thresholds."

You might ask where these people are going to go. "There is a purge on Wall Street," says York Capital's Parish. "The new dream job is a salary, health care, and Jamie Dinan buys you lunch every day."

"Five years ago, if you'd gone to start a fund, people would have fought over you," says another manager. "Now they won't return your phone call."

Nor is it clear when the purge will be over. In the coming year, private-equity firms will ask investors to pony up more capital, which will force more redemptions from hedge funds. People may also try to redeem in order to pay their taxes. "No silver lining in any of this cloud," says a hedge-fund trader. "The first quarter of 2009 is going to be another eyepopper for the industry."

As another manager says to me dryly, "The new $500 million is $50 million."

It isn't clear what the future holds for Fortress. In my admittedly 100 percent unscientific survey of the industry, I found that redemption requests are usually unrelated to the size of a fund's losses, and may have more to do with how investors feel about a particular manager, or about their need for cash.

While there are complaints that the Fortress principals are arrogant, there are clearly a lot of people who are willing to trust them with their hard-earned cash. Even during the meltdown of 2008, the firm raised a net $6.2 billion in new capital for its funds, a figure that includes $3 billion Briger raised during the tumultuous month of November.

Some of those familiar with Fortress say that while in the good times the people who worked there got along—who wouldn't, when the money is flowing?—the culture has turned brutal. "Hell," one hedge-fund manager puts it succinctly. Just before things turned truly rotten, Fortress committed more than $300 million to the film finance company Grosvenor Park, which last summer released the genre spoof *Disaster Movie*. "I think they are starring," jokes a former investor.

But, for now, it appears that the principals are sticking together. Fortress's filings note that several of its funds have "keyman" provisions, meaning that if one or more of the principals ceased to be actively involved in the business, that could give investors the right to get their money out—and, in the case of some of the hedge funds, might result in the acceleration of the debt. There are rumors that the principals might, as Cooperman predicted, buy their company back from the public. But it isn't clear how they'd repay the $675 million in debt on the balance sheet at the end of the third quarter.

Fortress, for its part, denies any issues. "I have known Pete [Briger] for 15 years. I talk to Pete 20 times a day," says Edens. "Any notion of divisiveness or a split is absurd." Nor, in truth, does Edens seem like the kind of guy who would give up easily. He comes in early in the morning, works until late at night, and often spends his weekends at the office. He'd be the first to say that he doesn't cure cancer or teach kids to read, but as he puts it, "I do take pensioners' money and try to give them back a good return."

For those basking in Schadenfreude—and, oh, it's hard not to—it is unlikely that hedge funds are going away. "Our cynicism has bounds," says AQR's Asness. "We don't think that no one has skill. It's just that skill is more scarce than the hedge-fund industry sold it as." There are plenty of funds, from the well known to the not so well known, that did just what they promised, even last year. Star manager Bruce Kovner's Caxton fund returned a reported 13 percent. The tiny Bearing Fund, which is managed by Kevin Duffy, returned 72 percent in 2007 and 134 percent in 2008—net of fees.

And even for the funds that did lose big sums, some have loyal investors who have made enough over time that they're willing to forgive one bad year. One manager, who posted a loss of more than 20 percent last year, says that 82 percent of his investors have been with him for more than five years. "I have gotten more handwritten notes saying, 'Hang in there,' " he says. Another manager points to Steve Mandel, of Lone Pine Capital, who lost money last year—but got requests for only a sliver of the capital he manages. "That says it all," says another manager.

Says Cooperman, despite his criticism of the industry, "They weren't the gods you made them into, but they aren't the whale turds they're being portrayed as now."

It's also worth noting that, despite all the problems in hedge-fund land and the clamor for more regulation (and there will be more regulation), you don't see any hedge-fund managers in Washington with their hands outstretched for a piece of the bailout pie.

Some managers, like Edens, even argue that, for those who survive the current shakeout, the future is more golden than ever before. After all, many hedge funds are gone, as are the in-house trading desks at many Wall Street firms that served as competitors to hedge funds. Meanwhile, opportunity abounds.

The hedge-fund king is dead. Long live the hedge-fund king.

· 5 ·

Wall Street's $18.4 Billion Bonus

By *MICHAEL SHNAYERSON*

March 2009

O n December 8, *The Wall Street Journal* reported that John Thain, the 53-year-old chairman and C.E.O. of Merrill Lynch, had let it be known he wanted a $10 million bonus.

And why not? After all, Thain had made the brutally pragmatic decision, over the mid-September weekend that changed Wall Street forever, to sell the 94-year-old firm to Bank of America for $50 billion, averting the bankruptcy that awaited Lehman Brothers that Monday and saving Merrill's shareholders billions of dollars. Surely, even in a bad year, he was entitled to the equivalent of a 25-cent tip on the deal.

But the directors balked. Wouldn't that send the wrong signal after Merrill's net losses for three quarters of $11.67 billion? Especially after Bank of America had taken $15 billion of federal bailout money and was due to take the $10 billion earmarked for Merrill as well? When as many as 30,000 jobs may be lost from the acquisition?

The same day came a scathing letter to the board from New York attorney general Andrew Cuomo. Soon after, a grim Thain walked into Merrill's boardroom and apparently told the directors he'd had a change of mind: no bonus for him, thank you.

Thain had gotten the message at last: bonus season would be different this year. At least, it would have to *look* different.

Only a year before, Wall Street's financial firms had paid out $33.2 billion in bonuses—down a mere rounding error from the $33.9 billion bestowed in 2006—even as the credit crisis spread and $74 billion in shareholders' equity went poof. But now one firm after another had teetered or collapsed. And Treasury Secretary Henry Paulson had stridden to the podium for his Al Haig moment, inflicting upon already hard-hit 401(k)-holding Americans the unfortunate acronym TARP (Troubled Assets Relief Program), and through it propping up nine large banks with $125 billion in federal bailout money. Paulson had taken the Cabinet post, in July 2006, with only the noblest of motives, but in hindsight, the move had been fortuitous; the former Goldman Sachs C.E.O. had been forced to sell his Goldman Sachs stock, then worth almost $500 million, at pretty close to its market peak.

For many U.S. taxpayers, the bailout was infuriating enough on its own terms: $700 billion of public money in all ($5,073 for every taxpayer) given to Wall Street for bingeing on risky bets and pocketing the profits, living high and leaving the government to mop up the losses. But . . . bonuses! That was an incitement to riot.

And so, Thain's misstep notwithstanding, the top officers at six large TARP-infused firms declared they were forgoing bonuses this year. The headlines were dramatic, and they seemed to work. Editorial writers held their fire, public outrage cooled. But did all this falling on swords really mean no bonus season on Wall Street this year?

It did not.

The first cause for concern came well before the formal bonus season. It was the much-reported $440,000 junket last September to the Tuscan-style St. Regis resort at Dana Point, California, enjoyed by 70 high-performing employees of insurance giant A.I.G. The retreat, which included $23,000 for spa charges, was held less than a week after the company was promised its first $85 billion from a TARP fund separate from the one helping the banks.

In his office at 120 Broadway, Attorney General Andrew Cuomo started strategizing with his deputy counselor, Benjamin Lawsky, about how to stop what he would soon call "unwarranted and outrageous expenditures" by A.I.G. Civil charges could be brought, he decided—and would, if A.I.G. persisted in exploiting taxpayers. And so began a campaign on Cuomo's part to rein in A.I.G. that would broaden to include nine TARP-infused financial firms and their top officers' lingering hopes for bonus season.

Summoning A.I.G.'s new C.E.O., Edward Liddy, to his office, Cuomo demanded an immediate end to junkets. He threatened the company with legal action for "fraudulent conveyances": engaging in business transactions without sufficient capital on hand. A.I.G.'s legal team saw that as a stretch, as the law seemed more relevant to bankruptcy proceedings, and A.I.G., thanks to taxpayer money, wasn't bankrupt. But Liddy got the point and agreed to no more junkets.

Liddy had started at A.I.G. only a month before. He'd come from All-state, and, at the Treasury Department's request, had agreed to work for $1 a year, at least until the company's fortunes improved. His predecessor was the problem. A.I.G. had let Martin Sullivan go last June after three quarters of hideous losses totaling $18 billion—but had not fired him. Its directors had reasoned Sullivan wasn't responsible for the mountains of credit-default swaps—unregulated insurance-like contracts—that A.I.G. had written on mortgage-backed securities and had to make good on now that the supposedly risk-free securities had tanked. So Sullivan had been free to leave with a package that included a $4 million pro-rated bonus, $15 million in severance, and other benefits then valued at $28 million, for a total of $47 million.

As for Joseph Cassano, the executive whose Financial Products division *was* responsible for all those C.D.S.'s, he'd left in February with a $1-million-a-month consulting contract (since discontinued) and $69 million in deferred compensation. Only six months before, in a widely reported quote, Cassano had said of the $441 billion portfolio of C.D.S.'s he'd bet would not default, "It is hard for us, without being flippant, to even see a scenario with any kind of realm of reason that would see us losing one dollar in any of those transactions." He is reported to have since repaired to his three-story town house in London's Knightsbridge district, on a bucolic square with a private garden, and his lawyer declined to respond to an e-mail from *Vanity Fair*.

The word that's giving top Wall Street officers angina these days is "clawback." Cuomo wanted A.I.G. to claw back those packages, along with those of Sullivan's other top officers, even though A.I.G.'s board had approved them.

On October 29, Cuomo went further. He wrote a letter to the boards of nine big financial firms—Goldman Sachs, Morgan Stanley, Merrill Lynch, Wells Fargo, Bank of New York Mellon Corp., Bank of America, Citigroup, J. P. Morgan Chase, and State Street—and expressed grave concerns about executive bonuses.

That letter may have become a subject of dinner talk between the C.E.O.'s of two arch-rival firms. Goldman Sachs's Lloyd Blankfein and Morgan Stanley's John Mack had taken to commiserating at the Palm, the Manhattan steak house favored by bankers and traders. The two men had a lot in common. With Lehman's fall, they led the last two major investment banks, both soon to become bank holding companies (meaning more financial backup from the government, but more regulation too). Together, they could rue the end of windfall profits from leveraging assets nearly 30 to 1. An era was over.

To forgo or not to forgo bonuses: that was the decision that fell first to Blankfein and Mack because of their late-November fiscal-year end, an investment-bank tradition to be followed one last time before converting to the standard year. Goldman, as always, set the tone. On November 16, Goldman announced that neither Blankfein nor the firm's other six top officers would take bonuses for 2008: only their base pay of $600,000 each.

The Street was rocked. In 2007, Blankfein had set an investment-bank record for C.E.O. compensation by taking home $68.5 million in cash and equity. His two co-presidents, Gary D. Cohn and Jon Winkelried, had gotten $67.5 million each. Now here he was coolly refusing to take more, even though Goldman had stopped bingeing on toxic securities long before the other banks. Its write-down on them was just $7.2 billion.

Except that with Goldman stock's huge drop—65 percent—how large would the top officers' 2008 bonuses, weighted to the stock, have been in any event? And does forsaking a bonus even matter when Blankfein alone had earned $210,169,732 in total compensation from 2003 to 2007, according to Equilar, a compensation-tracking firm? "If they really want to forgo, give back the last two years' bonuses and give back half of your deferred compensation," suggests Gustavo Dolfino, founder and president of the WhiteRock Group, a Wall Street recruiting firm. Without a bonus this year, Blankfein might have to tighten his belt a bit—no more shopping, perhaps, for $40 million Southampton estates, as he'd done the year before—but still, he had the consolation of a new, $26 million apartment at 15 Central Park West. The suddenly bonus-less Winkelried has reportedly put his 5.9-acre Nantucket estate up for sale at $55 million, after annoying his neighbors by closing off a long-used lane that runs along the property.

As for Goldman's 440 partners, they *are* getting bonuses this year. Maybe in many cases not the $12 to $15 million each got in 2007—more like packages worth $3 to $4 million, according to *The New York Times*. Goldman has 30,000 employees in all, so some of the company's overall $10.9 billion in compensation and benefits this year will go to assistants, junior analysts, and the like, who will share a pool that's 46 percent smaller than last year's. But what's striking about the figure is that it's exactly as much as U.S. taxpayers just handed over to the firm. "For Goldman Sachs to get billions in TARP money and then three months later pay out a fortune in bonuses . . . is political tone-deafness," says Richard Cellini, of Integrity Interactive, an adviser on corporate ethics and compliance.

Goldman spokesman Michael DuVally says no TARP money is going to bonuses: "The compensation that was paid to employees came out of our business activities." Charles Geisst, finance professor at Manhattan College and author of the upcoming *Collateral Damaged: The Marketing of Consumer Debt to America,* begs to differ. "If they didn't have the TARP money, they would be forced to raise fresh capital," he says. "Now, I agree it's a long-term item on the balance sheet. But [without the government money] they would have to take a dip into what operating profits they have left, and reduce those salaries. So the TARP money *is* a substitute. Theirs is an extremely disingenuous argument." Counters DuVally, "Professor Geisst is wrong. We paid bonuses out of earnings, not capital." But as former compensation consultant Graef Crystal put it on Bloomberg.com, "The argument of saying we're not using the bailout money is just crap because money's fungible. Money's money. It exposes them to ridicule."

Just as hard to buy is the old mantra that Goldman has to pay staggering sums to its partners to keep them from being poached by other firms. To date, some 200,000 jobs have been lost in the financial sector, many of them at the executive level. Where are all those partners going to go?

Some, says a recruiter who has clients at Goldman Sachs, are actually in deep financial trouble. "Hypothetically, they had $100 million of stock at its 2007 value," the recruiter says. "I've heard stories where people have borrowed $30 to $40 million to invest in real estate or private equity or hedge funds. Well, that $100 million is worth maybe $25 million. So you have some partners and senior directors who are really hurting."

Three weeks after Blankfein's bonus announcement, John Mack sent out a memo to Morgan Stanley worldwide: he, too, would forgo his bonus, as would his two top lieutenants. The next 35 or so officers of the firm would have their compensation cut by 65 to 75 percent. It was the second year in a row that Mack had scrapped his own bonus: for Wall Street, that was pretty close to noble.

At the same time, Morgan Stanley had had to take $15.2 billion in write-downs on toxic securities through the third quarter of 2008, all on Mack's watch. The share price had dropped by 70 percent, and the firm had come close to bankruptcy last September before securing a lifesaving $9 billion infusion of Japanese capital. Now Morgan, like Goldman, had $10 billion in TARP money, and, like Goldman, it would be paying bonuses to many of its 47,000 employees and partners. Morgan noted that, overall, the bonus pool would be cut by 50 percent, but that would still mean an estimated $5 billion in bonuses for 2008—more than the company's modest $1.59 billion profit for the year.

Just since his return to Morgan Stanley in 2005 from a short stint at Credit Suisse, Mack has been awarded, according to Equilar, $69,565,233, more than enough for greens fees at the Apawamis golf course, in Rye, New York, where his home, resembling a French château, looks out on the 18th hole. Forgoing his 2008 bonus would hurt, but perhaps not that much.

How had it come to this? Huge bonuses in good years leading, or so it seemed, to terrifying drops and talk of clawbacks? For, not so long ago, investment bankers were like dentists and lawyers, toiling in the upper middle class for 40 or 50 years before retiring to their nice homes in Connecticut. Their firms were partnerships. In a good year the partners got bonuses; in a bad they wrote checks to the partnership to cover the shortfall.

Then, in the 1980s and 90s, the firms went public, and everything changed. "They shared the downside risk with their investors, yet seemed to keep the upside for themselves," says Charles Elson, director of the Weinberg Center for Corporate Governance, at the University of Delaware. "It's a lousy deal for shareholders."

Only, the shareholders didn't seem to mind as long as the stock went up and the stakes grew larger and larger. By the late 1990s, investment bankers were no longer Cheever-esque commuters. The best were more like star professional baseball players, aiming to make their fortunes in 5 or 10 years of high-pressure trading or deal-making. The higher the risks, the higher the bonuses. The game was to win—and get out before those risks came home to roost. And then came the 00s, with the seemingly no-risk game of securities backed by subprime real-estate mortgages. For the banks, it was a lot like printing their own money—and all of it led to the year-end bonus, which by this time wasn't a bonus so much as expected pay. By tradition the firms paid out nearly half their revenues in compensation and benefits each year, so as the revenues skyrocketed, so did the "pay."

"As bonuses grew and grew, thinking beyond the next quarter became irrelevant to the management of the firm," says Richard Ferlauto, director of corporate governance and pension investment at the American Federation of State, County and Municipal Employees union, for whose 1.6 million members he works as a shareholder activist. "Pay became so large that it was decoupled from providing incentives to drive long-term strategic planning."

The worst part, says Russ Gerson, of the Gerson Group, a Wall Street recruiter, was that there was no disincentive for taking major risks. "Think about it: if you're a Wall Street professional and you know that if you can create $100 million of revenues you'll get $15 million, while if you lose $100 million you'll still get paid $2 to $3 million, what would you do?"

Or what if as C.E.O. you could drive your firm to take maximum risks in mortgage securities, rack up $8 billion of write-downs, and still be allowed to resign, not be fired, so you could leave with $161 million in deferred compensation and stock? Wouldn't you do that?

Merrill Lynch's E. Stanley O'Neal did, leaving the storied firm in tatters in late 2007 with no successor in place. Desperate for top talent, Merrill's board threw Thain a $15 million signing bonus and a multi-year pay package worth between $50 million and $120 million, depending on how high he pushed Merrill's share price. Unfortunately, Thain was stuck with O'Neal's mountain of toxic debt. By the time he reached out to Bank of America's Kenneth D. Lewis last September, he was presiding over another roughly $40 billion in write-downs and watching the share price plummet from more than $50 to $17. All he had to show for saving Merrill was his $750,000 base pay and that $15 million signing bonus.

Thain, like Blankfein, had built up quite a lifestyle. There was a $27.5 million duplex at 740 Park Avenue—the late philanthropist Enid Haupt's old place. Plus a huge Westchester estate. Before he was forced out by Bank of America, in mid-January, Thain reportedly spent $1.22 million of company money redecorating his new office with such items as an $87,000 area rug, $11,000 window shades, and a $68,000 credenza. And the two top lieutenants he'd hired away from Goldman to help him turn Merrill around hauled home as much as or more than $100 million between them in contractually agreed-upon pay and bonuses.

Thomas K. Montag, 51, started in August as Merrill's new global-sales-and-trading head, after a signing bonus of $39.4 million and a pledge to have Merrill buy his $50 million of Goldman stock. This was money no board or public official would shame Montag into surrendering. Some of it may have gone to redecorating the six-story, Stanford White–designed 1903 town house on East 73rd Street that Montag had purchased earlier in the year. The house, listed at $38 million, reportedly has a wood-paneled basketball court and a capacious climate-controlled wine cellar.

At least Montag is still on the job. Peter S. Kraus, 55, reported for duty at Merrill in early September as head of growth-and-acquisitions strategy. Soon Merrill was sold to Bank of America, and Kraus left, pocketing, for his three months of work, a contractual severance package that *The Wall Street Journal* reports could be as high as $25 million. On December 18, Kraus's wife, Jill, closed for $36.63 million on the seventh-floor apartment at 720 Park Avenue that used to be owned by onetime adman and former ambassador to Slovakia Carl Spielvogel and his wife, Barbaralee Diamonstein-Spielvogel.

That seems to be where the big money is still going this bonus season: to the executives a level or two below the C.E.O.'s. Some make news when jealous or appalled colleagues leak to the press. But most avoid public scrutiny. The trading floors of one large New York firm are abuzz about the $15 million bonus due to go to the head of one trading desk. Rank-and-file traders who work for the guy are used to getting bonuses of between $300,000 and $700,000 above their $150,000 base salaries. This year it's rumored they're getting nothing.

What *are* the restrictions on executive compensation and bonuses demanded of the TARP recipients by Henry M. Paulson Jr.? A paltry few. Pay of more than $500,000 for the top five executives can't be booked as a tax deduction by their employers, for example. And a severance package can't be greater than three times the annual base pay. "Annual bonuses or discretionary bonuses—those aren't directly regulated or restricted," says David M. Lynn, a Washington lawyer and former S.E.C. official. For that matter, he says of the banks and their TARP money, "there's nothing in the law itself that prevents them from doing what they want with the money."

The bigger the TARP infusion, the more galling the lack of bonus restrictions. Take Citigroup, so sodden with toxic securities that the Treasury's first $25 billion in TARP funds had to be followed in less than a month with another $15 billion, as well as a separate guarantee of $5 billion: $45 billion in all. In December, as Thain decided to embrace relative penury and fellow C.E.O.'s such as Jamie Dimon, of J. P. Morgan Chase, were hinting they'd follow, Citigroup's Vikram S. Pandit stayed mum on the bonus question. Even a stern admonition from Cuomo failed to budge him.

Pandit, like Thain, could attribute his firm's mess to his predecessor, Charles O. Prince III, who'd pushed the pedal to the metal on mortgage-backed securities and, like Merrill's O'Neal, walked away in late 2007 with a whopping bundle, in his case $68 million, because Citi, like Merrill and A.I.G., had declined to fire its C.E.O. for cause. Pandit, in his one year as C.E.O., chalked up more write-downs (more than $30 billion to date), and a net loss of $18.72 billion for 2008. Surely weighing on the issue of a bonus for Pandit after this performance were the terms of his triumphal arrival.

And no one at Citi had forgotten the terms of that arrival. At the suggestion of resident wise man Robert Rubin, Treasury secretary in the

Clinton administration, Citi had brought Pandit in by buying his fledgling hedge fund, Old Lane Partners, for $800 million, of which Pandit reportedly pocketed $165 million. (Last June, Citi announced it was closing Old Lane, incurring a $202 million write-down.) At about the same time he paid $17.9 million for the 10-room apartment at the Beresford, on Central Park West, formerly owned by actor Tony Randall.

Rubin, oddly enough, let it be known in early December that *he* would forgo his $14 million bonus package for the second year in a row. Still, it was a piddling gesture. Rubin had pocketed an annual compensation package totaling $14 million or more from 2000 through 2006. One of Wall Street's highest-paid directors, he had professed in interviews that he had no operating responsibility, yet reportedly pushed Citi to take ever higher risks on what proved to be toxic securities. Now the company's market cap was down from $244 billion in 2006 to $20.5 billion, some 75,000 jobs had vaporized, and its share price was down to $3.77, a low not seen in more than a decade. Finally, on December 31, Pandit coughed up the bilious words: no bonus for him or chairman Winfried F. W. Bischoff, 40 percent less for other top officers, and a drastically reduced bonus pool for everyone else.

Well, not everyone. At Citi, as at the rest of Cuomo's TARP nine, the bonus pool has shrunk, but hardly evaporated. And, as at other banks, a lot of bonuses are contractual, tied to performance, so some have actually grown. One standout is that of Andrew J. Hall, a low-profile British-born commodities trader at Citi's Phibro who reportedly pocketed around $125 million. About five years ago, Hall bet big on oil futures, locking in prices he thought would look low as demand in China and India grew. He made so much money that Citi let him create his own corporate fiefdom in Westport, Connecticut—and set his own terms. Hall declined to explain to *Vanity Fair* how he made last year's fortune, but energy analyst John Kilduff, of MF Global, suggests a scenario: "You would have bought in January and hopefully sold at the all-time highs, and sold more than you had, went short the market, and rode it all the way down the $100 drop." Hall, a contemporary-art collector, has fought a long, losing battle with his Southport, Connecticut, neighbors for the right to place an 80-foot-long concrete sculpture on the lawn of his Greek Revival home. Last year's windfall will doubtless help him fill the walls and grounds with art at another of his properties: Schloss Dernberg, a 1,000-year-old German castle.

"As previously announced, we will not use TARP funding for compensation," notes a recent Citigroup statement. Others disagree. "I don't see how to separate the $45 billion bailout that Citigroup gets from the $125 million bonus paid to the Phibro commodities trader," says corporate-governance gadfly Graef Crystal. "Obviously if the government hadn't bailed these people out they would have gone bankrupt and the Phibro guy wouldn't have gotten a bonus—no one would have."

For A.I.G., which took three times as much TARP money, that point was at least three times as true. Yet so many versions of the company's own bonus story emerged that Representative Elijah E. Cummings (Democrat, Maryland), of the House Oversight and Government Reform Committee, declared, "It pains me to say this, but I begin to wonder if it has been made intentionally confusing. The arrogance here is unbelievable." (A.I.G. spokesman Nick Ashooh says, "It was certainly not our intention to cause confusion, and we sincerely apologize if we did.")

Perhaps A.I.G.'s game was to distract the lawmakers' attention from junkets. (Ashooh says that wasn't the intention.) If so, it succeeded. By then, Cuomo had persuaded A.I.G. to freeze $600 million of deferred compensation and bonus pools for the company's high-flying financial-products division—the toxic-securities risktakers—including Joe Cassano's $69 million. A.I.G. was also persuaded to freeze $19 million of former C.E.O. Sullivan's $47 million package. (Other clawbacks are under review.) Still, bonuses of one sort or another would be given to top executives. And that reckoning, as Cummings learned, failed to include the artful introduction of *retention* payments (i.e., bonuses).

To those who now follow the company's S.E.C. filings, an 8-K on September 22, 2008, shortly after the government's first injection, of $85 billion, was of interest. About 130 executives would be given retention awards. The specific award to be granted to one Jay Wintrob was noted, since Wintrob is one of the public company's five top-earning officers, for whom compensation details must be disclosed. Wintrob was to receive $3 million. He is A.I.G.'s V.P. of retirement services. His total 2007 compensation was $7,632,352.

In a letter, Cummings asked A.I.G.'s new C.E.O., Edward M. Liddy, to explain the 130 retention awards. On December 5, Liddy replied, noting that A.I.G. intended to sell businesses that made up 65 percent of the company—in order to pay back its loan from the government—and that keeping key employees of those businesses was crucial to their value. Helpfully, he mentioned that the pool of recipients had since grown to 168, and that the retention awards ranged from $92,500 to $4 million.

Days later, reporter Hugh Son of Bloomberg News broke an astounding story. According to sources inside A.I.G., the company planned to bestow retention awards not just on 168 employees but on 2,000, who had been advised to keep their awards secret. If they discussed them with anyone but their families and financial advisers, they would lose them. The Bloomberg story noted that as many as 7,000 A.I.G. employees might receive retention awards.

Cummings was livid. "A.I.G. came to the U.S. government and said they were about to go out of existence," he fumes. "They were on the respirator and the plug was just about out of the wall. None of them would be employed if it were not for the U.S. government and the taxpayers of this country." And here was A.I.G. dispensing public money—$481 million was the latest figure Cummings had gleaned—for secret bonuses? A.I.G.'s Ashooh says the final number of retention-award winners will more likely be about 5,000, receiving about $600 million in all. He does acknowledge that this doesn't include the roughly 380 employees of A.I.G.'s now moribund financial-products division, which traded all those toxic securities. He has no idea what their awards will be. Ashooh says the "secrecy" of the awards was merely an intramural matter, to keep recipients from spreading envy among their colleagues. "It's confidentiality, not secrecy, that's the issue."

Cummings takes umbrage at that. "If they give a bonus, it's public money," he declares. "They are owned by the taxpayers of America, the same ones who are losing their jobs and homes and damned sure didn't have a bonus for Christmas."

Here's the bottom line on Wall Street bonuses for 2008—according to the New York State Comptroller's Office. They're estimated to be 44 percent lower than last year's. That's a sharp cut, except that it's still $18.4 billion. Taxpayers may see that money as theirs. Bankers and traders see it as pay for work done. "There's no sympathy for us anywhere," says one thirtysomething trader, "but it's not as if we weren't working hard." Working hard and, in many cases, earning good money for the firm. "The system was: if we pay you $2 million for a job, it's because you helped us make $20 million."

All too often, unfortunately, those profits were of the short-term sort, generated by risky securities now turned to ashes. Bonus-bagging bankers may be loath to admit it, but the answer is obvious: tie bonuses to longer-term profitability. Have them vest in two years, maybe three. Meanwhile, keep them in escrow. The question is: Will the bankers stand for it? "If the government says you can't pay people who are successful, then game over," says executive-compensation consultant Alan Johnson. Second-raters may let their bonuses be tied up, but "the people who are good," says Gustavo Dolfino, the Wall Street recruiter, "will say, 'Screw that, I'll start my own firm or start a restaurant in Greece.'" Or, adds fellow Wall Street recruiter Gary Goldstein of Whitney Partners L.L.C., they'll be poached by unlikely new players: regional banks. "The regionals aren't encumbered by subprime stuff . . . They've done so well they're becoming national."

For all the upper-middle bankers still taking bonuses this year, a lot of younger, lower-middle types are getting goose eggs; as one puts it: No bonuses at all. "Now suddenly I have to think about living on my salary," says one mid-30s trader glumly. "It's $140,000 a year—with two kids, and parents who want to retire." Peter Singer, a prominent bioethics professor at Princeton and author of the newly published *The Life You Can Save: Acting Now to End World Poverty*, suggests the bonus-deprived take a hard look at themselves. "How much happier does it make them to have $10 million rather than $200,000? . . . Have they got enough from that salary to provide them and their families with the basics of what they need to live? And by that I don't mean a six-bedroom apartment on Park Avenue."

For a lot of them, apparently not. Dolfino says the choice for some mid-level bankers and their families isn't some firm across the street that will pay more, because none will. That game *is* over, at least in Manhattan. "The market for them is Mumbai, Dubai, Hong Kong, Singapore, Shanghai. We've been moving them out there for a year."

Highfliers who traded the riskiest of securities face a grimmer prospect. In his memo to staff, John Mack declared a new Morgan Stanley claw-back policy starting with cash bonuses for 2008. The policy is ominously broad: awards could be clawed back not just for risky trading that results in long-term losses but also for "reputational harm to the Firm"—a pretty vague definition. Soon that policy may be industry-wide.

At least the Morgan Stanley guys have cash bonuses, provisional though they may be, for now. Credit Suisse—not a TARP recipient—is handing out the market equivalent of just deserts. Its bonuses this year are the same toxic securities its bankers and traders sold their customers last year. However, since the securities have already been marked down to 65 cents on the dollar, there may be nowhere for their value to go but up. Shareholders have borne the losses to date; the Credit Suisse–ers may do quite well.

For thirtysomethings and fortysomethings, the worst may still be to come: not just one bad year, but another. "That," says one Wall Street recruiter, "is when it will hit them." But for top officers? Maybe not so bad. After all, when a company's stock has gotten beat down to $2 a share, and the top officers who helped drive it down get a few million shares in stock options, how hard is it to double that money?

A.I.G.'s Ed Liddy, for one, will be eligible for a "special bonus for extraordinary performance" in 2010. What does that mean? No one, including TARP officials, seems to know.

Shortly after our story went to press, Wall Street was rocked by the disclosure that Merrill Lynch in December 2008 had dispensed $3.6 billion in bonus money to its top bankers—allegedly without the knowledge of the shareholders of Bank of America, which would then become Merrill Lynch's new parent company. The bonuses had been paid a month prior to Merrill's usual bonus period, fueling suspicions that John Thain had rushed to get the deed done before Bank of America took over Merrill's operations in January. Along with the S.E.C., New York's attorney general spent the next months investigating further, and a different picture began to emerge.

Then, in August 2009, the S.E.C. announced that Bank of America had agreed to pay $33 million for making "materially false and misleading" disclosures about bonus payments in a proxy statement to shareholders. But a month later, U.S. District Court judge Jed S. Rakoff rejected the proposed settlement, calling the penalty unfair and questioning why the S.E.C. hadn't pursued its case against the bank's executives and lawyers. The case has become the poster child for regulators looking to rein in executive pay.

In September 2009, Bank of America chief Kenneth D. Lewis announced he would soon step down.

·6·

The Man Who Crashed the World

Joe Cassano and A.I.G.

By Michael Lewis

August 2009

Six months ago, I received an odd phone call from a man named Jake DeSantis at A.I.G. Financial Products—the infamous unit of the doomed insurance company, staffed by expensively educated, highly paid traders, whose financial ineptitude is widely suspected of costing the U.S. taxpayer $182.5 billion and counting. At the time A.I.G. F.P.'s losses were reported, it became known that a handful of traders in this curious unit had sold trillions of dollars of credit-default swaps (essentially unregulated insurance policies) on piles of U.S. subprime mortgages, but its employees hadn't yet become the leading examples of Wall Street greed. And so this was before Jake DeSantis and his colleagues found themselves suburban-Connecticut outcasts, before their first death threats, before the House of Representatives passed a bill because of them (taxing 90 percent of their large bonuses), before New York attorney general Andrew Cuomo announced he was going after their paychecks, and before Iowa senator

Charles Grassley said that A.I.G.'s leaders should follow the Japanese example and "either do one of two things, resign or go commit suicide."

DeSantis turned out to be a friend of a friend. He'd called because he didn't know anyone else "in the media." As a type he was instantly recognizable: a "quant," a numbers guy who was allowed to take financial risks because of his superior math skills, but who had no taste for company politics or public exposure. He'd grown up in the Midwest, the son of schoolteachers, and discovered Wall Street as a scholarship student at M.I.T. The previous seven years he'd spent running A.I.G. F.P.'s profitable stock-market-related trades. He wasn't looking for me to write about him or about A.I.G. F.P. He just wanted to know why the public perception of what had happened inside his unit, and the larger company, was so different from the private perception of the people inside it, who actually knew what had happened.

The idea that the employees of A.I.G. F.P. had conspired to maximize their short-term gains at the company's longer-term expense, for instance. He and the other traders had been required to defer about half of their pay for years, and intertwine their long-term interests with their firm's. The people who lost the most when A.I.G. F.P. went down were the employees of A.I.G. F.P.: DeSantis himself had just watched more than half of what he'd made over the previous nine years vanish. The incentive system at A.I.G. F.P., created in the mid-1990s, wasn't the short-term-oriented racket that helped doom the Wall Street investment bank as we knew it. It was the very system that U.S. Treasury secretary Timothy Geithner, among others, had proposed as a *solution* to the problem of Wall Street pay.

Even more oddly, the public explanation of A.I.G.'s failure focused on the credit-default swaps sold by traders at A.I.G. F.P., when A.I.G.'s problems were clearly broader. There was the mortgage-insurance unit in North Carolina, United Guaranty, that had taken on all sorts of silly risks in the past two years, lost several billion dollars, and replaced their C.E.O. There were the fund managers at A.I.G., the parent company, who had blown nearly $50 billion on trades in subprime mortgages—that is, they had lost more than A.I.G. F.P., whose losses stood around $45 billion. And there was a pattern: all of this stuff had happened since 2005, after an accounting scandal forced C.E.O. Maurice "Hank" Greenberg to resign. Greenberg, who had headed A.I.G. since 1968, was a bullying, omnipotent ruler—one of those bosses who did not so much build a company as tailor it to his character and render it incapable of being run by anyone else. After he was forced out, Greenberg said, "The new management wanted to prove that they could continue to grow without former management" and so turned a blind eye to all sorts of risks. So how come most of the senior management at A.I.G. was left in place by the U.S. Treasury after the bailout? Why were officials, both public and private, so intent on leading others to believe all the losses at A.I.G. had been caused by a few dozen traders in this fringe unit in London and Connecticut?

I had no idea, was busy doing other things, and had no special interest in Jake DeSantis's predicament. I listened politely, made my excuses—and went back to whatever it was I'd been doing. But then, on March 19, the new C.E.O. of A.I.G., Edward Liddy, went to Washington to testify. The story broke—or, rather, rebroke, as it had been reported two weeks earlier, without stirring much notice—that A.I.G. F.P. had just shelled out $450 million in bonuses to the 400 employees of A.I.G. F.P., including to Jake DeSantis. It must have been an otherwise slow news day because all hell broke loose, in a way it hadn't before and hasn't since in this financial crisis. The perception was that the very same people who had made these insane, greed-driven decisions that might cost the U.S. taxpayer $182.5 billion were still paying themselves big bucks! An exchange between C.E.O. Liddy and Florida congressman Alan Grayson captured the spirit of that moment:

> GRAYSON: Mr. Liddy, you said before that there's 20 or 25 people who were involved in the credit default business. What are their names, please?
>
> LIDDY: I don't have their names at my disposal, sir.
>
> GRAYSON: Well, I'm sure you remember a few of the names. I mean, they did cause your company to crash.
>
> LIDDY: You know, I've been at the company, as you know, for six months. I don't know all the people that were in AIG F.P., and many of them are gone.
>
> GRAYSON: Well, there or gone, it doesn't really matter. I want to know who they are. Names, please. . . .

LIDDY: If it's possible to provide you the names, we will. We will cooperate with you.

GRAYSON: That's good, but I want to know the names that you know right now.

LIDDY: I don't know them, sir.

GRAYSON: Not a single one. You're talking about a group, a small group of people who caused your company to lose $100 billion, as you sit here today, you can't give me one single name.

LIDDY: The single name I would give you is Joseph Cassano, who ran . . .

GRAYSON: That's a good start. You already gave that name. Give me another name.

LIDDY: I just don't know them. I do not know those names. I don't have them all at my command.

GRAYSON: Well, how can you propose to solve the problems of the company that you're now running if you don't know the names of the people who caused that problem? . . . I would expect you'd at least know more than one name. How about two names? Give us one more name.

LIDDY: I'm just not going to do that, sir, because that will provide—that'll be the—that could be a list of people that we could do—individuals who want to do damage to them could do that. It's just not . . .

GRAYSON: Well, listen, these same people could now be working right now today at Citibank. Is it more important to protect them, the ones who caused the $100 billion loss, or protect us? Which is more important to you right now?

For a brief moment you had a glimpse of how harshly financial people might be treated if Wall Street ever lost its political influence. Just days before, Larry Summers had gone on the morning talk shows to explain that a contract is a contract and the government couldn't just go in and void it and take back A.I.G.'s paychecks, but that "every legal step possible to limit those bonuses is being taken by Secretary Geithner and by the Federal Reserve System." Then Obama himself went out of his way to denounce the greed at A.I.G. F.P. and say he was looking for a way to get the bonus money back—and even that failed to slake the public anger. "On A.I.G.," a journalist asked Obama at a press conference, "why did you wait—why did you wait days to come out and express that outrage? It seems like the action is coming out of New York and the attorney general's office. It took you days to come public with Secretary Geithner and say, Look, we're outraged. Why did it take so long?"

"It took us a couple of days because I like to know what I'm talking about before I speak," Obama said testily. "All right?"

It's unlikely that he actually did know what he was talking about, except in the broadest outlines. Nor, for that matter, did the people who had engineered the bailout. How could they? At no point did anyone from the U.S. Treasury or the U.S. Congress, or any of the various New York State authorities that had gotten involved, call them up, much less visit A.I.G. F.P.—as, say, someone might who was genuinely curious to know what, exactly, had happened there. Not even A.I.G. C.E.O. Ed Liddy had bothered to make the drive from Manhattan to Wilton, Connecticut, where many of the offending trades had been done, and most of the offending bonuses were being paid, to ask questions of the people still on the scene—people who could have told him a great deal about what had happened and why. Everyone seemed to be operating on whatever they read in the newspapers—and the people inside A.I.G. F.P., who had the best view of the action, did not appear to be talking to reporters. Depending on which account you read, you thought they had lost $40 billion, or $100 billion, or $152 billion. They had done this by selling credit-default swaps on subprime-mortgage bonds—which is to say, they had insured Goldman Sachs, Deutsche Bank, Merrill Lynch, and the rest against Americans with weak credit histories defaulting on their mortgages. But why? Apparently, because they were greedy: the premiums they took in from the insurance allowed them to pay themselves big bonuses, which they'd grown so accustomed to that they now were reduced to stealing from the U.S. taxpayer. And that, it seemed, was that.

The day after Liddy's testimony, I got another call from Jake DeSantis. (I was still the only person "in the media" with whom he felt any connection.) He was upset. He'd turned down offers of more money from other people. He'd stayed only because the company had begged him to help clean up the mess: the bonus he was paid was the result of profits he had generated by selling off his trades in global equities—profits which almost surely would have been losses had he not hung around. He'd had nothing to do with the trades that lost money; the handful of people who'd known about them, when they happened, were long gone, and even they had been guided by a certain understandable logic. Now A.I.G.'s new leader, who had accepted these bonuses and run them by both the Treasury and the Federal Reserve, flies down to Washington and tells the world that he found the bonuses "distasteful."

"You go to church and you go to soccer practice and people look at you funny," said DeSantis. "This is changing people's views on who I am as a person." He'd decided to resign, write a letter to Liddy, and, as he put it, "release it to the media."

It sounded like the sort of thing that might work on a TV show. "What does that mean: 'Release it to the media'?" I asked. That, he said, was why he'd called me: he thought I knew how. Having no clue, I put him in touch with the editor of the *New York Times* op-ed page, who published Jake DeSantis's letter of resignation on March 25 at the top of his page under the headline: DEAR A.I.G., I QUIT! In it Jake repeated what he'd told me, offered a bit of his life story, and confessed the size of his after-tax bonus ($742,006.40). He also explained that he had for a year spent up to 14 hours a day helping to dismantle the company and that he and the others who had nothing to do with the losses had agreed to do so based on the promise their contracts would be honored.

It's never easy to prove that a piece of writing causes anything, but Jake's letter was an instant sensation. Bits of it were reprinted in major publications around the world. Within a few days it was the most sent, most blogged, and most read item on the *Times*'s Web site, and remained so for the entire month. Three point nine million browsers clicked on it and read it, and the tone of the public discussion changed. New York attorney general Andrew Cuomo stopped saying he intended to hound the millions paid to the people who worked at A.I.G. F.P., and started saying he was more interested in the $12.9 billion A.I.G. had paid out to Goldman Sachs, and others, to cover the massive bets against U.S. subprime mortgages that they had made with A.I.G. The House tax bill stalled in the Senate. I didn't really know Jake DeSantis, but I thought, That was just incredibly brave. He stepped out alone in front of the mob and compelled it to disband, at least for the moment. But I never heard back from him. After a few days of not being able to open a newspaper or go to a Web site without seeing some reference to Jake DeSantis and his letter, I phoned him. "Oh hey," he said cheerily. "They published my letter."

No shit, Jake.

"Has it worked out O.K.?" I asked.

"Oh yeah," he said, "but I had to move my family out of our house."

He had woken up the morning his piece ran to find media trucks jamming the end of his driveway. He took his family out back through the woods—"We live in the middle of nowhere"—and secreted them at a friend's house. "I've been going back and standing on the porch down the road and pretending to be a gawking neighbor," he said, "but they're all still there blocking the end of the driveway. They're waiting for me to come back, I guess." His voice mail, he said, was also jammed. "All these media people keep calling," he said. "Like who?" I asked. "We don't watch TV, so I don't know who they are," he said. I pressed him. "Well, there's one guy who has been calling a bunch. Matt Lauer. I don't know who he's with." The only caller he could completely identify was Katie Couric: "She called our mayor personally and tried to butter her up to get her to tell her where I am," he said. (A Couric producer says, "Katie placed a brief call to the mayor, expressed interest in the interview, and nothing further happened.") He suspected, probably rightly, that the media wanted him to play the role of the greedy Wall Street trader who had stolen millions and now claimed to feel misunderstood. "O.K.," he said. "I can do this and probably not make an ass of myself. But I can do nothing and not make an ass of myself. I'll stick with that."

With that, A.I.G. F.P. went dark again, which, I now realized, was a shame. DeSantis had established, sort of, what the people in his unit didn't do. He'd left unexplained what exactly they did do.

Here is an amazing fact: nearly a year after perhaps the most sensational corporate collapse in the history of finance, a collapse that, without the intervention of the government, would have led to the bankruptcy of every major American financial institution, plus a lot of foreign ones, too, A.I.G.'s losses and the trades that led to them still haven't been properly explained. How did they happen? Unlike, say, Bernie Madoff's pyramid scheme, they don't seem to have been raw theft. They may have been an outrageous departure from financial norms, but, if so, why hasn't anyone in the place been charged with a crime? How did an insurance company become so entangled in the sophisticated end of Wall Street and wind up the fool at the poker table? How could the U.S. government simply hand over $54 billion in taxpayer dollars to Goldman Sachs and Merrill Lynch and all the rest to make good on the subprime insurance A.I.G. F.P. had sold to them—especially after Goldman Sachs was coming out and saying that it had hedged itself by betting against A.I.G.? Since I had him on the phone I asked Jake DeSantis for what Congressman Grayson had asked Edward Liddy: names. He obligingly introduced me to his colleagues in London and Connecticut, and they walked me through what had happened—all of them speaking to someone from the outside for the first time. All, for obvious reasons, were terrified of seeing their names in print, and asked not to be mentioned by name. That was fine by me, as their names are not what's interesting. What's interesting is their point of view on the event closest to the center of the financial crisis. For while they disagreed on this and that, they all were fairly certain that if it hadn't been for A.I.G. F.P. the subprime-mortgage machine might never have been built, and the financial crisis might never have happened.

A.I.G. F.P. was created back in 1987 by refugees from Drexel Burnham, led by a trader named Howard Sosin, who claimed to have a better model to trade and value interest-rate swaps. Nineteen-eighties financial innovation had all sorts of consequences, but one of them was a boom in the number of deals between big financial firms that required them to take each other's credit risks. Interest-rate swaps—in which a party swaps a stream of income from a floating rate of interest for one from a fixed rate of interest—was one such innovation.

The Man Who Crashed the World   113

Once upon a time Chrysler issued a bond through Morgan Stanley, and the only people who wound up with credit risk were the investors who had bought the Chrysler bond. Now Chrysler might sell its bonds and simultaneously enter into a 10-year interest-rate-swap transaction with Morgan Stanley—and just like that, Chrysler and Morgan Stanley were exposed to each other. If Chrysler went bankrupt, its bondholders obviously lost; depending on the nature of the swap and the movement of interest rates, Morgan Stanley might lose, too. If Morgan Stanley went bust, Chrysler along with anyone else who had done interest-rate swaps with Morgan Stanley stood to suffer. Financial risk had been created, out of thin air, and it begged to be either honestly accounted for or disguised.

Enter Sosin, with his supposedly new and improved interest-rate-swap model (even though Drexel Burnham was not at the time a market leader in interest-rate swaps).

There was a natural role for a blue-chip corporation with the highest credit rating to stand in the middle of swaps and long-term options and the other risk-spawning innovations. The traits required of this corporation were that it not be a bank—and thus subject to bank regulation and the need to reserve capital against the risky assets—and that it be willing and able to bury exotic risks on its balance sheet. There was no real reason that company had to be A.I.G.; it could have been any AAA-rated entity with a huge balance sheet. Berkshire Hathaway, for instance, or General Electric. A.I.G. just got there first.

In a financial system that was rapidly generating complicated risks, A.I.G. F.P. became a huge swallower of those risks. In the early days it must have seemed as if it was being paid to insure against events extremely unlikely to occur—how likely was it that all sorts of companies and banks all over the globe would go bust at the same time? Its success bred imitators: Zurich Re F.P., Swiss Re F.P., Credit Suisse F.P., Gen Re F.P. All of these places were central to what happened in the last two decades; without them the new risks being created would have had no place to hide, but would have remained in full view of bank regulators. All of these places have been washed away by the general nausea now felt in the presence of complicated financial risks, but there was a moment when their existence seemed cartographically necessary to the financial world. And A.I.G. F.P. was the model for them all.

The division's first 15 years were consistently, amazingly profitable—there wasn't the first hint that it might be running risks that would cause it to lose money, much less cripple its giant parent. Its traders were able to claim that they were "hedged," and even if the term was misleading, they never sold exactly the same thing as the thing they had bought—there was always some slight difference. The risks it ran were probably trivial in relation to its capital, because the risks that the financial system wanted to lay off on it were, in fact, not terribly risky. One indication of this is that, even in the middle of the calamity, the 95 percent of A.I.G. F.P. that had nothing to do with subprime-mortgage bonds continued to generate profits. By 2001, A.I.G. F.P. could be counted on to generate $300 million a year, or 15 percent of A.I.G.'s profits.

Meanwhile, the people who worked at A.I.G. F.P. got rich. Exactly how rich is hard to say, but there are plenty of hints. One is that a company lawyer—a mere lawyer!—took home a $25 million bonus at the end of one year. Another is that in 2005, when Howard Sosin and his wife divorced, she received more than $40 million of an estate valued at $168 million—and Sosin had left A.I.G. in 1993, receiving $182 million from the company! He had been replaced that year as C.E.O. by a gentler soul named Tom Savage, who had allowed Hank Greenberg to take some of the sugar out of F.P., but even then the small band of traders had, arguably, a sweeter deal than any money managers in the world. The typical hedge fund kept 20 percent of profits; the traders at A.I.G. F.P. kept 30 to 35 percent. The typical hedge fund or private-equity fund has to schlep around and raise money all the time, and post collateral with big Wall Street firms for all the trades they do. The traders at A.I.G. F.P. had essentially unlimited capital on tap from the parent company, along with the AAA rating, rent-free. For the people who worked there, A.I.G. F.P. was a financial miracle. They were required to leave 50 percent of their bonuses in the company, but they were happy to do so; many of them, viewing it as the best way to grow their own savings, invested far more than the minimum back in the company. When it collapsed, the employees lost more than $500 million of their own money.

How and why their miracle became a catastrophe, A.I.G. F.P.'s traders say, is a complicated story, but it begins simply: with a change in the way decisions were made, brought about by a change in its leadership. At the end of 2001 its second C.E.O., Tom Savage, retired, and his former deputy, Joe Cassano, was elevated. Savage is a trained mathematician who understood the models used by A.I.G. traders to price the risk they were running—and thus ensure that they were fairly paid for it. He enjoyed debates about both the models and the merits of A.I.G. F.P.'s various trades. Cassano knew a lot less math and had much less interest in debate.

It's impossible to deliver the full flavor of a man's character without talking to him, and relying instead upon a bunch of people who remain afraid of seeing their names in print. That Joe Cassano is the son of a police officer and was a political-science major at Brooklyn College seems, in retrospect, far less relevant than that he'd spent most of his career, both at Drexel and A.I.G. F.P., in the back office, doing operations. Across A.I.G. F.P. the view of the boss was remarkably consistent: a guy with a crude feel for financial risk but a real talent for bullying people who doubted him. "A.I.G. F.P. became a dictatorship," says one London trader. "Joe would bully people around. He'd humiliate them and then try to make it up to them by giving them huge amounts of money."

"One day he got me on the phone and was pissed off about a trade that had lost money," says a Connecticut trader. "He said, 'When you lose money it's my fucking money. Say it.' I said, 'What?' 'Say "Joe, it's your fucking money!"' So I said, 'It's your fucking money, Joe.'"

"The culture changed," says a third. "The fear level was so high that when we had these morning meetings you presented what you did not to upset him. And if you were critical of the organization, all hell would break loose." Says a fourth, "Joe always said, 'This is my company. You work for my company.' He'd see you with a bottle of water. He'd come over and say, 'That's my water.' Lunch was free, but Joe always made you feel he had bought it." And a fifth: "Under Joe the debate and discussion that was common under Tom [Savage] ceased. I would say what I'm saying to you. But with Joe over my shoulder as the audience." A sixth: "The way you dealt with Joe was to start everything by saying, 'You're right, Joe.'"

According to traders, Cassano was one of those people whose insecurities manifested themselves in a need for obedience and total control. "One day he came in and saw that someone had left the weights on the Smith machine, in the gym," says a source in Connecticut. "He was literally walking around looking for people who looked buff, trying to find the guy who did it. He was screaming, 'Who left the fucking weight on the fucking Smith machine? Who left the fucking weight on the fucking Smith machine?' " If that rings a bell it may be because you read *The Caine Mutiny* and recall Captain Queeg scouring the ship to find out who had stolen the strawberries. Even by the standards of Wall Street villains, whose character flaws wind up being exaggerated to fit the crime, Cassano was a cartoon despot.

Oddly, he was as likely to direct his anger at profitable traders as at unprofitable ones—and what caused him to become angry was the faintest whiff of insurrection.

Even more oddly, his anger had no obvious effect on the recipient's paycheck; a trader might find himself routinely abused by his boss and yet delighted by his year-end bonus, determined by that same boss. Every one of the people I spoke with admitted that the reason they hadn't taken a swing at Joe Cassano, before walking out the door, was that the money was simply too good. A man who valued loyalty and obedience above all other traits had not any tools to command them except money. Money worked, but only up to a point. If you were going to be on the other side of a trade from Goldman Sachs, you had better know what, exactly, Goldman Sachs was up to. A.I.G. F.P. could attract extremely bright people, whose success depended on precision of both calculation and judgment. It was now run, roughly, by a man who didn't fully understand all the calculations and whose judgment was clouded by his insecurity. The few people willing to question that judgment wound up quitting the firm. Left behind were people who more or less accommodated Cassano. "If someone is a complete asshole," one of them puts it to me, "you seek his approval in a way you don't if he's a nice guy."

All of which raises an obvious question: Who put a man like Joe Cassano in charge of such an enterprise as A.I.G. F.P.? The simple answer is Hank Greenberg, the C.E.O. of A.I.G.; the more complicated one is A.I.G. F.P.'s board, consisting of many smart people, including Harvard economist Martin Feldstein. "Tom Savage proposed Joe to replace him," says Greenberg, "and we had no reason to think he wasn't able to do the job."

A.I.G. F.P.'s employees for their part suspect that the only reason

Greenberg promoted Cassano was that he saw in him a pale imitation of his own tyrannical self and felt he could control him. "So long as Greenberg was there, it worked," says one trader, "because he watched everything Joe did. After the Nikkei collapsed [in the 1990s], a trader in Japan lost $20 million. Greenberg personally flew to Tokyo and took him into a room and grilled him until he was satisfied." In March 2005, however, Eliot Spitzer forced Greenberg to resign. And, as one trader puts it, "the new guys running A.I.G. had no idea." They thought the money machine ran on its own, and Cassano did nothing to discourage the view. By 2005, A.I.G. F.P. was indeed, in effect, his company.

But even here the story's messier than its broad outlines. For a start, the guy who had the most invested in A.I.G. F.P. was Joe Cassano. Cassano had been paid $38 million in 2007, but left $36.75 million of that inside the firm. His financial interest in A.I.G. F.P. struck those who worked for him as secondary to his psychological investment: the firm was, by all accounts, Cassano's sole source of self-worth, its success his lone status symbol. He wore crappy clothes, drove a crappy car, and spent all of his time at the office. He had made huge piles of money ($280 million!), but so far as anyone could tell he didn't spend any of it. "Joe wasn't a trader and now he wasn't a risktaker, in his personal life," says one of the traders. "With the money he didn't have in the company he bought Treasury bonds." He had no children, no obvious social ambition; his status concerns seemed limited to his place in the global financial order. He entertained a notion of himself as the street-smart guy who had triumphed over his social betters—which of course implied that he wasn't quite sure that he had. "Joe had Goldman envy," one trader tells me—which was strange, as Cassano's brother and sister both worked for Goldman Sachs. "His whole life was F.P.," another trader says. "Without F.P. he had nothing." That was another reason, in addition to fear, that the highly educated, highly intelligent people who worked for Joe Cassano were slow to question whatever he was doing: he was the last person, they assumed, who would blow the place up.

The more subtle change inside A.I.G. F.P. occurred not long after Cassano assumed control. In 1998, A.I.G. F.P. had entered the new market for credit-default swaps: it sold insurance to banks against the risk of defaults by huge numbers of investment-grade public corporations. As

Gillian Tett tells it in her new book, *Fool's Gold,* bankers at J. P. Morgan, having invented credit-default swaps, went looking for an AAA-rated company to assume the bulk of the risk associated with them, and discovered A.I.G. The relationship began innocently enough, by Wall Street standards. The risk in these early deals was indeed small: it was unlikely that large numbers of investment-grade companies in different countries and different industries would default on their debt at the same time. (Even now A.I.G. F.P.'s $450 billion portfolio of corporate credit-default swaps, which dwarfs the $75 billion portfolio of subprime-mortgage credit-default swaps, has avoided losses.) But it made explicit what until then had only been implicit: A.I.G. F.P. was the most receptive dumping ground for new risks created by big Wall Street firms.

And in the early 2000s, the big Wall Street firms performed this fantastic bait and switch in two stages. Stage One was to apply technology that had been dreamed up to re-distribute corporate credit risk to *consumer* credit risk. The banks that used A.I.G. F.P. to insure piles of loans to IBM and G.E. now came to it to insure much messier piles that included credit-card debt, student loans, auto loans, prime mortgages, and just about anything else that generated a cash flow. "The problem," as one trader puts it, "is that something else came along that we thought was the same thing as what we'd been doing." Because there were many different sorts of loans, to different sorts of people, the logic applied to corporate credit seemed to apply to this new pile of debt: it was sufficiently diverse that it was unlikely to all go bad at once. But then, these piles, at least at first, contained almost no subprime-mortgage loans.

Toward the end of 2004, that changed dramatically—but just how dramatically A.I.G. F.P. was extremely slow to realize. In the run-up to the financial crisis there were several moments when an intelligent, disinterested observer might have realized that the system was behaving strangely. Maybe the most obvious of these was the effects of U.S. monetary policy on borrowing and lending. The combination of the dot-com bust and the 9/11 attacks had led Alan Greenspan to pump money into the system, and to lower interest rates. In June 2004 the Fed began to contract the money supply, and interest rates rose. In a normal economy, when interest rates rise, consumer borrowing falls—and in the normal end of the U.S. economy that happened: from June 2004 to June 2005 prime-mortgage lending fell by half. But in that same period subprime lending doubled—and then doubled again. In 2003 there had been a few tens of billions of dollars of subprime-mortgage loans. From June 2004 until June 2007, Wall Street underwrote $1.6 trillion of new subprime-mortgage loans and another $1.2 trillion of so-called Alt-A loans—loans which for some reason or another can be dicey, usually because the lender did not require the borrower to supply him with the information typically required before making a loan. The subprime sector of the financial economy clearly was responding to different signals than the others—and the result was booming demand for housing and a continued rise in house prices. Perhaps the biggest reason for this was that the Wall Street firms packaging the loans into bonds had found someone to insure against what turned out to be the rather high risk that they'd go bad: Joe Cassano.

A.I.G. F.P. was already insuring these big, diversified, AAA-rated piles of consumer loans; to get it to insure subprime mortgages was only a matter of pouring more and more of the things into the amorphous, unexamined piles. They went from being 2 percent subprime mortgages to being 95 percent subprime mortgages. And yet no one at A.I.G. said anything about it—not C.E.O. Martin Sullivan, not Joe Cassano, not Al Frost, the guy in A.I.G. F.P.'s Connecticut office in charge of selling his firm's credit-default-swap services to the big Wall Street firms. The deals, by all accounts, were simply rubber-stamped by Cassano and then again by A.I.G. brass—and, on the theory that this was just more of the same, no one paid them special attention. It's hard to know what Joe Cassano thought and when he thought it, but the traders inside A.I.G. F.P. are certain that neither Cassano nor the four or five people overseen directly by him, who worked in the unit that made the trades, realized how completely these piles of consumer loans had become, almost exclusively, composed of subprime mortgages.

Gene Park worked in the Connecticut office and sat close enough to the credit-default-swap traders to have a general idea of what they were up to. In mid-2005 he'd read a front-page story in *The Wall Street Journal* about the mortgage lender New Century. He noted how high its dividend was and thought he might like to buy some of its stock for himself. As he dug into New Century, however, Park saw that it owned all these subprime mortgages—and he could see from its own statements that the quality of the loans was frightening. Just after that he got a phone call from a penniless, jobless old college friend who had been offered a package of loans to buy a house he couldn't afford. At the same time, Park saw Al Frost announcing new credit-default-swap deals at an alarming rate. A year before, Frost might have had one half-billion-dollar deal each month; now he was doing 20, all on piles of consumer loans. "We were doing every single deal with every single Wall Street firm, except Citigroup," says one trader. "Citigroup decided it liked the risk and kept it on their books. We took all the rest." When traders asked Frost why Wall Street was suddenly so eager to do business with A.I.G., says a trader, "he would explain that they liked us because we could act quickly." Park put two and two together and guessed that the nature of these piles of consumer loans insured by A.I.G. F.P. was changing, that they contained a lot more subprime mortgages than anyone knew, and that if U.S. homeowners began to default in sharply greater numbers A.I.G. didn't have anywhere near the capital required to cover the losses. He told Andy Forster, Cassano's right-hand man in London, who brought this up at a meeting, but Cassano dismissed the concerns as overblown.

Oddly, this dramatic increase in the amount of risk A.I.G. F.P. was assuming came at exactly the moment when it lost the reason for its existence. The day after Hank Greenberg was forced to resign, in March 2005, the credit-rating agencies downgraded A.I.G. from AAA to AA. The AAA rating was the competitive advantage; without it, the natural course of action would have been to close or dramatically shrink A.I.G. F.P.'s business. Instead, Cassano grew it.

Toward the end of 2005, Cassano promoted Al Frost, then went looking for someone to replace him as the ambassador to Wall Street's subprime-mortgage-bond desks. As a smart quant who understood abstruse securities, Gene Park was a likely candidate. That's when Park decided to examine more closely the loans that A.I.G. F.P. had insured. He suspected Joe Cassano didn't understand what he had done, but even so Park was shocked by the magnitude of the misunderstanding: these piles of consumer loans were now 95 percent U.S. subprime mortgages. Park then conducted a little survey, asking the people around A.I.G. F.P. most directly involved in insuring them how much subprime was in them. He asked Gary

Gorton, a Yale professor who had helped build the model Cassano used to price the credit-default swaps. Gorton guessed that the piles were no more than 10 percent subprime. He asked a risk analyst in London, who guessed 20 percent. He asked Al Frost, who had no clue, but then, his job was to sell, not to trade. "None of them knew," says one trader. Which sounds, in retrospect, incredible. But an entire financial system was premised on their not knowing—and paying them for their talent!

By the time Joe Cassano invited Gene Park to London for the meeting in which he would be "promoted" to the job of creating even more of these ticking time bombs, Park knew he wanted no part of it. He announced that, if he was made to take the job, he'd quit. (Had he taken it he would now be a magazine cover.)

This, naturally, infuriated Joe Cassano, who, says one trader, thought Park was being lazy, dreaming up reasons not to do the deals that would require work. Confronted with the new development—his company was insuring not consumer credit generally but subprime mortgages—Cassano didn't blink. He simply claimed that the fact was irrelevant: for the bonds to default, U.S. house prices had to fall, and Cassano didn't believe house prices could ever fall everywhere in the country at once. After all, Moody's and S&P still rated this stuff AAA!

Still, Cassano agreed to meet with all the big Wall Street firms and discuss the logic of their deals—to investigate how a bunch of shaky loans could be transformed into AAA-rated bonds. Together with Park and a few others, Cassano set out on a series of meetings with Morgan Stanley, Goldman Sachs, and the rest—all of whom argued how unlikely it was for housing prices to fall all at once. "They all said the same thing," says one of the traders present. "They'd go back to historical real-estate prices over 60 years and say they had never fallen all at once." (The lone exception, he said, was Goldman Sachs. Two months after their meeting with the investment bank, one of the A.I.G. F.P. traders bumped into the Goldman guy who had defended the bonds, who said, Between you and me, you're right. These things are going to blow up.) The A.I.G. F.P. executives present were shocked by how little actual thought or analysis seemed to underpin the subprime-mortgage machine: it was simply a bet that U.S. home prices would never fall. Once he understood this, Joe Cassano actually changed his mind. He agreed with Gene Park: A.I.G. F.P. shouldn't insure any more of these deals. And at the time it didn't really seem like all that big of an issue. A.I.G. F.P. was generating around $2 billion year in profits. At the peak, the entire credit-default-swap business contributed only $180 million of that. He was upset, it seemed, mainly that he had been successfully contradicted.

What no one realized was that it was too late. A.I.G. F.P.'s willingness to assume the vast majority of the risk of all the subprime-mortgage bonds created in 2004 and 2005 had created a machine that depended for its fuel on subprime-mortgage loans. "I'm convinced that our input into the system led to a substantial portion of the increase in housing prices in the U.S. We facilitated a trillion dollars in mortgages," says one trader. "Just us." Every firm on Wall Street was making fantastic sums of money from this machine, but for the machine to keep running the Wall Street firms needed someone to take the risk. When Gene Park informed them that A.I.G. F.P. would no longer do so—*Hello, my name is Gene Park and I'm closing down your business*—he became the most hated man on Wall Street.

The big Wall Street firms solved the problem by taking the risk themselves. The hundreds of billions of dollars in subprime losses suffered by Merrill Lynch, Morgan Stanley, Lehman Brothers, Bear Stearns, and the others were hundreds of billions in losses that might otherwise have been suffered by A.I.G. F.P. Unwilling to take the risk of subprime-mortgage bonds in 2004 and 2005, the Wall Street firms swallowed the risk in 2006 and 2007. Lending standards had fallen, property values had risen, and the more recent loans were thus far riskier than the earlier ones, but still they gobbled them up—for if they didn't, the machine would have ceased to function. The people inside the big Wall Street firms who ran the machine had made so much money for their firms that they were now, in effect, in charge. And they had no interest in anything but keeping it running. A.I.G. F.P. wasn't an aberration; what happened at A.I.G. F.P. could have happened anywhere on Wall Street . . . and did.

As recently as August 2007, A.I.G. F.P. traders were feeling almost smug: all these loans made in 2006 and 2007 were going bad, but the relatively more responsible 2005 vintage that they had insured didn't look as if it would suffer any credit losses. They were, they thought, the smart guys at the poker table. Joe Cassano even went on an investor conference call and said, famously, "It is hard for us, without being flippant, to even see a scenario within any kind of realm of reason that would see us losing $1 on any of those transactions."

What no one realized is that Joe Cassano, in exchange for the privilege of selling credit-default swaps on subprime-mortgage bonds to Goldman Sachs and Merrill Lynch and all the rest, had agreed to change the traditional terms of trade between A.I.G. and Wall Street. In the beginning, A.I.G. F.P. had required its counter-parties simply to accept its AAA credit: it refused to post collateral. But in the case of the subprime-mortgage credit-default swaps, Cassano had agreed to several triggers, including A.I.G.'s losing its AAA credit rating, that would require the firm to post collateral. If the value of the underlying bonds fell, it would fork over cash, so that, for instance, Goldman Sachs would not need to be exposed for more than a day to A.I.G. Worse still, Goldman Sachs assigned the price to the underlying bonds—and thus could effectively demand as much collateral as it wanted. In the summer of 2007, the value of everything fell, but subprime fell fastest of all. The subsequent race by big Wall Street banks to obtain billions in collateral from A.I.G. was an upmarket version of a run on the bank. Goldman Sachs was the first to the door, with shockingly low prices for subprime-mortgage bonds—prices that Cassano wanted to dispute in court, but was prevented by A.I.G. from doing so when he was fired. A.I.G. couldn't afford to pay Goldman off in March 2008, but that was O.K. The U.S. Treasury, led by the former head of Goldman Sachs, Hank Paulson, agreed to make good on A.I.G.'s gambling debts. One hundred cents on the dollar.

A pair of ancient maples shade Joe Cassano's London home. It's a tasteful, almost inconspicuous place on a square, one of the best in London, just around the corner from Harrods. Only the living-room drapes are left open, to let in the spring light. Four black porcelain elephants decorate the windowsill. Behind them a shadow moves through the room.

Cassano resigned from A.I.G. F.P. early last year, but he didn't simply leave. He continued to turn up at his desk and spend the day staring at his Bloomberg TV. The traders thought it strange; only later did they learn that

A.I.G. was still paying him $1 million a month to consult. As far as anyone could tell, he had nothing to do. And then one day he simply stopped showing up. From time to time they spotted him cycling past their Mayfair office. Every now and again some British newspaper snapped a picture of him exiting his house with his racing bike. Apart from that he had as good as vanished. His absence is as frustrating as it is expected—the people best positioned to explain this financial disaster have all similarly vanished from view. It would be nice if Joe Cassano came out of hiding and tried to explain what he did and why, but there is little chance of that.

The people still left inside A.I.G. F.P. like to list just how many things had to go wrong for their business to implode. Any one of a number of things might have sufficed to avert their catastrophe: our political leaders might have decided against the Wall Street argument not to regulate credit-default swaps; the ratings agencies might have resisted the Wall Street argument to rate subprime bonds AAA; Wall Street banks, in 2006 and 2007, might have declined to replace A.I.G. F.P. in the role of subprime risktaker of last resort; and on and on. Their list is mostly a catalogue of large, impersonal forces. But impersonal forces require people to conspire with them. Joe Cassano was the perfect man for these times—as responsible for a series of disastrous trades as a person in a big company can be. He discouraged the dissent of subordinates who understood them better than he did. He acted with the approval of A.I.G., but he also must have known that A.I.G. wasn't able to evaluate his trades. Once he was persuaded to stop insuring subprime-mortgage bonds, the logical course of action was to reverse the deals he had already done. In 2006 he might have found a way to do this, if he had been willing to accept the costs involved, but he wasn't. Had he been, the machine he helped to create would have kept running—by then it had a life of its own—and the losses would have simply wound up more concentrated inside the big banks. But he'd have saved his company. No one would be blaming Jake DeSantis for blowing up the world.

And yet the A.I.G. F.P. traders left behind, much as they despise him personally, refuse to believe Cassano was engaged in any kind of fraud. The problem is that they knew him. And they believe that his crime was not mere legal fraudulence but the deeper kind: a need for subservience in others and an unwillingness to acknowledge his own weaknesses. "When he said that he could not envision losses, that we wouldn't lose a dime, I am positive that he believed that," says one of the traders. The problem with Joe Cassano wasn't that he knew he was wrong. It was that it was too important to him that he be right. More than anything, Joe Cassano wanted to be one of Wall Street's big shots. He wound up being its perfect customer.

PART TWO

WASHINGTON

· 7 ·

Good Billions After Bad

The Bailout Money

By *Donald L. Barlett* and *James B. Steele*

October 2009

Just inside the entrance to the U.S. Treasury, on the other side of a forbidding array of guard stations and scanners that control access to the Greek Revival building, lies one of the most beautiful interior spaces in all of Washington. Ornate bronze doors open inward to a two-story-high chamber. Chandeliers line the coffered ceiling, casting a soft glow on the marble walls and richly inlaid marble floor.

In this room, starting in 1869 and for many decades thereafter, the U.S. government conducted many of its financial transactions. Bags of gold, silver, and paper currency arrived here by horse-drawn vans and were carted upstairs to the vaults. On the busy trading floor, Treasury clerks supplied commercial banks with coins and currency, exchanged old bills for new, cashed checks, redeemed savings bonds, and took in government receipts. In those days, anyone could observe all this activity firsthand—could actually witness the government and the nation's bankers doing business. The public space where this occurred became known as the Cash Room.

Today the Cash Room is used for press conferences, ceremonial functions, and departmental parties. And that's too bad. If Treasury still used the room as it once did, then perhaps we'd have more of a clue about what happened to the billions of dollars that flew out of Treasury to selected American banks in the waning days of the Bush administration.

Last October, Congress passed the Emergency Economic Stabilization Act of 2008, putting $700 billion into the hands of the Treasury Department to bail out the nation's banks at a moment of vanishing credit and peak financial panic. Over the next three months, Treasury poured nearly $239 billion into 296 of the nation's 8,000 banks. The money went to big banks. It went to small banks. It went to banks that desperately wanted the money. It went to banks that didn't want the money at all but had been ordered by Treasury to take it anyway. It went to banks that were quite happy to accept the windfall, and used the money simply to buy other banks. Some banks received as much as $45 billion, others as little as $1.5 million. Sixty-seven percent went to eight institutions; 33 percent went to the rest. And that was just the money that went to banks. Tens of billions more went to other companies, all before Barack Obama took office. It was the largest single financial intervention by Treasury into the banking system in U.S. history.

But once the money left the building, the government lost all track of it. The Treasury Department knew where it had sent the money, but nothing about what was done with it. Did the money aid the recovery? Was it spent for the purposes Congress intended? Did it save banks from collapse? Henry Paulson's Treasury Department had no idea, and didn't seem to care. It never required the banks to explain what they did with this unprecedented infusion of capital.

Exactly one year has elapsed since the onset of the financial crisis and the passage of the bailout bill. Some measure of scrutiny and control has since been imposed by the Obama administration, but even today it's hard to walk back the cat and trace the money. Up to a point, though, it's possible to reconstruct some of what happened in the first chaotic and crucial three months of the bailout, when Treasury was still in the hands of Paulson and most of the money was disbursed. Needless to say, there is no central clearinghouse for information about the TARP (Troubled Asset Relief Program) money. To get details of any kind means starting with the hundreds of individual recipients, then poring over S.E.C. filings, annual reports, and other documentation—in other words, performing the standard due diligence that the government itself failed to perform. In the report that follows, we have no more than dipped a toe into the morass, but one fact emerges clearly: a lot of the money wound up in the coffers of some very surprising institutions—institutions that should have been seen as "troubling" as much as "troubled."

The intention of Congress when it passed the bailout bill could not have been more clear. The purpose was to buy up defective mortgage-backed securities and other "toxic assets" through TARP. But the bill was in fact broad enough to give the Treasury secretary the authority to do whatever he deemed necessary to deal with the financial crisis. If TARP had been a credit card, it would have been called Carte Blanche. That authority was all Paulson needed to switch gears, within a matter of days, and change the entire thrust of the program from buying bad assets to buying stock in banks.

Why did this happen? Ostensibly, Treasury concluded that the task of buying up toxic assets would take too long to help the financial system and unlock the credit markets. So, theoretically, something more immediate was needed—hence the plan to inject billions into banks, whether or not they wanted or needed the money. To be sure, Citigroup and Bank of America were in precarious condition. So was the insurance giant A.I.G., which had already received an infusion from the Federal Reserve and ultimately would receive more TARP money—$70 billion—than any single bank. But rather than just aiding institutions in distress, Treasury set out to disburse money in a more freewheeling way, hoping it would pass rapidly into the financial system and somehow address the system-wide credit crunch. Even at this early stage, it was hard to escape the feeling that the real strategy was less than scientific—amounting to a hope that if a massive pile of money was simply thrown at the economy some of it would surely do something useful.

On Sunday, October 12, between 6:30 and 7 P.M., Paulson made a series of calls to the C.E.O.'s of the biggest banks—the so-called Big 9—and asked them to come to Treasury the next afternoon for a meeting on the financial crisis. He was short on details, as he would be throughout the crisis. A series of e-mails obtained by Judicial Watch, a Washington public-interest group, offers a window on the moment. The C.E.O. of Citigroup, Vikram Pandit, had agreed to attend, but asked his staff to scope out the purpose. "Can you find out soon as possible what Paulson invite to VP [Vikram Pandit] for meeting at Treasury this afternoon is about?" a Citigroup executive in New York wrote the bank's Washington office. When Citi's high-powered lobbyist Nicholas Calio called Paulson's office, he was told only that Pandit should attend.

Top Treasury staffers were likewise in the dark. Paulson's chief of staff, James Wilkinson, sent out a 7:30 A.M. e-mail: "Can someone tell Michele Davis, [Kevin] Fromer and me who the 'Big 9' are?"

By midmorning, people finally had the names—Vikram Pandit, of Citigroup; Jamie Dimon, of J. P. Morgan Chase; Kenneth Lewis, of Bank of America; Richard Kovacevich, of Wells Fargo; John Thain, of Merrill Lynch; John Mack, of Morgan Stanley; Lloyd Blankfein, of Goldman Sachs; Robert Kelly, of the Bank of New York Mellon; and Ronald Logue, of State Street bank. Their destination was Room 3327, the Secretary's Conference Room, on the third floor.

Paulson laid before them a one-page memo, "CEO Talking Points." He wasn't there to ask for their help, Paulson would say; he was there to tell them what he expected from them. To "arrest the stress in our financial system," Treasury would unveil a $250 billion plan the next day to buy preferred stock in banks. Paulson's memo told the bankers bluntly that "your nine firms will be the initial participants." Paulson wasn't calling for volunteers; he made it clear the banks had no choice but to allow Treasury to buy stock in their companies. It was basically a reverse holdup, with Paulson holding the gun and forcing the banks to take the money.

Some of the C.E.O.'s had misgivings, fearing that by accepting TARP money their banks would be perceived as shaky by investors and customers. Paulson explained that opting out wasn't an option. "If a capital infusion is not appealing," the memo continued, "you should be aware that your regulator will require it in any circumstance." Paulson gave the bankers until 6:30 P.M. to clear everything with their boards and sign the papers.

Treasury had prepared a form with blank spaces for the name of the bank and the amount of TARP money requested. Each C.E.O. filled in the two blanks by hand—$10 billion, $15 billion, $25 billion, whatever—and then signed and dated the document. That was all it took.

B ut this was just the beginning. It's one thing to call nine big banks into a room and give them what turned out to be a total of $125 billion. That required little more than a few hours. It's quite a different matter to look out over the landscape of 8,000 other U.S. banks and decide which ones should get slices of the TARP pie. Moreover, the guiding principle was never clear. Was it to give money to essentially sound banks, so that they could help inject more money into the credit markets? Was it to pull troubled banks into the clear? Was it both—and more?

Regardless, the mechanism to disburse all this money even more widely was an entity called the Office of Financial Stability. Unfortunately, it wasn't a functioning office yet—it was just a name written into a piece of legislation. To lead it, Paulson picked Neel Kashkari, a 35-year-old former Goldman Sachs banker who had followed Paulson to Treasury when he became secretary, in July 2006. Kashkari was an odd choice to oversee a federal bailout of private companies. A free-market Republican, he had downplayed the gravity of the subprime-mortgage crisis only months before his appointment, reportedly sending the message to one gathering of bankers, "There is no problem here."

Kashkari and other Paulson aides cobbled together the Office of Financial Stability under immense time pressure. They press-ganged people from elsewhere in Treasury and from far-flung government departments. By the end of the year, there were more "detailees" on loan from other offices (52) than there were permanent staff (38). They were spread out all over Treasury, from the ground floor to the third. Some occupied space in leased offices six blocks away. It was a strange agglomeration of people—stretching from Washington to San Francisco—who had never worked together before.

There were no internal controls to gauge success or failure. The goal was simply to dispense as much money as possible, as fast as possible. When Treasury began giving billions to the banks, the department had no policies in place to ensure that the banks were using the money in ways that met the purposes of the program, however defined. One main purpose, as noted, was to free up credit, but there was no incentive to lend and nothing to stop a bank from simply sitting on the money, bolstering its balance sheet and investing in Treasury bills. Indeed, Treasury's plan was expressly *not* to ask the banks what they did with the money. As the Government Accountability

Office later learned, "the standard agreement between Treasury and the participating institutions does not require that these institutions track or report how they plan to use, or do use, their capital investments." When the G.A.O. asked Treasury if it intended to ask all TARP recipients to provide such an accounting, Treasury said it did not—and would not. "There's not a bank in this country that would lend money under [these] terms," Elizabeth Warren, the chair of a Congressional Oversight Panel that was eventually charged by Congress with overseeing TARP activities, would tell a Senate committee.

There wasn't even anyone within the TARP office to keep track of the money as it was being disbursed. TARP gave that job—along with a $20 million fee—to a private contractor, Bank of New York Mellon, which also happened to be one of the Big 9. So here was a case of a beneficiary helping to oversee a process in which it was a direct participant. Most of the TARP contracts—for everything from legal services to accounting—were awarded under an expedited procedure that government watchdogs regard as "high-risk," because it lacks a wide array of routine safeguards. In its first three months of operation, the Office of Financial Stability awarded 15 contracts worth tens of millions of dollars to law firms, fiscal agents, management consultants, and providers of various other services. There was enormous potential for conflicts of interest, and no procedure to deal with them. When the possibility of conflict of interest was raised, two of the contractors voiced vague promises to maintain an "open dialog" and "work in good faith" with Treasury, and left it at that.

When Henry Paulson unveiled the bank-rescue plan, he emphasized that it wasn't a bailout. "This is an investment, not an expenditure, and there is no reason to expect this program will cost taxpayers anything," he declared. For every $100 Treasury invested in the banks, he maintained, it would receive stock and warrants valued at $100. This claim proved optimistic. The Congressional Oversight Panel that later reviewed the 10 largest TARP transactions concluded that Treasury "paid substantially more for the assets it purchased under the TARP than their then-current market value." For each $100 spent, Treasury received assets worth about $66.

In those first few weeks, money gushed out of Treasury and into the TARP pipeline at a torrential rate. After giving $125 billion to the big banks, Treasury moved on to the second round, wiring $33.6 billion to 21 other banks on November 14 in exchange for preferred stock. A week later it sent $2.9 billion to 23 more banks. As noted, by the time Barack Obama took office, the TARP tab totaled more than a quarter of a trillion dollars. In its first six months, the new administration disbursed an additional $125 billion to banks, mortgage companies, A.I.G., and the big auto manufacturers.

To the public, the bailout looked like a gold rush by banks competing for TARP money. It was indeed partly that, but the reality is more complex. While some banks lobbied aggressively for TARP money, many others that had no interest in the money were pressured to take it. Treasury's explanation is that regulators knew which banks were strongest and wanted to get more capital into their hands in order to free up credit. But it's also true that spreading the money around to a large number of small and medium-size banks helped create the impression that the bailout wasn't just for a few big boys on Wall Street.

It's impossible to overstate how casual the process was, or how little Treasury asked of the banks it targeted. Like most bankers, Ray Davis, the C.E.O. of Umpqua Bank, a solid, respectable local bank in Portland, Oregon, followed with great interest all the news out of Washington last fall. But he didn't see that TARP had much relevance to his own bank. Umpqua was well run. It wasn't bogged down by a portfolio of bad loans. It had healthy reserves.

Then he got a call from a Treasury Department representative asking if Umpqua would like to participate in the Treasury program and suggesting it would be a good thing for Umpqua to do. Davis listened politely, but the fact was, he says, that Umpqua "didn't need the funds. Our capital resources were very high."

The next day, Davis was in his office when another call came through from the same Treasury representative. "Basically what he said was that the secretary of the Treasury would like to have your application on his desk by five o'clock tomorrow afternoon," Davis recalls.

The "application" was the paperwork for a capital infusion, and Davis was told it would be faxed over right away. By now he was sold on participating. "Here was somebody from the secretary of the Treasury calling," Davis says, "and complimenting us on the strength of our company and saying you need to do this, to help the government, to be a good American citizen—all that stuff—and I'm saying, 'That's good. You've got me. I'm in.'"

The most urgent task was to complete the application and get it back to Treasury the next day, and this had Davis in a sweat: "I pictured this 200-page fax that would take me three weeks of work crammed into one evening." Imagine Davis's surprise when a staff member walked in soon afterward with the official "Application for TARP Capital Purchase Program." It consisted of two pages, most of it white space.

If TARP accomplishes nothing else, it has struck a mighty blow for simplicity in government. The application was only 24 lines long, and asked such tough questions as the name and address of the bank, the name of the primary contact, the amount of its common and preferred stock, and how much money the bank wanted. Anyone who has filled out the voluminous federal forms required in order to be eligible for a college loan would die for such an application. Davis recalls that, when the two faxed pages were brought to him, all he could say was "Really?" As soon as Umpqua's application was approved, Treasury wired $214 million to Umpqua's account.

What happened in Portland happened elsewhere across the country. Peter Skillern, who heads the Community Reinvestment Association, a nonprofit group in North Carolina, describes a conference he attended where bankers explained that they had been "contacted by their regulators and told by them that they would be taking TARP."

One policy that TARP did decide to adopt was to keep confidential the name of any bank that was denied TARP funds—but it never had to invoke this rule. In those early months, with billions being wired all across the country, no financial institution that asked for TARP money was turned away.

With few restrictions or controls in place, bailout money found its way not only to banks that didn't really need it but also to banks whose business practices left much to be desired. On November 21, $180 million in TARP money wound up in the affluent seaside community of Santa Barbara, California. The TARP dollars flowed mostly into the coffers of a beige, Spanish-style building on Carrillo Street, home to the Santa Barbara Bank & Trust.

This might appear to be just the kind of regional bank that Treasury had in mind as an ideal beneficiary of TARP. The bank has been a fixture in Santa Barbara for decades, serving small businesses as well as wealthy individuals. It sponsors Little League teams, funds scholarships to send local kids to college, and takes an active role in community groups. It plays up its "longstanding commitment to giving back to the communities we serve."

How much TARP money made its way through S.B.B.&T. and into the local community is not known. But, as it happens, the bank also operates a little-known and controversial program far from the lush enclaves of Santa Barbara. Like an absentee landlord, the community bank with the "give back" philosophy in Santa Barbara turns out to be a big player in poor neighborhoods throughout the country. And not in a nice way. Outside Santa Barbara, S.B.B.&T. peddles what are known as refund-anticipation loans (RALs)—high-interest loans to the poor that are among the most predatory around.

A RAL is a short-term loan to taxpayers who have filed for a tax refund. Rather than waiting one or two weeks for their refund from the I.R.S., they take out a bank loan for an amount equal to their refund, minus interest, fees, and other charges. Banks operate in concert with tax preparers who complete the paperwork, and then the banks write the taxpayer a check. The loan is secured by the taxpayer's expected refund. RALs are theoretically available to everyone, but they are used overwhelmingly by the working poor. Ordinarily, the loans have a term of only a few weeks—the time it takes the I.R.S. to process the return and send out a check—but the interest charges and fees are so steep that borrowers can lose as much as 20 percent of the value of their tax refund. A recent study estimated that annual rates on some RALs run as high as 700 percent.

Santa Barbara is one of three banks that dominate this obscure corner of the banking market—the other two being J. P. Morgan Chase and HSBC. But unlike the two big banks, for which RALs are but one facet of a broad-based business, Santa Barbara has come to rely heavily for its financial well-being on these high-interest loans to poor people. Interest earned from RALs accounted for 24 percent of the banking company's interest earnings in 2008, second only to income generated by commercial-real-estate loans. Under pressure from consumer groups, some banks, including J. P. Morgan Chase, have lowered their RAL fees. Not Santa Barbara. Chi Chi Wu, of the National Consumer Law Center, in Boston, calls Santa Barbara Bank & Trust "a small bank with sharp teeth."

The U.S. Department of Justice and state authorities in California, New

Jersey, and New York have taken action against tax preparers with whom
S.B.B.&T. works, charging them with deceptive advertising and with preparing fraudulent returns. Santa Barbara later took a $22 million hit on its
books because of unpaid refund-anticipation loans.

The bank insists that its TARP money didn't go to finance RALs. "The
capital received by Santa Barbara Bank & Trust under the U.S. Treasury Department's Capital Purchase Program was not intended nor is it being used
to fund or provide liquidity for any Refund Anticipation Loans," according to Deborah L. Whiteley, an executive vice president of Pacific Capital
Bancorp, Santa Barbara's parent company. Other banks that have received
TARP money have made similar statements, contending that money received
from Washington simply became part of their capital base and was not earmarked for any specific purpose. But in a conference call with analysts on
November 21, Stephen Masterson, the chief financial officer of Pacific Capital Bancorp, admitted that TARP "obviously helps us. . . . We didn't take the
TARP money to increase our RAL program or to build our RAL program, but it
certainly helps our capital ratios."

Indeed, the infusion from Treasury may well have been a lifeline for
Santa Barbara. The Community Reinvestment Association of North Carolina, which has been tracking S.B.B.&T.'s finances and its RAL program
for years, concluded in 2008 that S.B.B.&T. would be losing money if it
weren't putting the squeeze on poor people around the country.

KeyBank of Cleveland is another institution that was given the nod
by Treasury officials—and another bank whose lending practices
prompt the question: What *were* they thinking?

Last fall KeyBank received $2.5 billion in TARP money. Its parent com-
pany is KeyCorp, a major bank holding company headquartered in Cleveland. With 989 full-service branches spread across 14 states, KeyCorp
describes itself as "one of the nation's largest bank-based financial services
companies," with assets of $98 billion. It also ranks as the nation's seventh-
largest education lender. In the summer of 2008, as banks and Wall Street
firms were unraveling faster than they could count up their losses, KeyCorp
delivered a decidedly upbeat report on its condition to investors. "Our costs
are well controlled," the company stated. "Our fee revenue is strong. . . .
Our reserves are strong. . . . We remain well capitalized."

What the report did not mention was a host of other problems. Key-Corp was in the midst of negotiations with the I.R.S. over questionable tax-leasing deals, and had had to deposit $2 billion in escrow with the government—forcing it to raise emergency capital and slash dividends after 43 consecutive years of annual growth. Meanwhile, consumer advocates had KeyBank in their sights because of the way it conducted its student-loan business, which they described as nakedly predatory. *The Salt Lake Tribune* reported that "KeyBank not only funds unscrupulous schools, it seeks them out, strikes up lucrative partnerships, and, in the process, suckers students into thinking the schools are legitimate."

Over the years, thousands of students have secured education loans from KeyBank to attend a broad range of career-training schools—schools offering instruction in how to use or repair computers, how to become an electronics technician or even a nurse. One of the schools was Silver State Helicopters, which was based in Las Vegas and operated flight schools in a half-dozen states. During high-pressure sales pitches, people looking to change careers were encouraged to simultaneously sign up for flight school and complete a loan application that would be forwarded to KeyBank. Once approved, KeyBank, in keeping with long-standing practice, would give all the tuition money up front directly to Silver State. If a student dropped out, Silver State kept the tuition and the student remained on the hook for the full amount of the loan, at a hefty interest rate.

The same rule applied if Silver State shut itself down, which it did without warning on February 3, 2008. "Because the monthly operating expenses, even at the recently streamlined levels, continue to exceed cash flow," an e-mail to employees explained, "the board has elected to suspend all operations effective at 5 p.m. today." More than 750 employees in 18 states were out of work. More than 2,500 students had their training (for which they had paid as much as $70,000) cut short.

Silver State Helicopters was a flight school, but it might more accurately be thought of as a Ponzi scheme, according to critics. As long as there was a continual source of loan money, keeping the scheme afloat, all was well. KeyBank bundled the loans into securities, just as the subprime-mortgage marketers had done, and sold them on Wall Street. But when Wall Street failed to buy at an adequate interest rate, the money supply evaporated. As KeyBank dryly put it, "In 2007, Key was unable to securitize its student loan portfolio at cost-effective rates." Without the loans—in other words, without the cooperation of Wall Street—the school had no income.

In February 2009, Fitch Ratings service, which rates the ability of debt issuers to meet their commitments, placed 16 classes of KeyCorp student-loan transactions totaling $1.75 billion on "Ratings Watch Negative," signaling the possibility of a future downgrade in their creditworthiness.

The credit-card behemoth Capital One, an institution that many Americans probably don't even realize is a bank, maintains its headquarters in McLean, in northern Virginia. Over the years, Capital One's phenomenally successful marketing strategy has made the company the fifth-largest credit-card issuer in the U.S., and it has used its profits to expand into retail banking, home-equity loans, and other kinds of lending.

Capital One never revealed what it planned to do with the $3.5 billion TARP check it received from the U.S. Treasury on November 14, 2008, but three weeks later, the company bought one of Washington's premier financial institutions, Chevy Chase Bank. To Washingtonians, Chevy Chase was a model corporate citizen. But outside Washington, it had a different reputation. The company's mortgage subsidiary had engaged in practices that were at the core of the nation's mortgage meltdown—risky loans with teaser interest rates that later went bad. The bank's portfolio of mortgages from around the country was stuffed with a high percentage of so-called option ARMs—adjustable-rate mortgages with many different payment options. One of the most common kept a homeowner's monthly payment the same for years, but the interest rate rose almost immediately. When the interest exceeded the amount of the monthly payment, the excess was tacked onto the principal, pushing homeowners ever deeper into debt. Having been lured by what a federal judge would call the "siren call" of this kind of mortgage, many Chevy Chase mortgage holders were on the brink of foreclosure, or had already fallen over the edge. By mid-2008, Chevy Chase's "nonperforming" assets had tripled to $490 million since the previous September.

With Chevy Chase rapidly deteriorating, along came Capital One. Flush with TARP money, Capital One became a bailout czar of its own. It bought Chevy Chase for $520 million and assumed $1.75 billion of its bad loans. The purchase price was a fraction of what Chevy Chase would have brought before it wandered off into the wilderness of exotic mortgages and risky lending.

Meanwhile, even as it was bailing out Chevy Chase, Capital One was putting the squeeze on many thousands of its own credit-card holders, sharply raising their interest rates and imposing other conditions that made credit far more expensive and difficult to obtain. For many cardholders, rates jumped overnight from 7.9 percent to as much as 22.9 percent. Rather than using its multi-billion-dollar government infusion to prime the credit pump, Capital One in fact began turning off the spigot.

Capital One's actions enraged its customers, many of whom had been cardholders for decades. The bank was engulfed with complaints. "The last I checked you were given money from the government for the specific purpose of freeing up credit to stimulate spending and help move the economy out of recession," wrote a woman in Holland, Michigan. This was "just the opposite of what you did." But other credit-card companies that received federal bailout money, such as Bank of America, J. P. Morgan Chase, and Citibank, would take the same route as Capital One, sharply raising interest rates, cutting off credit to millions of people, and frustrating the stated rationale for Treasury's bailout.

Because all dollar bills are alike, and because follow-up tracking by the government has been so minimal, it's often impossible to determine if any bank or other financial institution used TARP money for any particular, discernible purpose. Only A.I.G., Bank of America, and Citigroup were subject to any reporting requirements at all, and the reporting has been spotty. But what is possible to say is that TARP allowed many recipients to spend money in ways they would have been unable to do otherwise. It's also the case that recipients of TARP money continued to behave as if a financial earthquake hadn't just shaken the world economy.

The Riviera Country Club is about a mile from the Pacific Ocean, in a scenic canyon north of Los Angeles. Riviera is home to one of the most storied tournaments on the P.G.A. tour. This year the tournament was sponsored by a TARP recipient, the Northern Trust Company of Chicago. Northern was founded more than a century ago to cater to wealthy Chicagoans, and not much about its clientele has changed since then, except that now the company caters to the wealthy not just in Chicago but everywhere.

According to the bank, its wealth-management group caters to those "with assets typically exceeding $200 million." The company manages $559 billion in assets—a sum nearly as great as what has so far been spent on the TARP program itself.

When Northern Trust received $1.6 billion in TARP funds, a spokesman for the bank said that it was "too soon to say specifically" how the money would be used. But the company's president and C.E.O., Frederick Waddell, noted that "the program will provide us with additional capital to maximize growth opportunities." Three months later, the bank sponsored the Northern Trust Open, flying in wealthy clients from around the country. To entertain them, the bank brought in Sheryl Crow, Chicago, and Earth, Wind & Fire. A Northern Trust spokesman declined to say how much all this cost, but explained that it was really just a business decision "to show appreciation for clients."

Northern Trust was acting no differently from many other TARP recipients. One of the most blatant examples was Citigroup's plan to buy a $50 million private jet to fly executives around the country. A public outcry forced Citigroup to abandon that scheme, but the bank quietly went ahead with a $10 million renovation of its executive offices on Park Avenue, in New York. Given that Citigroup had already gone to the government three times for TARP assistance totaling $45 billion, and was not a paragon of public trust, retrofitting the windows with "Safety Shield 800" blastproof window film may have just been common sense.

The excesses weren't confined to big-city banks. A subsidiary of North Carolina–based B.B.&T., after accepting $3.1 billion in TARP money, sent dozens of employees to a training session at the Ritz-Carlton hotel in Sarasota, Florida. TCF Financial Corp., based in Wayzata, Minnesota, sent 40 "high-performing" managers, lenders, and other employees on a junket in February to Cancún, soon after receiving more than $360 million in TARP funds.

But let's face it: episodes like these, infuriating as they may be, aren't the real issue. The real issue is TARP itself, one of the most questionable ventures the U.S. government has ever pursued. Adopted as a plan to buy up toxic assets—one that was quickly deemed impractical even by those who first proposed it—it evolved into something more closely resembling an all-purpose slush fund flowing out to hundreds of institutions with their own interests and goals, and no incentive to deploy the money toward any clearly defined public purpose.

By and large, the cash that went to the Big 9 simply became part of their capital base, and most of the big banks declined to indicate where the money actually went. Because of the sheer size of these institutions, it's simply impossible to trace. Bank of America no doubt used a portion of its $25 billion in TARP funds to help it absorb Merrill Lynch. Citigroup revealed in its first quarterly report after receiving $45 billion in TARP funds that it had used $36.5 billion to buy up mortgages and to make new loans, including home loans.

A.I.G., the largest single TARP beneficiary, wasn't even a bank. The insurance company used its $70 billion in TARP funds to pay off a previous government infusion from the Federal Reserve. The original bailout money had flowed through A.I.G. to Wall Street firms and foreign banks that had incurred big losses on credit-default swaps and other exotic obligations. These were basically the casino-style wagers made by A.I.G. and the counterparties—wagers they lost. The government justified the help by saying it was necessary to prevent disruption to the economy that would be caused by a "disorderly wind-down" of A.I.G. The collapse of Lehman Brothers had occurred just days before the Fed took action, and the shock waves on Wall Street from yet another implosion might have been catastrophic. Bankruptcy court, where troubled corporations routinely wind down their disorderly affairs, would have been another option, though that prospect might not have quickly enough addressed the gathering sense of urgency and doom. We'll never know. Certainly bankruptcy court would not have allowed A.I.G.'s clients to get full value for their bad investments.

Instead, A.I.G. was able to pay off its counterparties 100 cents on the dollar. The largest payout—$12.9 billion—went to Goldman Sachs, the Wall Street investment house presided over by Paulson before he moved into his Treasury job. Merrill Lynch, the world's largest brokerage—then in the process of being taken over by Bank of America—received $6.8 billion. Bank of America itself received $5.2 billion. Citigroup, the nation's largest bank, received $2.3 billion. But it wasn't just Wall Street that benefitted. A.I.G. also funneled tens of billions of TARP dollars to banks on the other side of the Atlantic.

Some banks receiving TARP funds bristle at the notion that the taxpayer-funded program is a bailout. They say it is an investment in banks by the federal government, one that requires them to pay interest and ultimately pay back the money or face a financial penalty. In fact, many banks are making their scheduled payments to Treasury, and others have paid off billions of dollars in TARP funds (as well as interest). To TARP supporters, this is evidence of a sound investment. But at this stage it isn't clear that every institution will be able to make the interest payments and buy back the government's holdings. As of this writing, some banks, including Pacific Capital Bancorp, the parent of Santa Barbara Bank & Trust, have not been able to make their scheduled payments. No one can predict how many banks will ultimately come up short. But in the meantime TARP has been a very good deal for banks, because it gave them, courtesy of the taxpayers, access to capital that would have cost them substantially more in the private market, while exacting nothing from the beneficiaries in the form of a quid pro quo.

Based on the reluctance of many banks to take the money in the first place, and the swiftness with which other banks have repaid TARP funds, the main conclusion to be drawn is that relatively few were actually endangered. Rather than targeting the weak for relief—or allowing them to fail, as the government allowed millions of ordinary Americans to fail—Paulson and Treasury pumped hundreds of billions of dollars into the financial system without prior design and without prospective accountability. What was this all about? A case of panic by Treasury and the Federal Reserve? A financial over-reaction of cosmic proportions? A smoke screen to take care of a small number of Wall Street institutions that received 100 cents on the dollar for some of the worst investments they ever made?

More than five months after the bulk of the bailout money had been distributed into bank coffers, Elizabeth Warren plaintively raised the central and as yet unanswered question: "What is the strategy that Treasury is pursuing?" And she basically threw up her hands. As far as she could see, Warren went on, Treasury's strategy was essentially "Take the money and do what you want with it."

·8·

Capitalist Fools

Five Key Mistakes That Led Us to the Collapse

By JOSEPH E. STIGLITZ

January 2009

There will come a moment when the most urgent threats posed by the credit crisis have eased and the larger task before us will be to chart a direction for the economic steps ahead. This will be a dangerous moment. Behind the debates over future policy is a debate over history—a debate over the causes of our current situation. The battle for the past will determine the battle for the present. So it's crucial to get the history straight.

What were the critical decisions that led to the crisis? Mistakes were made at every fork in the road—we had what engineers call a "system failure," when not a single decision but a cascade of decisions produce a tragic result. Let's look at five key moments.

No. 1: FIRING *the* CHAIRMAN

In 1987 the Reagan administration decided to remove Paul Volcker as chairman of the Federal Reserve Board and appoint Alan Greenspan in his place. Volcker had done what central bankers are supposed to do. On his watch, inflation had been brought down from more than 11 percent to under 4 percent. In the world of central banking, that should have earned him a grade of A+++ and assured his re-appointment. But Volcker also understood that financial markets need to be regulated. Reagan wanted someone who did not believe any such thing, and he found him in a devotee of the objectivist philosopher and free-market zealot Ayn Rand.

Greenspan played a double role. The Fed controls the money spigot, and in the early years of this decade, he turned it on full force. But the Fed is also a regulator. If you appoint an anti-regulator as your enforcer, you know what kind of enforcement you'll get. A flood of liquidity combined with the failed levees of regulation proved disastrous.

Greenspan presided over not one but two financial bubbles. After the high-tech bubble popped, in 2000–2001, he helped inflate the housing bubble. The first responsibility of a central bank should be to maintain the stability of the financial system. If banks lend on the basis of artificially high asset prices, the result can be a meltdown—as we are seeing now, and as Greenspan should have known. He had many of the tools he needed to cope with the situation. To deal with the high-tech bubble, he could have increased margin requirements (the amount of cash people need to put down to buy stock). To deflate the housing bubble, he could have curbed predatory lending to low-income households and prohibited other insidious practices (the no-documentation—or "liar"—loans, the interest-only loans, and so on). This would have gone a long way toward protecting us. If he didn't have the tools, he could have gone to Congress and asked for them.

Of course, the current problems with our financial system are not solely the result of bad lending. The banks have made mega-bets with one another through complicated instruments such as derivatives, credit-default swaps, and so forth. With these, one party pays another if certain events happen—for instance, if Bear Stearns goes bankrupt, or if the dollar soars. These instruments were originally created to help manage risk—but they can also be used to gamble. Thus, if you felt confident that the dollar was going to fall, you could make a big bet accordingly, and if the dollar indeed fell, your profits would soar. The problem is that, with this complicated intertwining of bets of great magnitude, no one could be sure of the financial position of anyone else—or even of one's own position. Not surprisingly, the credit markets froze.

Here too Greenspan played a role. When I was chairman of the Council of Economic Advisers, during the Clinton administration, I served on a committee of all the major federal financial regulators, a group that included Greenspan and Treasury Secretary Robert Rubin. Even then, it was clear that derivatives posed a danger. We didn't put it as memorably as Warren Buffett—who saw derivatives as "financial weapons of mass destruction"— but we took his point. And yet, for all the risk, the deregulators in charge of the financial system—at the Fed, at the Securities and Exchange Commission, and elsewhere—decided to do nothing, worried that any action might interfere with "innovation" in the financial system. But innovation, like "change," has no inherent value. It can be bad (the "liar" loans are a good example) as well as good.

No. 2: TEARING DOWN *THE* WALLS

The deregulation philosophy would pay unwelcome dividends for years to come. In November 1999, Congress repealed the Glass-Steagall Act—the culmination of a $300 million lobbying effort by the banking and financial-services industries, and spearheaded in Congress by Senator Phil Gramm. Glass-Steagall had long separated commercial banks (which lend money) and investment banks (which organize the sale of bonds and equities); it had been enacted in the aftermath of the Great Depression and was meant to curb the excesses of that era, including grave conflicts of interest. For instance, without separation, if a company whose shares had been issued by an investment bank, with its strong endorsement, got into trouble, wouldn't its commercial arm, if it had one, feel pressure to lend it money, perhaps unwisely? An ensuing spiral of bad judgment is not hard to foresee. I had opposed repeal of Glass-Steagall. The proponents said, in effect, Trust us: we will create Chinese walls to make sure that the problems of the past do not recur. As an economist, I certainly possessed a healthy degree of trust, trust in the power of economic incentives to bend human behavior toward self-interest—toward short-term self-interest, at any rate, rather than Tocqueville's "self interest rightly understood."

The most important consequence of the repeal of Glass-Steagall was indirect—it lay in the way repeal changed an entire culture. Commercial banks are not supposed to be high-risk ventures; they are supposed to manage other people's money very conservatively. It is with this understanding that the government agrees to pick up the tab should they fail. Investment banks, on the other hand, have traditionally managed rich people's money—people who can take bigger risks in order to get bigger returns. When repeal of Glass-Steagall brought investment and commercial banks together, the investment-bank culture came out on top. There was a demand for the kind of high returns that could be obtained only through high leverage and big risktaking.

There were other important steps down the deregulatory path. One was the decision in April 2004 by the Securities and Exchange Commission, at a meeting attended by virtually no one and largely overlooked at the time, to allow big investment banks to increase their debt-to-capital ratio (from 12:1 to 30:1, or higher) so that they could buy more mortgage-backed securities, inflating the housing bubble in the process. In agreeing to this measure, the S.E.C. argued for the virtues of self-regulation: the peculiar notion that banks can effectively police themselves. Self-regulation is preposterous, as even Alan Greenspan now concedes, and as a practical matter it can't, in any case, identify systemic risks—the kinds of risks that arise when, for instance, the models used by each of the banks to manage their portfolios tell all the banks to sell some security all at once.

As we stripped back the old regulations, we did nothing to address the new challenges posed by 21st-century markets. The most important challenge was that posed by derivatives. In 1998 the head of the Commodity Futures Trading Commission, Brooksley Born, had called for such regulation—a concern that took on urgency after the Fed, in that same year, engineered the bailout of Long-Term Capital Management, a hedge fund whose trillion-dollar-plus failure threatened global financial markets. But Secretary of the Treasury Robert Rubin, his deputy, Larry Summers, and Greenspan were adamant—and successful—in their opposition. Nothing was done.

No. 3: APPLYING *the* LEECHES

Then along came the Bush tax cuts, enacted first on June 7, 2001, with a follow-on installment two years later. The president and his advisers seemed to believe that tax cuts, especially for upper-income Americans and corporations, were a cure-all for any economic disease—the modern-day equivalent of leeches. The tax cuts played a pivotal role in shaping the background conditions of the current crisis. Because they did very little to stimulate the economy, real stimulation was left to the Fed, which took up the task with unprecedented low-interest rates and liquidity. The war in Iraq made matters worse, because it led to soaring oil prices. With America so dependent on oil imports, we had to spend several hundred billion more to purchase oil—money that otherwise would have been spent on American goods. Normally this would have led to an economic slowdown, as it had in the 1970s. But the Fed met the challenge in the most myopic way imaginable. The flood of liquidity made money readily available in mortgage markets, even to those who would normally not be able to borrow. And, yes, this succeeded in forestalling an economic downturn; America's household saving rate plummeted to zero. But it should have been clear that we were living on borrowed money and borrowed time.

The cut in the tax rate on capital gains contributed to the crisis in another way. It was a decision that turned on values: those who speculated (read: gambled) and won were taxed more lightly than wage earners who simply worked hard. But more than that, the decision encouraged leveraging, because interest was tax-deductible. If, for instance, you borrowed a million to buy a home or took a $100,000 home-equity loan to buy stock, the interest would be fully deductible every year. Any capital gains you made were taxed lightly—and at some possibly remote day in the future. The Bush administration was providing an open invitation to excessive borrowing and lending—not that American consumers needed any more encouragement.

No. 4: FAKING *the* NUMBERS

Meanwhile, on July 30, 2002, in the wake of a series of major scandals—notably the collapse of WorldCom and Enron—Congress passed the

Sarbanes-Oxley Act. The scandals had involved every major American accounting firm, most of our banks, and some of our premier companies, and
made it clear that we had serious problems with our accounting system.
Accounting is a sleep-inducing topic for most people, but if you can't have
faith in a company's numbers, then you can't have faith in anything about
a company at all. Unfortunately, in the negotiations over what became
Sarbanes-Oxley a decision was made not to deal with what many, including the respected former head of the S.E.C. Arthur Levitt, believed to be a
fundamental underlying problem: stock options. Stock options have been
defended as providing healthy incentives toward good management, but
in fact they are "incentive pay" in name only. If a company does well, the
C.E.O. gets great rewards in the form of stock options; if a company does
poorly, the compensation is almost as substantial but is bestowed in other
ways. This is bad enough. But a collateral problem with stock options is
that they provide incentives for bad accounting: top management has
every incentive to provide distorted information in order to pump up share
prices.

The incentive structure of the rating agencies also proved perverse.
Agencies such as Moody's and Standard & Poor's are paid by the very
people they are supposed to grade. As a result, they've had every reason
to give companies high ratings, in a financial version of what college professors know as grade inflation. The rating agencies, like the investment
banks that were paying them, believed in financial alchemy—that F-rated
toxic mortgages could be converted into products that were safe enough to
be held by commercial banks and pension funds. We had seen this same
failure of the rating agencies during the East Asia crisis of the 1990s: high
ratings facilitated a rush of money into the region, and then a sudden reversal in the ratings brought devastation. But the financial overseers paid
no attention.

No. 5: LETTING IT BLEED

The final turning point came with the passage of a bailout package on October 3, 2008—that is, with the administration's response to the crisis itself.
We will be feeling the consequences for years to come. Both the administration and the Fed had long been driven by wishful thinking, hoping that the

bad news was just a blip, and that a return to growth was just around the corner. As America's banks faced collapse, the administration veered from one course of action to another. Some institutions (Bear Stearns, A.I.G., Fannie Mae, Freddie Mac) were bailed out. Lehman Brothers was not. Some shareholders got something back. Others did not.

The original proposal by Treasury Secretary Henry Paulson, a three-page document that would have provided $700 billion for the secretary to spend at his sole discretion, without oversight or judicial review, was an act of extraordinary arrogance. He sold the program as necessary to restore confidence. But it didn't address the underlying reasons for the loss of confidence. The banks had made too many bad loans. There were big holes in their balance sheets. No one knew what was truth and what was fiction. The bailout package was like a massive transfusion to a patient suffering from internal bleeding—and nothing was being done about the source of the problem, namely all those foreclosures. Valuable time was wasted as Paulson pushed his own plan, "cash for trash," buying up the bad assets and putting the risk onto American taxpayers. When he finally abandoned it, providing banks with money they needed, he did it in a way that not only cheated America's taxpayers but failed to ensure that the banks would use the money to re-start lending. He even allowed the banks to pour out money to their shareholders as taxpayers were pouring money into the banks.

The other problem not addressed involved the looming weaknesses in the economy. The economy had been sustained by excessive borrowing. That game was up. As consumption contracted, exports kept the economy going, but with the dollar strengthening and Europe and the rest of the world declining, it was hard to see how that could continue. Meanwhile, states faced massive drop-offs in revenues—they would have to cut back on expenditures. Without quick action by government, the economy faced a downturn. And even if banks had lent wisely—which they hadn't—the downturn was sure to mean an increase in bad debts, further weakening the struggling financial sector.

The administration talked about confidence building, but what it delivered was actually a confidence trick. If the administration had really wanted to restore confidence in the financial system, it would have begun by addressing the underlying problems—the flawed incentive structures and the inadequate regulatory system.

Was there any single decision which, had it been reversed, would have changed the course of history? Every decision—including decisions not to do something, as many of our bad economic decisions have been—is a consequence of prior decisions, an interlinked web stretching from the distant past into the future. You'll hear some on the right point to certain actions by the government itself—such as the Community Reinvestment Act, which requires banks to make mortgage money available in low-income neighborhoods. (Defaults on C.R.A. lending were actually much lower than on other lending.) There has been much finger-pointing at Fannie Mae and Freddie Mac, the two huge mortgage lenders, which were originally government-owned. But in fact they came late to the subprime game, and their problem was similar to that of the private sector: their C.E.O.'s had the same perverse incentive to indulge in gambling.

The truth is most of the individual mistakes boil down to just one: a belief that markets are self-adjusting and that the role of government should be minimal. Looking back at that belief during hearings this fall on Capitol Hill, Alan Greenspan said out loud, "I have found a flaw." Congressman Henry Waxman pushed him, responding, "In other words, you found that your view of the world, your ideology, was not right; it was not working." "Absolutely, precisely," Greenspan said. The embrace by America—and much of the rest of the world—of this flawed economic philosophy made it inevitable that we would eventually arrive at the place we are today.

· 9 ·

Fannie Mae's Last Stand

By Bethany McLean

February 2009

"The chairman of the universe."

"Washington, D.C.'s Medici."

"The face of the Washington national establishment."

"One of the most powerful men in the United States."

All those phrases were used to describe a man you may never have heard of: Jim Johnson, the C.E.O. of mortgage giant Fannie Mae in the 1990s. Fannie was then one of the largest, most profitable companies in the world, with a stock-market value of more than $70 billion and more earnings per employee than any other company in America. (By comparison, G.M. at its peak, in 2000, was worth only $56 billion.) On one level, Johnson, now 65 years old, was just another businessman with a lot of money and multi-million-dollar houses in desirable locations from D.C. to Sun Valley, Idaho, to Palm Desert, California. Chairman of D.C.'s premier arts venue, the Kennedy Center, and one of its top think tanks, the Brookings Institution, Johnson was out "wearing white-tie and black-tie every night," says Bill Maloni, Fannie's former chief lobbyist. "Everyone wanted a little bit of Jim."

But Johnson was also a political force, because the company he ran had a public mission—literally. It had been chartered by Congress to help homeownership. Johnson liked to paraphrase the old motto about General Motors: "What's good for American housing is good for Fannie Mae," he'd say. Accordingly, he built Fannie into what former congressman Jim Leach, a Republican from Iowa and longtime Fannie gadfly, calls "the greatest, most sophisticated lobbying operation in the modern history of finance."

He may be right. John McCain was embarrassed last summer by revelations that his campaign manager, Rick Davis, had served as the president of the Homeownership Alliance, an advocacy group for Fannie and Freddie Mac, Fannie's smaller brother. The "revolving door," as people call it, between the Hill and Fannie and Freddie spun so quickly that it's actually more surprising when someone isn't on the list than when they are. Rahm Emanuel served on Freddie's board! Right-wing godfather Grover Norquist lobbied for Fannie! Newt Gingrich was a consultant for Freddie, and Ralph Reed was a consultant for Fannie!

The Princeton-educated son of a Minnesota state legislator, Johnson has silver hair and round tortoiseshell glasses, which give him a warm appearance that is belied by the hard planes of his face. Indeed, he was "very warm, very nice," in the words of one former Fannie executive, but also "very hard-ass." In 1996, Richard Baker, a Republican representative from Louisiana, complained that the preface to a Treasury Department report on Fannie had been watered down to make it friendlier to the company. Rumors flew that this had been accomplished after Johnson, or someone else high up in the company, had simply made a call to Treasury Secretary Robert Rubin or President Bill Clinton, both of whom were Johnson's personal friends. (Johnson and Clinton had met at a 1969 gathering on Martha's Vineyard.) Johnson has denied calling either man, and has said that he and Rubin had a policy while Rubin was Treasury secretary that they would not discuss business. But, under Johnson, Fannie Mae had a reputation for never losing a fight. "The old political reality was that we always won, we took no prisoners, and we faced little organized political opposition" is how Daniel Mudd, son of journalist Roger Mudd and Fannie's last real C.E.O., later described Fannie's golden years.

On December 15, 1998, Jim Johnson's retirement dinner was held at the National Museum for Women in the Arts. That seems to have been the second choice—according to *The Washington Post,* the gala was supposed to have been in the U.S. State Department's Benjamin Franklin Room, which could be used by outsiders only if a government official requested it. The *Post* began making calls after it got hold of an invitation, at which point State Department lawyers pulled the plug. But the dinner was grand in any event. Rubin spoke, as did comedian Bill Cosby and Fannie board member Bill Daley, the brother of Chicago's current mayor.

The press reported Johnson's compensation in his final year as around $7 million, but an internal Fannie Mae analysis (which assumed a high stock price) said that the real number was closer to $21 million. Plus, he got perks that could add up to half a million a year: a consulting agreement, two support-staff employees paid for by Fannie Mae, a car, and partial payment for a driver.

There were rumors that Johnson was angling to become Treasury secretary. Instead, in 1999, he became one of the first outside directors of the investment bank Goldman Sachs, where Rubin had been C.E.O., and where current Treasury secretary Henry Paulson presided at the time. Johnson became the head of the compensation committee, making him the closest thing Hank Paulson had to a boss.

Flash forward to just 10 years later. On Friday, September 5, 2008, Treasury Secretary Paulson sat in a conference room at an obscure government agency known as the Federal Housing Finance Agency (F.H.F.A.), which had been charged with regulating Fannie and Freddie. Next to Paulson sat Jim Lockhart, the director of F.H.F.A. On Lockhart's other side was Ben Bernanke, chairman of the Federal Reserve. Across the table sat Dan Mudd, who had become Fannie's C.E.O. in late 2004. By the summer of 2008, Fannie and Freddie owned or guaranteed $5.2 trillion of American mortgages, roughly half the $12 trillion total. Just six weeks before the September 5 meeting, Lockhart had said publicly that Fannie Mae's capital was "well in excess" of what it needed to survive the mortgage storm that was engulfing the nation. But at the meeting he announced that the company's capital was, in fact, insufficient. The government officials told Mudd that his company had to give its consent to something called conservatorship, which meant that the government would take it over, pretty much wiping out shareholders—not because Fannie needed capital at that moment, but because they believed Fannie would need it in the future. Mudd was out.

The message to Fannie executives, says one person who was in the room, was crystal clear: "If you oppose us, we will fight publicly and fight hard, and do not think that your share price will do well with all of the forces of the government arrayed against you."

There was also a threat that F.H.F.A. would make life very unpleasant for both the board and management if they didn't agree to the government's terms, says another Fannie executive. "That's really not true—there were no threats," claims Lockhart, although he adds, "We were very firm." Steve Ashley, former chairman of Fannie's board, asked what the government wanted Fannie to do that it wasn't already doing. The Fannie team didn't feel that any good answers were given.

A lot of people assume they already know the story of Fannie's fall from grace. In a narrative that has been repeated incessantly in op-eds and on cable TV, there were good guys and bad guys. The good guys were the Republicans, who had tried to rein in Fannie and Freddie (which was also put into conservatorship that same day), and the bad guys were the Democrats, who wanted to put people into houses they couldn't afford with subprime mortgages, and Fannie itself, which took advantage of its supposed mission to enrich its executives at the expense of taxpayers. Some even argue that Fannie and Freddie—"the toxic twins," former Connecticut Republican representative Chris Shays called them—are to blame for the entire economic meltdown. They were "the match that started this forest fire," according to John McCain. On October 21, a group of House Republicans wrote to Attorney General Michael Mukasey, requesting that the Justice Department appoint a special counsel to investigate Fannie and Freddie executives. (The F.B.I. is investigating both Fannie and Freddie.) Jim Johnson, by last June the vetter of vice-presidential candidates for Barack Obama, had to resign the post due to allegations that he had gotten more than $7 million of loans—some at favorable rates—from scandal-ridden Countrywide Financial, a major Fannie Mae customer whose former C.E.O., Angelo Mozilo, was a friend of Johnson's. (Johnson said at the time that he received no special favors.)

But there's a very different—albeit equally radical—version of reality. In this version, which is told by former Fannie executives and shareholders, Fannie was shot not because it had to be, but because it could be. "The weekend massacre" is how one former Freddie lobbyist describes the events of the September 5 weekend. "My view is [the Bush] administration said we've got four months to remove this thorn in our side," says Tim Howard, who was Fannie's chief financial officer from 1990 to 2004. "There will never be another time. We've got to do it now."

It is worth noting that thus far the government has put not a dime into Fannie and only $13.8 billion into Freddie—which is a drop in the bucket compared to the taxpayer dollars that have gone to some other firms, such as the $45 billion Hank Paulson has handed Citigroup. In this alternative narrative, it was Paulson's rash action of taking over Fannie and Freddie that helped cause the financial meltdown. As famous money manager Bill Miller, the chief investment officer of Legg Mason Capital Management, wrote in a recent letter to his investors: "When the government preemptively seized [Fannie and Freddie] not because they needed capital and could not get it, but because the government believed they would run out in the future, then shareholders of every other institution that needed or was perceived to need capital did the only rational thing they could do—sell, in case the government decided to pre-emptively wipe them out as well."

In truth, Fannie was a company with extraordinarily powerful enemies. They spanned the decades, the two parties, and the ideological spectrum, from Reagan budget director David Stockman to Clinton Treasury secretary Larry Summers to President George W. Bush, and from Ralph Nader to former Federal Reserve chairman Alan Greenspan. These enemies, who detested the privileges Fannie got from its congressional charter, had long wanted to drastically curtail the company—or kill it outright. Johnson called the battle a "philosophical dispute with deep roots and many, many branches," and it was, but it was also a personal dispute based on rivalries and jealousies. "The War of the Roses" is how a former Fannie executive describes it.

As in most wars, there is fault on both sides. Although in 2000 the Department of Housing and Urban Development (HUD), under Andrew Cuomo, increased the requirements that Fannie and Freddie buy loans made to lower-income people, a dramatic increase came in 2004—under the Bush administration. Some people believe it did so merely in order to pressure the companies into agreeing to new regulation. But Fannie itself isn't a hapless victim, either. In the end, it was Fannie executives who made a business decision to stake their future on risky mortgages that had nothing to do with helping people own homes. The company used its political power to stymie effective regulation, and its extreme aggressiveness and arrogance gave its enemies license to do things they never would have done to a normal company. And, oh, did they ever.

Gary Gensler, the Treasury undersecretary for domestic finance in the final years of the Clinton administration, likes to tell a story about the deal Alexander Hamilton cut with Thomas Jefferson and James Madison back in 1790. Jefferson and Madison agreed that the nation would assume the debt of the states; Hamilton agreed that the capital of the country would not be in New York, but rather on the Potomac. "This was a very wise move," says Gensler, "because for about two centuries it separated the nation's financial capital from its political capital." Then he chuckles a little. "It worked until Fannie Mae and Freddie Mac came along."

The Federal National Mortgage Association (Fannie Mae) was founded in 1938, a creature of F.D.R.'s New Deal. The Federal Home Loan Mortgage Corp. (Freddie Mac) came along in 1970, when the thrift industry decided that Fannie needed a competitor. Referred to as Government Sponsored Enterprises, or G.S.E.'s, they were created to help homeownership, but that has never been because they lend money directly to homeowners. Instead, Fannie and Freddie bought mortgages from the local institutions—banks, thrifts, and mortgage originators—that had made them, which relieved those mortgage-makers of both the credit risk (the risk that the homeowner wouldn't pay) and the interest-rate risk (the risk that the bank would earn less on the mortgage than it paid on its debt). This enabled the mortgage-makers to go out and make more loans.

In addition to having a congressional mandate to aid homeownership, Fannie and Freddie also had shareholders who wanted to see profits, just like Citigroup or General Electric or any publicly traded company. That's because in 1968 President Lyndon Johnson, who needed money to pay for the Vietnam War, decided to remove Fannie from the government's balance sheet by having it sell shares to the public. Freddie followed suit in 1989.

And yet, Fannie and Freddie weren't just like Citigroup or General Electric, or any normal company, because they kept an array of special perks that came with their congressional charters. Among those perks: an exemption from state and local income taxes, presidential appointees on their boards of directors, and a line of credit with the U.S. Treasury. This last was by far the most important, because the line of credit—eventually $2.25 billion for each company—implied to many investors that the full faith and credit of the U.S. government stood behind Fannie and Freddie. Officially, everyone denied that that was the case, but this "double game"—as Rick Carnell, the Treasury undersecretary for domestic finance in the 1990s, called it—enabled the companies to raise money at a cost that was just a smidgen higher than that of the government itself, thereby providing them with an enormous competitive advantage over ordinary financial institutions.

As the mortgage market evolved, and finance grew more sophisticated, Fannie and Freddie came to make their money in two ways. One was supposedly conservative: they were paid a small fee by the mortgage-makers to guarantee that the homeowner wouldn't default. And for most of their history, they wouldn't buy just any loans, but rather loans that conformed to certain size limits (thereby excluding so-called jumbo loans, more than $417,000) and fairly strict credit standards. Then they repackaged these loans into what are known as mortgage-backed securities, and sold them to other investors. The new investors were willing to take the interest-rate risk, but didn't have to worry about evaluating each and every homeowner's ability to pay—a task of enormous proportions—because Fannie and Freddie guaranteed that. Today, this is the $3.7 trillion in mortgages Fannie and Freddie guarantee.

The other way Fannie and Freddie made money was when they began to repurchase their own mortgage-backed securities, and to buy similar securities that were created by Wall Street without the G.S.E. guarantee, and hold them in a portfolio. Then Fannie and Freddie pocketed the difference—what Greenspan called "the big fat gap"—between what the mortgages yielded and the companies' own cost of borrowing funds. This was an immensely profitable business: Wall Street analysts estimated that it provided up to three-fourths of Fannie's and Freddie's earnings, and today the portfolio business comprises most of the $1.5 trillion in mortgages that Fannie and Freddie own.

This second way of making money became the source of great controversy. Critics, most notably Alan Greenspan, argued that the portfolio wasn't worth any risk at all because it did nothing to put people in homes and existed only to make money for the companies' executives and shareholders.

He and other critics didn't want just to modify Fannie's and Freddie's business. They wanted to drastically curtail it—or, better yet, wipe out the two G.S.E.'s altogether. And so it was only human nature that Fannie and Freddie fought back—hard. Or, as former Fannie chief lobbyist Bill Maloni, whose Friday-night poker games for Washington power players were the stuff of legend, wrote on a blog, "One fact of the GSE world is that you will be slaughtered either for being a sheep or a wolf, and I'd much rather meet my fate as a predator than as a lamb chop provider."

Maloni and his bosses felt that they couldn't lose any battle, no matter how small. "You punch my brother in the face, I'll burn down your house" was one Fannie Mae saying. Another was "It's better to throw one brick too many than one brick too few."

But Fannie, no matter how aggressive it was, could never stop the criticism. Within Fannie, people called the desire to shrink them or kill them the "vampire issue"—because Fannie could never make it go away.

Jim Johnson had come to Fannie in 1990. His predecessor, David Maxwell, had been on the tennis team at Yale and was "the kind of man who sends only handwritten notes," recalls Maloni. But Maxwell was also a tough cookie who knew how to get what he wanted. When he left, in 1991—with a $19.5 million retirement package—a humorous going-away video showed corporate cars leaving Fannie's offices with body bags in the trunks.

Maxwell had met Johnson at a small Washington dinner party in 1985. Johnson was a partner at Shearson Lehman, where he'd landed after he and Richard Holbrooke (who would go on to become ambassador to the U.N. under President Clinton) sold a consulting firm they'd founded to the investment bank. Johnson's world encompassed both business and politics. He had worked on the campaigns of Eugene McCarthy and George McGovern, and then served in the Carter administration as Walter Mondale's executive assistant (and later the chair of his presidential campaign), during which time he married Mondale's press secretary, Maxine Isaacs, now a lecturer at the Harvard Kennedy School. When Maxwell retired, he chose Johnson as his successor over protests from President George H. W. Bush's people, who claimed Johnson was a partisan Democrat.

It was Johnson who "took the seeds that David Maxwell sowed and

[grew] them far beyond what David Maxwell dreamed," as Countrywide chief Angelo Mozilo later told a reporter. Like Maxwell, Johnson cut a charming, suave figure in society, but under his Minnesota-nice exterior was the heart of a born fighter. "In daily life, he'd say things like 'We're going to cut them off at the knees,'" says a former Fannie executive.

A key test for Johnson came early in his tenure, when Congress began work on how best to regulate Fannie and Freddie. The resulting legislation, which allowed the G.S.E.'s to hold lower amounts of capital than other financial institutions, was what one analyst later called Johnson's "finest moment." Fannie lobbied relentlessly, using a letter from former Fed chairman Paul Volcker, who said that if Fannie reached its proposed capital standards it would be able to maintain its solvency.

Fannie's allies in Congress also made sure that the new regulator—which was known as the Office of Federal Housing Enterprise Oversight (OFHEO) until its name was changed to the F.H.F.A. in the summer of 2008—was placed inside HUD, which had no experience regulating a financial-services company, and that OFHEO, unlike any other regulator, would be subject to the appropriations process, meaning its funding was at the mercy of politicians— politicians who often took their cues from Fannie.

Not surprisingly, OFHEO was a notoriously weak regulator. For almost three years, from February 1997 to September 1999, the agency didn't even have a director. "The goal of [Fannie's] senior management was straightforward: to force OFHEO to rely on [Fannie itself] for information and expertise to such a degree that Fannie Mae would essentially be regulated only by itself," wrote OFHEO in a report years later.

Johnson also addressed Fannie's other big problem, which was that homeowners and politicians never really understood what it did. "There's nothing in the homeowner's life called Fannie Mae," he'd say. So he had to show homeowners that the company was indispensable. The cornerstones of his strategy were the Fannie Mae Foundation and the Partnership Offices. In 1994, Fannie began opening offices in congressional districts around the country. They issued thousands of press releases, which usually featured a local politician prominently assisting Fannie in some good housing-related deed.

In 1995, Johnson seeded the Fannie Mae Foundation with $350 million in Fannie stock. In the ensuing years, the foundation gave away millions of dollars to organizations ranging from the Cold Climate Housing Research Center, in Fairbanks, Alaska, to the Congressional Hispanic Caucus Institute. All of this, along with the alliances Johnson built with others in housing, including homebuilders and real-estate agents, helps explain all the outcry today about Fannie's and Freddie's lobbying dollars—$170 million over the past decade, or just a little less than what the American Medical Association spent, according to the Associated Press. But that misses the point. It's like counting only one arm on a giant octopus. "They ran a battle plan that would make Patton proud. It was 24-7 and never anything left to chance," says former congressman and Fannie antagonist Richard Baker today.

Despite what right-wing critics now charge, however, Fannie and Freddie weren't big risktakers, even after the 1992 legislation in which Congress also mandated that they had to buy a certain number of mortgages made to people with lower incomes. Critics now charge that this was when Fannie began to engage in risky lending practices. But, in reality, Fannie was extremely careful about the credit risks it took. Johnson was a master at announcing plans that sounded very grand—such as the trillion-dollar initiative, in which Fannie would buy a trillion dollars' worth of mortgages to help housing—but didn't really cost much. "About 98 percent were done at market rates [i.e., mortgages they would have bought anyway]," says a former employee. "We were giving away a little at the edge of the big machine." Or, as Maloni puts it, Johnson could say to a member of Congress, " 'Have you seen our initiative for the handicapped?' It might have only been for a few dozen loans, but our intent mattered." Johnson would tell people that "the [congressional] housing goals had no teeth." Indeed, during those years, Fannie and Freddie faced harsh criticism that they did less—not more—to support affordable housing than private lenders did.

This wasn't because Fannie people were cynical about affordable housing. Quite the contrary: many referred to themselves as "housers," which is slang for those who believe that better housing is the cure to all of society's ills. But the company's leaders knew that they couldn't afford to make many unsafe loans, because any sign of financial weakness would be grist for their critics.

If the 1990s were a golden time for Fannie's political power, they were for its financial power as well. Fannie's market valuation grew from $10.5 billion at the beginning of the decade to more than $70 billion by the end. On Wall Street, Fannie and Freddie were big business—all those mortgage-backed securities and all that debt to fund their growth were sold through Wall Street firms—and "people dealt with them as if they were sovereign credits," says one former banker. There was even talk, in those days of no federal deficit, that Fannie and Freddie debt would become the substitute for U.S. Treasuries.

The G.S.E.'s also became the place for ex-politicians to work. The *Washington Monthly* once declared that after he left the White House, Bill Clinton should go to Fannie because "scoring an executive post at Fannie Mae is recognized around establishment Washington as the equivalent of winning the lottery." After all, where else could you make Wall Street–type money with no financial skills? And where else could you make so much money as a lobbyist?

In retrospect, this was a balancing act that was almost destined to fail. As Fannie and Freddie got bigger and more powerful, they struck even more fear into the hearts of those who resented their size and power. "We became dominant so quickly that we scared people," says former Fannie chief financial officer Tim Howard today. And as a former top lobbyist for Fannie says, "A company like Fannie Mae, which has defined itself in Washington through its public mission, but which also has very well-paid executives, will have a hard time staying in the sweet spot."

Every winter, Fannie Mae held a conference for Wall Street analysts and major investors. One year, right before Johnson retired, the theme song was a customized version of the song "The Best Is Yet to Come," popularized by Frank Sinatra. Fannie Mae executives dressed up in top hats and tails to perform it. Frank Raines, who took over from Johnson as C.E.O., told investors that "the future's so bright that I'm willing to set as a goal that our earnings per share will double over the next five years." A report by the research firm Sanford Bernstein noted that the combined assets of Fannie Mae and Freddie Mac exceeded, in dollar terms, the G.D.P. of any nation except the U.S., Japan, and Germany.

When Franklin Delano Raines was named Johnson's successor, he became the first African-American C.E.O. of a Fortune 500 company.

Born in 1949 in Seattle to blue-collar parents—his mother cleaned offices at Boeing and his father was a custodian at the Seattle Parks Department—Raines went to Harvard, where he joined *both* the Young Democrats and the Young Republicans, and was named a Rhodes scholar. He interned in the Nixon White House and then served in the Carter administration, before leaving government to become a partner at the investment bank Lazard Frères. After 11 years at Lazard, Raines was spending four days a week on the road. He left, without his next move planned, in order to spend more time with his three young children. In 1991, when Johnson offered him the vice-chairmanship of Fannie Mae, Raines said yes—Fannie's offices were just a mile and a half from Raines's seven-bedroom Colonial home in Virginia.

In 1996, President Clinton lured Raines away from Fannie by appointing him the director of the Office of Management and Budget. Raines asked Clinton how long the job would last, and Clinton replied, "Until you balance the budget." Within two years Raines produced the first balanced budget the U.S. had seen in 30 years. Later, he would be amazed to find himself painted as a partisan Democrat, because, during his time at O.M.B., Democrats had been angered by what they saw as his support for Republican fiscal policies. In 1995, Raines was appointed to the board of Boeing, where his mother had scrubbed floors. In 1998 he returned to Fannie Mae. At the time, there was talk that one day he would become the first black president of the United States.

There is no one who says that Franklin Raines isn't incredibly smart. But praise for Raines's intelligence is often accompanied by criticism of his interpersonal skills. "He's very introverted," says one former executive. "He cannot lower himself to make nice to people he considers intellectually inferior." "Frank hurt himself," says another. "He lacks a certain understanding of how to best position the other person so that you get what you want."

Inside Fannie, there was also skepticism about the promise Raines made to Wall Street to double Fannie's earnings from $3.23 per share in 1998 to $6.46 per share in 2003. "All the V.P.'s in the company looked at each other and said, 'How is that going to happen?'" says a former executive. The promise, combined with the lure of financial rewards, created an unhealthy pressure throughout the company. In 2000 the head of Fannie's office of auditing gave a speech to the company's internal auditors. "By now, every one of you must have 6.46. . . . branded in your brains," he said. "You must be able to say it in your sleep, you must be able to recite it forwards and backwards, you must have a raging fire in your belly that burns away all doubts, you must live, breathe, and dream 6.46. . . . After all, thanks to Frank, we all have a lot of money riding on it."

Almost immediately in Raines's tenure, the criticism of the G.S.E.'s took on a new ferocity. One of the first salvos was fired by the Clinton Treasury Department under Larry Summers, who had replaced Rubin in the summer of 1999. Treasury workers knew that taking on Fannie was akin to political suicide, but "everyone jumped off together," in the words of one former appointee, because they were all so convinced that Fannie and Freddie would eventually fall on top of taxpayers with a crushing thud. One of Summers's goals was to weaken the perceived ties between the G.S.E.'s and the U.S. government, which was enabling the G.S.E.'s to take on too much risk. Most notably, on March 22, 2000, in congressional testimony, Gary Gensler said that the U.S. Treasury should consider cutting the lines of credit that Fannie and Freddie had with the government.

The response from Fannie Mae was immediate and furious. Tim Howard called Gensler's comments "inept" and "irresponsible." Fannie even tried to get the White House to distance itself from the Treasury, according to one person.

What has never been disclosed before is that, even before Gensler's comments, and through the summer of 2000, Treasury held a series of meetings—some in a room just down the hall from Summers's office—with Fannie's top executives, in which Fannie tried to get Treasury to sign off publicly on a set of initiatives Fannie had devised in the hopes of appeasing its critics. Both sides describe Fannie's strategy in the same way: keep your friends close and your enemies closer. But the negotiations came to nothing. One explanation is that the chemistry between Summers and Raines was "horrible," in the words of one former executive. "The two of them were so alike," says this person. "They were both arrogant, stubborn sons of bitches, and they both viewed themselves as the smartest guy in the room."

Another explanation is that Summers realized that if Treasury supported

Fannie in any public way it would only strengthen its apparent ties to the U.S. government, so he backed off. "Treasury was too smart," Howard says now. "Larry wouldn't bite."

But perhaps the best explanation is that there just wasn't a deal to be cut. Treasury officials simply didn't believe Fannie's arguments. As for Fannie, "you have to have some level of trust that they're not trying to do you in, and there wasn't that level of trust," says another former Fannie executive.

As the critics became more vehement, Fannie's responses became ever tougher. Its customers, including major banks, who were terrified of its rapid growth and Raines's grand plans, set up a group called FM Watch, which began its own anti-G.S.E. lobbying effort. Fannie responded by comparing FM Watch to Slobodan Milošević, the Serb dictator who was charged with crimes against humanity for his role in the Balkan wars. "I think Frank was scared that he couldn't be as tough as Jim, and so he overcompensated," says a former executive.

When George W. Bush ran for president, part of the Republican Party platform was that "homeownership is central to the American Dream." Those words were manna for Fannie and Freddie. And Bush appointed people to their boards, including Yale classmate Victor Ashe and campaign donor Manuel Justiz. ("It is a great honor to be appointed by the President to serve on the board of a company with such an important housing mission," wrote the Bush appointees in a letter to OFHEO in late 2001.) In 2002, Karl Rove invited Raines to Bush's economic summit in Waco. Raines still keeps a "Doonesbury" cartoon on his wall that features an admiring Bush saying, "Franklin can tell you . . . "

Perhaps most notably, after a 2002 event in Atlanta in which Bush announced his efforts to help 5.5 million black and Hispanic families buy homes before the end of the decade, both Raines and Freddie C.E.O. Leland Brendsel flew back with him on Air Force One.

Then the Bush administration's attitude changed dramatically. Both sides point to the same catalyst: Enron. "It was as if someone flipped a switch," Raines says today. A former Bush-administration official says that the last thing the president wanted was to be at the center of another corporate scandal, and if you were looking for likely candidates, how could you miss Fannie and Freddie, with their longtime critics and thin capitalization? Raines, for his part, thought that the administration wanted to deflect the criticism it got for its ties to Enron by pointing at what it could claim was a Democratic scandal in the making. In 2003, Bush's chief of staff Andrew Card was put in charge of a policy-review group. Soon thereafter, Bush pulled his presidential appointees from the G.S.E.'s boards.

And then there was Fed chairman Alan Greenspan. He was friendly with Raines, had regular lunches with him, and came to the grand Christmas parties at Raines's home—but he never got past his deep suspicion of the G.S.E.'s. To wit: the portfolio business was a ticking time bomb, and who needed Fannie and Freddie anyway? Big banks, which were supposedly subject to the discipline of the market, were better holders of mortgage risks than the G.S.E.'s.

Although it didn't happen immediately, Greenspan's thinking on the G.S.E.'s soon came to dominate the Bush administration's thinking on them. "[Greenspan and the Bush administration] weren't interested in having a strong regulator," says Howard today. "They were interested in constraining Fannie and Freddie. Obviously, Fannie and Freddie weren't going to agree to that." So someone had to win, and someone had to lose.

The fight became both nasty and personal in early 2004, when Raines sent what one person calls a "fuck you" letter to Andrew Card. This came about after the homebuilders complained to Raines that Card had told them Raines had agreed to regulatory compromises the homebuilders didn't want. After that the White House took on Fannie and Freddie in an organized, orchestrated way that was akin to how Fannie itself had long operated. Some of those on the inside jokingly referred to their assault as "Noriega"—as in Manuel Noriega, the former Panamanian dictator and drug kingpin whom the U.S. military blasted with loud, incessant rock music during its attempt to get him to leave a Vatican compound and surrender.

Congressman Barney Frank, a Massachusetts Democrat and longtime supporter of the G.S.E.'s, told a Wall Street analyst that "the [Bush] administration is engaged in a strategy of political attacks on the G.S.E.'s, designed to pressure them into accepting the administration's regulatory-reform bill by depressing their stock prices."

But the best weapon the G.S.E.'s opponents could have had was handed to them by Freddie Mac itself. On June 9, 2003, Freddie's entire top management team was ousted after the company confessed to needing to re-state its earnings for the past three years. They had understated—not overstated, but understated—earnings in order to produce the smoothly growing earnings that investors most valued.

Just days before Freddie announced its accounting error, OFHEO had signed off on Freddie's management and internal controls. This very public mistake was a huge black eye—a "humiliating experience," in the words of Steve Blumenthal, then OFHEO's deputy director—for an agency that was already smarting from years of perceived and real condescension.

Not that anyone would have guessed that OFHEO's director at the time, Armando Falcon, was a guy to take on the G.S.E. machine. A Texas Democrat who was appointed by Clinton to head OFHEO in 1999, Falcon had been raised near San Antonio by a father who was an aircraft mechanic. On the surface, he seemed like a shy, gentle soul—but he was far more politically savvy and ambitious than anyone would have expected. And he had Steve Blumenthal, a longtime Republican Hill staffer who viewed himself as a warrior, by his side. Even OFHEO's supporters say that Falcon and Blumenthal were emotionally invested in getting Fannie. And even though Falcon is a Democrat, he and the White House both wanted the same thing. In early 2004, over Fannie's protests that "there should be no question about our accounting" in the wake of Freddie's problems, OFHEO launched a review of Fannie's finances.

Fannie fought back in classic Fannie fashion. They tried to get Falcon and Blumenthal fired. Via a staffer who was a longtime friend and poker buddy of Maloni's, Fannie got Republican senator Kit Bond of Missouri to launch a counter-investigation into OFHEO. The resulting 2004 report from the HUD inspector general (I.G.) came to some startling conclusions that couldn't be dismissed as politics as usual, however. It claimed that Falcon and Blumenthal's campaign against the G.S.E.'s was both ugly and relentless. It accused OFHEO of taking what one source within OFHEO called a "publicity-driven approach to oversight" with a "very strong intent to embarrass Fannie Mae." A witness recalled that Blumenthal was "almost gleeful" when Fannie's stock went down. (Blumenthal denied being gleeful, but did say, "You can't hurt them enough to matter.") Even more troubling was that both OFHEO's chief accountant, Wanda DeLeo, and its chief examiner, Scott Calhoun, complained that Falcon and Blumenthal were overstating Fannie's problems or prematurely reporting some of OFHEO's findings, partly for political purposes. Another witness, who wanted to remain anonymous, had this way of explaining OFHEO's strategy: "Everybody runs for cover if somebody's accusing a company of some impropriety in terms of their accounting. All of a sudden, they don't have any friends anymore."

An online exchange that took place in December 2007 shows how bitter emotions were, and still are, between Fannie publicist Bill Maloni and Blumenthal.

Maloni: "A HUD IG in a GOP Administration—with no Dems involved in the process—revealed the game you and your friends were playing. . . . Why would a regulator turn to guerilla tactics and try and financially injure one of its regulated institutions?"

Blumenthal, who didn't directly answer the question, responded: "It has been my privelege [*sic*] to fight people like you all my life. Corrupt, fundamentally dishonest, cowards. . . . The HUD IG didn't intimidate me, and a Chevy Chase wanna-be thug doesn't either." (Maloni now lives in Chevy Chase.)

Falcon and Blumenthal accused Fannie's management of seeking to "misapply and ignore accounting principles" in order to meet Wall Street's earning expectations. Although much of this was due to the implementation of a complicated new accounting rule for derivatives—one that caused hundreds of other companies to re-state their results as well—Falcon also accused Fannie of improperly deferring $200 million of expenses in 1998 to the following year in order to meet earnings targets and pay management's bonuses. Both the Department of Justice and the S.E.C. opened investigations into possible accounting fraud at Fannie Mae.

At a congressional hearing on October 6, 2004, Raines and Falcon faced off. Falcon defended his work; Raines defended himself and his company. At the end of the hearing, longtime G.S.E. antagonist Richard Baker, the Republican from Louisiana, threw a curveball. More than a year earlier, he had requested information from OFHEO on the compensation of Fannie's top executives. He hadn't released it, because Fannie had hired Ken Starr—the former special prosecutor who investigated Bill Clinton—to represent it, and had gone so far as to threaten "criminal proceedings" against anyone who supposedly violated privacy laws to disclose the information. Now Baker had found his moment. He put up a chart showing that 20 of Fannie's top executives—including three lobbyists—had earned more than $1 million in 2002, and 9 had made more than $3 million. Today, Baker says that when he brought the chart out "the whole room blew up. It was the most animated room I'd ever seen in a hearing."

If Fannie had any hope of prevailing, that was demolished on December 15, 2004, when the S.E.C. sided with OFHEO and said that Fannie would have to re-state years of earnings, wiping out as much as $9 billion in profits. Under pressure from the board, which was itself under pressure from OFHEO, Raines retired and Howard resigned.

One and a half years later, on May 23, 2006, OFHEO issued its final report on Fannie Mae. The agency claimed that Fannie's executives "deliberately and systematically" created earnings "illusions" to hit Fannie's earnings-per-share targets from 1998 through 2004. Fannie agreed to pay the government $400 million. Christopher Cox, chairman of the S.E.C., promised to "vigorously pursue" the people responsible for this "extensive financial fraud."

At the end of that year, OFHEO sued Frank Raines, along with Tim Howard and controller Leanne Spencer, demanding the payment of $100 million in civil fines and returned bonuses that could exceed $115 million. OFHEO said that Raines, in particular, had gotten $90 million in total compensation from 1998 to 2003, of which more than $52 million was directly tied to achieving earnings-per-share targets.

But astonishingly, given the extreme rhetoric from OFHEO—Falcon even called Fannie a "government-sponsored Enron"—no criminal charges were filed against Fannie Mae or any of its executives. And despite Cox's promises, the S.E.C. never filed civil charges against any Fannie Mae executive, either. This past spring, OFHEO trumpeted the news that the former Fannie executives had paid $31.4 million to settle the charges against them, with Raines agreeing to forgo cash, stock, and other benefits of $24.7 million. But the headline number was an illusion. In Raines's case, the bulk of his settlement consisted of stock options that were so out of the money they would never be worth anything, along with $5.3 million that OFHEO called "other benefits," but which Raines says was a "totally made up number." Nor did Raines agree to keep his mouth shut. In fact, he wanted to respond to the settlement by saying that "the process against me began with lies and ended with lies," but was persuaded by his lawyers to say instead that "the process invoked against me by OFHEO was fundamentally unfair."

Raines "had to settle because something was wrong," says current F.H.F.A. director Jim Lockhart. He adds, "It was not one of my happier days. Over 20 percent of the agency's budget was legal expenses. We were just being eaten up, and [Raines] knew it."

To this day, Raines insists that he was sabotaged by his enemies. He tells friends that he told Clinton, "They spent more time and money investigating me than you!" In 2007, in a civil suit that is still proceeding against Fannie and its former executives, Raines subpoenaed the White House for what his lawyers called "evidence that officials in the most powerful office in the country were part of a plan to influence the political debate about Fannie Mae." (Of course, Raines can afford to be aggressive, because as part of his "retirement," Fannie Mae is paying his legal bills.)

"Frank Raines continues to try to re-write history to protect his reputation, but the history is clear," counters White House deputy press secretary Tony Fratto.

But, in fact, the history isn't perfectly clear. There is no question that Fannie Mae's accounting problems were real, and that under Raines the company had an unhealthy focus on earnings growth, but, still, one has to wonder about the solidity of the charge that Raines led an Enron-like enterprise. While some believe the lack of prosecution merely reflects the Justice Department's unwillingness to take on a deeply complicated accounting case, others argue that it didn't have a case, because there is a line between aggressive accounting and intentional fraud. And, in fact, an internal Fannie Mae investigation led by former senator Warren Rudman found no evidence that Raines knew the company's accounting policies departed significantly from generally accepted principles. For Fannie Mae, the distinction didn't much matter, because its reputation was tarnished beyond repair.

Despite that, no new legislation for regulation of the G.S.E.'s made it through Congress. While it is true that votes often broke along partisan lines, with the Democrats siding with Fannie and Freddie, it's also true that Republicans often broke ranks. In one instance, Senator Bob Bennett, a Republican from Utah, sabotaged a bill by adding an amendment that favored the G.S.E.'s. (Bennett's son worked for Fannie's partnership office in Utah.) Congressman Mike Oxley, an Ohio Republican and a recipient of much campaign cash from the G.S.E.'s, also introduced bills that the administration thought were too weak. "I think the administration, for whatever reason, wants to do a lot more than is possible," said Oxley. Says former congressman Richard Baker today, "There were Democrats and Republicans who had reservations. It was not a partisan thing."

Maybe the truth is that, as one person puts it, "everyone was still scared of Fannie Mae and Freddie Mac." Or maybe the truth is that everyone— not just Democrats, and not just Republicans—was terrified that hurting Fannie and Freddie would, as the G.S.E.'s always said, hurt the housing market. "Everybody had a fear of the unknown," says consultant Bert Ely, another longtime G.S.E. critic.

When Raines was dethroned, the board called Dan Mudd, then the company's chief operating officer, at seven A.M., just as Mudd was getting dressed for work, and asked him to step in. Mudd couldn't be more different from Raines and Johnson. He's "not a rock star," as one former Fannie employee puts it, he's not a Democrat, and he's all businessman. (He ran G.E. Capital Japan before joining Fannie, in 2000.) A self-deprecating ex-Marine, he was not close to Raines, and he had thought about leaving the company because he didn't like what he called the "arrogant, defiant, my-way Fannie Mae." But he stayed because, as he later said, "I'm not a quitter."

Mudd immediately embarked on a strategy of conciliation with OFHEO. He visited members of its staff and Congressman Baker, and he even gave OFHEO examiners their own badges so they wouldn't need a Fannie Mae escort when they were at the company's offices. "I thought for a very long time that it was our fault, because we were heavy-handed, because we had a propaganda machine," he says now. "I thought the only way to solve it was to make it Fannie's problem. It's like having an argument with your spouse. There's no use in being right. You have to find the way forward."

There are some who think Mudd had no choice, and some who are far more critical. Says Maloni, "Dan's attitude is great if you don't live in a jungle where all the other animals are trying to eat you." Even Mudd himself says today, "I thought there were things we could do to be a normal company. I did some, and it turned out they didn't make a difference." It was perhaps telling that during his years as C.E.O., he says, no one in the White House would ever take his calls.

By mid-2006 there was a new actor in this long-running drama: Hank Paulson, the former Goldman Sachs C.E.O. who had just become Treasury secretary. Unlike the advisers who surrounded Bush, Paulson did not believe that the G.S.E.'s were the bogeymen of the financial system. After all, they had been major clients of his for years, and the ties between Goldman and Fannie ran deep. Nor did Paulson want any part of what he called "the closest thing I've witnessed to a Holy War."

Paulson quickly began to move away from what one observer calls the "extreme rigidity" of the administration's position. Then, on the Tuesday night before the 2006 Thanksgiving weekend, he "threw down the gauntlet to change course on where the administration was going," says someone familiar with the events. He "aggressively argued that the White House should soften its position" and cut a deal for new regulation—which Paulson strongly believed was necessary—with Barney Frank, who had just been named the chairman of the House Financial Services Committee. Bush, who had granted Paulson an unprecedented degree of independence in exchange for his taking the job, soon gave him the authority to change existing policy, according to one inside source.

"I was aghast," says a longtime G.S.E. foe, expressing a common attitude. "Here we were fighting trench warfare with Fannie and Freddie, and Paulson says, 'Let's cut a deal and say we won.' Some of us really did believe they were a house of cards."

That fall, Barney Frank told *The Washington Post* that Paulson had told him he wasn't going to use the Treasury's authority to limit Fannie's and Freddie's ability to raise money by issuing new bonds. The Bush administration had won that right in 2004, and other Treasury officials had been saying the government would use it. With Paulson's backing down from Treasury's position, the White House had lost one of its major clubs against the G.S.E.'s.

At the same time, a critical change was occurring in Fannie's and Freddie's businesses. By the mid-2000s, the mortgage market was radically different than it had been in Fannie's and Freddie's golden years. What we now all know as the subprime business had taken off, and a whole new breed of opportunistic lenders, such as IndyMac and Washington Mutual, were selling their mortgages to Wall Street, which churned out its own mortgage-backed securities. These were often referred to as private-label securities, or P.L.S.'s, because they bypassed Fannie and Freddie and didn't have the G.S.E. imprimatur. As a result, Fannie and Freddie, which had always been selective as to which mortgages met their criteria for purchase, saw their market share plunge. Shareholders and customers were begging them to dive into this new, highly profitable world.

Although both companies resisted due to their worries about the riskiness of the new products, eventually senior executives disregarded internal warnings, because the lure of big profits was too great. "We're rushing to get back into the game," Mudd told analysts in the fall of 2006. "We will be there." Both companies did two major things. For their portfolios, they bought Wall Street's P.L.S.'s. They also began to guarantee so-called Alt-A mortgages—loans made to people who had better credit scores than a subprime customer's, but who might lack a standard job and pay stub. (These mortgages came to be known as "liar loans," because either the customers or the brokers, or both, were often just making up the information on the applications.) By the spring of 2008, the companies owned a combined $780 billion of the riskiest mortgages, according to the Congressional Budget Office, even though they had bought P.L.S.'s that were rated Triple A by the rating agencies and they thought their Alt-A product was conservative. But they bought in bulk.

For a brief time, in the summer and fall of 2007, it did look as if the G.S.E.'s would be the saviors of the mortgage market. That is, if you didn't look too closely and instead just listened to what congressional Democrats were pushing hard, and what the powers that were, including Paulson, Bernanke, Lockhart, and, yes, even President Bush, started saying. As the banks that everyone had said could handle mortgage risk better than the G.S.E.'s deserted the market, stumbling under the weight of billions of dollars in losses on subprime mortgages, there wasn't anyone else to turn to. Even so, "is there anything dumber than the suggestion that the institutions to rescue the U.S. mortgage market are institutions that are leveraged 60 to 1 and only own U.S. mortgages?" asks one G.S.E. opponent.

Not surprisingly, Fannie and Freddie—egged on by Democrats—seized the opportunity to prove how critical they were to the market. By the first quarter of 2008, they were buying 80 percent of all U.S. mortgages, roughly double their market share from two years earlier.

To some observers, the most remarkable moment came on March 19, 2008, when OFHEO held a press conference to announce a deal that Bob Steel—a former Goldman Sachs partner who had joined the Treasury Department shortly after Paulson—had brokered with Fannie and Freddie. The deal was that the G.S.E.'s, which had already sold a combined $14 billion in preferred stock in late 2007, would raise as much as another $10 billion in capital. In return, new OFHEO director Jim Lockhart agreed to *lower* the amount of capital the G.S.E.'s were required to hold, enabling them to acquire another $200 billion in mortgages. Several people who were involved with the discussions say that the theme was that they were all in this together. They say Steel would use the line "We want to come out of this with everyone on the green team." (Possibly Mudd used the phrase first.) Says Lockhart today, "We could not afford them not being able to provide funding to the housing market."

OFHEO (with Treasury's support) cut this deal despite the fact that the G.S.E.'s losses from mortgages' going bad were already escalating. By the spring of 2008, the two had reported combined losses of $9.5 billion over the previous year. And they had just $81 billion in capital, which was 1.5 percent of the $5.2 trillion in mortgages they owned or guaranteed. In other words, if they had to make good on their promises, they had very little money with which to do so. (Skeptics on the Street believed that OFHEO's calculation of Fannie's and Freddie's capital was deeply flawed and made the G.S.E.'s look healthier than they were.)

Fannie's $300 billion Alt-A portfolio accounted for roughly 50 percent of its credit losses. At Freddie, the numbers were similar. Although both companies justified their purchases of risky loans based on their need to meet HUD's affordable-housing goals, former Fannie employees say that, while the P.L.S. purchases did aid in meeting the goals (which, given the abusiveness of these loans, is an abomination), the Alt-A loans did not. In other words, Fannie dove into Alt-A not because of its mission but because of its bottom line—and because its executives feared that Fannie would become irrelevant if it continued to say no to this brave new world.

B y the summer of 2008, the market was going from bad to worse, and Fannie's and Freddie's stocks were plunging. International banks, which held big chunks of both companies' debt, were panicking, and asking if the U.S. government stood behind the debt. On July 13, Paulson announced a plan under which Treasury would backstop all of the G.S.E.'s debt and buy equity if needed. "If you've got a bazooka, and people know you've got it, you may not have to take it out," Paulson told lawmakers.

Said President Bush about Fannie and Freddie, "We must ensure that they can continue providing access to mortgage credit during this time of financial stress."

Said Lockhart, "At a very difficult time in the market, the enterprises have the flexibility and sound operations needed to support their mission." That was when he also said that their capital levels were "well in excess" of federal requirements.

Paulson's plan was signed into law as part of legislation that—finally!—created a new G.S.E. regulator: the F.H.F.A. This legislation was based on a deal Paulson had cut with Barney Frank. (Despite the criticism of Paulson and Steel, they did succeed where their predecessors had failed, and helped create a far tougher regulator—although by then it was too late.) Slipped in was a provision that exempted Fannie's and Freddie's boards from shareholder lawsuits—which was an enormous threat—if they agreed to conservatorship in time of crisis. Fannie didn't fight this provision, because Mudd thought that conservatorship would require a negotiation. "It's like the president has the right to fire a nuclear weapon, but it's unlikely he'll do so," as Mudd put it. And maybe there was also a little hubris at work. "I used to say that if two accounting scandals [and] a Republican Congress and White House couldn't kill us, how could you kill us ever?" says a former executive.

Others knew better. "Fannie Mae figured they could give the government an enormous loaded gun and they'd never fire it," says Tim Howard.

P aulson's bazooka to help Fannie and Freddie failed. It failed for a mixture of reasons. Investors were unsure what their eventual losses would be. Both companies announced terrible 2008 second-quarter results, with Fannie losing $2.3 billion and Freddie losing $821 million. But investors were also unsure what the new legislation meant. No one wanted to risk putting money into the G.S.E.'s, only to have the government radically raise capital requirements—or step in and wipe the shareholders out. And so, as if the second-quarter results hadn't caused enough alarm on their own, the legislation had the perverse effect of ensuring the companies would be unable to raise new capital, even as everyone began to say that they had to do so.

Maybe Fannie's executives should have anticipated what happened next, but they didn't. After taking the red-eye back from a short family trip over Labor Day weekend—a trip he'd had to reschedule four times—Mudd got a letter from Lockhart that abruptly changed the tone. It "condemned everything we'd ever done," says one person familiar with the letter's contents. (Lockhart agrees it was a "severe letter" but says he had given "verbal warnings" about what his agency saw as a "significant deterioration" in their financial position.) On Friday morning, Mudd was summoned to the meeting at F.H.F.A. at three P.M. that day. When the Fannie contingent arrived, there had been no preparation for the meeting, so they were wandering around the lobby when Bernanke came in the front door. The Fannie people also spotted a *Wall Street Journal* reporter, who had been given advance notice of the meeting, lurking outside the door. It was "almost comical if it weren't tragic," Mudd has since joked.

In a conference room off his office, Lockhart told Fannie, he says today, that "pending losses . . . were going to make it such that [Fannie and Freddie] could not function and fulfill their mission" of supporting the housing market. Then government officials told Fannie that the company had to give its consent to conservatorship.

As for the terms, they were fairly straightforward, with one exception. The government would acquire $1 billion of preferred shares, giving it 80 percent of the company and pretty much wiping out the existing shareholders.

Although the government would provide no upfront cash, it would put in money up to a combined $200 billion for Fannie and Freddie if needed. Both Mudd and Syron were out, and in short order they were told to forfeit their "golden parachutes." The exception was an odd detail: Fannie and Freddie would be allowed to grow their portfolios through 2009 in order to help the mortgage market, but then would have to shrink them to $250 billion each. To Fannie people, that provision seemed like a clear indication that their adversaries had had a hand in the battle that ended the war.

Although Freddie agreed to conservatorship at a separate meeting that same day, the Fannie contingent headed to Sullivan & Cromwell's law offices and called all of their board members to fly to Washington on Saturday for a deliberation. The board came to the conclusion that they had no choice. They could not "single-handedly declare war on the federal government!" Mudd said. Added board chairman Steve Ashley, according to people who were present: "We've closed the book on 70 years of housing policy in this country."

There are a lot of conflicting views on why Paulson abruptly stopped supporting the G.S.E.'s. The best explanation is probably that he was convinced they needed large amounts of capital, and there was no way, given what a Treasury official calls the polarizing quality of the G.S.E.'s in Washington, that he could simply cut them a check without punishing their shareholders and executives.

When a CNBC host asked Paulson what he thought the losses would be, he said, "We didn't sit there and figure this out with a calculator." In truth, there's no way to know, because the ultimate number will depend on what happens with the housing market, and on what activities Fannie and Freddie undertake at the direction of their new owner: you! Estimates, which depend on whether you talk to a G.S.E. friend or foe, range from as low as $30 billion for Fannie to well over the $100 billion the government has allocated to each G.S.E.

But a few things are clear. One is that the argument that Fannie and Freddie caused our entire economic calamity is absurd. Yes, the volume of bad mortgages that Fannie and Freddie bought may have blown the bubble bigger than it otherwise would have been. But to put the blame entirely on Fannie and Freddie is to exempt all the other players, including the mortgage originators who sold subprime mortgages and Wall Street, which packaged up the bad mortgages and sold them to investors around the globe.

Another thing that's clear is that the critics were both right and very wrong about Fannie and Freddie. Yes, their executives and shareholders made fortunes in the glory years, and, yes, taxpayers are now bearing the brunt of whatever losses there are. Just as critics always warned, it's "the privatization of profits and the socialization of risks." But what the critics missed is that that wasn't unique to Fannie and Freddie. It turns out our entire financial sector was operating under that same premise—and to a far greater degree than Fannie and Freddie.

The last thing is that what happened on September 7 didn't solve anything. In fact, quite the opposite. "It is a hodgepodge of nothing," says one Wall Streeter. One key idea was, as the Treasury put it, that Fannie and Freddie would "work to increase the availability of mortgage finance." In other words, the government takeover would reduce the cost of Fannie's and Freddie's funds, thereby enabling them to raise money at cheap rates and pump that money into the mortgage market. In a great irony, almost everyone, even some longtime critics, now agree that's necessary. As Larry Summers recently said, "They have to be used to keep the flow of capital going to the housing market."

But the terms of the conservatorship are confusing, because the government backing lasts only through 2009, and government officials refuse to confirm that the U.S. actually guarantees Fannie's and Freddie's debt. Instead, they say there is an "effective guarantee"—which means nothing in a market as untrusting as this one. And so, Fannie's and Freddie's cost of funds has shot higher, making it economically unfeasible for them to buy up a slew of mortgages. (Lockhart continues to defend the conservatorship. "If we hadn't done it, there would probably have been a run on the bank," he says, adding, "My view is that conservatorship is working at this point. We prevented a downward spiral.")

In other words, in the greatest irony of all, the G.S.E.'s critics have finally gotten what they wanted—Fannie's and Freddie's perceived ties to the government have been weakened—just when no one wants that anymore. "There is culpability somewhere," says a former Fannie executive. "Whether it is a conspiracy or incompetence, I don't know." And in some ways, that sums up the entire story—on both sides.

· 10 ·

Henry Paulson's Longest Night

By *TODD S. PURDUM*

October 2009

It was February 2008, and Henry M. Paulson Jr., a prince of Wall Street turned secretary of the Treasury, was reflecting on his biggest achievement to date: a $168 billion economic-stimulus package that had passed Congress four days earlier after swift, bipartisan progress through both houses. In light of all the later twists and turns that the global financial system and the national economy took, this measure would come to seem quaint and fainthearted. But at the time, it was a very big deal indeed, and Paulson felt justifiably proud. The stimulus had been his baby. Paulson had persuaded George W. Bush, whose relations with both parties in Congress were by then close to toxic, to articulate only the broadest principles, and not to present a detailed plan. Paulson himself, in endless night and weekend negotiations with congressional leaders, had delivered the final package.

"Nancy Pelosi to me was a wonder in this deal, and she was available 24-7, anytime I called her on the cell phone," Paulson told me, his hulking frame unfolding in a comfortable chair in his office at the Treasury, dominated by an oil portrait of his first predecessor, Alexander Hamilton. "She was engaged, she was decisive, and she was really willing to just get involved with all of her people on a hands-on basis." Paulson paused. "Now let me . . . I'll be there in one minute . . . Let me just make a . . . I have been, you know . . . I finished this thing on Thursday night, flew over to Tokyo, flew back, and I'm battling a bit of a stomach problem."

And with that Paulson ducked into the private bathroom adjoining his office, closed the big paneled door, and audibly, violently, and repeatedly threw up. He emerged a moment later as if nothing had happened, but in a few minutes he did the same thing all over again. I asked if he wouldn't rather stop and resume our conversation another time. "That's O.K.," he said. "I'm just going to go through this all. I won't remember it. You know, I barely remember the details now."

In the months to come, I would think of Paulson's perseverance in the face of gastric distress as a metaphor for the way he persevered through the worst global financial crisis since the Great Depression. He never missed a day of work due to illness or indisposition in two and a half years, though he often awoke at one or two A.M., unable to go back to sleep. "I don't mean to make light of this, because I felt awesome responsibility," he told me on one occasion. "But as I said to someone—it may not be a great analogy, but once you're boiling in oil, it doesn't make much difference" what the temperature is.

Like the Dartmouth offensive lineman he once was (his nickname had been "The Hammer"), Paulson spent most of his time at Treasury slogging down the field, facing one crisis after another. History will decide whether Paulson's policy choices were wise or ill-advised. Economists and politicians are already deeply divided. But watching him over many months, it was hard not to be impressed by the resolve with which this moderate old-line Republican—a man with a threshold faith in the wisdom of markets—became the greatest economic interventionist of his generation.

Henry Paulson's memoir, *On the Brink: Inside the Race to Stop the Collapse of the Global Financial System,* will reopen all the old debates over his tenure. I began sitting down with Paulson on a regular basis just as the economic crisis started to unfold. In the summer of 2006 he had left Goldman Sachs to become George W. Bush's third Treasury secretary. In an administration that had concentrated economic policymaking in the political shop of the White House and had slighted its first two Treasury chiefs, Paul O'Neill and John Snow, to the point of near irrelevance, here at last was a player of undisputed accomplishment who wouldn't be relegated to the Cabinet's second tier—the C.E.O. of one of Wall Street's most powerful and respected investment banks, a Tom Wolfe "Master of the Universe" come vividly to life. Paulson had joined the Bush administration with the greatest reluctance; his previous job in government, as an office assistant to John Ehrlichman in the Nixon White House, had ended 33 years earlier in what could mildly be called disappointment. (Watergate brought Ehrlichman down before finally snaring Nixon himself.)

It was not clear what even a figure of Paulson's achievements could do for a lame-duck president with sagging approval ratings, miserable relations with much of his own party, and Democrats poised to regain control of both houses of Congress for the first time since 1994. I approached his staff with a proposal: Could I come and talk to him every couple of months or so, on the record, about whatever was on his mind or mine, with the proviso that nothing would appear in print until after he left office? His staff at first resisted, for whatever reason—Paulson would later tell me, "I hate good press and I abhor bad press"—and I suspect aides were fearful that the boss might wind up looking good at the president's expense. But eventually he agreed to the idea, which ultimately produced more than eight hours of taped interviews over 15 months. The account that follows is based on those sessions—sometimes episodic, often impressionistic, ranging from the forced sale of Bear Stearns to the collapse of Lehman Brothers and beyond. Typically, we talked about fast-moving events in the news, and if I had ever broken the ground rules, there were times when I could have moved the markets, as when Paulson told me last fall, days before he announced the decision publicly, that he had concluded it would not be enough to use the $700 billion in federal bailout funds to buy up toxic bank assets, and that the government would have to inject capital directly into the biggest banks (as it would turn out, whether they wanted the money or not). Sometimes Paulson was in a reflective mood: on the very day that Congress passed a multi-billion-dollar plan to prop up Fannie Mae and Freddie Mac, the government-blessed mortgage-finance agencies, Paulson wanted to talk about nothing so much as his years and years of dealing with China.

In many ways, Paulson was a most unlikely tribune for the cause that became his to carry. He rose to the heights on Wall Street but once told his Dartmouth alumni magazine that he was not an inspirational leader, and that is true. He is tall and striking, with piercing blue eyes and a head that is nearly bald. When he crosses his arms, he looks like Mr. Clean. But he is not articulate, especially in public, and as he gropes to find the words he wants, his features often contort into expressions that project a kind of caged and edgy consternation, when quiet confidence may be what's called for. He is fully aware of the effect, noting how news photographers always seemed to catch him when he was wiping his eyes, or "where I look like I was in anguish." He is a nonsmoker, non-drinker, and devout Christian Scientist in a business whose captains typically have subscriptions to *Cigar Aficionado* and *Wine Spectator.* "Home" to him is still the relatively modest house he built for himself in Barrington, Illinois. "I would have friends visit from Goldman Sachs," he recalled, "and they were used to looking at these palatial Goldman Sachs homes, and they could hardly believe this." He came of age in a trade in which secrecy is honored and billion-dollar deals are sealed with handshakes—he has never kept a journal, doesn't believe in "kiss-and-tell kinds of things"—yet found himself working in a frantic environment in which senators and congressmen can be blabbermouths who say one thing in private and do just the opposite in public. During the heated presidential primary contests of 2008—to a political addict, the most consequential and riveting campaign in a generation—he admitted that electoral politics left him cold: "I find public policy interesting, and I find the *result* very interesting—who gets elected. But how that happens is not."

After his swift, unanimous confirmation, in June 2006, Paulson's next congressional testimony did not come until February 2007—when the pace picked up markedly, driven by the press of events. He never became fully comfortable in a committee setting, in part because hearings seemed to try his patience. As he noted, "There's a great lack of financial literacy and understanding in this nation, even among college-educated people." But Paulson did figure out how to behave on the Hill. "There's a way, keeping full integrity, of answering the questions you want to answer," Paulson told me in one of our conversations, reflecting on what he had learned about committee hearings. "The thing that scared me was not a question I didn't know the answer to. Just say, 'I don't know.' The thing that scared me was some question that I knew, and answered correctly, and I'd be in deep doo-doo!" As his tenure wore on, Paulson confessed, "I amuse myself a lot by sitting there sometimes and thinking what would happen if I said, 'Do you realize what an idiotic question that is?'"

My first on-the-record session with Paulson came in November 2007, when he was roughly a year and a half into the job, and just months after the subprime-mortgage meltdown had begun to hint at the scale of the worldwide trouble to come. The headlines in *The New York Times* that morning had to do with tightening global credit markets. Much of our conversation revolved around his unwillingness to take the Treasury post in the first place, and around his palpable surprise at the ways of the capital. For a person whose baptism in Washington included an up-close look at the unfolding Watergate scandal, Paulson often seemed astonishingly naïve about the realities of big-time national politics.

When Paulson's old Goldman colleague Josh Bolten, the White House chief of staff, first approached him, "the idea of being Treasury secretary in the abstract appealed to me, but my initial inclination was that it wasn't right for me to take that step." Paulson had sized up the issues he cared about—reforming Social Security and Medicare, overhauling the tax code, rethinking trade and investment policy—and concluded that all were essentially non-doable. He would be right about that. Paulson resisted the offer, strongly recommending someone else. (He wouldn't say whom.) By the spring of 2006, Bolten was so eager for Paulson to sign on that he offered something almost unheard of for the Bush team: a private meeting with the president even before Paulson decided whether he wanted the job. Paulson agreed, then changed his mind, thinking, "Wait a minute—what am I smoking? You know, how could I possibly presume to take the president's time," only to turn him down. A month or so later he relented, after concluding that he should not shrink from a challenge and that, as a friend told him, "there are no dress rehearsals in life." He put prescient misgivings aside: "Part of the reason I hadn't then taken this on was I said, How many Cabinet secretaries had I seen come to Washington and leave in recent times with a better reputation than they came with?" The answer was: Not many. Paulson laughed when he remembered calling Lloyd Blankfein to tell him that he'd be taking the Treasury job after all, and that Blankfein in turn would take over as head of Goldman Sachs. "I think I surprised and delighted him," Paulson said. He "thought it was great for the country—and for *him*."

Paulson is the kind of Republican who barely exists anymore—an economic conservative, yes, but also a strong environmental advocate who has given more than $100 million to conservation causes. He laid down a few conditions for coming on as secretary in a midterm-election year, the first of which was that he would not do any campaigning—a brave stance in the hyper-politicized Bush White House: "Treasury secretary to me, just the Treasury secretary, is not a political position."

Paulson's confirmation took barely a month from the announcement of his nomination to his swearing-in—a snap of the fingers by Washington's clock—but to him it felt like an eternity, "like I'd jumped into the abyss." He knew he'd had it easy, but it was intolerable all the same: "Oh, it's terrible. You're staying in a hotel. You can't meet with anybody, you know, that's got anything to do with running the government." He added, "I just realized what a baby I would have been if I had been subjected to what some others are subject to. . . . There were a couple of times during the process—where there were no serious hiccups, just people asking questions about this matter or that, you know—if I could have had a do-over, I would have gone right back to C.E.O. of Goldman Sachs."

For Paulson, in his first months on the job, the biggest adjustment was having a boss for the first time in a decade, and not just any boss, but the president of the United States. "Everything depends on a good relationship with the president," he told me. "The onus is on me to build that relationship, not him. I told him, 'There's just never going to be any daylight between you and me on any issue in public, just isn't.'" During our conversation Paulson spoke in the next breath of his having needed to build a relationship with the White House staff and Cabinet as well, and I asked how that had gone. He smiled a bit. "I have a different management style" from what you usually find in the White House, he said. "Many of them like the fact that I'm straightforward and predictable." But the ponderous pace of the executive branch, the need for multiple sign-offs, the "interagency process," the ideological litmus tests applied to every last policy—this he never got used to, calling it a "ball and chain." The saving grace for Paulson ended up being the skills he had honed as an investment banker, calling on clients in industries all across the country and the world, building relation-ships that would pay off later. "I've done that for a living for a very long time. We're down on our knees with clients all the time."

At Goldman, Paulson had played his share of high-stakes office politics (he got the top job in a coup against his colleague Jon Corzine, who went on to become a Democratic senator from New Jersey and subsequently the state's governor), and he had dealt with high-powered C.E.O.'s and government leaders all over the planet. Members of Congress are a more slippery lot. When it came to Washington, Paulson found he had much to learn. "It's directionally the same, but the extent of it is very different," he would tell me. "Here's what I mean: I found that at Goldman Sachs, to be effective as a leader, you had to build consensus when you're managing smart people who've got other alternatives. . . . I'm in that situation today to a much greater extent than I ever was at Goldman Sachs, because the people I'm trying to bring together are *truly* independent. Oftentimes, they may even agree [with me] in private, but because of their constituencies or because of their parties or because of their committee chairmen or because of what the American people think, you know, won't agree in public. So I have to get used to people saying, 'Boy, that's reasonable—I really think a trade agreement with Colombia is great, but I can't be for it.'" Repeat-edly, phone conversations with members of Congress would go as follows. Paulson would ask, What do you think we should do?, and the reply would come: "Exactly what you're doing. If you need my vote to get it done, I'll vote with you, but, fortunately, you don't, and I can take a pass."

Paulson was appalled by the two-facedness of some members of Con-gress. "And they say—they're calling—'Oh, sorry to do that,' 'I hate to do it,' 'We're so glad you're here,' 'There's such a burden on you,' 'Thank you for being here. Don't worry. We'll get this done. We'll work this through.' And then, up there . . . my God!" It took a year to get acclimated, "because I didn't understand the system."

As I look back over our conversations, one man whose name comes up frequently and stands out as an exception to everything that left Paulson cold about Washington's way of doing business is Barney Frank, the Demo-cratic congressman from Massachusetts and chairman of the House Finan-cial Services Committee, who was a key player in almost all the actions

Paulson took as the crisis unfolded. "This is a guy that's got the intellect, he's got the energy, he cares, and he wants to legislate, knows how to legislate," Paulson said. "He's interested in getting across the finish line. Now, I just wish he were a Republican and we all shared the same policy principles, and you'd cut a wide swath!"

For a person long used to dealing with the hard, rational facts of a business deal—accustomed to assessing value, the upside and downside potential of any transaction, and then striking at precisely the right moment—Paulson had to struggle to grasp the intricacies of Washington, where appearance often *is* reality and even the easy things can be difficult. Should this have come as a surprise to a man of the world—someone who, at a young age, had seen the Nixon White House from the inside? The nature of the capital is no secret, and many pairs of young eyes have quickly scoped it out and conquered it. Think of the accounts left by John Hay, Lincoln's personal secretary, or the mastery of the young Clark Clifford advising Harry Truman, or, for that matter, the precocity of George Stephanopoulos.

That said, Paulson the outsider sometimes described Washington's essential character with memorable clarity. "I see nothing easy in Washington," he said at one point. "I see either analytically simple things that are politically complex, or those that are politically complex *and* analytically complex. I mean, look at immigration reform, you know? It is, I think, analytically easy, but politically very, very complex and very difficult."

If Paulson was taken aback by the ways of Washington, he was just as surprised at how the crisis in the subprime-mortgage market became, by the fall of 2008, a global economic meltdown. He told me repeatedly that he had always known that, because the country had gone eight years without a major financial shock, "the next shock we had was going to really stress the modern financial system." He was certainly aware, and frequently mentioned, that the subprime-mortgage problem had the potential to spread. He recalled telling President Bush that "there's a dry forest, and we don't know what's going to ignite the fire or set the spark," but suspected that housing might be it. During a conversation late in his tenure, Paulson said he believed that he and Ben Bernanke, the chairman of the Federal Reserve Board, "were ahead of a lot of people in understanding how serious" the gathering economic crisis was. But, he added, "it was always bigger and more systemic even than I had for a good while anticipated it to be, or expected it to be." At another point, he said simply, "We've been late on everything."

When I went to see Paulson in January 2008—just as he was putting together the Bush administration's stimulus package—he was eager to talk about how he hoped to respond to a slowdown that he himself acknowledged was "pretty significant." So eager to respond, in fact, that it was often difficult to get a question in edgewise. This turned out to be a pattern in all our conversations, and I couldn't help thinking of those old photographs of Lyndon Johnson, leaning in and bearing down on some wavering Senate colleague, as if to persuade his listener by sheer physical force. Paulson, like Johnson, comes across far more persuasively, and more effectively, in private than in public, where his remarks tend to be bland and a bit impenetrable. Television is definitely not Paulson's medium. He mentioned once the reaction of friends he'd run into at the peak of the crisis: "I have people say, 'Oh, you look so good. You look relaxed, much better than you look on TV.' And I think, What do I look like on TV?" Associates have described him as an occasional table pounder in meetings (on at least one occasion, apparently, he even turned into a table thrower), and though I never glimpsed that side of him, I did sense a bluntness and a frankness that might have served him well, had the public ever been able to see it.

"It was in August, O.K., where there was real stress, where credit spreads blew out, and there was fear," he told me, referring to the late summer of 2007, when the mortgage crisis began. "I always talk publicly about 'extreme risk aversion,' or something. Treasury secretaries don't use 'fear.' But there was this—you know—there was *fear*, O.K.?"

By the winter of 2008, this extreme risk aversion—this *fear*—had prompted Paulson to persuade reluctant free marketeers in the Bush administration that it was time to devise some kind of government package of tax rebates and other actions aimed at stimulating the economy. On January 16, he gave me a preview of his thinking and a summary of his forecast for the future. He was clearly trying to get ahead of economic trouble, though it turned out that his forecasts were well wide of the mark.

"We've said, let's proceed with—that I can tell you because this is confidential and longer-term, because right now we haven't announced that it's official—but, let's proceed with a stimulus package," Paulson explained. "This would not be one where we're doing it because we're in recession or because we know we're going to go into recession. As a matter of fact, if I had to guess, I would say the odds are that we will continue to grow." He saw the stimulus package more as an "insurance policy" against recession rather than a lifeline out of one. A month later, in February, he referred to the "likelihood" that the economy was "going to be growing." A month after that, in March, he told me that recession was "not the most likely case," and repeated that he believed the economy would continue to grow. He didn't minimize the impact of home foreclosures, but insisted that they be seen in perspective: "You know, last year, there were a million and a half, maybe. This year people are estimating up to two million. So this increment of un- usual foreclosures is not huge relative to the 55 million mortgage holders. There's 2 percent in default. You wouldn't get that from reading the news- papers, would you?" The National Bureau of Economic Research, a private group of leading economists charged with charting the country's official economic condition, would eventually determine that the United States had entered a period of recession the previous December, before Paulson spoke any of these words.

When I asked Paulson how conditions had deteriorated to this point, his answer was succinct. "Going back for some good period of years, housing prices have appreciated at a rate that's clearly not sustain- able. And as in any situation like this that's got global-like aspects, the in- vestors all assume that prices will keep going up, and so they do things that don't seem foolish at the time, but in retrospect seem utterly ridiculous. And it's not so ridiculous to buy a home with little money down or negative amortization or whatever, if the price is going to keep going up. And then we have in our capital markets—in general, innovation precedes regulation, and that's generally been good because we grow quicker because of it. But then regulation policy needs to catch up with innovation." In short, Paul- son said, the go-go vehicles—the credit-default swaps, the hedge funds, the mortgage-backed securities, and other devices—had made the world finan- cial system more interconnected than ever. "This is the first time we've gone through a crisis where we've had this level of complexity and this degree of global integration of the capital markets."

Paulson was determined to approach the problem in a bipartisan way, in contrast to the often heavy-handed and divisively partisan pattern of the Bush administration. To some degree, this was an acknowledgment of reality; both houses of Congress had been in Democratic hands for a year by this point, and Democratic cooperation was essential. Paulson had a larger goal, too—he believed a display of bipartisanship would in itself be good for the markets and for the economy. "It's not enough to just sit there and say, 'I'm right, the other guys are wrong,'" he told me at one point, explaining why it was often so difficult working with some of the more doctrinaire members of the White House staff. "It's not that there's anything wrong with ideology. I've got my ideology and my philosophy. But those that say, 'I won't compromise,' to prove a point, and then 'I'm going to point a finger afterwards and say, See, I was right . . .'" Paulson was impatient with such people.

The stimulus proposal passed, though it would have no discernible impact. By March, Paulson had a fresh crisis on his hands: Bear Stearns, the weakest of the nation's major investment banks, was teetering near collapse because of its deepening losses in the mortgage market. By Thursday, March 13, it became apparent that Bear would have to file for bankruptcy—with potentially devastating consequences for investor confidence—unless a willing buyer could be found. Over the weekend, together with the Federal Reserve, which approved a $30 billion credit line to ease the purchase, Paulson helped engineer the sale of Bear to J. P. Morgan Chase at a fire-sale price that wiped out 90 percent of the firm's value in a matter of days. Paulson's strong ally in the deal was Timothy Geithner, then the president of the Federal Reserve Bank of New York. (Paulson told me just after the sale, "My own view—he's going to be a terrific Treasury secretary someday.") Shortly after the Bear Stearns deal, Paulson still seemed to be in a bit of shock from the speed with which the intervention had unfolded, though he wasn't surprised at the speed of Bear's collapse. "When financial institutions die, it's liquidity, O.K.? If you're an investment-banking firm, it's liquidity. And when the run starts, it happens, it's over quickly."

Paulson expressed frustration at the Treasury's limited powers—his lack of what he always referred to as "the authorities"—to deal with such a crisis at a non-bank financial institution: "Our infrastructure—legal and regulatory—hasn't changed in a long time." Since the 1930s, federal deposit insurance has made bank failures no big deal for most depositors: the government insures the accounts and is empowered to take over, or sell, the bad bank to a stronger one. No such safety net exists for investment banks, or for the high-flying financial products they market and sell.

There had been a moment, Paulson said, when he worried that the government might simply have to let Bear Stearns file for bankruptcy, "put foam on the runway," and hope for the best. "And then things came together," he said. "Would it have been nice if J. P. Morgan had bought it without any government help? You bet. Were we fortunate that they were there with government help? You bet."

Hank Paulson does not have an in-box mind. No one could have gotten as far on Wall Street as he did by simply dealing with whatever happened to cross his desk. On major questions—such as U.S. relations with China—he has passionate views and ambitious agendas. "I can't think of a single big issue, national-security issue, whether it be with Iran or when we're dealing with, what do you call it, Myanmar or Burma, or North Korea, that we're not going to be able to solve it better with China," he said. Paulson can go on (and on) about China, and does. He made nearly 70 trips there between the time he became co-head of investment banking at Goldman and the time he assumed his job at Treasury. He won President Bush's backing to consolidate some 40 extant bilateral economic dialogues between China and Washington into one strategic effort that he himself led, and that met with some limited success.

As noted, when he went to Washington, Paulson had hoped, forlornly, that he might have a hand in overhauling Social Security and Medicare, reforming the tax code, and addressing other issues of fundamental long-term importance. He was far from an authority on housing: "I'm not a housing expert. We don't have housing experts at Treasury." He was also far from an expert on financial regulation: "I knew a lot about regulation, but not nearly as much as I needed to know, and I knew very little about regulatory powers and authorities." But these and other matters became his to deal with. "Would it be more satisfying if we were solving fundamental, long-term structural economic issues?" he asked at one point. "Of course. But it's my job to play the hand that I've been dealt, and to play it as well as I can."

The hand that Paulson was dealt, as everyone knows, was the greatest disruption in the world economy in nearly 80 years—a disruption that manifested itself above all as turmoil in the global financial markets. Paulson's entire career had been spent in the marketplace, and, indeed, his understanding of broader economic themes was almost wholly a reflection of his understanding of markets. In coping with the cascade of crises that confronted him in 2008, Paulson took a deal-maker's approach, moving from day to day and bailout to bailout, with the consistently stated goal of shielding the global economy from greater shock, but often—as critics and supporters alike contended—without a clear or coherent overarching philosophy or worldview. Paulson is certainly no Henry Kissinger—a man who combined an interest in grand strategy on the heights of Olympus with an equal taste for manipulative scheming down here on earth. Paulson is, above all, a pragmatist. "I tend to be a person that is very focused on the matter at hand," he explained at one point. And again: "Focus on the immediate, you know: what you're doing right now. And if you do a good job, things take care of themselves." And yet again: "It's my weakness and my strength: I have a focus. I have a one-track mind when I'm working on something. I've never tried to look ahead." One step at a time. Address this problem, then the next one. If Paulson had an overarching strategy, it amounted simply to this: "First and foremost, let's get through the night. Let's get through this period with as little spillover into the global economy as possible."

The rescue of Fannie Mae and Freddie Mac—which together touched more than half of the nation's $12 trillion in mortgages, by either backing them or owning them outright—proved to be all-consuming. "Mind-numbing" was the term Paulson used more than once. Beginning in the fall of 2006, Paulson had pressed for systemic reform of Fannie and Freddie, and had run into fierce opposition from the White House, which drew the line at any compromise with Congress. But by midsummer 2008, the mortgage meltdown had left Fannie and Freddie on the verge of collapse. In July, Paulson proposed a rescue package that gave the government sweeping powers to inject capital into the two institutions through investments and loans, and extended a total credit line of some $300 billion. Paulson told lawmakers that the measure would give him a "bazooka in my pocket" whose mere existence would mean the government might never have to act.

By September, that assessment turned out to be completely wrong, and Paulson fired the bazooka, staging a government takeover of both Fannie and Freddie and ousting their leadership.

September 2008 was Paulson's *mensis horribilis,* the cruelest month of his tenure. It was the month in which Ben Bernanke declared, "There are no atheists in foxholes and no ideologues in financial crises." Paulson—the staunch foe of government intervention—would intervene more massively than any Treasury secretary in modern times. Ten days after the takeover of Fannie Mae and Freddie Mac, Paulson let Lehman Brothers file for bankruptcy—the largest bankruptcy in American history—because, unlike Bear Stearns, the firm could not find a willing buyer and, Paulson said, the Treasury lacked any adequate mechanism for providing funds. Then, the very next day, with Paulson's support, the Federal Reserve approved an $85 billion buyout of the troubled insurance giant A.I.G., the most radical intervention into private business in the Fed's history. The distinction between the two cases has never been especially clear to the average American, much less to many experts. For Paulson, part of the difference seemed to be that A.I.G. had some assets that could be disposed of, but, more important, had sold rafts of esoteric insurance contracts to holders of complicated debt securities all over the world. If A.I.G. had failed, and been unable to pay its insurance claims, investors would have been forced to lower the valuations of the securities they held—and thus to dramatically reduce their own capital. "A meltdown there would have been just catastrophic," Paulson said.

The meltdown at Lehman was catastrophic enough, and Paulson took enormous heat for its failure. Barclays, the British bank, had hoped to buy it, but British regulators blocked the deal, and Paulson saw no alternative. "Lehman Brothers was something that we had been focused on and worked on and worried about for a year. And we knew, and Dick Fuld [the Lehman C.E.O.] knew, and we kept telling him every way we knew how that if he announced earnings like he thought he was going to announce—right after he announced the second-quarter earnings—the company would fail. And when you've got an investment bank, no one had any powers to deal with that. I certainly didn't have any powers to deal with that."

In the months since the A.I.G. bailout, some of Paulson's critics have suggested that he had a particular interest in protecting A.I.G., because its failure would have threatened Goldman Sachs, where he spent his entire career. In August, *The New York Times* reported that Paulson had sought, and received from Treasury lawyers, permission to talk with Lloyd Blankfein, his successor as Goldman's C.E.O., and ultimately spoke with him 24 times in the six days following the A.I.G. crisis. In Paulson's conversations with me, many casual references gave the impression of a man continually on the phone with players on Wall Street, and at one point he singled out Blankfein (along with Ben Bernanke) as someone "at a different intellect level than some of the rest of us." It would be natural enough for Paulson to talk with a trusted former colleague about such momentous events, and Paulson's aides have insisted that he showed Goldman no special favors. No evidence to the contrary has ever emerged, but Paulson's harshest critics have focused their attention on Goldman's ties to A.I.G. Paulson has taken pains to note—most recently in congressional testimony this summer— that he himself didn't fashion the A.I.G. deal. As he told me right after the A.I.G. bailout, "Much of what has been done hasn't been done with any power we had at Treasury. It's been done with the Fed. I've been a good team player. I've given them advice. I've been willing to take the hits for things that weren't done with my authorities." The truth is, coordination among all the relevant parties—Ben Bernanke, Tim Geithner, financiers outside government—was intense throughout the crisis. In addition to countless phone calls, Paulson said he and Bernanke had lunch once a week. Sometimes, Paulson said, he spoke to Geithner "every hour." In this environment of mutual consultation, even the principals sometimes seem to have trouble delineating their roles. Once, in explaining the purchase of Bear Stearns by J. P. Morgan, Paulson began, "So anyway, the deal was, we cut the deal—," then corrected himself. "*We* didn't cut the deal. Tim cut the deal."

By the end of that third week in September, Paulson and Bernanke were at last proposing a structural response, albeit an ad hoc one, to the ongoing crisis of liquidity and the resulting crisis of confidence. The response came in the form of a $700 billion emergency program that would give the government broad—indeed, almost unfettered—authority to intervene in the financial sector. The initial idea was to buy toxic assets of financial institutions—the bad mortgages and other investments—in order to restore confidence and get credit flowing again. The program was called the Troubled Assets Relief Program, which quickly became known as TARP.

196 The Great Hangover

A surreal atmosphere had descended on Washington. The Republican presidential nominee, John McCain, "suspended" his campaign and joined a contentious emergency meeting at the White House, along with Barack Obama. The process degenerated into partisan bickering and stalemate. There was such outrage among the public at the idea of a bailout for Wall Street—with calls running 60 to 1 against—that on September 29 the House Republicans succeeded in initially defeating the bill. Paulson and administration officials were shocked, though Barney Frank read the situation correctly, as Paulson recalled: "He said, 'Well, sometimes, you know, kids have got to run away from home and be hungry before they come back.'" Four days later, the runaways came home, and a barely revised version of the program passed. "It was one of the most difficult things I've ever done, to go up there, to go through these hearings, which are all about . . . it's entertainment, and it's speaking to the people back home, and it's sound bites. And to be doing that at the same time you're trying to negotiate something this important was exhausting."

By early October, when we talked about the episode, Paulson had just returned from a short weekend on the Georgia shore, catching redfish and banding a peregrine falcon. It was a rare reminder of Paulson as an outdoorsman, and of the fact that what had given some Republicans pause about Paulson when he was nominated was that he was a potential conservationist, not a potential interventionist. Paulson reflected on what he had just been through: "Republicans, in particular in the House, were very vulnerable, and so it was against their philosophy, against everything they've been saying about markets." But there was another reason the Republicans were unhappy: "Because the Democrats would rub their noses in it and say, You know, we're working closely with Paulson. And so every time Barney Frank would say, 'I'm working closely with Paulson,' that was like waving a red flag in front of a bull." Around this time, *Newsweek* ran a cover story on Paulson with the headline KING HENRY. It was not helpful. "After that article, I had a number of people I was dealing with, and they all say, 'You're not king, O.K.?' In private, on the phone, 'You're not king.' And I'm saying to myself, Thank you, *Newsweek*, you know? You really made my job easier."

Paulson was castigated by many economists for the bluntness of the tools he was wielding, and by people within his own party for the sheer scale of his intervention. Looking back, he would tell me, without apology, "The lessons of history are such that the biggest mistake you can make is not doing enough." Bush was a non-presence—the conservative columnist Peggy Noonan likened him to the cuckoo in a Swiss clock that makes regular but ritualistic appearances and is ignored. Paulson told me that this strategy had been deliberate—that having the president involved simply would have been counterproductive, and the president himself knew it. "Given the political dynamics, given where we were in the election year, given his relationship, you know, with the people up there, he said to me, 'You will be more successful if we do it this way.' " The damage to Bush's prestige—from Iraq, from Katrina, from the general perception of incompetence—diminished his influence on economic matters. Paulson put it bluntly: "The president didn't have the stick to get some of the things we would have liked to have gotten."

By this point in the crisis, Paulson was deeply fatigued—"It wasn't the hours in bed. It was the hours I spent sleeping in bed!" he told me at one point when I asked him how much rest he was getting. He felt, he said, resorting again to a stock image from his repertoire, as if he'd been boiling in oil for a year. He was also increasingly frustrated. "As I look back—and I'm a great second-guesser—I would not second-guess any of these, because we did everything we've been able to do. But none of them have been sufficient. . . . We've been late on everything, because it just is the kind of thing—it's just impossible to get ahead of with the authorities we have in particular. And I think I've been pretty consistent since I've been down here to say now we have a broken regulatory system, but we don't have the authorities and powers we need." Paulson acknowledged that the country was indeed facing the prospect of a full-blown recession.

Just five days after passage of the TARP plan, and a week before he would announce it publicly, Paulson told me he had made what would turn out to be perhaps the most controversial decision of his tenure: he decided he would have to invest government rescue money directly into equity stakes in banks.

"One thing I can say to you—because this is embargoed—is we very much are going to need to inject capital and come up with programs to do that. This has now moved to the point where $700 billion acquiring assets isn't going to be as effective as we need it to be. So we're going to do that"—

inject capital—"and we just haven't figured out how to get the Congress and the American people ready for it. But that will be something we're going to need to figure out how to do."

In many ways, the Obama administration is still figuring out how to do that very same thing.

T wice in the course of our conversations Paulson came back to the subject of how reluctant he had been to take the job, and why: "I thought it could be pretty unpleasant to be down here the last two and a half years," he told me right before the 2008 elections. But having formed that thought, he went on, he realized that it wasn't a rationale he could ever be proud of. "I'm going to be embarrassed if I look back and think I turned down my country."

I went to see Paulson a few days before the inauguration of Barack Obama. Paulson was reflective, but also preoccupied with the prospect of one last bailout, for a bank he did not name. "I'm sitting here with a major bank, with an unpleasant earnings surprise coming," he told me. It turned out to be Bank of America, which would take another $20 billion, to help cope with the effects of its merger with Merrill Lynch.

Because Paulson had worked so closely with Tim Geithner, he would be leaving the Treasury in what he considered friendly hands, despite the partisan transfer. Is "partisan transfer" even the right term for this transition? Geithner's name came up so frequently in Paulson's conversation that one began to think of the pair of them—and others formed by the same Wall Street culture—as representatives of some extra-partisan third force. Early in his own tenure, Paulson had approached Geithner about serving as his deputy, but Geithner felt it was better to stay at the New York Fed. "He was very helpful to me from day one. He understands Treasury. He's an internationalist. You know, he's a guy that comes in a package where he doesn't have a big or imposing figure. He's smooth, but there's . . . inside, he's tough as steel."

Paulson's experience during the economic crisis had left him sounding decidedly post-partisan. He told me he was "normally not a big proponent" of having partisan majorities in both houses of Congress and the White House and "the same party in control." But, he added, "I think if there's ever a time when we need action . . . I'm just hopeful that, with President-

Elect Obama's popularity and with a strong economic team, they'll be able to get some things done." Paulson seemed more or less optimistic as he looked into the middle distance—"We are a rich country. So we will get through this just fine, because we have the resources to devote to it"—and he hoped that the administration would do more rather than less, "because the cost in terms of the economic growth that is lost is something you will never get back."

Paulson knew that the Obama administration was bound to face continuing criticism as it dispensed the second $350 billion in funds from the TARP program. He said he thought it was all too possible that the system would need more than that. This was in January, and Paulson knew his words would not become public for many months. "I'd never say it publicly right now," he told me. "In my judgment, $350 billion is not enough."

I asked Paulson what sort of new paradigm might emerge in the financial system. "There's always a tendency to over-react—or to take what's happening at any one point in time and then look at a trend and get an extreme result that doesn't happen. I can think of times over the last 10 years when it was all the mega-banks that were going to inherit the world. Then it was, you know, private equity and hedge funds. So I think there will be big changes, but I think the changes we're going to see are going to have to do much more with the shape of the regulatory system, the regulatory powers that are acquired, the financial architecture globally and domestically."

Henry Paulson arrived in Washington hoping to find the sliver of daylight that might help his party redeem itself, and to help a president who he hoped might yet do good things. He came to believe that in the face of turmoil the biggest mistake that economic policymakers could make was to do too little. Some of his furious fellow Republicans came to believe he did too much—as do some furious critics on the left, though for different reasons. Paulson himself is relieved just to have gotten us through the night.

PART THREE

BEYOND

Wall Street on the Tundra

The Implosion of Iceland's Economy

By *MICHAEL LEWIS*

April 2009

Just after October 6, 2008, when Iceland effectively went bust, I spoke to a man at the International Monetary Fund who had been flown in to Reykjavík to determine if money might responsibly be lent to such a spectacularly bankrupt nation. He'd never been to Iceland, knew nothing about the place, and said he needed a map to find it. He has spent his life dealing with famously distressed countries, usually in Africa, perpetually in one kind of financial trouble or another. Iceland was entirely new to his experience: a nation of extremely well-to-do (No. 1 in the United Nations' 2008 Human Development Index), well-educated, historically rational human beings who had organized themselves to commit one of the single greatest acts of madness in financial history. "You have to understand," he told me, "Iceland is no longer a country. It is a hedge fund."

An entire nation without immediate experience or even distant memory of high finance had gazed upon the example of Wall Street and said, "We can do that." For a brief moment it appeared that they could. In

2003, Iceland's three biggest banks had assets of only a few billion dollars, about 100 percent of its gross domestic product. Over the next three and a half years they grew to over $140 billion and were so much greater than Iceland's G.D.P. that it made no sense to calculate the percentage of it they accounted for. It was, as one economist put it to me, "the most rapid expansion of a banking system in the history of mankind."

At the same time, in part because the banks were also lending Icelanders money to buy stocks and real estate, the value of Icelandic stocks and real estate went through the roof. From 2003 to 2007, while the U.S. stock market was doubling, the Icelandic stock market multiplied by nine times. Reykjavík real-estate prices tripled. By 2006 the average Icelandic family was three times as wealthy as it had been in 2003, and virtually all of this new wealth was one way or another tied to the new investment-banking industry. "Everyone was learning Black-Scholes" (the option-pricing model), says Ragnar Arnason, a professor of fishing economics at the University of Iceland, who watched students flee the economics of fishing for the economics of money. "The schools of engineering and math were offering courses on financial engineering. We had hundreds and hundreds of people studying finance." This in a country the size of Kentucky, but with fewer citizens than greater Peoria, Illinois. Peoria, Illinois, doesn't have global financial institutions, or a university devoting itself to training many hundreds of financiers, or its own currency. And yet the world was taking Iceland seriously. (March 2006 Bloomberg News headline: ICELAND'S BILLIONAIRE TYCOON "THOR" BRAVES U.S. WITH HEDGE FUND.)

Global financial ambition turned out to have a downside. When their three brand-new global-size banks collapsed, last October, Iceland's 300,000 citizens found that they bore some kind of responsibility for $100 billion of banking losses—which works out to roughly $330,000 for every Icelandic man, woman, and child. On top of that they had tens of billions of dollars in personal losses from their own bizarre private foreign-currency speculations, and even more from the 85 percent collapse in the Icelandic stock market. The exact dollar amount of Iceland's financial hole was essentially unknowable, as it depended on the value of the generally stable Icelandic krona, which had also crashed and was removed from the market by the Icelandic government. But it was a lot.

Iceland instantly became the only nation on earth that Americans could point to and say, "Well, at least we didn't do *that*." In the end, Icelanders amassed debts amounting to 850 percent of their G.D.P. (The debt-drowned United States has reached just 350 percent.) As absurdly big and important as Wall Street became in the U.S. economy, it never grew so large that the rest of the population could not, in a pinch, bail it out. Any one of the three Icelandic banks suffered losses too large for the nation to bear; taken together they were so ridiculously out of proportion that, within weeks of the collapse, a third of the population told pollsters that they were considering emigration.

In just three or four years an entirely new way of economic life had been grafted onto the side of this stable, collectivist society, and the graft had overwhelmed the host. "It was just a group of young kids," said the man from the I.M.F. "In this egalitarian society, they came in, dressed in black, and started doing business."

Five hundred miles northwest of Scotland the Icelandair flight lands and taxis to a terminal still painted with Landsbanki logos—Landsbanki being one of Iceland's three bankrupt banks, along with Kaupthing and Glitnir. I try to think up a metaphor for the world's expanding reservoir of defunct financial corporate sponsorships—water left in the garden hose after you've switched off the pressure?—but before I can finish, the man in the seat behind me reaches for his bag in the overhead bin and knocks the crap out of me. I will soon learn that Icelandic males, like moose, rams, and other horned mammals, see these collisions as necessary in their struggle for survival. I will also learn that this particular Icelandic male is a senior official at the Icelandic stock exchange. At this moment, however, all I know is that a middle-aged man in an expensive suit has gone out of his way to bash bodies without apology or explanation. I stew on this apparently wanton act of hostility all the way to passport control.

You can tell a lot about a country by how much better they treat themselves than foreigners at the point of entry. Let it be known that Icelanders make no distinction at all. Over the control booth they've hung a charming sign that reads simply, ALL CITIZENS, and what they mean by that is not "All Icelandic Citizens" but "All Citizens of Anywhere." Everyone is from somewhere, and so we all wind up in the same line, leading to the guy behind the glass. Before you can say, "Land of contradictions," he has pretended to examine your passport and waved you on through.

Next, through a dark landscape of snow-spackled black volcanic rock that may or may not be lunar, but that looks so much as you would expect the moon to look that NASA scientists used it to acclimate the astronauts before the first moon mission. An hour later we arrive at the 101 Hotel, owned by the wife of one of Iceland's most famous failed bankers. It's cryptically named (101 is the city's richest postal code), but instantly recognizable: hip Manhattan hotel. Staff dressed in black, incomprehensible art on the walls, unread books about fashion on unused coffee tables—everything to heighten the social anxiety of a rube from the sticks but the latest edition of *The New York Observer.* It's the sort of place bankers stay because they think it's where the artists stay. Bear Stearns convened a meeting of British and American hedge-fund managers here, in January 2008, to figure out how much money there was to be made betting on Iceland's collapse. (A lot.) The hotel, once jammed, is now empty, with only 6 of its 38 rooms occupied. The restaurant is empty, too, and so are the small tables and little nooks that once led the people who weren't in them to marvel at those who were. A bankrupt Holiday Inn is just depressing; a bankrupt Ian Schrager hotel is tragic.

With the financiers who once paid a lot to stay here gone for good, I'm given a big room on the top floor with a view of the old city for half-price. I curl up in silky white sheets and reach for a book about the Icelandic economy—written in 1995, before the banking craze, when the country had little to sell to the outside world but fresh fish—and read this remarkable sentence: "Icelanders are rather suspicious of the market system as a cornerstone of economic organization, especially its distributive implications."

That's when the strange noises commence.

First comes a screeching from the far side of the room. I leave the bed to examine the situation. It's the heat, sounding like a teakettle left on the stove for too long, straining to control itself. Iceland's heat isn't heat as we know it, but heat drawn directly from the earth. The default temperature of the water is scalding. Every year workers engaged in street repairs shut down the cold-water intake used to temper the hot water and some poor Icelander is essentially boiled alive in his shower. So powerful is the heat being released from the earth into my room that some great grinding, wheezing engine must be employed to prevent it from cooking me.

Then, from outside, comes an explosion.

Boom!

Then another.

Boom!

As it is mid-December, the sun rises, barely, at 10:50 A.M. and sets with enthusiasm at 3:44 P.M. This is obviously better than no sun at all, but subtly worse, as it tempts you to believe you can simulate a normal life. And whatever else this place is, it isn't normal. The point is reinforced by a 26-year-old Icelander I'll call Magnus Olafsson, who, just a few weeks earlier, had been earning close to a million dollars a year trading currencies for one of the banks. Tall, white-blond, and handsome, Olafsson looks exactly as you'd expect an Icelander to look—which is to say that he looks not at all like most Icelanders, who are mousy-haired and lumpy. "My mother has enough food hoarded to open a grocery store," he says, then adds that ever since the crash Reykjavík has felt tense and uneasy.

Two months earlier, in early October, as the market for Icelandic kronur dried up, he'd sneaked away from his trading desk and gone down to the teller, where he'd extracted as much foreign cash as they'd give him and stuffed it into a sack. "All over downtown that day you saw people walking around with bags," he says. "No one ever carries bags around downtown." After work he'd gone home with his sack of cash and hidden roughly 30 grand in yen, dollars, euros, and pounds sterling inside a board game.

Before October the big-name bankers were heroes; now they are abroad, or laying low. Before October Magnus thought of Iceland as essentially free of danger; now he imagines hordes of muggers en route from foreign nations to pillage his board-game safe—and thus refuses to allow me to use his real name. "You'd figure New York would hear about this and send over planeloads of muggers," he theorizes. "Most everyone has their savings at home." As he is already unsettled, I tell him about the unsettling explosions outside my hotel room. "Yes," he says with a smile, "there's been a lot of Range Rovers catching fire lately." Then he explains.

For the past few years, some large number of Icelanders engaged in the same disastrous speculation. With local interest rates at 15.5 percent and the krona rising, they decided the smart thing to do, when they wanted to buy something they couldn't afford, was to borrow not kronur but yen and

Swiss francs. They paid 3 percent interest on the yen and in the bargain made a bundle on the currency trade, as the krona kept rising. "The fishing guys pretty much discovered the trade and made it huge," says Magnus. "But they made so much money on it that the financial stuff eventually overwhelmed the fish." They made so much money on it that the trade spread from the fishing guys to their friends.

It must have seemed like a no-brainer: buy these ever more valuable houses and cars with money you are, in effect, paid to borrow. But, in October, after the krona collapsed, the yen and Swiss francs they must repay are many times more expensive. Now many Icelanders—especially young Icelanders—own $500,000 houses with $1.5 million mortgages, and $35,000 Range Rovers with $100,000 in loans against them. To the Range Rover problem there are two immediate solutions. One is to put it on a boat, ship it to Europe, and try to sell it for a currency that still has value. The other is set it on fire and collect the insurance: *Boom!*

The rocks beneath Reykjavík may be igneous, but the city feels sedimentary: on top of several thick strata of architecture that should be called Nordic Pragmatic lies a thin layer that will almost certainly one day be known as Asshole Capitalist. The hobbit-size buildings that house the Icelandic government are charming and scaled to the city. The half-built oceanfront glass towers meant to house newly rich financiers and, in the bargain, block everyone else's view of the white bluffs across the harbor are not.

The best way to see any city is to walk it, but everywhere I walk Icelandic men plow into me without so much as a by-your-leave. Just for fun I march up and down the main shopping drag, playing chicken, to see if any Icelandic male would rather divert his stride than bang shoulders. Nope. On party nights—Thursday, Friday, and Saturday—when half the country appears to take it as a professional obligation to drink themselves into oblivion and wander the streets until what should be sunrise, the problem is especially acute. The bars stay open until five A.M., and the frantic energy with which the people hit them seems more like work than work. Within minutes of entering a nightclub called Boston I get walloped, first by a bearded troll who, I'm told, ran an Icelandic hedge fund. Just as I'm recovering I get plowed over by a drunken senior staffer at the Central Bank. Perhaps because he is drunk, or perhaps because we had actually met a few hours earlier, he stops to tell me, "Vee try to tell them dat our problem was not a solfency problem but a likvitity problem, but they did not agree," then stumbles off. It's exactly what Lehman Brothers and Citigroup said: If only you'd give us the money to tide us over, we'll survive this little hiccup.

A nation so tiny and homogeneous that everyone in it knows pretty much everyone else is so fundamentally different from what one thinks of when one hears the word "nation" that it almost requires a new classification. Really, it's less a nation than one big extended family. For instance, most Icelanders are by default members of the Lutheran Church. If they want to stop being Lutherans they must write to the government and quit; on the other hand, if they fill out a form, they can start their own cult and receive a subsidy. Another example: the Reykjavík phone book lists everyone by his first name, as there are only about nine surnames in Iceland, and they are derived by prefixing the father's name to "son" or "dottir." It's hard to see how this clarifies matters, as there seem to be only about nine first names in Iceland, too. But if you wish to reveal how little you know about Iceland, you need merely refer to someone named Siggor Sigfusson as "Mr. Sigfusson," or Kristin Petursdottir as "Ms. Petursdottir." At any rate, everyone in a conversation is just meant to know whomever you're talking about, so you never hear anyone ask, "Which Siggor do you mean?"

Because Iceland is really just one big family, it's simply annoying to go around asking Icelanders if they've met Björk. Of course they've met Björk; who *hasn't* met Björk? Who, for that matter, didn't know Björk when she was two? "Yes, I know Björk," a professor of finance at the University of Iceland says in reply to my question, in a weary tone. "She can't sing, and I know her mother from childhood, and they were both crazy. That she is so well known outside of Iceland tells me more about the world than it does about Björk."

One benefit of life inside a nation masking an extended family is that nothing needs to be explained; everyone already knows everything that needs to be known. I quickly find that it is an even greater than usual waste of time to ask directions, for instance. Just as you are meant to know which Bjornjolfer is being spoken of at any particular moment, you are meant to know where you are on the map. Two grown-ups—one a banker whose office is three blocks away—cannot tell me where to find the prime minister's office. Three more grown-ups, all within three blocks of the National Gallery of Iceland, have no idea where to find the place. When I tell the sweet middle-aged lady behind the counter at the National Museum that no Icelander seems to know how to find it, she says, "No one actually knows anything about our country. Last week we had Icelandic high-school students here and their teacher asked them to name an Icelandic 19th-century painter. None of them could. Not a single one! One said, 'Halldor Laxness?'!" (Laxness won the 1955 Nobel Prize in Literature, the greatest global honor for an Icelander until the 1980s, when two Icelandic women captured Miss World titles in rapid succession.)

The world is now pocked with cities that feel as if they are perched on top of bombs. The bombs have yet to explode, but the fuses have been lit, and there's nothing anyone can do to extinguish them. Walk around Manhattan and you see empty stores, empty streets, and, even when it's raining, empty taxis: people have fled before the bomb explodes. When I was there Reykjavík had the same feel of incipient doom, but the fuse burned strangely. The government mandates three months' severance pay, and so the many laid-off bankers were paid until early February, when the government promptly fell. Against a basket of foreign currencies the krona is worth less than a third of its boom-time value. As Iceland imports everything but heat and fish, the price of just about everything is, in mid-December, about to skyrocket. A new friend who works for the government tells me that she went into a store to buy a lamp. The clerk told her he had sold the last of the lamps she was after, but offered to order it for her, from Sweden—at nearly three times the old price.

Still, a society that has been ruined overnight doesn't look much different from how it did the day before, when it believed itself to be richer than ever. The Central Bank of Iceland is a case in point. Almost certainly Iceland will adopt the euro as its currency, and the krona will cease to exist. Without it there is no need for a central bank to maintain the stability of the local currency and control interest rates. Inside the place stews David Oddsson, the architect of Iceland's rise and fall. Back in the 1980s, Oddsson had fallen under the spell of Milton Friedman, the brilliant economist who was able to persuade even those who spent their lives working for the government that government was a waste of life. So Oddsson went on a quest to give Icelandic people their freedom—by which he meant freedom from government controls of any sort. As prime minister he lowered taxes, privatized industry, freed up trade, and, finally, in 2002, privatized the banks. At length, weary of prime-ministering, he got himself appointed governor of the Central Bank—even though he was a poet without banking experience.

After the collapse he holed up in his office inside the bank, declining all requests for interviews. Senior government officials tell me, seriously, that they assume he spends most of his time writing poetry. (In February he would be asked by a new government to leave.) On the outside, however, the Central Bank of Iceland is still an elegant black temple set against the snowy bluffs across the harbor. Sober-looking men still enter and exit. Small boys on sleds rocket down the slope beside it, giving not a rat's ass that they are playing at ground zero of the global calamity. It all looks the same as it did before the crash, even though it couldn't be more different. The fuse is burning its way toward the bomb.

When Neil Armstrong took his small step from Apollo 11 and looked around, he probably thought, Wow, sort of like Iceland—even though the moon was nothing like Iceland. But then, he was a tourist, and a tourist can't help but have a distorted opinion of a place: he meets unrepresentative people, has unrepresentative experiences, and runs around imposing upon the place the fantastic mental pictures he had in his head when he got there. When Iceland became a tourist in global high finance it had the same problem as Neil Armstrong. Icelanders are among the most inbred human beings on earth—geneticists often use them for research. They inhabited their remote island for 1,100 years without so much as dabbling in leveraged buyouts, hostile takeovers, derivatives trading, or even small-scale financial fraud. When, in 2003, they sat down at the same table with Goldman Sachs and Morgan Stanley, they had only the roughest idea of what an investment banker did and how he behaved—most of it gleaned from young Icelanders' experiences at various American business schools. And so what they did with money probably says as much about the American soul, circa 2003, as it does about Icelanders. They understood instantly, for instance, that finance had less to do with productive enterprise than trading bits of paper among themselves. And when they lent money they didn't simply facilitate enterprise but bankrolled friends and family, so that they might buy and own things, like real investment bankers: Beverly Hills condos, British soccer teams and department stores, Danish airlines and media companies, Norwegian banks, Indian power plants.

That was the biggest American financial lesson the Icelanders took to heart: the importance of buying as many assets as possible with borrowed money, as asset prices only rose. By 2007, Icelanders owned roughly 50 times more foreign assets than they had in 2002. They bought private jets and third homes in London and Copenhagen. They paid vast sums of money for services no one in Iceland had theretofore ever imagined wanting. "A guy had a birthday party, and he flew in Elton John for a million dollars to sing two songs," the head of the Left-Green Movement, Steingrimur Sigfusson, tells me with fresh incredulity. "And apparently not very well." They bought stakes in businesses they knew nothing about and told the people running them what to do—just like real American investment bankers! For instance, an investment company called FL Group—a major shareholder in Glitnir bank—bought an 8.25 percent stake in American Airlines' parent corporation. No one inside FL Group had ever actually run an airline; no one in FL Group even had meaningful work experience at an airline. That didn't stop FL Group from telling American Airlines how to run an airline. "After taking a close look at the company over an extended period of time," FL Group C.E.O. Hannes Smarason, graduate of M.I.T.'s Sloan School, got himself quoted saying, in his press release, not long after he bought his shares, "our suggestions include monetizing assets . . . that can be used to reduce debt or return capital to shareholders."

Nor were the Icelanders particularly choosy about what they bought. I spoke with a hedge fund in New York that, in late 2006, spotted what it took to be an easy mark: a weak Scandinavian bank getting weaker. It established a short position, and then, out of nowhere, came Kaupthing to take a 10 percent stake in this soon-to-be-defunct enterprise—driving up the share price to absurd levels. I spoke to another hedge fund in London so perplexed by the many bad LBOs Icelandic banks were financing that it hired private investigators to figure out what was going on in the Icelandic financial system. The investigators produced a chart detailing a byzantine web of interlinked entities that boiled down to this: A handful of guys in

Iceland, who had no experience of finance, were taking out tens of billions of dollars in short-term loans from abroad. They were then re-lending this money to themselves and their friends to buy assets—the banks, soccer teams, etc. Since the entire world's assets were rising—thanks in part to people like these Icelandic lunatics paying crazy prices for them—they appeared to be making money. Yet another hedge-fund manager explained Icelandic banking to me this way: You have a dog, and I have a cat. We agree that they are each worth a billion dollars. You sell me the dog for a billion, and I sell you the cat for a billion. Now we are no longer pet owners, but Icelandic banks, with a billion dollars in new assets. "They created fake capital by trading assets amongst themselves at inflated values," says a London hedge-fund manager. "This was how the banks and investment companies grew and grew. But they were lightweights in the international markets."

On February 3, Tony Shearer, the former C.E.O. of a British merchant bank called Singer and Friedlander, offered a glimpse of the inside, when he appeared before a House of Commons committee to describe his bizarre experience of being acquired by an Icelandic bank.

Singer and Friedlander had been around since 1907 and was famous for, among other things, giving George Soros his start. In November 2003, Shearer learned that Kaupthing, of whose existence he was totally unaware, had just taken a 9.5 percent stake in his bank. Normally, when a bank tries to buy another bank, it seeks to learn something about it. Shearer offered to meet with Kaupthing's chairman, Sigurdur Einarsson; Einarsson had no interest. (Einarsson declined to be interviewed by *Vanity Fair.*) When Kaupthing raised its stake to 19.5 percent, Shearer finally flew to Reykjavík to see who on earth these Icelanders were. "They were very different," he told the House of Commons committee. "They ran their business in a very strange way. Everyone there was incredibly young. They were all from the same community in Reykjavík. And they had no idea what they were doing."

He examined Kaupthing's annual reports and discovered some amazing facts: This giant international bank had only one board member who was not Icelandic, for instance. Its directors all had four-year contracts, and the bank had lent them £19 million to buy shares in Kaupthing, along with options to sell those shares back to the bank at a guaranteed profit. Virtually the entire bank's stated profits were caused by its marking up assets it had bought at inflated prices. "The actual amount of profits that were coming from what I'd call banking was less than 10 percent," said Shearer.

In a sane world the British regulators would have stopped the new Icelandic financiers from devouring the ancient British merchant bank. Instead, the regulators ignored a letter Shearer wrote to them. A year later, in January 2005, he received a phone call from the British takeover panel. "They wanted to know," says Shearer, "why our share price had risen so rapidly over the past couple of days. So I laughed and said, 'I think you'll find the reason is that Mr. Einarsson, the chairman of Kaupthing, said two days ago, like an idiot, that he was going to make a bid for Singer and Friedlander.'" In August 2005, Singer and Friedlander became Kaupthing Singer and Friedlander, and Shearer quit, he said, out of fear of what might happen to his reputation if he stayed. In October 2008, Kaupthing Singer and Friedlander went bust.

In spite of all this, when Tony Shearer was pressed by the House of Commons to characterize the Icelanders as mere street hustlers, he refused. "They were all highly educated people," he said in a tone of amazement.

Here is yet another way in which Iceland echoed the American model: all sorts of people, none of them Icelandic, tried to tell them they had a problem. In early 2006, for instance, an analyst named Lars Christensen and three of his colleagues at Denmark's biggest bank, Danske Bank, wrote a report that said Iceland's financial system was growing at a mad pace, and was on a collision course with disaster. "We actually wrote the report because we were worried our clients were getting too interested in Iceland," he tells me. "Iceland was the most extreme of everything." Christensen then flew to Iceland and gave a speech to reinforce his point, only to be greeted with anger. "The Icelandic banks took it personally," he says. "We were being threatened with lawsuits. I was told, 'You're Danish, and you are angry with Iceland because Iceland is doing so well.' Basically it all had to do with what happened in 1944," when Iceland declared its independence from Denmark. "The reaction wasn't 'These guys might be right.' It was 'No! It's a conspiracy. They have bad motives.'" The Danish were just jealous!

The Danske Bank report alerted hedge funds in London to an opportunity: shorting Iceland. They investigated and found this incredible web of cronyism: bankers buying stuff from one another at inflated prices, borrowing tens of billions of dollars and re-lending it to the members of their little Icelandic tribe, who then used it to buy up a messy pile of foreign assets. "Like any new kid on the block," says Theo Phanos of Trafalgar Funds in London, "they were picked off by various people who sold them the lowest-quality assets—second-tier airlines, sub-scale retailers. They were in all the worst LBOs."

But from the prime minister on down, Iceland's leaders attacked the messenger. "The attacks . . . give off an unpleasant odor of unscrupulous dealers who have decided to make a last stab at breaking down the Icelandic financial system," said Central Bank chairman Oddsson in March of last year. The chairman of Kaupthing publicly fingered four hedge funds that he said were deliberately seeking to undermine Iceland's financial miracle. "I don't know where the Icelanders get this notion," says Paul Ruddock, of Lansdowne Partners, one of those fingered. "We only once traded in an Icelandic stock and it was a very short-term trade. We started to take legal action against the chairman of Kaupthing after he made public accusations against us that had no truth, and then he withdrew them."

One of the hidden causes of the current global financial crisis is that the people who saw it coming had more to gain from it by taking short positions than they did by trying to publicize the problem. Plus, most of the people who could credibly charge Iceland—or, for that matter, Lehman Brothers—with financial crimes could be dismissed as crass profiteers, talking their own book. Back in April 2006, however, an emeritus professor of economics at the University of Chicago named Bob Aliber took an interest in Iceland. Aliber found himself at the London Business School, listening to a talk on Iceland, about which he knew nothing. He recognized instantly the signs. Digging into the data, he found in Iceland the outlines of what was so clearly a historic act of financial madness that it belonged in a textbook. "The Perfect Bubble," Aliber calls Iceland's financial rise, and he has the textbook in the works: an updated version of Charles Kindleberger's 1978 classic, *Manias, Panics, and Crashes,* a new edition of which he's currently editing. In it, Iceland, he decided back in 2006, would now have its own little box, along with the South Sea Bubble and the Tulip Craze—even though Iceland had yet to crash. For him the actual crash was a mere formality.

Word spread in Icelandic economic circles that this distinguished professor at Chicago had taken a special interest in Iceland. In May 2008, Aliber was invited by the University of Iceland's economics department to give a speech. To an audience of students, bankers, and journalists, he explained that Iceland, far from having an innate talent for high finance, had all the markings of a giant bubble, but he spoke the technical language of academic economists. ("Monetary Turbulence and the Icelandic Economy," he called his speech.) In the following Q&A session someone asked him to predict the future, and he lapsed into plain English. As an audience member recalls, Aliber said, "I give you nine months. Your banks are dead. Your bankers are either stupid or greedy. And I'll bet they are on planes trying to sell their assets right now."

The Icelandic bankers in the audience sought to prevent newspapers from reporting the speech. Several academics suggested that Aliber deliver his alarming analysis to Iceland's Central Bank. Somehow that never happened. "The Central Bank said they were too busy to see him," says one of the professors who tried to arrange the meeting, "because they were preparing the Report on Financial Stability." For his part Aliber left Iceland thinking that he'd caused such a stir he might not be allowed back into the country. "I got the feeling," he told me, "that the only reason they brought me in was that they needed an outsider to say these things—that an insider wouldn't say these things, because he'd be afraid of getting into trouble." And yet he remains extremely fond of his hosts. "They are a very curious people," he says, laughing. "I guess that's the point, isn't it?"

Icelanders—or at any rate Icelandic men—had their own explanations for why, when they leapt into global finance, they broke world records: the natural superiority of Icelanders. Because they were small and isolated it had taken 1,100 years for them—and the world—to understand and exploit their natural gifts, but now that the world was flat and money flowed freely, unfair disadvantages had vanished. Iceland's president, Olafur Ragnar Grimsson, gave speeches abroad in which he explained why Icelanders were banking prodigies. "Our heritage and training, our culture and home market, have provided a valuable advantage," he said, then went on to list nine of these advantages, ending with how unthreatening to others Icelanders are. ("Some people even see us as fascinating eccentrics who can do no harm.") There were many, many expressions of this same sentiment, most of them in Icelandic. "There were research projects at the university to explain why the Icelandic business model was superior," says Gylfi Zoega, chairman of the economics department. "It was all about our informal channels of communication and ability to make quick decisions and so forth."

"We were always told that the Icelandic businessmen were so clever," says university finance professor and former banker Vilhjalmur Bjarnason. "They were very quick. And when they bought something they did it very quickly. Why was that? That is usually because the seller is very satisfied with the price."

You didn't need to be Icelandic to join the cult of the Icelandic banker. German banks put $21 billion into Icelandic banks. The Netherlands gave them $305 million, and Sweden kicked in $400 million. U.K. investors, lured by the eye-popping 14 percent annual returns, forked over $30 billion—$28 billion from companies and individuals and the rest from pension funds, hospitals, universities, and other public institutions. Oxford University alone lost $50 million.

Maybe because there are so few Icelanders in the world, we know next to nothing about them. We assume they are more or less Scandinavian—a gentle people who just want everyone to have the same amount of everything. They are not. They have a feral streak in them, like a horse that's just pretending to be broken.

After three days in Reykjavík, I receive, more or less out of the blue, two phone calls. The first is from a producer of a leading current-events TV show. All of Iceland watches her show, she says, then asks if I'd come on and be interviewed. "About what?" I ask. "We'd like you to explain our financial crisis," she says. "I've only been here three days!" I say. It doesn't matter, she says, as no one in Iceland understands what's happened. They'd enjoy hearing someone try to explain it, even if that person didn't have any idea what he was talking about—which goes to show, I suppose, that not everything in Iceland is different from other places. As I demur, another call comes, from the prime minister's office.

Iceland's then prime minister, Geir Haarde, is also the head of the Independence Party, which has governed the country since 1991. It ruled in loose coalition with the Social Democrats and the Progressive Party. (Iceland's fourth major party is the Left-Green Movement.) That a nation of 300,000 people, all of whom are related by blood, needs four major political parties suggests either a talent for disagreement or an unwillingness to listen to one another. In any case, of the four parties, the Independents express the greatest faith in free markets. The Independence Party is the party of the fishermen. It is also, as an old schoolmate of the prime minister's puts it to me, "all men, men, men. Not a woman in it."

Walking into the P.M.'s minute headquarters, I expect to be stopped and searched, or at least asked for photo identification. Instead I find a single policeman sitting behind a reception desk, feet up on the table, reading a newspaper. He glances up, bored. "I'm here to see the prime minister," I say for the first time in my life. He's unimpressed. Anyone here can see the prime minister. Half a dozen people will tell me that one of the reasons Icelanders thought they would be taken seriously as global financiers is that all Icelanders feel important. One reason they all feel important is that they all can go see the prime minister anytime they like.

What he might say to them about their collapse is an open question. There's a charming lack of financial experience in Icelandic financial-policymaking circles. The minister for business affairs is a philosopher. The finance minister is a veterinarian. The Central Bank governor is a poet. Haarde, though, is a trained economist—just not a very good one. The economics department at the University of Iceland has him pegged as a B-minus student. As a group, the Independence Party's leaders have a reputation for not knowing much about finance and for refusing to avail themselves of experts who do. An Icelandic professor at the London School of Economics named Jon Danielsson, who specializes in financial panics, has had his offer to help spurned; so have several well-known financial economists at the University of Iceland. Even the advice of really smart central bankers from seriously big countries went ignored. It's not hard to see why the Independence Party and its prime minister fail to appeal to Icelandic women: they are the guy driving his family around in search of some familiar landmark and refusing, over his wife's complaints, to stop and ask directions.

"Why is *Vanity Fair* interested in Iceland?" he asks as he strides into the room, with the force and authority of the leader of a much larger nation. And it's a good question.

As it turns out, he's not actually stupid, but political leaders seldom are, no matter how much the people who elected them insist that it must be so. He does indeed say things that could not possibly be true, but they are only the sorts of fibs that prime ministers are hired to tell. He claims that the krona is once again an essentially stable currency, for instance, when the truth is it doesn't currently trade in international markets—it is assigned an arbitrary value by the government for select purposes. Icelanders abroad have already figured out not to use their Visa cards, for fear of being charged the real exchange rate, whatever that might be.

The prime minister would like me to believe that he saw Iceland's financial crisis taking shape but could do little about it. ("We could not say publicly our fears about the banks, because you create the very thing you are seeking to avoid: a panic.") By implication it was not politicians like him but financiers who were to blame. On some level the people agree: the guy who ran the Baugur investment group had snowballs chucked at him as he dashed from the 101 Hotel, which his wife owns, to his limo; the guy who ran Kaupthing Bank turned up at the National Theater and, as he took his seat, was booed. But, for the most part, the big shots have fled Iceland for London, or are lying low, leaving the poor prime minister to shoulder the blame and face the angry demonstrators, led by folksinging activist Hordur Torfason, who assemble every weekend outside Parliament. Haarde has his story, and he's sticking to it: foreigners entrusted their capital to Iceland, and Iceland put it to good use, but then, last September 15, Lehman Brothers failed and foreigners panicked and demanded their capital back. Iceland was ruined not by its own recklessness but by a global tsunami. The problem with this story is that it fails to explain why the tsunami struck Iceland, as opposed to, say, Tonga.

But I didn't come to Iceland to argue. I came to understand. "There's something I really want to ask you," I say.

"Yes?"

"Is it true that you've been telling people that it's time to stop banking and go fishing?"

A great line, I thought. Succinct, true, and to the point. But I'd heard about it thirdhand, from a New York hedge-fund manager. The prime minister fixes me with a self-consciously stern gaze. "That's a gross exaggeration," he says.

"I thought it made sense," I say uneasily.

"I never said that!"

Obviously, I've hit some kind of nerve, but which kind I cannot tell. Is he worried that to have said such a thing would make him seem a fool? Or does he still think that fishing, as a profession, is somehow less dignified than banking?

At length, I return to the hotel to find, for the first time in four nights, no empty champagne bottles outside my neighbors' door. The Icelandic couple whom I had envisioned as being on one last blowout have packed and gone home. For four nights I have endured their Orc shrieks from the other side of the hotel wall; now all is silent. It's now possible to curl up in bed with "The Economic Theory of a Common-Property Resource: The Fishery." One way or another, the wealth in Iceland comes from the fish, and if you want to understand what Icelanders did with their money you had better understand how they came into it in the first place.

The brilliant paper was written back in 1954 by H. Scott Gordon, a University of Indiana economist. It describes the plight of the fisherman—and seeks to explain "why fishermen are not wealthy, despite the fact that fishery resources of the sea are the richest and most indestructible available to man." The problem is that, because the fish are everybody's property, they are nobody's property. Anyone can catch as many fish as they like, so they fish right up to the point where fishing becomes unprofitable—for everybody. "There is in the spirit of every fisherman the hope of the 'lucky catch,'" wrote Gordon. "As those who know fishermen well have often testified, they are gamblers and incurably optimistic."

Fishermen, in other words, are a lot like American investment bankers. Their overconfidence leads them to impoverish not just themselves but also their fishing grounds. Simply limiting the number of fish caught won't solve the problem; it will just heighten the competition for the fish and drive down profits. The goal isn't to get fishermen to overspend on more nets or bigger boats. The goal is to catch the maximum number of fish with minimum effort. To attain it, you need government intervention.

This insight is what led Iceland to go from being one of the poorest countries in Europe circa 1900 to being one of the richest circa 2000. Iceland's big change began in the early 1970s, after a couple of years when the fish catch was terrible. The best fishermen returned for a second year in a row without their usual haul of cod and haddock, so the Icelandic government took radical action: they privatized the fish. Each fisherman was assigned a quota, based roughly on his historical catches. If you were a big-time Icelandic fisherman you got this piece of paper that entitled you to, say, 1 percent of the total catch allowed to be pulled from Iceland's waters that season. Before each season the scientists at the Marine Research Institute would determine the total number of cod or haddock that could be caught without damaging the long-term health of the fish population; from year to year, the numbers of fish you could catch changed. But your percentage of the annual haul was fixed, and this piece of paper entitled you to it in perpetuity.

Even better, if you didn't want to fish you could sell your quota to someone who did. The quotas thus drifted into the hands of the people to whom they were of the greatest value, the best fishermen, who could extract the fish from the sea with maximum efficiency. You could also take your quota to the bank and borrow against it, and the bank had no trouble assigning a dollar value to your share of the cod pulled, without competition, from the richest cod-fishing grounds on earth. The fish had not only been privatized, they had been securitized.

It was horribly unfair: a public resource—all the fish in the Icelandic sea—was simply turned over to a handful of lucky Icelanders. Overnight, Iceland had its first billionaires, and they were all fishermen. But as social policy it was ingenious: in a single stroke the fish became a source of real, sustainable wealth rather than shaky sustenance. Fewer people were spending less effort catching more or less precisely the right number of fish to maximize the long-term value of Iceland's fishing grounds. The new wealth transformed Iceland—and turned it from the backwater it had been for 1,100 years to the place that spawned Björk. If Iceland has become famous for its musicians it's because Icelanders now have time to play music, and much else. Iceland's youth are paid to study abroad, for instance, and encouraged to cultivate themselves in all sorts of interesting ways. Since its fishing policy transformed Iceland, the place has become, in effect, a machine for turning cod into Ph.D.'s.

But this, of course, creates a new problem: people with Ph.D.'s don't want to fish for a living. They need something else to do.

And that something is probably not working in the industry that exploits Iceland's other main natural resource: energy. The waterfalls and boiling lava generate vast amounts of cheap power, but, unlike oil, it cannot be profitably exported. Iceland's power is trapped in Iceland, and if there is something poetic about the idea of trapped power, there is also something prosaic in how the Icelanders have come to terms with the problem. They asked themselves: What can we do that other people will pay money for that requires huge amounts of power? The answer was: smelt aluminum.

Notice that no one asked, What might Icelanders want to do? Or even: What might Icelanders be especially suited to do? No one thought that Icelanders might have some natural gift for smelting aluminum, and, if anything, the opposite proved true. Alcoa, the biggest aluminum company in the country, encountered two problems peculiar to Iceland when, in 2004, it set about erecting its giant smelting plant. The first was the so-called "hidden people"—or, to put it more plainly, elves—in whom some large number of Icelanders, steeped long and thoroughly in their rich folkloric culture, sincerely believe. Before Alcoa could build its smelter it had to defer to a government expert to scour the enclosed plant site and certify that no elves were on or under it. It was a delicate corporate situation, an Alcoa spokesman told me, because they had to pay hard cash to declare the site elf-free but, as he put it, "we couldn't as a company be in a position of acknowledging the existence of hidden people." The other, more serious problem was the Icelandic male: he took more safety risks than aluminum workers in other nations did. "In manufacturing," says the spokesman, "you want people who follow the rules and fall in line. You don't want them to be heroes. You don't want them to try to fix something it's not their job to fix, because they might blow up the place." The Icelandic male had a propensity to try to fix something it wasn't his job to fix.

Back away from the Icelandic economy and you can't help but notice something really strange about it: the people have cultivated themselves to the point where they are unsuited for the work available to them. All these exquisitely schooled, sophisticated people, each and every one of whom feels special, are presented with two mainly horrible ways to earn a living: trawler fishing and aluminum smelting. There are, of course, a few jobs in Iceland that any refined, educated person might like to do. Certifying the nonexistence of elves, for instance. ("This will take at least six months—it can be very tricky.") But not nearly so many as the place needs, given its talent for turning cod into Ph.D.'s. At the dawn of the 21st century, Icelanders were still waiting for some task more suited to their filigreed minds to turn up inside their economy so they might do it.

Enter investment banking.

For the fifth time in as many days I note a slight tension at any table where Icelandic men and Icelandic women are both present. The male exhibits the global male tendency not to talk to the females—or, rather, not to include them in the conversation—unless there is some obvious sexual motive. But that's not the problem, exactly. Watching Icelandic men and women together is like watching toddlers. They don't play together but in parallel; they overlap even less organically than men and women in other developed countries, which is really saying something. It isn't that the women are oppressed, exactly. On paper, by historical global standards, they have it about as good as women anywhere: good public health care, high participation in the workforce, equal rights. What Icelandic women appear to lack—at least to a tourist who has watched them for all of 10 days—is a genuine connection to Icelandic men. The Independence Party is mostly male; the Social Democrats, mostly female. (On February 1, when the reviled Geir Haarde finally stepped aside, he was replaced by Johanna Sigurdardottir, a Social Democrat, and Iceland got not just a lady prime minister but the modern world's first openly gay head of state—she lives with another woman.) Everyone knows everyone else, but when I ask Icelanders for leads, the men always refer me to other men, and the women to other women. It was a man, for instance, who suggested I speak to Stefan Alfsson.

Lean and hungry-looking, wearing genuine rather than designer stubble, Alfsson still looks more like a trawler captain than a financier. He went to sea at 16, and, in the off-season, to school to study fishing. He was made captain of an Icelandic fishing trawler at the shockingly young age of 23 and was regarded, I learned from other men, as something of a fishing prodigy—which is to say he had a gift for catching his quota of cod and haddock in the least amount of time. And yet, in January 2005, at 30, he up and quit fishing to join the currency-trading department of Landsbanki. He speculated in the financial markets for nearly two years, until the great bloodbath of October 2008, when he was sacked, along with every other Icelander who called himself a "trader." His job, he says, was to sell people, mainly his fellow fishermen, on what he took to be a can't-miss speculation: borrow yen at 3 percent, use them to buy Icelandic kronur, and then invest those kronur at 16 percent. "I think it is easier to take someone in the fishing industry and teach him about currency trading," he says, "than to take someone from the banking industry and teach them how to fish."

He then explained why fishing wasn't as simple as I thought. It's risky, for a start, especially as practiced by the Icelandic male. "You don't want to have some sissy boys on your crew," he says, especially as Icelandic captains are famously manic in their fishing styles. "I had a crew of Russians once," he says, "and it wasn't that they were lazy, but the Russians are always at the same pace." When a storm struck, the Russians would stop fishing, because it was too dangerous. "The Icelanders would fish in all conditions," says Stefan, "fish until it is impossible to fish. They like to take the risks. If you go overboard, the probabilities are not in your favor. I'm 33, and I already have two friends who have died at sea."

It took years of training for him to become a captain, and even then it happened only by a stroke of luck. When he was 23 and a first mate, the captain of his fishing boat up and quit. The boat owner went looking for a replacement and found an older fellow, retired, who was something of an Icelandic fishing legend, the wonderfully named Snorri Snorrasson. "I took two trips with this guy," Stefan says. "I have never in my life slept so little, because I was so eager to learn. I slept two or three hours a night because I was sitting beside him, talking to him. I gave him all the respect in the world—it's difficult to describe all he taught me. The reach of the trawler. The most efficient angle of the net. How do you act on the sea. If you have a bad day, what do you do? If you're fishing at this depth, what do you do? If it's not working, do you move in depth or space? In the end it's just so much feel. In this time I learned infinitely more than I learned in school. Because how do you learn to fish in school?"

This marvelous training was as fresh in his mind as if he'd received it yesterday, and the thought of it makes his eyes mist.

"You spent *seven* years learning every little nuance of the fishing trade before you were granted the gift of learning from this great captain?" I ask.

"Yes."

"And even then you had to sit at the feet of this great master for many months before you felt as if you knew what you were doing?"

"Yes."

"Then why did you think you could become a banker and speculate in financial markets, without a day of training?"

"That's a very good question," he says. He thinks for a minute. "For the first time this evening I lack a word." As I often think I know exactly what I am doing even when I don't, I find myself oddly sympathetic.

"What, exactly, was your job?" I ask, to let him off the hook, catch and release being the current humane policy in Iceland.

"I started as a . . . "—now he begins to laugh—"an adviser to companies on currency-risk hedging. But given my aggressive nature I went more and more into plain speculative trading." Many of his clients were other fishermen, and fishing companies, and they, like him, had learned that if you don't take risks you don't catch the fish. "The clients were only interested in 'hedging' if it meant making money," he says.

In retrospect, there are some obvious questions an Icelander living through the past five years might have asked himself. For example: Why should Iceland suddenly be so seemingly essential to global finance? Or: Why do giant countries that invented modern banking suddenly need Icelandic banks to stand between their depositors and their borrowers—to decide who gets capital and who does not? And: If Icelanders have this incredible natural gift for finance, how did they keep it so well hidden for 1,100 years? At the very least, in a place where everyone knows everyone else, or his sister, you might have thought that the moment Stefan Alfsson walked into Landsbanki 10 people would have said, "Stefan, you're a fisherman!" But they didn't. To a shocking degree, they still don't. "If I went back to banking," he says, with an entirely straight face, "I would be a private-banking guy."

Back in 2001, as the Internet boom turned into a bust, M.I.T.'s *Quarterly Journal of Economics* published an intriguing paper called "Boys Will Be Boys: Gender, Overconfidence, and Common Stock Investment." The authors, Brad Barber and Terrance Odean, gained access to the trading activity in over 35,000 households, and used it to compare the habits of men and women. What they found, in a nutshell, is that men not only trade more often than women but do so from a false faith in their own financial judgment. Single men traded less sensibly than married men, and married men traded less sensibly than single women: the less the female presence, the less rational the approach to trading in the markets.

One of the distinctive traits about Iceland's disaster, and Wall Street's, is how little women had to do with it. Women worked in the banks, but not in the risktaking jobs. As far as I can tell, during Iceland's boom, there was just one woman in a senior position inside an Icelandic bank. Her name is Kristin Petursdottir, and by 2005 she had risen to become deputy C.E.O. for Kaupthing in London. "The financial culture is very male-dominated," she says. "The culture is quite extreme. It is a pool of sharks. Women just despise the culture." Petursdottir still enjoyed finance. She just didn't like the way Icelandic men did it, and so, in 2006, she quit her job. "People said I was crazy," she says, but she wanted to create a financial-services business run entirely by women. To bring, as she puts it, "more feminine values to the world of finance."

Today her firm is, among other things, one of the very few profitable financial businesses left in Iceland. After the stock exchange collapsed, the money flooded in. A few days before we met, for instance, she heard banging on the front door early one morning and opened it to discover a little old man. "I'm so fed up with this whole system," he said. "I just want some women to take care of my money."

It was with that in mind that I walked, on my last afternoon in Iceland, into the Saga Museum. Its goal is to glorify the Sagas, the great 12th- and 13th-century Icelandic prose epics, but the effect of its life-size dioramas is more like modern reality TV. Not statues carved from silicon but actual ancient Icelanders, or actors posing as ancient Icelanders, as shrieks and bloodcurdling screams issue from the P.A. system: a Catholic bishop named Jon Arason having his head chopped off; a heretic named Sister Katrin being burned at the stake; a battle scene in which a blood-drenched Viking plunges his sword toward the heart of a prone enemy. The goal was verisimilitude, and to achieve it no expense was spared. Passing one tableau of blood and guts and moving on to the next, I caught myself glancing over my shoulder to make sure some Viking wasn't following me with a battle-ax. The effect was so disorienting that when I reached the end and found a Japanese woman immobile and reading on a bench, I had to poke her on the shoulder to make sure she was real. This is the past Icelanders supposedly cherish: a history of conflict and heroism. Of seeing who is willing to bump into whom with the most force. There are plenty of women, but this is a men's history.

When you borrow a lot of money to create a false prosperity, you import the future into the present. It isn't the actual future so much as some grotesque silicon version of it. Leverage buys you a glimpse of a prosperity you haven't really earned. The striking thing about the future the Icelandic male briefly imported was how much it resembled the past that he celebrates. I'm betting now they've seen their false future the Icelandic female will have a great deal more to say about the actual one.

·12·

Rich Harvard, Poor Harvard

By *NINA MUNK*

August 2009

Early last May, I attended a town-hall meeting of undergraduates at Harvard University in Cambridge, Massachusetts. The topic that evening: cost-cutting. As I settled into my chair, in Boylston Hall, student activists, members of the "Student Labor Action Movement," were making their way through the auditorium, handing out flyers. "Rethink. Resist," urged the bold black letters. It was a call to action. "NO LAYOFFS!" At the top of the printed page was Harvard's historic coat of arms: three small open books. Cleverly, the university's Latin motto—normally inscribed on the books as "VE-RI-TAS"—had been replaced with a near anagram, "AV-AR-ICE."

Ignoring the agitators as best he could, Michael Smith, dean of the Faculty of Arts and Sciences, Harvard's biggest division, called the meeting to order. Sitting casually on a desk, wearing jeans and a short-sleeved polo shirt, Smith, a professor of engineering and applied sciences, and a former competitive swimmer, looked more like an athlete than an administrator. He got straight to the point: his division—which includes Harvard College, the Graduate School of Arts and Sciences, and the School of Engineering and Applied Sciences—was facing a budget deficit of $220 million.

That's a huge sum: $220 million! Nearly 20 percent of the Faculty of Arts and Sciences' current budget had to be cut. "That frightens me," Smith said forthrightly. "It should frighten you. We obviously can't sit around and do nothing. We've got to find a way to try and get the income back in alignment with the expenses."

Smith's audience listened intensely. Already, they had seen evidence of the cutbacks Smith was alluding to. All across campus, as a preliminary measure, thermostats had been lowered during the winter months, from 72 degrees to 68 degrees. Students and faculty were no longer entitled to free coffee at the university's Barker Center. The Quad Express, which shuttles students between the Radcliffe Quadrangle and Memorial Hall, would soon be running every 20 minutes, not every 10 minutes. More recently, despite loud protests from Harvard's athletes, among others, it was announced that hot breakfasts would no longer be served on weekdays at undergraduate residential houses. Instead of bacon, poached eggs, and waffles, students would have to get by on cold ham, cottage cheese, cereal, and fruit.

Such cost-cutting measures—"alignments" and "resizements," as Harvard prefers to call them—are painful for everyone involved. In the words of a university staff member, as quoted by *The Harvard Crimson,* "Harvard's the richest place around here. If they can't even afford the coffee, it makes us wonder, you know."

But this evening at Boylston Hall, Michael Smith seemed to be suggesting something bigger, more serious, than the absence of free coffee. "What will that mean for students in practical terms?" asked one coolheaded member of the audience. "Are we going to have fewer resources in terms of advisers? Are we going to have fewer office hours for our professors? Are we going to have fewer professors?"

Smith would not be specific. "The resizing that we've done is nothing compared to what we've got coming up," he said, hinting at imminent upheaval.

Someone else asked a tough question: Instead of cutting undergraduate budgets, why not cut the salaries of Harvard's top administrators?

Smith sighed. *If only it were that easy.* His colleague Evelynn Hammonds, dean of Harvard College, answered this time round: "I'd rather use the words 'reduction,' 'shifting things around,' 'reorganizing'—rather than saying something that says 'cuts,' which implies you whack the heads off flowers," she said. "What we're trying to do is make those kinds of priority-driven changes."

Smith looked at the audience. "Are we done?" he asked. Then, glancing at the clock, he stood up. It was eight o'clock. "We're done!" he concluded.

Outside, along the Charles River, the cherry trees were in bloom. In Harvard Yard, the wide grassy lawn was soft and green. To my left was a bronze statue of John Harvard, the university's first major benefactor, his shoe polished to a high gloss by passersby. Then something else caught my eye: discarded paper cups, torn and crumpled candy wrappers, an empty Evian bottle. The trash can in front of the stately, granite University Hall was overflowing. It was a bad sign.

"There are going to be a hell of a lot of layoffs. Courses will be cut. Class sizes will get bigger," conceded a Harvard insider, who, like every other administrator on campus, was not permitted to speak openly to me on the classified subject of alignments and resizements and belt-tightenings.

Radical change is coming to Harvard. Fewer professors, for one thing. Fewer teaching assistants, janitors, and support staff. Shuttered libraries. Less money for research and travel and books. Cafés replaced by vending machines. Junior-varsity sports teams downgraded to clubs. No raises. No bonuses. No fresh coats of paint or new carpets. Overflowing trash cans.

The recession has been hard on most Americans. We know that. At Harvard, however, adjusting to the end of the gilded age, the champagne age, is proving especially wrenching: the university's endowment has collapsed, donations are down, budgets are overstretched. With so many enormous fixed costs—and with much of its endowment restricted by the narrowly defined wishes of donors—there's almost no room left to maneuver.

What's more, the university is facing the onerous financial consequences of over-building. Consider this: Over the 20-year period from 1980 to 2000, Harvard University added nearly 3.2 million square feet of new space to its campus. But that's nothing compared with the extravagance that followed. So far this decade, from 2000 through 2008, Harvard has added another 6.2 million square feet of new space, roughly equal to the total number of square feet occupied by the Pentagon. All across campus, one after another, new academic buildings have shot up. The price of these optimistic new projects: a breathtaking $4.3 billion.

In Allston, a Boston neighborhood just across the Charles River from the school's main campus, you can view Harvard's billion-dollar hole in the ground, a vast construction pit. It's the foundation of Harvard's most ambitious project of all: the sprawling Allston Science Complex, once scheduled to be completed by 2011 at a cost of $1.2 billion—but now on hold.

It's become a symbol, that vast hole in the ground, yet another indication that Harvard University is facing the worst, most dangerous financial crisis in its 373-year history. Adding to the instability: the university is on its fourth president in eight years. And every few weeks, or so it seems, Harvard announces the departure of yet another administrator—most recently the university's executive vice president, Edward Forst, who just last year came to Harvard from Goldman Sachs and intends to step down on August 1.

"They have to do what business people do—they have to make hard decisions," one Harvard business professor told me, referring to the university's administrators. But, of course, Harvard is not a business, nor is it being run like a business; it's a distinguished, high-minded research university, arguably the greatest university in the nation. "Balancing their budget is going to be very traumatic for them," the professor added, in case I'd missed his point.

Already, the inevitable recriminations and backbiting have started. Harvard is in trouble, and no one can decide who's to blame, or what to do next. In reporting this story, I found myself caught up in a nasty, self-serving whisper campaign: back and forth, "on background," Harvard's hostile fiefdoms are pointing anonymous fingers, each accusing another of "pulling the trigger" on this and that high-ticket capital project. They disagree about who made the flawed investment decisions in the first place, insisting that they themselves had never been consulted on the matter, or had been overruled, or pushed aside and ignored. Invariably, somebody else had the "ultimate fiduciary responsibility."

Meanwhile, the campus itself is in turmoil. Faculty members are angry. Students feel betrayed. "Why haven't the faculty been asked to sacrifice at all?" reads one typical comment posted on the *Crimson*'s Web site. "The lowest paid professors make over 150k+, and yet they have the nerve to tell students to suck it all up."

"Were the judgments we made reasonable ones?" a former top Harvard administrator asked me, rhetorically, addressing the sharp increase in expenses and capital commitments of the last decade. "At the time, I think they were reasonable judgments. It turns out, with the benefit of hindsight, you might have preferred less ambitious plans." (Which is not to say that the administrator in question accepts a grain of responsibility for those judgments.)

Incensed, one member of the board of Harvard Management Company, the fund that manages Harvard's endowment, told me, "This story is about leadership. It isn't about money." He may be right. At some point in the last five years, the men and women who run Harvard convinced themselves that the endowment would grow at double-digit rates forever. If Harvard were a publicly traded company, those people would have been fired by now.

"Apparently nobody in our financial office has read the story in Genesis about Joseph interpreting Pharaoh's dream—you know, during the seven good years you save for the seven lean years," remarked Alan Dershowitz, a professor at Harvard Law School since 1967. "And now they're coming hat in hand, pleading to the faculty and students to bear the burden of cutbacks. It's a scandal! It's an absolute scandal, the way Harvard has handled this financial crisis."

O nce upon a time—that is, the fiscal year ending June 30, 2008— Harvard's endowment stood at $36.9 billion, way, way up from $4.8 billion in 1990. No other university endowment in the world comes close to matching Harvard's. Yale's endowment, the second-largest in the nation—$22.9 billion for fiscal 2008—is nearly 40 percent smaller than Harvard's. Stanford's is less than half the size: $17.2 billion, as of last year.

Then came the Great Recession. In the second half of 2008, even more quickly than it had taken off, Harvard's overheated endowment collapsed. Last December, in a letter written to the university's deans, Harvard's president, the historian Drew Gilpin Faust, and its executive vice president, Ed Forst, revealed that Harvard's endowment had lost $8 billion, or 22 percent, in the first four months of the fiscal year, from July through October

2008. To put that number in context: $8 billion is greater than Columbia University's entire endowment ($7.1 billion as of fiscal 2008). Not since 1974, when Harvard's endowment shrank by 12.2 percent, had the university seen losses of such magnitude. Anticipating more dire financial news, Faust warned her deans to expect a 30 percent loss in the endowment for the year. Other universities were showing big losses in 2008, but at Harvard, given the scale and size of its endowment, the numbers seemed inconceivably large.

Right away, some commentators said that Faust was being far too optimistic. On the Huffington Post, the financial journalist Edward Jay Epstein argued that, adjusted for the true value of Harvard's illiquid assets—that is, its private-equity partnerships and other assets that don't sell on the open market—the endowment's losses for those first four months alone were closer to 50 percent, or $18 billion. *Forbes* magazine, noting that Harvard faces a staggering $11 billion of unfunded commitments—money promised, but not yet paid, to various private-equity funds, real-estate funds, and hedge funds—concluded that the university was in a kind of death spiral, forced to sell healthy portions of its portfolio just to stay afloat.

If Harvard were a serious business facing a liquidity crisis, it would have done something drastic by now: fired senior employees, closed departments, sold off real estate. But Harvard, like most other leading universities, is stubborn and inflexible. "None of these schools has the ability to cut expenses fast enough" is how a hedge-fund manager who counts Harvard among his investors explained the problem. Running the numbers for me, proving how impossible it is for a shrinking endowment to keep up with the university's bloated, immovable costs, the hedge-fund manager concluded, "They are completely fucked."

Here's what we do know about Harvard's response to the crisis: at some point in the fall of 2008, Harvard Management Company tried to sell off a big chunk of its private-equity portfolio, about $1.5 billion worth of investments that were locked up in such long-term buyout funds as Apollo Investment Fund VI and Bain Capital Fund IX, among many others. The planned auction was a fiasco: no one was willing to pay anywhere near the asking price for those assets.

A money manager I spoke to described his meeting late last year with Jane Mendillo, who in July 2008 became president and chief executive officer of Harvard Management Company. Knowing that Mendillo was trying to unload assets, he offered to buy back Harvard's sizable stake in his private fund. As he recalls, the surreal dialogue went something like this:

HE: "Hey, look, I'll buy it back from you. I'll buy my interest back."

SHE: "Great."

HE: "Here, I think it's worth—you know, today the [book] value is a dollar, so I'll pay you 50 cents."

SHE: "Then why would I sell it?"

HE: "Well, why are you? I don't know. You're the one who wants to sell, not me. If you guys want to sell, I'm happy to rip your lungs out. . . . If you are desperate, I'm a buyer."

SHE: "Well, we're not desperate."

Was Harvard desperate then? Is Harvard desperate now? One clue is this: last December, the university sold $2.5 billion worth of bonds, increasing its total debt to just over $6 billion. Servicing that debt alone will cost Harvard an average of $517 million *a year* through 2038, according to Standard & Poor's.

To be clear, even if you'd tried hard, you could not have picked a worse time to sell bonds than December 2008; that was the precise moment when credit markets seized up. But Harvard, it seems, had no choice. Unwilling to sell its assets at fire-sale prices, it needed immediate cash to cover, among other things, what my sources say was approximately a $1 billion unrealized loss from interest-rate swaps. That's a staggering figure: $1 billion, roughly a third of the university's entire operating budget for last year.

Those swaps, put in place under Harvard's then president, Lawrence "Larry" Summers, in the early 2000s, were intended to protect, or hedge, the university against rising interest rates on all the money it had borrowed. The idea was simple: if interest rates went up, the swaps would bring in enough money to cover Harvard's higher debt payments.

Instead, interest rates went down. And for reasons no one can explain to me, even as interest rates were plunging in 2007 and 2008, the university simply forgot, or neglected, or chose not to cancel its swaps—with the result that Harvard wound up facing that $1 billion loss! Whose responsibility was that? Where were Harvard's chief financial officer and treasurer while all this was going on?

In the financial press, it's been suggested that Larry Summers is to blame for the interest-rate-swaps crisis, despite the fact that he left Harvard in 2006, long before interest rates plunged. The university flatly refuses to speak publicly on the subject. Which leaves journalists free to turn Summers into a scapegoat. But that's too easy: the real story of Harvard's financial catastrophe, and of Larry Summers, is far more nuanced.

In the days when Harvard's endowment provided only a fraction of the university's operating budget, a loss would have been unfortunate, but not tragic. In recent years, however, Harvard's soaring endowment has become the engine fueling the university's growth. In 2008 alone, so-called distributions from the endowment were $1.2 billion, representing more than a third of Harvard's total operating income, up from only 16 percent two decades ago.

During the boom years, it was assumed without question that the value of Harvard's endowment would keep rising. Trusting in that false certainty, the already profligate university went wild, increasing its annual operating budget by 67 percent, from an inflation-adjusted $2.1 billion in 1998 to $3.5 billion in 2008—this, even as the number of students remained constant. While I was reading through Harvard's financial reports from the past decade, the word "delusional" sprang to mind. So did "unsustainable." It was like feeding an addiction, having access to so much quick and easy money.

Harvard's biggest operating expense is salaries and benefits, which eat up almost half the operating budget. In the past year alone, that single expense jumped 7.5 percent. Today, on average, a full professor at Harvard earns $192,600, before benefits; that's more than he or she would make at any other school in the nation. (At Yale, for example, the average salary is $174,700. At the University of California, Berkeley: $143,500.)

Harvard is also generous with its financial aid to students. In the past decade, the cost of subsidizing students has increased nearly threefold, from $125 million a year to $338 million.

Officially, the university charges $48,868 a year for undergraduate tu-

tuition, room, and board—that's an increase of 50 percent over the last 10 years—but only a small number of students actually pays that much. Back in 2004, under growing pressure from Washington, and in response to outsiders who accused the school of (a) elitism and (b) hoarding its immense wealth, Larry Summers shook up the world of higher education by announcing that students whose parents earned $40,000 a year or less would be able to attend Harvard gratis. Two years later, that cutoff was increased to $60,000, a figure well above the median U.S. household income.

Still, Harvard pressed ahead in its efforts to ease the growing burden of tuition. In December 2007, declaring that "excellence and opportunity must go hand in hand," the university's new president, Drew Faust, made another stunning announcement: henceforth, students whose parents earn as much as $180,000 a year would pay no more than 10 percent of their family's annual income in tuition fees.

"Harvard's new financial aid policy is the boldest move yet to mitigate the soaring costs of a college education," applauded an editorial in *The New York Times*.

No one could have known it then, but two months before Faust's munificent offer to the upper middle class, the Dow Jones Industrial Average had peaked. By the time Harvard's new financial-aid initiative took effect, last September, right at the start of the school year, Lehman Brothers had filed for bankruptcy and the stock market was in a sickening free fall. By year-end, the Dow Jones Industrial Average had plunged almost 40 percent from its 2007 high, dragging with it Harvard's overheated endowment.

Years ago, when I was a reporter for *Forbes*, we revered Jack Meyer, the man who ran Harvard Management Company from 1990 to 2005. Together with his competitor David Swensen, Yale's long-serving chief investment officer, Meyer transformed the way universities manage their endowments.

When Meyer arrived at Harvard, the endowment was in a deep rut, going nowhere. Walter Cabot, who'd run Harvard Management Company since its founding, in 1974, had survived the stock-market crash of 1987 magnificently. But afterward, weakened by a heart attack, Cabot remained cautiously on the sidelines, even as the market took off again. His time was up. Meyer, then 45, a Harvard M.B.A. and the former chief investment officer for the Rockefeller Foundation, was hired to take charge.

Meyer was a pioneer. He was daring, or reckless, depending on your point of view. Instead of abiding by the old, prosaic rule of 65/35 (whereby 65 percent of your portfolio is invested in U.S. equities and 35 percent in bonds), Meyer and his team of portfolio managers moved Harvard's money into all sorts of things: private equity, real estate, oil, gas, fixed-income arbitrage, timberland, hedge funds, high-tech start-ups, foreign equities, credit-default swaps, interest-rate swaps, cross-currency swaps, commodities, venture-capital funds, junk bonds. As if all those exotic, illiquid investments weren't enough to amplify the returns, Meyer added a heap of leverage. It was dizzying, Harvard's portfolio.

The best money managers in the country dreamed of working for Meyer. "It was an intellectually charged place," recalls a portfolio manager who worked at Harvard Management Company in the 1990s. "They were the brightest people that I have ever met," I was told by another portfolio manager who worked under Meyer.

If outsiders viewed the money managers at Harvard Management Company as cowboys—and they did—it may be because Meyer demanded performance above all. "Jack basically said he had no use for anybody who couldn't contribute value," said an admiring Frank Dunau, who worked for Meyer until 2001. "Unless you can beat the S&P, there's no reason for you to be here" is how Meyer put it, according to Dunau. "I mean, if you're not adding value, why am I paying you?"

For a long time, Meyer's daring strategy worked flawlessly. Between fiscal 1990 and 2008, Harvard's endowment boasted an average annual growth rate of 14.3 percent. That's a spectacular performance. The Wilshire TUCS index, which tracks the performance of 1,200 U.S. foundations and endowments, grew by a median annual rate of only 9.7 percent over that same time frame.

For all that, the long-term performance of Harvard's endowment doesn't tell us the whole story. What really happened is that somewhere along the line, around the year 2000 by most accounts, Harvard Management Company, like the university itself, lost its way.

In droves, the best portfolio managers started to leave Harvard Management Company. For most of them, the issue was money, pure and simple. Under Meyer, what Harvard paid his people was based on performance—in most cases, about 10 percent of what they made for the university. As the endowment got bigger, their incentive bonuses got bigger, too. And before long, the (mostly) men at Harvard Management Company were by far out-earning any administrator or professor at the university they were working for.

Jon Jacobson, aged 34, was Harvard's top earner in 1995. He made $6 million that year, roughly 25 times more than the university's then president, Neil Rudenstine. Two years later, in 1997, Jacobson, a former trader at Shearson Lehman Brothers, made $7.6 million. By 1998, Jacobson was making $10.2 million.

Resentment followed. At first, articles criticizing Harvard's well-paid or overpaid money managers were limited to *The Harvard Crimson* and *The Boston Globe*. Then *The Wall Street Journal* got its hands on the story. Soon after that, in 1998, and backed by $500 million of seed capital from Harvard's endowment, Jacobson quit to start his own hedge fund; no one had to know how much money he was earning.

Complaints about excessive compensation at Harvard Management Company gathered force, like an avalanche or a mudslide. By the early 2000s, Harvard's top moneymen were making as much as $30 million to $40 million a year. Finally, in 2003, seven members of Harvard's class of 1969 wrote a strong letter of protest to the university's president, Larry Summers. They spoke out loudly, publicly, informing any member of the media who would listen that compensation at Harvard Management Company was "obscene."

At other American universities, where investing money for the institution is regarded as a kind of public service, Harvard's swagger raised deep suspicion. "Harvard became a bunch of mercenaries," the chief investment officer of another big private university told me.

One day in late April, I visited Walter Cabot—Harvard College class of 1955, first president of Harvard Management Company, and a descendant of one of Boston's most distinguished First Families. Almost 20 years have passed since Cabot was pushed out of Harvard Management Company and replaced by Jack Meyer. He's now 76 years old and semi-retired. "I always told people I had the greatest job in the world," Cabot said, nostalgically. "I could've probably made a lot more money doing something else, but my goal was to do something unique and different for an institution that I went to."

For nearly two hours, as I sat in his modest office in Wellesley, Massachusetts, Cabot reminisced, in monologue. Again and again, he kept returning to the subject of money and its discontents: "I mean, unlike New York, I guess we weren't greedy. We didn't know any better." Wearing a blue oxford-cloth shirt and khaki trousers, Cabot moved slowly across the room, supported by two metal canes. "We tried to run an honest, simple business. We tried to abide by the rules," he continued. "Obviously, we weren't there to go to the poorhouse, but you were there to do an honest trade and work hard and produce results and take pride in what you did. And money for the sake of money, or power, or whatever money is, was really not the objective."

Under Jack Meyer, making money was the sole objective of Harvard Management Company. That was its job. Located in a modern skyscraper in downtown Boston, well insulated from Harvard's right-thinking campus, on the other side of the river, Harvard Management Company resembled a typical Wall Street trading floor. That its portfolio managers were being paid according to the rules of Wall Street should have surprised no one.

In response to the growing protests about "obscene" compensation, Meyer tried to reason with the Harvard community. If Harvard were to outsource its portfolio to various hedge funds, instead of managing its money in-house, he argued, the fees would amount to at least twice what he paid his traders. The end justified the means: consider the billions of dollars that his team was earning for the university!

Meyer's pragmatic line of reasoning was ignored. Meanwhile, more of his best people left in disgust. "You get to the point where you just don't want the ugly calls or the press coverage," I was told by one of Meyer's former portfolio managers. "I just said enough's enough."

There were other pressures on Meyer. Ever since Larry Summers, a renowned economist who'd served as secretary of the Treasury under Bill Clinton, had become president of Harvard, in 2001, he'd been questioning Meyer's investment strategies. Meyer, who was used to running things his own way, was insulted. Something else: Summers implied that Meyer was encouraging his top money managers to strike out on their own. By investing Harvard's money in their new hedge funds, and allowing them to keep their deferred compensation, Meyer was making it far too easy for his best traders to quit. "I think Larry is largely responsible for blowing up the place," one Meyer loyalist told me, still bitter at the memory of Summers's meddling. "Harvard Management Company worked perfectly when the board left them alone!"

Another critic should be cited: Robert Rubin, Summers's mentor and his predecessor as secretary of the Treasury under Bill Clinton. Rubin—a powerful member of the Harvard Corporation (the university's executive governing body), a former director of Harvard Management Company, and a graduate of Harvard College, class of 1960—was contemptuous of Meyer's daring investment strategies. As one person put it to me, Rubin was on the "warpath." To anyone who would listen—Harvard's board, Wall Street, Larry Summers—Rubin kept chipping away at Meyer's credibility.

By 2005, Jack Meyer had had enough. After 15 years at Harvard Management Company, frustrated by the circular fights about compensation, and sick of justifying himself to Summers and Rubin, he walked out and started his own giant hedge fund. Shamelessly, he took many of Harvard Management Company's best people with him, about 30 portfolio managers and traders, along with the chief risk officer, chief operating officer, and chief technology officer. Harvard's trading floor was decimated. It was "like a Ferrari without the engine," I was told by a portfolio manager who arrived after Meyer left. Rubin, for one, was furious, according to someone who knows him well: "In Rubin's opinion, Meyer crippled the institution."

It took almost a year for Harvard Management Company to find someone to replace Meyer; few qualified people wanted the job. Meanwhile, under an interim manager, Harvard invested more and more of its money passively, in pools of stocks, bonds, and commodities intended to mirror the performance of the markets as a whole. It was safer that way; as long as Harvard's portfolio managers didn't underperform the broader stock market, no one could blame them for making bad calls.

But the bigger issue for Harvard was timing: Meyer's departure coincided with the peak of hedge-fund mania. With a reduced staff, and no particular investment strategy, Harvard foolishly sank huge sums of money into the latest, most glamorous hedge funds: notably, $500 million went to Old Lane Partners, a "multi-strategy" fund co-founded by Vikram Pandit in early 2006.

Some of these investments were a disaster—Old Lane folded last year after posting giant losses. Moreover, like other investors late to the game, Harvard was paying its outside managers preposterously high fees: typically an annual management fee of 2 percent of assets under management, plus a performance fee equal to 20 percent of that year's return. Harvard Management Company agreed to other conditions—conditions that contributed to Harvard's frantic scramble for cash late last year: long "lockup periods," whereby investors can't take back their money for five years, more or less, and "gate provisions," which limit how much money investors can withdraw at the end of the lockup period.

Finally, in February 2006, Meyer was replaced by Mohamed El-Erian, an economist with a Ph.D. from Oxford, whose most recent job had been overseeing $28 billion in emerging-market debt at PIMCO, the big money-management firm. Hoping to improve relations with his bosses across the Charles River, El-Erian lectured at Harvard Business School; he also spoke regularly with the editors of *Harvard Magazine*, and he created a Web site devoted to news and information about Harvard Management Company.

In terms of his investment strategy, El-Erian largely followed Meyer's aggressive approach to Harvard's portfolio. In fact, in some respects, El-Erian turned up the dial on risk: moving heavily into emerging markets, for example, he invested in a fund with EFG-Hermes, an investment bank based in Cairo that specializes in the Middle East and North Africa. At the same time, guarding against a possible downturn, he put in place more and more "tail-risk hedging," insurance against risk. In El-Erian's book *When Markets Collide*, written during his time at Harvard, he describes his hedging strategy as "Armageddon protection."

El-Erian stayed at Harvard for less than two years. In September 2007, having barely settled in, he announced that he was returning to his former employer, PIMCO, as co–chief executive officer. According to a friend, El-Erian felt suffocated at Harvard and couldn't wait to get out.

Under El-Erian, Harvard's endowment climbed 23 percent in fiscal 2007, comfortably above that year's 20 percent increase in the Dow Jones Industrial Average. Despite that success, El-Erian, an outsider, quickly became the subject of unsubstantiated attacks, many of them based on rumor and malice. Harvard tends to be like that. He was "a complete fraud," a former Harvard Management Company employee assured me. He "wrecked the place." "He's not an investor," opined someone else. *He didn't belong.*

On July 1, 2008, after a drawn-out search for yet another leader, Jane Mendillo took charge of Harvard Management Company. Having spent 15 years there, from 1987 to 2002, working for Walter Cabot and then Jack Meyer, Mendillo was a safe choice, a well-connected insider. That said, her only experience running an endowment was at Wellesley College, where for six years she capably oversaw the school's relatively modest endowment, helping it grow from $1 billion to $1.6 billion.

Congeniality and competence may or may not be assets in the money-management business. If they are, no one I've spoken to has a bad word to say about Mendillo. "She's a very pleasant and analytic person," attested Scott Sperling, co-president of Thomas H. Lee Partners, who worked with Mendillo at Harvard Management Company in the 1980s and 1990s. Said someone else who used to work with Mendillo, "You know, she was someone that always was there early, always there late. I think she was very dedicated." A third source: "She's very orderly. She's organized."

Is Jane Mendillo the right person to lead Harvard Management Company? It's too early to tell. During the crisis of the past year, she's performed as inadequately as everyone else, nor has she given her nervous public much in the way of reassurance. We do know that she's laid off about a quarter of her staff and that she's cautiously moved more of Harvard's portfolio into cash, even as the market climbs. Otherwise, there has been no news, good or bad, from Harvard Management Company since late 2008.

On May 2, at the annual gathering of Harvard's Committee on University Resources—a privileged group of donors who have each given $1 million or more to the university—Mendillo was the luncheon speaker. According to one discouraged alumnus who was present, Mendillo used nothing but empty rhetoric and dodged all the tough questions. A "pep talk" is the way her speech was described to me.

Any week now, Harvard will be releasing its final year-end results. One of my sources on the board of Harvard Management Company reports the endowment is down less than predicted and in line with losses at other universities: in the range of 23 to 25 percent. Give or take a few percentage points, however, what really matters is that Harvard's endowment is way down, and, more, thanks to (1) the unhappy arithmetic of investing and (2) the need to withdraw money from the endowment to fund the university's operations, it will probably take more than a decade for the value of the endowment to return to where it was in the heady days of 2008.

Let's back up for a moment and return to more prosperous times. It's 2001 and Larry Summers has just been named president of Harvard University. Unapologetically combative, Summers is determined to lead (or force) the university into a glorious renaissance. Gazing into the future, Summers envisions smaller class sizes, a more diverse student body, a younger and more energetic faculty, a revitalized core curriculum, cooperation among Harvard's Balkanized divisions, and a greatly expanded campus. Above all, at a university best known for its focus on the humanities, business, and law, Summers hopes to make science a priority. Belatedly, Harvard will match and even surpass the lavish investments that Princeton and Stanford have plowed into the sciences.

As Summers recently remarked to one of his colleagues, "I held out the hope that Boston would be to this century what Florence was to the 15th century."

Harvard's soaring endowment was the key to Summers's blueprint for the future. Instead of promoting fiscal restraint, he argued, Harvard should loosen its purse strings. The endowment should be used for "priorities of transcendent importance," he proclaimed to *The New York Times* in 2008, after resigning as Harvard's 27th president. "There is a temptation to go for what is comfortable," he added, "but this would be a mistake. The universities have matchless resources that demand that they seize the moment."

Caught up in the exuberance of the new millennium, and guided by Summers's transcendent vision for the university, Harvard embarked on a plan of action. In September 2003, Summers cut a crimson ribbon marking the opening of the $260 million New Research Building, at Harvard Medical School: at 525,000 square feet, it was the largest building in Harvard's history. The previous year, construction had started on the 249,000-square-foot Center for Government and International Studies

(CGIS). Designed by Henry N. Cobb, architect of Boston's John Hancock Tower, CGIS, with its two identical buildings covered in fragile terra-cotta panels, ended up costing a reported $140 million, more than four times what the planners had first anticipated.

The New College Theatre came next—a beautiful 272-seat space, built on the site of the Hasty Pudding Theatre of 1888 and retaining, at great expense, the Hasty Pudding's historic façade. A few months later, in November 2007, Harvard's Laboratory for Integrated Science and Engineering was completed. Its vital stats: 137,000 square feet, an internationally esteemed architect (1996 Pritzker winner Rafael Moneo), and a $155 million price tag, funded almost entirely with debt.

To be fair, when the Laboratory for Integrated Science and Engineering was still in the planning stage, Harvard intended to defray the cost of the building by selling naming rights. Nevertheless, for some now hazy reason, construction was well under way before a willing donor had been secured, and by then it was too late to seize the moment. "It is a lot harder to raise money for a building that has already been built" is how a former dean of Harvard College explained the situation at the time.

Where in the world were the voices urging restraint? "Some people really wondered at the expanse of the new buildings and the pace at which it was happening," I was informed by Everett Mendelsohn, a professor emeritus in the Department of the History of Science, who's been at Harvard since 1960. "Periodically, discussions would take place at the Faculty Council, and one of the deans or the presidents would come, and there would be questions asked. But there wasn't a regular give-and-take.... I'd say there was a sense that the critics were not being heard."

Even today construction is going on at Harvard. The polished 520,000-square-foot Northwest Science Building, designed by Skidmore, Owings & Merrill, has just opened. Over at Harvard Law School, a $250 million project, designed by the firm of Robert A. M. Stern, is a work in progress: a giant limestone building with a 700-car underground garage.

On the subject of Harvard's billion-dollar construction pit in Allston: over the years, quietly, the university had been assembling and buying hundreds of acres in the Allston-Brighton area, more land than it owns in Cambridge. Once home to slaughterhouses and stockyards and stench, Allston seemed the most likely place for Harvard to expand. In a 2006 interview with *Harvard Magazine,* Summers described Allston as "the launching pad for something new that reflects the dreams of the most creative young scientists in the world."

The university's master plan called for a "seminal" transformation of 220 acres in Allston over the next 50 years: in place of broken pavement and abandoned warehouses, Harvard would build new walkways and bicycle lanes. A paved piazza would be surrounded by theaters and museums. A new pedestrian bridge would span the Charles River. Here and there, landscapers would plant abundant, well-tended gardens. Small, charming shops would be adjacent to outdoor cafés. All that and more was the Utopian plan.

After decades of planning, construction began in Allston in 2007. Part one was to be the $1.2 billion Allston Science Complex. At 589,000 square feet it would include four buildings designed to house the Harvard Stem Cell Institute, the Harvard Medical School's Department of Systems Biology, the Department of Stem Cell and Regenerative Biology, and the new Wyss Institute for Biologically Inspired Engineering.

Earlier this year, however, when it became clear to everyone at Harvard that the effects of the global recession would be profound, construction at Allston was abruptly stopped. Not, mind you, that the verb "to stop" is part of Harvard's current vocabulary—the project is being "re-assessed" and "recalibrated." Once its mammoth foundation has been poured (for otherwise the unstable mud walls could cave in), the Allston Science Complex will be on hold.

Meanwhile, as Harvard pauses to recalibrate, five huge and silent cranes, like prehistoric relics, like monoliths, dominate the local skyline—or at least they did when I was there in May. Residents of Allston are furious; they think they've been double-crossed. YOU DIRTY RATS, screamed a cover of the *Boston Herald,* referring to Allston's growing rodent problem and, subversively, to "rats" at Harvard jumping ship.

In theory, Larry Summers, who now heads the National Economic Council under Barack Obama, may have been the right person to lead Harvard into a glorious renaissance. In reality, however, when Summers was president of Harvard, he alienated just about every faculty member who crossed his path. Instead of being admired as a visionary, he was said to be arrogant. Instead of being recognized as a bold and fearless leader, he was perceived as a cerebral bully. That Summers suggested women lacked a natural ability for sciences did not help matters one bit. Nor did his very public feud with the professor of African-American studies Cornel West, who decamped for Princeton. In early 2006, anticipating a vote of no confidence by the Faculty of Arts and Sciences, Summers resigned.

"The fact that they fired him is a symptom of everything that's wrong with Harvard," one of Harvard's big donors told me. "He's not politically correct or diplomatic—he's incredibly provocative. What he really got fired for was attacking waste and abuse in the Faculty of Arts and Sciences."

Above all, what Harvard needs right now is stability. "Harvard, institutionally, never had change when I first came here," the law professor Alan Dershowitz told me. "It was like the old baseball teams; you were born here and you died here. . . . But the turnover now has become like corporate turnover—and that always takes a toll."

The need to restore calm may explain why the unprovocative Drew Gilpin Faust, a well-respected academic and the founding dean of Harvard's Radcliffe Institute for Advanced Study, was installed as president in 2007 (following a year in which Derek Bok, a former Harvard president, temporarily led the university).

Faust is not known as a visionary. In fact, outside of academia, no one I've spoken to has any idea who Drew Faust is or why she got the job in the first place. One undergraduate I spoke to described Faust as "expressionless." An alumnus, having recently attended a dinner where Faust was the guest speaker, told me she was exceedingly dull—so dull he was reminded of those animated Peanuts cartoons from the 1970s, the ones where adults appear offscreen as so many disembodied, insubstantial "voices" that say nothing but "wa-wa-wa."

To leave her imprint on Harvard, and possibly to distance herself from Summers with his tight focus on the sciences, Faust has dedicated herself to elevating the arts. Last December, outlining her vision of the future, Faust released a written statement: "In times of uncertainty, the arts remind us of our humanity and provide the reassuring proof that we, along with the Grecian urn, have endured and will continue to do so."

Of course Harvard will endure—but in contrast to Keats's Grecian urn, which is poetically frozen in time, Harvard must change. Aside from making speeches and releasing inspirational statements about the permanence of art, what is Drew Faust doing to change things in Cambridge? What is her vision? According to Dershowitz, "Her vision at this point is preserving the university. She's in a defensive posture."

As you may have guessed by now, Harvard refused to cooperate when I was reporting this story. At first, the university's public-relations apparatus ignored me. Week after week, e-mail after e-mail, I'd be assured that someone or someone else was unavailable—in meetings, or on vacation, or away from his desk, or out of the office, ill. When I did manage to track someone down, I was thrown a sop of evasive prose. ("I don't feel we've made a decision about how to best engage for your piece," the vice president for public affairs told me in an e-mail.) A formally scheduled interview with the dean of the business school was canceled at the very last minute. ("Glitch" was the subject heading of an e-mail informing me that the meeting was off.) Even requests for basic, public financial information were bungled. When I asked him a simple question about Harvard's debt, one of the university's many communications directors stonewalled: "I'm not a numbers person at all," he said, wide-eyed.

One day, desperate for someone in authority to talk on the record, I caught up with Michael Smith, dean of the Faculty of Arts and Sciences, as he was leaving the town-hall meeting of undergraduates at Boylston Hall. Unaware that I was *persona non grata* on the Harvard campus, he talked openly to me.

I walked with him from the meeting to his car. How did the university get into this mess? I asked as we cut across Harvard Yard. Smith stopped. "First of all," he remarked, reinforcing what I already knew, "the endowment growth did not keep up with the expenses. We hired faculty faster than we really should have. . . . We put up buildings based on debt financings—not fund-raising. And we decided the right thing to do was this financial-aid package, even though, again, we didn't have new finances behind it to actually do it."

A popular professor with an undergraduate degree from Princeton and a Ph.D. from Stanford, an expert in computer architecture, and co-founder of a data-security company called Liquid Machines, Smith, 47, is a driven and dedicated man. Yet even he conceded that his current job has been taxing. He's held the position for less than two years; still, as he remarked to me, it "seems like forever."

We were in the parking lot, Michael Smith and I. The sun had set. Smith looked tired. It can't be easy to be charged with cost-cutting at a university that refuses to use the term "cost-cutting" and instead goes on about "alignments" and "resizements." He added: "The hope was that the endowment would continue to increase, and we could get some support from our alumni base to help pay for those changes in the program."

He paused. "And then, of course, the bottom fell out of the market."

· 13 ·

Pirate of the Caribbean

The Mystery of Allen Stanford

By BRYAN BURROUGH[*]

July 2009

In 2006, a Miami attorney named Milton M. Ferrell Jr. boarded a private plane bound for the Caribbean island of Antigua. Ferrell had a meeting there with the country's top private banker, R. Allen Stanford, a muscular, boisterous Texan billionaire whose $8 billion Stanford Financial Group had grown so profitable he had attained the No. 205 spot on the Forbes Four Hundred. Ferrell represented a number of wealthy Latin Americans, and Stanford had invited him for a tour of his Antiguan bank, hoping to attract money from Ferrell's clients.

With Ferrell that day was a security consultant I'll call Trevor, an expert on the shadowy world of Caribbean banking. Trevor had heard the rumors about Stanford Financial—the suspiciously high returns on its certificates of deposit, the money-laundering investigations—but wanted to see Stanford's offices up close. Stanford himself—six feet four, with a mustache, close-cropped brown hair, wide-set eyes, and a crushing handshake—was

*With additional reporting by Christopher Bateman.

waiting at his hangar when they landed. After a tour of the adjacent complex some called Stanfordville, which included three bank buildings, a vast cricket field, and a restaurant called the Sticky Wicket, Stanford ushered the men into his crown jewel, Stanford International Bank, an imposing structure that resembled a columned mansion, overlooking the airport. Inside, the company's gold-eagle logo was everywhere—on doors, walls, coffee mugs, and lapel pins. It even appeared, it was whispered, on the toilet seats.

"The first thing Allen says is how they use all these sophisticated financial techniques to get such good returns on these C.D.'s, which consistently didn't make sense to me," Trevor recalls today. "So I said, 'Can I see your trading desk? Is it in London, New York?' Allen says, 'No, we do it right here in Antigua.' So he takes us into this room with a big desk, full of computers. There's a bunch of 300-pound Antiguan women in there, you know, like these women who sell fruit in the market. Milton and I looked at each other like, 'No way.'"

At that point, Trevor asked to meet the bank's compliance officer, the executive tasked with making sure the firm's trades conformed to securities regulations. "So Allen takes us back to a corner of this room," Trevor goes on. "And I swear, the door was creaking on its hinges, and out comes this 70-year-old guy who clearly had nothing to do with banking. I mean, he looked like a janitor. Milton and I, we said to ourselves, This is just a giant Ponzi scheme. Clearly this outfit doesn't have the facilities to support this kind of business."

They were right: it didn't—though it took an awfully long time for American authorities to realize it. On February 17, 2009, after years of rumor and several weeks of intense investigation, U.S. marshals raided Stanford Financial's Houston headquarters. Even as camera crews filmed them toting out boxes of paperwork, the Securities and Exchange Commission filed a suit charging Stanford and his two top aides with fraud, freezing all of Stanford Financial's assets and shutting down a financial empire that catered to 30,000 customers in 131 countries, though the bulk of its business was in Latin America. The company, the S.E.C. charged, was in fact little more than an $8 billion Ponzi scheme—the second largest of the era, it appears, after Bernard Madoff's. Billions of dollars in deposits, the agency alleged, were simply missing. Nine days later Stanford's chief investment officer, Laura Pendergest-Holt, was arrested for lying to the S.E.C. (Stanford and Pendergest-Holt deny any wrongdoing.)

It was an odd scandal, even as it broke. For two days Allen Stanford was thought to be a fugitive, until F.B.I. agents found him near his girlfriend's family's house in Virginia. Unlike Madoff or many of the other so-called mini-Madoffs, whose frauds surfaced in the wake of the global financial crisis, Stanford was not arrested. At the time of this writing, in fact, he remains a free man, though he may be indicted any day; his most notable appearance came in April, when he told ABC's Brian Ross that he would punch in the mouth anyone who said his bank was a money-laundering operation. By then the flash flood of media stories on Stanford had abated, and unlike in the Madoff scandal, there was no groundswell of public outrage, in large part because so many of Stanford's depositors were Latin American.

Yet Allen Stanford's is quite a tale. The story of his rise, in fact, is as improbable as any you're likely to read. Until February, "Sir" Allen—Antigua knighted him in 2006—sat atop a personal fortune valued at $2.2 billion, collected American and European politicians like stamps—a former president of Switzerland sat on his "international advisory board"—and in his spare time served as the world's foremost promoter of the sport of cricket, of all things. He had a mansion with a moat in South Florida and, apparently, one heck of a libido; according to an exhaustive investigation by London's *Daily Mail*, Stanford, a married man, fathered no fewer than five children by three women other than his wife.

But that's just the half of it. What is truly startling is how he did it. One might expect a financier running an $8 billion international banking colossus to have a background in, say, banking. Not Stanford. He founded his Caribbean empire 24 years ago after bankrupting his first business, a chain of upscale health clubs based in the central-Texas city of Waco, 25 miles from the Crawford hobby farm of former president George W. Bush. After that, there was even a brief spell where Stanford was seen flipping hamburgers at a burger joint his family owned for a short time before it too closed. Then, as far as many of his old Waco friends knew, he simply vanished.

"I worked out at his club in the late 70s. I knew Allen a little," says

K. Paul Holt, a Waco businessman. "So one day last February, I go online and out of the corner of my eye I see this headline, R. ALLEN STANFORD, CARIBBEAN BANKING KING, IN $8 BILLION SCANDAL. I said, 'There's no way in hell that can be Allen.' Then it says something about cricket, and I'm like, 'I don't think so.' And then I Googled him and there's something about a failed health club in Waco, Texas, and so I'm going, Whoa! How did somebody go from Total Fitness Center to being a knight in the Caribbean? Jesus Christ! But hey, you know, this is America. Anybody can be anything, I guess."

Nowhere is that more true than in the world of high finance; in the 25 years I've spent writing about bankers and their ilk, I've repeatedly been amazed by the humble backgrounds of even the most successful financiers. James Cayne, the fallen C.E.O. of Bear Stearns, was a cabbie when he got his first job on Wall Street. Ivan Boesky, the disgraced arbitrageur at the center of the great insider-trading scandals of the 1980s, stumbled onto a trading floor after bankrupting his family's Detroit strip joint. In terms of sheer strangeness, though, one would need to look long and hard to find a career quite like that of Robert Allen Stanford.

Perhaps unsurprisingly, the most revealing glimpses of Stanford come from the years before he ensconced himself in mansions and yachts and boardrooms. He was born in Mexia, Texas, a weary village of 7,000 or so south of Dallas. His father, James, who partnered with Stanford in his early ventures, owned an insurance agency. His mother, Sammie, wrote the society column for the local paper. By the time Stanford was nine his parents had divorced; his mother took Stanford and his younger brother to Fort Worth, where they grew up. After graduating from high school, in 1968, Stanford stumbled through a few small colleges before landing at Baylor University, in Waco, where he graduated in 1974. He has told some interviewers he was on the football team; he wasn't. He told others he taught scuba; he did. After college he briefly worked for his father, and married a pretty dental hygienist named Susan Williams.

Despite his unremarkable origins, by his mid-20s Stanford was already shaping up to be a classic Texas archetype: the swashbuckling entrepreneur, with a big smile, a roving eye, and a laserlike focus on making money. After the wedding the Stanfords moved into Apartment 204 at the Window Box Apartments in Waco. Not long after, Stanford acquired his first business, an exercise club called Mr. and Mrs. Health, on Lake Air Drive. According to former employees, Stanford had worked there in college and then bought it from his onetime boss.

The Total Fitness Center, as Stanford re-christened it, was one of the first clubs in central Texas to feature newfangled Nautilus machines. It proved immensely popular; Stanford was able to sell memberships to scores of Wacoans for up to $1,000 a year, which generated contracts he was able to sell for cash to a finance company. In short order he opened Total Fitness clubs in neighboring Temple and Killeen and purchased an expensive riverside home. By his 30th birthday, in 1980, Stanford was driving a white Jaguar through the streets of the bucolic Texas city.

It got him noticed, which he clearly loved. "One of his rules at the gym was you don't drop your weights—they can get damaged," recalls Tim Gardner, an assistant manager at Total Fitness, "but I can still see him sitting on the bench, doing curls, and then standing up and dropping these weights from as far up as he could do. And people would turn and look at him. It was just for the attention, see? He loved to be in the limelight like that. I think if you looked up 'narcissist' in the dictionary, you'd find Allen's picture."

"I'll never forget the first time I met Allen," says Gary Findley, who managed the gym for a time. "I was inside the gym, and I heard this loud noise outside. I mean, loud. I couldn't figure out what it was, so I walked outside. He was landing in the middle of our running track in a private helicopter with the name 'Total Fitness' on the side. That guy spent money like it was going out of style."

"I remember I had parties at this little apartment complex, and Allen was always there, laughing, joking," says a dentist named David Rhoden. "He was kind of wild, in a fun way, definitely one of the loudest ones at the party, a bright spirit, never gloomy, a guy who would yell at you across the room."

"He was really a likable ol' boy, big fella—he just had a presence about him, like a pro athlete," recalls Rick Hagelstein, one of Stanford's Waco bankers. "One story I do remember is he came into my office once with bandages all around his right forearm, big ol' bunch of bandages. What had happened was he had a Rottweiler and some redneck up in Mexia had a pit bull. This guy challenged Allen, said, 'My pit bull can beat your Rottweiler.'

Allen said, 'This is crazy.' The guy kept pushing him and got in Allen's face. So Allen hit the guy. And the pit bull lashed out at Allen and evidently did a good job on his forearm. He said, 'I had to beat that thang I don't know how many times to get it loose.' That was Allen."

That in-your-face combativeness was part of Stanford's persona from the outset. "Allen's a big guy. He uses his size to intimidate people, and he's extremely demanding," says Tim Gardner. "I remember he told me, 'Tim, I flat out don't like you, but as long as you make me money, I'll keep you. Once you stop making me money, you're out the door.' That was very much Allen's way."

If Stanford lived big, he dreamed even bigger. By 1980 he had opened two large health clubs featuring racquetball courts in Austin, plus another club in Galveston. "When I knew him, he had a girlfriend in every town, and he was married, and several of these girls—real stripper types with big boobs—he had bought them cars and put them up in apartments," remembers Royle Berry, who worked at the Austin facility. "He was a real player. He was so aggressive and so interested in making money. But it just felt a little sleazy at times. I remember when he would come into the club, the first thing he'd do is say, 'How much cash do we have?' And he'd take all the cash."

In about 1981, Stanford made his boldest move to date, announcing plans for his largest club yet, in the new Arena Towers development, on Houston's Southwest Freeway. According to Royle Berry, Stanford leveraged his other clubs to build the facility. His timing, however, couldn't have been worse. Falling oil prices triggered a statewide economic collapse, and by 1982, Stanford's athletic clubs were in Chapter 11. Two years later, he himself went bankrupt, listing $13.6 million in debt against barely $200,000 in assets. He left scores of angry creditors in the Waco area. It was the last most people in central Texas would hear of him for more than 20 years.

In fact, Stanford didn't flee Waco right away. In November 1984 a bankruptcy court cleared his debts, allowing him to start over. Gary Findley hadn't seen Stanford for months when he strode into a new restaurant in suburban Hewitt called Junior's Hamburgers. "I walked in there one night and who should I see flipping hamburgers but Allen—he had started the place," Findley remembers. Junior's, however, closed down before long, leaving big Allen Stanford, fresh out of bankruptcy, the guiding light behind not one but two shuttered businesses, without his Jaguar, his helicopter, or any way to make a living.

So he went to the Caribbean and opened a bank.

By 1985, Stanford and his wife were living in Houston. That's when he opened his first bank, on the Caribbean island of Montserrat. On its face, it is a startling transition: how on earth does a bankrupt Texas gym owner suddenly wake up one day and start an offshore bank?

The story Stanford told of how he entered Caribbean banking remained consistent over the years. During the mid-1980s, he explained, he and his father branched out into real estate, buying apartment complexes in the Houston area on the cheap and flipping them for big profits. It was with this money, Stanford told reporters—usually said to be about $6 million— that his father staked him to his first bank, in Montserrat, which became an incarnation of the family business, Stanford Financial.

In fact, little about this explanation makes sense. For one thing, Stanford Financial no longer existed; James Stanford had sold it in 1983, and for a lot less than $6 million. ("I wish I had had $6 million to pay him," says the Mexia businessman Bobby Forrest, who bought it. "It wasn't anywhere near that.") Wherever the family got the money—in a 1999 interview Stanford claimed it came from a group of Aruban oil-refinery workers—it's hard to imagine it came from Houston real estate. While the Stanfords did become small-time developers later in the 1980s, their projects appear to date from the period *after* the Montserrat bank's founding, in 1985. This suggests that the bank probably funded the real-estate deals, mostly apartment buildings, not the other way around.

But of all the businesses Stanford could have entered, why banking? And why in such an obscure spot as Montserrat? According to one former employee, it happened this way: After moving to Houston, Stanford was at loose ends and decided to return to one of his first loves, scuba-diving, taking a long vacation in the Caribbean during which he supported himself giving scuba lessons. It was beside a resort swimming pool, this employee says, that Stanford met a charming European expatriate named Frans Vingerhoedt, who dazzled him with stories of the easy money to be made operating a bank in the Caribbean.

In 1985, when Stanford first became interested in the Caribbean, the hottest new home for offshore banks was the tiny island of Montserrat, a British colony with a smoking volcano (that, in 1995, obliterated half the island) and barely 12,000 jittery residents. A notorious Beverly Hills broker named Jerome Schneider—later convicted of fraud—had discovered the colony's porous financial regulations and begun selling banking licenses; of Montserrat's 350 so-called instabanks, at least 200 arrived via Schneider.

By most accounts, it was a stunningly sleazy climate in which to operate. The vast majority of the Montserrat instabanks existed only on paper; their owners scarcely if ever visited the island. Scores of these banks would later be probed by British and U.S. authorities. One, Zurich Overseas Bank, whose owners would be indicted for fraud in Detroit, operated out of the Chez Nous tavern in the Montserrat town of Plymouth. "Almost every bank in Montserrat was operated illegally," says David Marchant, editor of *OffshoreAlert*, a newsletter that covers offshore banking. "They were all shell banks, and they were all pretty much involved in fraud. They were all the same: certificate-of-deposit frauds, money-laundering. The fact that Stanford had a banking license in Montserrat is all you needed to know about his credibility. It wasn't like most of the banks were good and you had a few bad eggs. The only reason you opened a bank in Montserrat was to commit fraud."

Stanford's new Guardian International Bank, however, was sharply different from other Montserrat banks. Rather than avoid the island itself, Stanford actually opened a bank building and hired local women to staff it. (The building and all its contents, alas, were destroyed by Hurricane Hugo in 1989.) The island facilities were augmented by a sales office in Miami and another in Houston, where Stanford worked with a small group including his college roommate James Davis, who would go on to become Stanford Financial's C.F.O. But what also distinguished Guardian from other Montserrat banks was how Stanford constructed a mythos to establish his credibility. He began telling customers the company had been founded by his grandfather Lodis B. Stanford (a barber turned insurance agent) in Mexia in 1932 and, once he renamed the bank Stanford International, he hung a photo of the gray-haired old man in the lobby.

From the beginning, little about Stanford International was what it seemed. A rare glimpse of its early years comes from one of the bank's first employees, a person I'll call Maria, whose job in Houston included assembling its first marketing brochures. "I remember the bank in Montserrat," Maria says. "It had two stories, with three or four African-American ladies and one white lady, this really pretty girl, maybe 17 or 18. They had all these computers, but the power was not even switched on. The computers didn't even work."

In those early days on Montserrat, Stanford attracted depositors, as he would throughout his career, by placing advertisements, some featuring attractive young women, in Latin-American newspapers. Far more alluring than the women, however, were the interest rates Stanford promised: two percentage points above American bank rates. "That was what Allen always said, 'Two points more,'" Maria says. "He told me, 'It is unbelievable. People are so stupid, they will risk all their money, give it to someone they don't even know, for two points.' One day he grabbed the calculator on my desk, ran the numbers for two points on a million dollars: it was $20,000 a year. He said it was just unbelievable what people would do for just two points more."

By 1988, Stanford had acquired his first three run-down Houston apartment complexes—possibly using depositors' money—as the bank's deposits began to skyrocket. By the end of 1989, Stanford claimed an astounding $55.5 million in accounts. By November 1990 the number hit $100 million. Even inside the bank, this kind of growth raised eyebrows. "Nobody knew if the numbers were true," Maria says. "If you asked Allen how he [managed to pay higher interest rates], he always said exactly the same thing he says now: 'It's only two points; our organization is very lean. We don't pay taxes in Montserrat.' Nobody believed that. But he paid very well. So the questions stopped.

"I was suspicious when we did the first annual report," Maria continues. "We used to do the work at night, when everybody was already gone. It was weird. You could see they were playing with the numbers and changing them right there in front of me. Jim [Davis] would come back to my office and look at the numbers, then go back to Allen, who would come in and say, 'Fine, let's just put this number down.' They were just making things up. Personally, I was hoping we could make enough money to cover up everything. But it just got worse and worse." Stanford, however, seemed without a care. He and his wife moved into a pink hacienda-style house in the northern suburb of Kingwood.

Then came trouble. According to David Marchant, it all began when an American computer programmer, hired to update another Montserrat bank's systems, complained to local authorities that his boss appeared to be transferring deposits into his personal account. A Scotland Yard man named Dick Marston was summoned to investigate; Marston brought in the F.B.I. A probe Marston expected to take a few weeks turned into a massive investigation that lasted years. By 1989 more than a hundred banks were under scrutiny by British and American agents for every conceivable financial crime.

Stanford's operation, by then one of the larger Montserrat banks, quickly became a target. Where, Marston wondered, were all those deposits coming from? Colombian drug money was flooding into banks across the region, and there were persistent rumors that this was the source of Stanford's growth. Marston called in an expert from the Office of the Comptroller of the Currency. As a onetime F.B.I. agent involved in the Montserrat probe recalls, "The O.C.C. guy went down there, stood across from the Stanford office for maybe several hours, came back and said, 'Yep, that's a money-laundering operation.' Marston goes, 'How can you tell from just standing across the street?' The guy goes, 'I'm telling you, it is.' Then, a little later, we got fairly detailed intelligence that they were indeed laundering for major Colombian drug traffickers. I remember very clearly that, when the governor [of Montserrat] heard this, we had to literally peel the guy off the ceiling." The Montserrat authorities were already tossing dozens of shady banks out of the colony when the government revoked Stanford's license, in May 1991.

It was a crushing blow. "Allen disappeared for six or eight months after that," Maria says. "For a long period nobody saw him. He would call in at one in the morning, and he always said he was working on this big deal, it would save everything." For once, Stanford was true to his word. In time he found a new home for Stanford Financial, one where fungible banking regulations would prove ideal for his ambitions:

Antigua.

An American vacationer who wants only to sip rum punches on its legendary pink-sand beaches may not realize—or care—that Antigua was long host to one of the Caribbean's most corrupt governments, under the two Bird administrations. A militant trade unionist with little formal education, Vere Bird led Antigua to independence in 1981 and for years ran the two-island country—officially named Antigua and Barbuda—as a personal fiefdom amid constant allegations of criminal activities. One of his sons was behind a scheme to sell Israeli weapons to Colombian drug traffickers. Another was arrested at V. C. Bird International Airport with 25 pounds of cocaine in his luggage. Another son, Lester Bird, eventually took control of the government, in 1994, as the U.S. began voicing concerns that the island was becoming not only a money-laundering center but also a haven for Russian organized crime.

Such was the Antiguan milieu when Allen Stanford introduced himself to the Birds, around 1990. He wanted to buy the local Bank of Antigua, on the verge of bankruptcy, and the Birds were happy to broker its sale to him. Soon after, Stanford opened a second Antiguan bank, a new incarnation of Stanford Financial, which he operated much as before, opening a bank building, hiring locals to staff it, and advertising high interest rates in Latin-American newspapers. From the outset Stanford worked diligently to forge a partnership with the Birds. He provided the money to build cricket fields and a hospital, a vast multicolored complex overlooking the capital of Saint John's. In 1995, Stanford went a step further, loaning the government several million dollars to cover salaries and pension contributions. The loans grew over the years. By the late 1990s, Stanford owned the *Antigua Sun*, one of the island's two daily newspapers, and when two editors protested Stanford's suppression of an article criticizing Lester Bird during the 1999 elections, he fired them. (Both sued successfully.)

"Stanford became Lester's go-to guy," says Winston Derrick, publisher of the competing *Daily Observer*. "When Lester needed a hospital, he turned to Stanford. When Lester needed anything, he turned to Stanford."

Stanford Financial boomed in its new home. By 1994 it claimed $350 million in assets, enough for Stanford, in the following years, to buy a Venezuelan bank and start a conventional broker-dealer operation in Houston; he eventually opened a corporate headquarters near Houston's

Galleria mall. Later, branches were added in Panama, Peru, Ecuador, and Mexico.

From the outset, U.S. authorities kept tabs on Stanford. The Internal Revenue Service sued Stanford and his wife for failing to file their 1990 return, and sought more than $420,000 in back taxes; 19 years later, the I.R.S. is claiming they owe over $226 million for returns from 1999 to 2003. After the money-laundering allegations on Montserrat, the F.B.I. too has kept a keen eye on Stanford, more or less nonstop, for more than 20 years.

"In terms of his notoriety, once that kind of information started coming in, he was known to a lot of folks in law enforcement," says a former F.B.I. agent who investigated Stanford. "He stayed very prominently on the radar for years—still is. There was a series of investigations. Obviously none of them ever ended in indictments. But we're talking various F.B.I. field divisions, with multiple agents, then multiple agencies, over 10 to 12 years."

Throughout Stanford's first decade on Antigua, the focus of U.S. investigators remained largely, perhaps exclusively, money-laundering. Questions of whether the bank was swindling investors wouldn't arise for years. "If you were in the metaphoric bushes outside Stanford anytime in the last 20 years," notes one U.S. security consultant, "you would literally have been bumping into team after team of U.S. government agencies, shouting at each other to get out of the way, you know, 'Be quiet, Stanford will hear you.' Those agencies would include the F.B.I., [U.S.] Customs, and the S.E.C. From everything I hear, there was endless interagency conflict over what to do and how serious this guy was."

The authorities' inability to mount a criminal case against Stanford—not to mention everyone's inability to sniff out fraud—has left many, inside and outside the government, outraged. "Clients would come to us and go, 'Oh, this guy is offering such great rates, he's never been in trouble, should we go with him?'" says the C.E.O. of one private-security firm. "And then you reach into your sources and they say, 'Stop, run, avoid this guy like the plague. He's hot—hot with the government.' Well Jesus, we're just private investigators, and we knew the guy was bad. Where was the government? Why didn't anyone hang a sign on this guy?"

One reason was Stanford's defenses. He became known for suing anyone, even journalists, who suggested Stanford Financial was anything but legitimate. In 1996, when a writer for *Caribbean Week* portrayed the company as a money-launderer, Stanford sued and won a front-page retraction. No critic was too small to ignore. He once sued a Catholic-school principal in New York after the man, active in Antiguan politics, termed him a "neo-colonialist."

Behind the scenes, Stanford was even more aggressive. As the company grew, he became renowned within law-enforcement circles for aggressive counter-intelligence. Stanford's security chief was a former head of the F.B.I.'s Miami office. But his greatest asset may have been a top security firm, Kroll Associates, whose Miami office worked with Stanford for years. "Stanford was spending millions of dollars a year trying to figure out who was looking at him, and aggressively combating whoever it was," recalls the former F.B.I. agent. "Kroll was essentially running a propaganda campaign in defense of Stanford's good name. They beat on me many times: 'Hey, you got this all wrong, he's not a money-launderer, he's a great guy, leave him alone.' "

Kroll's role in defending Stanford's reputation, in both law-enforcement circles and the wider banking community, was an example of a controversial practice known within the private-security world as "reputational self–due diligence," that is, vouching for a client's good name. It is, by all accounts, an exceedingly lucrative business. "What Kroll would do," says a former Kroll executive, "was put together a very detailed description of the bank, what it does, look over its balance sheet, the origin of the deposits, and produce this really thick report that says, 'This bank complies with the [U.S.] guidelines for combating money-laundering, and you, Bank A, should feel free to work with them.' It is controversial, even inside the firm. Kroll is considered—how to say this nicely—well, they're willing to take more controversial clients for this type of service."

"Kroll can confirm that it has provided routine professional services to various businesses related to Allen Stanford," the company said in a statement issued to *Vanity Fair.* "All such work was provided consistent with Kroll's reputation, internal controls, and its history of working with law enforcement. Suggestions to the contrary are incorrect. Confidentiality restrictions prevent any further comment on those assignments."

Kroll's work for Stanford dates back at least a decade, to the moment when U.S. concerns about the company finally burst into the open. That happened in 1999, when a Drug Enforcement Administration probe revealed that members of Mexico's vicious Juárez cartel had deposited more than $3 million in accounts at Stanford. The bank froze the accounts, while the Bird government announced formation of a committee to rewrite its anti-money-laundering laws. To the U.S. government's dismay, Stanford himself was named to the committee. Another member was Thomas Cash, a former D.E.A. chief for Florida and the Caribbean who headed Kroll's Miami office and, former associates say, was long Kroll's liaison with Stanford. The committee produced a set of new regulations that appeared to weaken Antigua's banking laws rather than strengthen them.

The State Department howled, complaining that "the Antiguan government has effectively ceded oversight of its offshore section to an offshore banker and his minions." When the Bird government shrugged, the U.S. Treasury officially designated Antigua a "money-laundering risk," just the second such warning ever issued against a sovereign country.

Under intense pressure, the Bird administration backed off and, after negotiations with U.S. authorities, tightened the island's laws. At the same time, according to a State Department cable obtained by *The Philadelphia Inquirer,* unnamed Stanford "allies" seized a sheaf of Antiguan banking records. "It appears that the U.S. offshore banker [Stanford] is taking advantage of loopholes . . . to seize the initiative and protect himself from any future inquiries or investigations," noted the cable, which labeled the incident "Filegate, Antiguan style." "The high-powered legal and investigative guns from the U.S. are likely being tasked with cleansing the files to make sure there is nothing in them that could damage or implicate the American offshore banker."

Having survived his first dustup with U.S. authorities, Stanford apparently realized he could use friends in Washington. Some of these new friends may have been inside the D.E.A.; a BBC broadcast in May claimed that Stanford became a D.E.A. informant. But his best friends were in politics. His political giving began about the time that a sweeping anti-money-laundering bill was introduced to Congress, around 2000. Stanford began donating large sums to a number of senators, including Minority Leader Tom Daschle, in an apparent effort to block it; in a later study, the public-interest group Public Citizen judged that Stanford's donations were probably crucial to the bill's eventual defeat in the Senate. Stanford's giving grew from there.

In 2002, his company gave $800,000 to the Democratic Senatorial Campaign Committee, the vice-chairman of which was Florida senator Bill Nelson, who received $45,900. In all, Stanford spent nearly $5 million lobbying Congress between 1999 and 2008 and dished out $2.4 million to federal candidates. He also sponsored dozens of free "fact-finding" trips to Antigua and other Caribbean islands for politicians and their staffs on his fleet of jets. Former Republican House majority leader Tom DeLay, of Texas, among the largest recipients of Stanford's largesse, flew 11 times on Stanford's jets, according to *The Dallas Morning News*.

What remains of Stanford's Antiguan empire today is a series of mostly empty buildings that line the periphery of the island's airport; in fact, the first half-dozen structures a visitor encounters, even the airport parking lot, are Stanford's. Turn right at the airport traffic circle and you see the offices of his newspaper, the *Antigua Sun*. To the left is the Stanford Cricket Ground, an expanse of grass lined with grandstands, video screens, and Stanford's restaurant, the Sticky Wicket, guarded by a statue of a cricket player. Looming over the traffic circle is Stanford International Bank itself, an immense building, engulfed in colorful tropical gardens; people working for a court-appointed receiver can be seen wandering in and out of its great mahogany front doors. Next door is another Stanford restaurant, the Pavilion, which features an 8,000-bottle wine cellar. Just up the street, past the observation tower and the botanical gardens, is a long, low plantation-style building, Stanford Trust. Across the way is the Bank of Antigua. The entire development has the just-built look and feel of a middle-class Miami subdivision.

By the early 2000s, Stanford's wealth, power, and visibility were all on the rise. As his company grew, Stanford became a distant, sometimes mercurial executive, a figure most employees saw only at official functions. "You would wait for hours to see him," recalls an executive, one of 15 who reported directly to the boss. "If you got called for a 10-o'clock-in-the-morning meeting, it might be 1 o'clock in the morning by the time you got to see him. Time didn't matter. He demanded respect too. [Every meeting was] basically a table of yes-men. His wish was our command."

In Antigua, Stanford had become a polarizing figure. Many on the island, citing the gifts and money he had given the government, adored him. But others viewed him as a sharp-elbowed Yankee imperialist, a view propagated by opposition politicians during the hard-fought 2004 election in which Lester Bird was tossed out of office; Bird's replacement, Baldwin Spencer, termed Stanford "haughty, arrogant, and obnoxious."

Yet Stanford's power endured, in large part because of the financial hammerlock he held on the government. By 2004 its debt to Stanford had grown to $87 million—nearly half its annual tax revenues. And in return for being allowed to put up the new buildings of an airport complex and purchase 19-acre Maiden Island (where he planned to build a new home), plus another islet, he supplied money to build a new national library and an education complex.

As his fortune grew, however, he began spending more time in South Florida—he seldom visited the Houston headquarters, former employees say—where in October 2003 he paid $10.5 million for a 57-room mansion, called Tyecliffe Castle, on the Coral Gables waterfront. It was there that, according to the *Daily Mail* investigation and various court filings, Stanford secreted one of the women some inside his company began calling "the outside wives."

By most accounts, there were at least three of them. The first was apparently a woman with the same name as his wife, Susan, whom he had dated in Houston. She lives today in a Dallas suburb with her and Stanford's 17-year-old son. A second woman, Beki Reeves-Stanford, lives in South Florida with their two teenage children. The third is Louise Sage, who lives in Kent, England. Stanford has two younger children with her. Their relationship became public when she sued for financial support.

With his wife, Stanford has a daughter, now in her 20s. According to reports, he and his wife separated in 1999; Susan filed for divorce in 2007. The case is pending. Stanford's current girlfriend was formerly a cocktail waitress at one of his Antiguan restaurants.

S tanford Financial, meanwhile, remained nearly as productive as its
founder, topping $3 billion in deposits in 2004. Over time the com-
pany grew into a high-pressure marketing powerhouse in which employees
worked in groups with colorful names such as Money Machine, Superstars,
and the Deal Hunters. Stanford offered several financial products, but its
mainstay remained the high-rate C.D.'s sold out of its Antiguan bank. According to *The Wall Street Journal,* Stanford salesmen earned commissions
of 1 percent for every dollar they brought in, a rate so rich some brokers
called it "bank crack"—it was that addictive. Top producers might also win
a luxury BMW sedan.

"He sort of burned through countries," notes an investigator working
for Stanford's court-appointed receiver. "If you look at the internals, early on
the money was coming from Brazil and Venezuela. Billions from Venezuela.
Then Peru, Ecuador. You know, you can only get so many investors in one
country to put in so much money before people start asking questions. So
from there he moved to trying to capture money in Panama, then the U.S.,
which was difficult, and then Mexico. That's where he was at the very end."

Stanford Financial's drive to "capture" American depositors shifted into
high gear in 2004. Between 2004 and 2007, the bank expanded its U.S.
branches from 6 to more than 25, opening offices in Denver, San Francisco,
and Boston, as well as in southern cities, such as Little Rock and Baton Rouge;
a second headquarters of sorts was established, in Memphis, close to the
northern-Mississippi home of Stanford's chief financial officer, Jim Davis.
Prospective investors were often ushered through the hushed mahogany-
and-marble corridors at the Houston headquarters, where they were led into
the Lodis Room—named for Stanford's barber grandfather—for a promotional film, then plied with champagne and cigars in the executive dining
room. The wealthiest prospects might be flown to Antigua aboard one of
Stanford's six private jets, be put up for a few nights at the luxurious Jumby
Bay resort, and, if they were lucky, get to meet Stanford himself.

B it by bit, Stanford Financial emerged from its shadowy Caribbean origins. To popularize the brand, Stanford began throwing money into
the usual kinds of corporate philanthropy and naming opportunities. He

sponsored the pro golfer Vijay Singh, along with two tournaments. There were Stanford banners in the Miami Heat's arena, a Stanford Field at the International Polo Club Palm Beach, plus millions given to hospitals, theaters, and museums, mostly in Memphis, Miami, and Houston. When it came to sports marketing, though, Stanford's passion was cricket, especially a fast-moving new version of the game called Twenty20 that can be played in hours instead of days.

In 2005, after completing his Antiguan cricket ground, Stanford announced a pan-Caribbean tournament. The hidebound cricket world, centered in England and India, snickered, but Stanford would not be deterred. He unveiled his own team, the Superstars, and, in a 2008 media event whose Texas-style audacity stunned the cricket community, challenged the English team to a match by landing a black "Stanford Financial" helicopter on London's most hallowed field, Lord's. He jumped out, promptly chest-bumped a British official, and thrust forward a Plexiglas box containing the match's prize: $20 million in cash. Stanford's Superstars won the big match, but the affair did little to ingratiate the Texan with the cricket establishment.

What kept attracting depositors, though, wasn't Stanford's publicity stunts. It was his profits. The first serious questions about Stanford's performance came as it began to hire dozens of veteran American brokers to staff its new American offices. One of those with suspicions was Lawrence DeMaria, a former *New York Times* reporter who, after enduring a six-hour grilling by an investigator from Kroll Associates, had been hired to supervise internal publications and write speeches for Stanford himself. DeMaria's "bullshit antennae," as he terms it, rose not long after he joined the company.

"I kept getting vibes throughout the company that nobody knew where the money was coming from or where it was going," he says today. "When I would ask about how the company made its money, not just the principals but the investment-banking divisions, the research department, I would get no answers. [Everyone] said they didn't know. . . . When I asked the investment people, they said, 'We can't tell you, but believe us—we have computers.'" Eventually DeMaria was fired. He sued and settled.

DeMaria's concerns were hardly unique. The executive who reported directly to Stanford recalls a talk with another executive in charge of the Antiguan bank: "I remember once having a conversation about how they make such great money. He said, You know, good investments, things like that. He told me right away it was not drug money. That it once had been drug money. But, you know, Oh they found out about it, paid a penalty, they would never do that again, right? [And he] told me it was not a Ponzi scheme. Everything was legit."

S till, the rumors persisted, especially among the new American hires. In Miami, a broker named Charles Hazlett asked too many pointed questions, including several of Stanford's 31-year-old chief investment officer, Laura Pendergest-Holt, and found himself dismissed; he too sued and won a settlement. In Houston, a pair of new Stanford brokers, Charles Rawl and Mark Tidwell, asked still more questions, and resigned just as they were dismissed. They eventually sued; their complaint reportedly triggered interest within the S.E.C.'s Fort Worth office, but for some reason the investigation went nowhere.

But it wasn't just U.S. brokers who raised questions. The most senior whistle-blower may have been Gonzalo Tirado, the longtime head of Stanford's Venezuelan bank, the company's largest outpost. After Tirado resigned, in 2005, he and the bank engaged in a hail of litigation, much of it centered on compensation matters. An investigator in Miami told me Tirado came to believe Stanford was engaged in criminal acts and alerted regulators in Venezuela and the U.S. In an e-mail exchange, Tirado confirms this, but declines to elaborate, noting, "I had more than three years telling the authorities in Venezuela and USA about his lack of loyalty and ethics."

Stanford Financial, however, easily weathered what few financial investigations it confronted. The S.E.C. and another agency began probes in 2005 and identified several technical infractions, but the probes neither received much attention in the press nor did anything to slow Stanford's growth. Buoyed by the U.S. economic boom, its assets roughly doubled between 2004 and 2008, to $8 billion.

In 2008 a magazine called *World Finance* named Stanford its Man of the Year. He was added to the University of Houston business school's Circle of Honor and spoke to a commencement class on the importance of ethics. "So," CNBC correspondent Carl Quintanilla asked Stanford in May 2008, "is it fun being a billionaire?"

"Well, uh, yes," he replied. "Yes, I have to say it is fun."

The fun, alas, was almost over.

One day last October, a 48-year-old independent financial analyst, Alex Dalmady, sitting in his office in South Florida, took a call from a friend. The friend, whom Dalmady refers to as Roberto, had much of his savings invested in Stanford C.D.'s, and in the wake of the financial meltdown, he asked Dalmady, as a favor, to examine the bank's financials and see if his money was safe. "So when I went over to the bank's Web site, I was stunned," Dalmady recalls in a blog item. "First, it looked so simple, so unsophisticated. The language used wasn't quite right." The explanation Stanford offered for its returns, Dalmady felt, made no sense; no one could achieve market returns like that year after year, and no reputable commercial bank would try. It was far too risky. As he later described it on his blog, Dalmady immediately called his friend and said, "Roberto, take your money out YESTERDAY!"

Once his friend was safe, Dalmady found himself returning to the Stanford Web site. In the interim, the Madoff scandal had hit, and his curiosity soon turned to suspicion. "It became obvious," Dalmady wrote. "No one was looking at stuff like this. The S.E.C. had its head up its butt. So I dug deeper and put some numbers on a spreadsheet—took me about 30 minutes. It just got worse. Where was the portfolio? What were they invested in? [Twenty percent plus] returns on their hedge funds? No way. Outperforming the S&P in stocks? No way. With 30 percent deposit growth [i.e., money constantly coming in]? No way."

Stanford Financial, Dalmady judged, had to be a fraud. He decided to write up his conclusions in an article and offered it to an old friend who edited a Venezuelan financial magazine called *Veneconomy*, which published it at the end of January. At first, the piece caused little stir. Titled "Duck Tales," it was front-loaded with complex financial analysis; Stanford Financial wasn't even mentioned until page 4. But on February 9, a financial blog called the Devil's Excrement republished it, at which point it was picked up by a popular Latin-American blog, the snarky Inca Kola News. The Inca Kola item, in turn, immediately became the focus of intense interest.

"So far today," a post on the blog read, "this humble blog has had several visits from major newswires, three visits from the US Federal Reserve and one from the SEC, all using [the terms] 'Alex Dalmady,' 'Stanford,' 'Madoff' etc as keyword entries. Not to mention all those people from an island called Antigua and plenty from a company called 'Stanford Eagle' in Houston. *Hi guys, having a nice day?"*

Subpoenas were already on the way. As an e-mail from a Stanford lawyer, included in court materials, explained, the S.E.C. wanted to confirm that "the bank is 'real,' the CDs are 'real,' that the money is actually invested as described in our documents, and that client funds in the CDs are safe and secure." Both Stanford and Jim Davis declined to be interviewed by the agency. Instead, they sent in their chief investment officer, tall, willowy Pendergest-Holt, a Davis protégée he had met at his rural Mississippi church. She would testify together with a team from Stanford International Bank.

At a prep meeting of Stanford executives, on February 4, according to materials filed in a Dallas federal court, Pendergest-Holt sat down in a Miami conference room to explain to one of the firm's outside attorneys just how Stanford operated. Its assets, she said, were divided into three "tiers." Tier I, about 10 percent of assets, was held in cash. Tier II, another 10 percent, was invested in mutual funds managed by outside firms; these holdings, Pendergest-Holt said, had fallen to $350 million from $850 million since just last June.

But it was the super-secret Tier III that most interested the S.E.C. Tier III held about 80 percent of Stanford Financial's assets, roughly $7 billion; its contents and day-to-day management appear to have been handled only by Stanford, Davis, and Pendergest-Holt. At the Miami meeting, Davis, who was also present, handed Pendergest-Holt a data drive that broke down Tier III's contents in detail. She showed it to the group. According to these numbers, Tier III at that moment was composed of $3 billion in real estate, a $1.6 billion "loan to shareholder"—Allen Stanford—and nothing else.

Nothing. Else.

The shortfall came to nearly $2.5 billion. The bank executives in the room, who had never peered inside Tier III, were aghast. When the meeting reconvened the next day, Stanford appeared. Two of the bank executives said they had no choice but to report this new information to the S.E.C. According to court materials, Stanford flew into a rage and pounded on the conference table.

"The assets are there!" he shouted.

On the third day things got stranger yet. Before Pendergest-Holt could even begin talking, another executive started to cry. "If you are going to go through more information I didn't know," he sniffed, "I don't want to be here, and I'm going to the authorities." One of the lawyers suggested they pray. Stanford, however, was unmoved. He insisted the bank still had $850 million more in assets than liabilities. For the first time, though, the group in the room could see their emperor had no clothes. A few hours later, the outside attorney walked into a Stanford man's office and said, "The party is over."

On February 10, Pendergest-Holt began giving sworn testimony to attorneys in the S.E.C.'s Fort Worth office. She played dumb. Asked whom she consulted with to prepare, she failed to mention either Davis or Stanford. "I have been to Antigua," she said. "I have reviewed statements and looked through, gosh, other issues." Time and again she insisted she knew nothing about Tier III. "I can state it as many ways as you would like me to," she said. "I don't know about Tier III, other than what I've already shared with you in about 20 different ways." There was a second interview a week later. "If I knew anything about Tier III, I'd tell you," she said. "God's honest truth."

As Pendergest-Holt spoke, federal agents were already raiding Stanford headquarters in Houston. A week later she was indicted for lying to the S.E.C. It was over.

Within hours there were runs on the Stanford branches in Antigua and Venezuela, and throughout Latin America long lines of worried people sweated in the tropical heat. Most will probably never see their money again; one investigator told me he believes maybe $1 billion out of Stanford's $8 billion in assets might eventually be recovered.

If Stanford Financial was in fact a Ponzi scheme, it was strikingly similar to Bernie Madoff's. As with Madoff's operation, only a handful of people appear to have known what was going on. Stanford's auditor, like Madoff's, was tiny, in this case a 14-person accounting firm in Antigua; its owner has recently died. Stanford's seven-member board was composed entirely of insiders, including Stanford's father and one of his elderly chums, disabled by a stroke. That such a scheme could grow so enormous, and last for so many years, is a devastating indictment of worldwide banking regulation. It took Alex Dalmady maybe two hours on the Internet to glean the amazing truth. It's not clear anyone in Washington ever seriously tried.

Allen Stanford declined to be interviewed for this article. But in an April publicity blitz clearly designed to head off his looming indictment, he told a number of interviewers, including ABC's Brian Ross, that his company was never a Ponzi scheme. If any money was missing, Stanford insisted, it was all Jim Davis's fault. (Davis is cooperating with the S.E.C. investigation and plans to enter in plea talks with government officials.) When Ross asked about comparisons to Madoff, Stanford began to tear up.

"Bullshit, that's bullshit," he said. "It makes me madder than hell and touches the core of my soul."

Stanford, who remains in seclusion in Houston, didn't display the first bit of guilt or remorse. Instead, he said he felt persecuted. "I'm the maverick rich Texan that they can put the moose head on the wall—and that's the only reason they went after me," Stanford told Ross. "I'm fighting for my survival and for my integrity." It's a fight, one suspects, that Allen Stanford should, and almost certainly will, lose.

Days after Vanity Fair's *story was published, Allen Stanford was arrested by the F.B.I. in Virginia. Over the following months, a number of the fallen financier's assets—including his beloved yacht,* Sea Eagle—*would be sold to help investors recover some of their money.*

In late August, as part of a plea agreement filed in Federal District Court in Houston, James Davis claimed that Antigua's head bank regulator, Leroy King, and Stanford had sealed their conspiracy in a blood oath. The same day, Stanford, suffering from an accelerated heart rate, was hospitalized and later given a heart catheterization. At this writing, Stanford remains in jail awaiting trial in Houston.

· 14 ·

The Inheritance

Arthur Sulzberger Jr.
and the Decline of
the Newspaper Business

By MARK BOWDEN

May 2009

I was in a taxi on a wet winter day in Manhattan three years ago when my phone rang, displaying "111 111 1111," the peculiar signature of an incoming call from *The New York Times*.

"Mark? It's Arthur Sulzberger."

For weeks I had been trying to talk with Arthur Ochs Sulzberger Jr., the publisher and chairman of the New York Times Company. We had met once before, on friendly terms, and sometime after that I had informed him that I was hoping to write a story about him. I figured he was calling now to set something up. Instead he asked, "Have you seen the *New Yorker* piece?"

The article in question, just published, was bruising. It had surely been painful for him to read. Among other indignities, it featured a remark by the celebrated former *Times* man Gay Talese, the author of one of the most popular histories of the newspaper, *The Kingdom and the Power*. Speaking of Arthur, the fifth member of the Ochs-Sulzberger dynasty to preside over the paper, Talese had said, "You get a bad king every once in a while."

I told Arthur that I had not yet fully read the story. "Well, I'm getting out of the business," he said. Startled, I gazed through the window at the cars and people shouldering through the cold rain, the headline already forming in my mind: PUBLISHING SCION RESIGNS! "Wait, Arthur," I said. "Is this a major scoop? Or are you just saying that you aren't talking to writers anymore?" He laughed his high-pitched, zany laugh. "The latter," he said.

Now, I respect people who avoid the spotlight, and a reluctance to be publicly vivisected is a sure sign of intelligence. But ducking interviews is an awkward policy for the leader of the world's most celebrated newspaper, one that sends a small army of reporters—approximately 400 of them—into the field every day asking questions. Still, I could understand Arthur's decision. After presiding or helping to preside over a decade of unprecedented prosperity, the publisher and chairman of the *Times* had recently begun to appear overmatched. Two of his star staffers were discovered to have violated basic rules of reporting practice; he had been bullied by the newsroom into firing his handpicked executive editor, Howell Raines; and he had spent much of the previous year in a confusing knot of difficulty surrounding one of his reporters and longtime friends, Judith Miller. For an earnest and well-meaning man, the hereditary publisher had begun to look dismayingly small.

He has been shrinking ever since. In 2001, *The New York Times* celebrated its 150th anniversary. In the years that have followed, Arthur Sulzberger has steered his inheritance into a ditch. As of this writing, Times Company stock is officially classified as junk. Arthur made a catastrophic decision in the 1990s to start aggressively buying back shares ($1.8 billion worth from 2000 to 2004 alone). This was considered a good investment at the time, and had the effect of increasing the stock's value. Shares were going for more than $50. Now they are slipping below $4—less than the price of the Sunday *Times*. Arthur's revenues are in free fall: the bottom has dropped out of both newspaper and Internet advertising. He has done more than anyone in the business to showcase newspaper journalism online. It hasn't helped much. The content and page views of the newspaper's Web site, nytimes .com, may be the envy of the profession, but as a recent report from Citigroup explained, "The Internet has taken away far more advertising than it has given." Layoffs have occurred in the once sacrosanct newsroom.

Having squandered billions during the newspaper's fat years—buying up all that stock, buying up failing newspapers, building a gleaming new headquarters—Arthur is scrambling to keep up with interest payments on hundreds of millions in debt, much of it falling due within the next year. To do so, he is peddling assets on ruinous terms. Arthur recently borrowed $250 million from Carlos Slim Helú, the Mexican telecommunications billionaire, who owns the fourth-largest stake in the Times Company. Controlling interest is held closely by the Sulzberger family, which owns 89 percent of the company's Class B shares. These shares, not traded publicly, are held by a family trust designed to prevent individual heirs from selling out, and ultimately to shelter editorial matters from strict concern for the bottom line. The family owns about 20 percent of the Class A shares, which is about the same percentage owned by the hedge funds Harbinger and Firebrand. The third-largest Class A shareholder is T. Rowe Price, with 10 percent. Slim comes next, with 7 percent. Given the current state of the investment and credit markets, Slim would appear to have the inside rail should the paper ever be sold, a prospect once unthinkable. It is now *very* thinkable. Among the other prospective buyers whose names have surfaced in the press are Michael Bloomberg, the billionaire mayor of New York; Google; and even, perish the thought, the press baron Rupert Murdoch, whose *Wall Street Journal* has emerged as journalistic competition for the *Times* in a way it never was before. (Murdoch has publicly dismissed reports of his interest in the *Times* as "crap," which has served only to heighten speculation.) This quarter, for the first time since Times Company stock went public, in 1969, the fourth- and fifth-generation Sulzbergers who hold shares (there are 40 of them in all) received no dividends. As recently as last year they divvied up $25 million.

Beyond these professional trials, Arthur has personal ones. He has separated from his wife of more than three decades, Gail Gregg, a painter, and embarrassing speculation about his sleeping partners has surfaced in the tabloid columns. His son, Arthur Gregg Sulzberger, is now working as a reporter at the paper, as his father and grandfather once did, but, for the first time in five generations, the heir apparent's inheritance is in doubt.

While the crushing forces at work in the newspaper industry are certainly not Arthur's fault, and many other newspapers have already succumbed to them, the fate of *The New York Times* is of special importance: it is the flagship of serious newspaper journalism in America. The *Times* sailed into the economic storm that began in 2001 in good financial shape, bearing the most respected brand name in the profession. It was far better equipped than most newspapers to adapt and survive. What is increasingly clear is that the wrong person may be at the helm. Arthur Sulzberger's heart has always been in the right place, but he assumed leadership from his father uniquely ill-equipped for this crisis—not despite but *because* of his long apprenticeship. To their credit, the Sulzbergers have long treated the *Times* less as a business than as a public trust, and Arthur is steeped in that tradition, rooted in it, trained by it, captive to it. Ever the dutiful son, he has made it his life's mission to maintain the excellence he inherited—to duplicate his father's achievement. He is a careful steward, when what the *Times* needs today is some wild-eyed genius of an entrepreneur.

The Sulzbergers embody one of the newsroom's most cherished myths: Journalism sells. Arthur says as much at every opportunity, and clearly believes this to his core. It encapsulates his understanding of his inheritance and of himself. But as a general principle, it simply isn't true. Rather: *Advertising sells, journalism costs.* Good journalism costs more today than ever, while ads have plummeted, particularly in print media. This is killing the *Times,* and every other decent newspaper in America. Arthur has manfully tied himself to the wheel, doggedly investing in quality reporting and editing even as his company loses more and more money. Few investors or analysts consider this to be sound business practice.

Many people are rooting for Arthur Sulzberger, and many people like him. It can be hard to persuade those who know him to talk candidly on the record. For this story, Arthur stuck by his decision to get out of the business of being interviewed, and he also declined to permit his employees to talk to me. Nevertheless, many did. I interviewed dozens of current and former *Times* reporters, editors, and business managers, as well as industry analysts, academics, and editors and publishers at rival newspapers. Nearly every one of them hopes that Arthur will succeed. Few expect that he can.

Only two years ago the New York Times Company moved into a new skyscraper on Eighth Avenue designed by Renzo Piano. Its façade rises into the clouds like an Olympian column of gray type. Whether owing to hubris or sheer distraction, the erection of a new headquarters often seems to spell trouble for corporations, and many had questioned the wisdom of this investment. The new *Times* building has now been sold, one more measure to relieve the company's mounting debt. Eyeing the handsome grove of birch trees planted in its soaring atrium, one reporter told me, "We used to joke about how many trees died for a story. Now we ask, How many stories died for those trees?"

America is not kind to the heir. He is a stereotypical figure in our literature, and not an appealing one at that. He tends to be depicted as weak, pampered, flawed, a diluted strain of the hardy founding stock. America celebrates the self-made. Unless an heir veers sharply from his father's path, he is not taken seriously. Even in middle age he seems costumed, a pretender draped in oversize clothes, a boy who has raided his father's closet. The depiction may be unfair, but it is what it is.

Arthur Ochs Sulzberger Jr. is fair-skinned with small, deep-set light-brown eyes. He has a high forehead with a steepening widow's peak, his crown topped with a buoyant crop of wavy hair, now turning to gray. He is a slight man who keeps himself fit, working out early in the morning most days of the week. He has a wide mouth that curls up at the edges, and when he grins he is slightly buck-toothed, which adds to an impression, unfortunate for a man in his position, of puerility. He is a lifelong New Yorker, but there is no trace whatsoever of region or ethnicity in his speech. When he chooses to be, Arthur is a fluent, eager, even urgent talker, someone who listens impatiently and who impulsively interrupts, often with a stab at humor. He has delicate hands with long fingers, which he uses freely and expressively in conversation. He is long-winded and, in keeping with a tendency toward affectation, is fussily articulate, like a bright freshman eager to impress, speaking in complex, carefully enunciated sentences sprinkled with expressions ordinarily found only on the page, such as "that is" and "i.e." and "in large measure," or archaisms like "to a fare-thee-well." He exaggerates. He works hard, endearingly, to put others at ease, even with those who in his presence are not even slightly intimidated or uncomfortable.

His witticisms are hit-and-miss, and can be awkward and inadvertently revealing. "Some character traits are too deep in the mold to alter," says one longtime associate. Arthur has the clever adolescent's habit of hiding behind a barb, a stinging comment hastily disavowed as a joke. Some find him genuinely funny. Others, particularly those outside his immediate circle, read arrogance—the witty king, after all, knows that his audience feels compelled to laugh. His humor can also be clubby. He will adopt, for instance, a pet expression that becomes an in-joke, which he will then deploy repeatedly. One of these is "W.S.L.," which stands for "We Suck Less," a self-deprecatory boast, which Arthur will use in discussions of the industry's woes as a reminder to those in the know that, for all its travails and failings, his newspaper remains, after all, *The New York Times.*

While clearly smart, Arthur is not especially intellectual. For what it's worth, he is a *Star Trek* fan. His mind wanders, particularly when pressed to concentrate on complicated business matters. Diane Baker, a blunt former investment banker who served for a time as the chief financial officer of the New York Times Company, has described him as having the personality of "a twenty-four-year-old geek." She did not long survive Arthur's ascension to the chairman's office. His 30-year marriage has reportedly foundered over a relationship Arthur had with a woman named Helen Ward, from Aspen, Colorado, whom he met on a group excursion to Peru. Since separating from Gail, he has been living alone and has not been involved with Ward or anyone else. Perturbations on the home front are also a family tradition. (Arthur's grandfather Arthur Hays Sulzberger was always, as the saying goes, a tough hound to keep on the porch. His father, Arthur Ochs Sulzberger, paid child support for 16 years to a newspaper-staff member who bore a child she claimed was his—this according to Susan E. Tifft and Alex S. Jones in *The Trust,* a history of the *Times.*) Arthur is provincial. Asked once if he had seen a story on the front page of that day's *Post,* he looked confused until it was explained that the item had appeared in *The Washington Post.* He said, "I only read the *Times, The Wall Street Journal,* and the *New York Post.*" He sometimes takes the bus or subway to work, and for many years jogged in Central Park. Recently his knees have started to bother him, so he now prefers exercising on an elliptical trainer. He also takes Pilates classes and can be evangelical about them, telling friends the practice wards off arthritis, which has begun to worry him. But he is not a complete health nut. He still enjoys unwinding with a cigar and a martini. He still goes on motorcycle treks with his cousin Dan Cohen and other friends. He is drawn to feats of personal daring, and is an avid rock climber, a vestige of his enthusiasm for Outward Bound. He has little interest in sports, particularly team sports, and dismissed as silly the effort to lure the Olympic Games to New York City, which included plans for a sports stadium in Manhattan. In a presentation at the *Times* building, Arthur greeted the scheme's promoters with cutting sarcasm, even though the paper's editorial board supported it.

He has been publisher for 17 years now, and chairman of the board for 12, yet no weight seems to adhere to him. What Arthur's manner does suggest is a hyper-self-awareness: he is one of those people who seem condemned to stand apart from themselves, watching. Arthur is theatrical. It shows in his public speeches, which can be impressive. He has a nice sense of comic timing, and enjoys attention and applause. This is a man who, after spending a few months living in London in his youth, returned home wearing wire-rimmed glasses and a broad-brimmed hat and carrying a cane. He long ago abandoned the Carnaby Street affectations, but the basic impulse for showmanship is still there, manifested in a very calculated ease. He prowls the *Times* building in his stocking feet, and will pounce on colleagues as they happen by his 16th-floor office, urging them to step in and visit, saying conspiratorially, "Let me show you something cool." His corner office in the new building is spare and sunny and much smaller and less imposing than his old one, the one his father had. The old office was musty and formal, with rich wooden bookcases and heavily sculpted furniture upholstered in leather. It was the *Citizen Kane* version of the publisher's lair. The new office has windows that stretch from floor to ceiling. On his desk is a Steuben crystal sculpture of a gold-handled Excalibur embedded in stone, a gift from his sisters when he was named publisher—the third Arthur in the line.

The plainer office is an expression of Arthur's desire to lessen the distance between himself and those he employs. He deliberately placed his office in the center of the floors inhabited by the *Times* in the new building. At his most romantically self-effacing, he speaks of the *Times* in the language of family. In an hour-long interview with Charlie Rose in 2001, to mark the newspaper's anniversary, he talked about how fortunate his own family was to have been "adopted" by the extraordinary talents who create the newspaper. He frets when people on his staff are unhappy, and he looks out for his friends, or tries to. When one of his old reporter pals was transferred and asked the *Times* to cover the loss on the sale of a residence, Arthur wanted to do it. When his business managers balked, complaining about the precedent it would set, he backed down, annoyed, and sent them to inform the reporter—"You handle it," he said. To a degree some of his top staff consider unwise, he tends to promote people based not on a cold-eyed assessment of their talent but on how comfortable he feels around them—on how much *fun* they are. As Arthur was deciding between Howell Raines and Bill Keller for the executive-editorship of the newspaper, in 2001, the reserved Keller kept a professional distance. The gregarious Raines sought to sweep Arthur off his feet. "I remember seeing them at the 2000 Democratic convention, in Los Angeles," said an editor at another newspaper. "Joe Lelyveld [then the *Times's* executive editor] was there. He was running the paper. But what everyone noticed most was how Howell Raines seemed glued to Arthur. It was evident that Howell was seducing Arthur, insinuating himself. Howell is a brilliant journalist, and he exudes confidence. You could watch him making this big impression on Arthur." Raines became the executive editor.

The defining fact of Arthur Sulzberger's life is his birth. His father, Arthur Ochs Sulzberger (known as "Punch"); his grandfather Arthur Hays Sulzberger; his uncle Orvil Dryfoos; and his great-grandfather Adolph Ochs were publishers and chairmen of the *Times*. Arthur was the firstborn male heir in a line that stretches back to 1896, when Adolph Ochs acquired the newspaper. In an era when merit generally counts for more than genes, Arthur is ill at ease about his medieval path to power, so he handles it the way he handles many things that make him uncomfortable. He jokes about it.

Near the end of his interview with Arthur, Charlie Rose scanned the long history of family ownership and success, and asked, "Does this make you believe in nepotism?" "To hell with nepotism!" said Arthur, smiling. "I'm a believer in primogeniture!" He was kidding . . . and he wasn't. He does in fact have two sisters with exactly the same genetic link to old Adolph, and while there is much discussion of Arthur's son eventually succeeding him, there is no such speculation about his daughter. On a stage before a big audience at the University of California, Berkeley, in 2002, Arthur was asked a question on the subject by his host, Orville Schell, then the dean of Berkeley's Graduate School of Journalism. Earlier, Arthur had joked with Schell about how he had achieved his position in the same way as Kim Jong Il, the North Korean dictator, who had succeeded his dictator father, Kim Il Sung.

Schell: "You said the difference was that they [the Kim dynasty] were only two generations, and your family was four."

"I don't like where this is going one damn bit!," Arthur protested comically, to much laughter. "And if you don't be a little more careful, I may nuke you!"

"My question is," Schell persisted, "really, I mean, *The New York Times* is governed and held in a very unique way in corporate America. It is a family company, and the family, I assume, decides who the successor is in a way that isn't either particularly corporate or democratic. Tell us a little bit about that, and what effect you think it has on how this great paper can comport itself in the world."

Arthur sighed.

"There's a lot behind that question," he said. "First of all, just to get it on the record, the family did go for talent." More laughter.

But Arthur wasn't just born to his position—the story is more complicated. He may have been the firstborn son in the line of succession, but he also staked his claim to the crown deliberately and dramatically, when he was only 14 years old. His mother, Barbara Grant, and Punch Sulzberger divorced when Arthur was just five. He lived throughout his early childhood on the Upper East Side with his mother and her new husband, David Christy, a warm and supportive stepfather. Punch is nominally Jewish, although not at all religious, while his son was raised Episcopalian. Arthur senior and Arthur junior were not close: Punch was generally aloof, even when Arthur was around. Yet, understanding what his famous name meant, and who his distant father actually was in the world, he packed up his things and moved himself the half-mile to his father's home on Fifth Avenue, to live with Punch and his stepmother and their daughters. He was not pulled by any strong emotional connection. It seemed more like a career move. His biological father and his stepmother were wealthy, socially connected, and powerful; his biological mother and his stepfather were not.

Arthur opted for privilege and opportunity. That his stepmother, Carol Sulzberger, despised Arthur—she would stick out her tongue at pictures of him—did not seem to matter. He was Arthur Ochs Sulzberger *Jr.*, and showing up on his father's doorstep was a way of asserting, consciously or not, that when Punch changed wives he had not washed his hands of an obligation to his son. While the inheritance was his by birth, it was also very much Arthur's choice.

Some heirs flee the burdens and expectations of family, determined to make their own way. Arthur chose to be defined by his name, and his father. When he went off to summer camp in 1966, the year he moved in with Punch, Arthur took his father's old portable typewriter case with him. It was stamped, "A. O. Sulzberger, *The New York Times*." This at a moment when many members of Arthur's generation were questioning received wisdom in all its forms, turning their backs on conventional careers, disdaining not just their parents but the entire Establishment. Arthur, too, would grow his bushy hair long, try drugs, demonstrate against the Vietnam War, and embrace the style and rhetoric of the 60s. He has said that he worked on his high-school newspaper but not his college paper, at Tufts, because "we had a war to stop." But even then Arthur, draped in Punch's old (and newly fashionable) Marine Corps fatigue jacket, was just acting out the editorial policy of the newspaper he planned someday to run. Appearances to the contrary, he was the exact opposite of a rebel.

Arthur has spent a lifetime faithfully placing his feet in his father's footsteps. Like Punch, he served a long apprenticeship on his inevitable rise. Perhaps "inevitable" is too strong a word. He began as a reporter for the *The Raleigh Times*, then moved on to the London bureau of the Associated Press. He was a hard worker and a cheerful colleague, and he produced competent if unspectacular work. His friend Steve Weisman, a former *Times* reporter (and now the editorial director for the Peterson Institute for International Economics), asked him once—when they were both in their late 20s and working as reporters in the *Times*'s Washington bureau, where Arthur landed after the A.P.—if he was going to be publisher one day. "Well, there's always the fuckup factor," said Arthur, which Weisman took to mean that, barring a serious misstep, Arthur's path was assured.

In *The Kingdom and the Power*, Gay Talese described the similar path taken by Arthur senior. He and Punch were roughly contemporaries. (Punch was six years older.) They both started working at the newspaper at about the same time, Punch having gone to college only after serving in the Marines. Talese, the son of a tailor, considered himself fortunate when he landed a job as copyboy at the *Times*, after distinguishing himself as a college journalist and a columnist for his hometown *Ocean City* (New Jersey) *Sentinel-Ledger*. He went on, one finely crafted story after another, to earn distinction as the best writer at the *Times*. What he wrote about Punch's apprenticeship could have been written about Arthur's:

> He would learn a good deal during the next few years, but he would never become a top reporter, lacking qualities that are essential and rarely cultivated by such men as himself, the properly reared sons of the rich. Prying into other people's affairs, chasing after information, waiting outside the doors of private meetings for official statements is no life for the scion of a newspaper-owning family. It is undignified, too alien to a refined upbringing. The son of a newspaper owner may indulge in reporting for a while, regarding it as part of his management training, a brief fling with romanticism, but he is not naturally drawn to it.

There is one other essential trait shared by ambitious reporters that the Sulzbergers, father and son, would never know: desperation. Reporting is a highly competitive craft where one's work is on display, sometimes on a daily basis. There is no faking it—not for long, anyway. When Arthur started working in Raleigh, the young men and women competing furiously for plum beats and a front-page showcase could only dream of someday working at *The New York Times*. For the ambitious, those early years at small newspapers were a scramble to get noticed, to shine brightly enough to catch the eye first of the local editors, then of those at bigger papers, and then on up the ladder to editors at the top newsrooms across the country. It was a fierce winnowing. Little wonder that his co-workers in those years found Arthur a man without an edge. He was charming, eager, cheerful, and ever willing to take on the most mundane assignments. He wore a leather jacket and roared to work on a motorcycle. He was having a ball. And why not? He wasn't competing; he was paying his dues. He didn't need front-page stories. He didn't need sources, a scoop, or any particular narrative flair to get ahead. It was easy to be Arthur. And it was smart to befriend Arthur.

His career progressed in prodigious and unearned leaps. He went from the Washington bureau, where he was close friends with Steve Rattner, Judith Miller, and a handful of other reporters, to New York, where he worked briefly as a very young assistant editor on the Metro desk, before moving on to stints in the advertising-and-production side of the paper, becoming deputy publisher in 1987. People liked Arthur everywhere he went, and he worked at being liked. But he was not deeply respected. Just as Arthur would never pass as an authentic reporter to those who have spent their lives in newsrooms, his brief apprenticeships in advertising, production, and various other departments were seen for exactly what they were: way stations on the road to publisher. The *Times*'s business managers do not enjoy the same status in their fields as the paper's top reporters and editors do among journalists. Newspapers do not attract top-tier business and financial talent, because it would be unseemly to pay those on the business side disproportionately more than the most senior editors, and the salary scale for even the highest-paid editors is a fraction of that for high-level C.E.O.'s and bankers. Yet even the mid-level talent around Arthur does not regard him as a peer, much less a suitable leader. He is accepted, of course. The family does own the newspaper, and there appears to be a consensus that—as one veteran *Times* man, no longer at the newspaper, told me—if a family member has to run the newspaper, Arthur is "the Sulzberger you would want."

There was an attempt by the business side of the Times Company to thwart his final ascent. On January 22, 1996, a front-page article in *The Wall Street Journal* by Patrick M. Reilly suggested that Arthur, then the *Times*'s publisher, might not succeed his father as the company's chairman, and that the company was considering looking outside the family for the next generation of leadership. One or another Sulzberger patriarch had held both jobs for a century, but Reilly's story indicated that the tradition could very well come to an end. It portrayed Arthur as someone who "sees himself as both a journalist and a businessman," but who in fact was fully neither. The story was based on highly placed but anonymous sources inside the building, and it quoted Judith Sulzberger, Arthur's aunt and a member of the board of directors, as saying that the job "might go to anyone."

Penny Muse Abernathy, who worked closely with Arthur on the business side of the *Times* before leaving for Harvard, *The Wall Street Journal*, and now a professorship at the University of North Carolina, remembers walking into Arthur's office at around 7:30 A.M. the day the article came out. He was crestfallen. "What are you going to do about that story?" she asked him. "I don't know," he said, and then made an attempt at gallows humor, suggesting that he might need to try an entirely new line of work. As they were speaking, Punch called. "Dad, can I come see you?" Arthur asked. It was the first time Abernathy had ever heard Arthur call his father "Dad." Around the office, he always referred to him as "the chairman."

The effort to end-run the dynasty proved to be short-lived. Many at the paper speculated that the company president, Lance Primis, was behind the *Journal* story. It had identified Primis as "a top prospect" for the chairmanship, and the article was interpreted as the opening salvo in a putsch—a play by the company's professional managers to wrest control of the business side from the amateurs. Family won. Arthur formed an alliance with Russ Lewis, then president of the newspaper, who would be named company C.E.O. when Punch retired and handed the top post to his son. Primis was invited to leave.

Here, in a nutshell, in the words of a veteran *Times* staffer, is what is supposedly wrong with Arthur: "He has no rays"—rays, as in the lines cartoonists draw around a character to suggest radiance, or power. In the comics trade these lines are called "emanata." The emanata deficit is a standard insider lament about Arthur, although most *Times* people need a few more words to make the point.

No one can plumb another's depths. Arthur certainly seems clever enough, but try as he might, he fails to impress. He comes off as a lightweight, as someone slightly out of his depth, whose dogged sincerity elicits not admiration so much as pity. While no one blames him for what is clearly a crisis afflicting all newspapers, he has made a series of poor business moves that now follow him like the tail of a kite. He has doubled-down on print over the last two decades, most notably with his own newspaper but also spending more than a billion dollars to buy *The Boston Globe* and the *International Herald Tribune*. These purchases appear to have been historically mis-timed, rather like sinking your life savings into hot-air balloons long after the first excited reports from Kitty Hawk. Back when he had the money to do it, Arthur failed to adequately diversify the Times Company's holdings, stranding it in an ocean of debt with no flotation device—unlike, say, *The Washington Post,* which is being buoyed through this industry-wide depression by the highly profitable Kaplan Inc., an education-services company that provides test-preparation classes and online instruction. (The *Post*'s diverse investments were made under a board that included Warren Buffett and like-minded business gurus.) Except for his admirable Web site, Arthur has failed to expand the *Times* effectively into other media. Back in 2000 he announced that television was "our next great frontier," but his one timid step in that direction, a partnership with the Discovery Channel to produce news-related documentaries, was halfhearted (and abbreviated). The *Times* still lacks a presence in television. Arthur has not missed the boat entirely with digital start-ups—his decision to buy the online information site About.com, which provides assisted Internet searching, has paid dividends—but he passed up (along with a lot of other people) early opportunities to invest in the great search engines, such as Google, which today is sucking ad revenue from the paper while at the same time giving away its content. Arthur's oft repeated assertion that he is "platform agnostic"— that is, doesn't care what medium delivers the *Times,* and is open to all of them—is both misguided and revealing. It sounds fancy and daring and forward-thinking but betrays a deep misunderstanding of the forces at play.

There are other knocks on his leadership. His choice for executive editor, Howell Raines, played favorites in the newsroom, overlooked shoddy journalism, and so alienated his reporters and editors that they forced Arthur to dump him. So goes one version of the story. Not everyone thinks jettisoning Raines was the right thing to do. Raines was shaking things up, presumably with Arthur's blessing, and when you shake things up you upset the rank and file. As one former *Times* man puts it, "If the sheriff of Nottingham gets mugged on his way through Sherwood Forest, and can't do anything about it, then the thieves are running the forest." Whichever take on Raines you prefer, Arthur's reversal looks bad. It suggests either poor judgment or a lack of conviction.

He is, or was, big on managerial gimmickry. There is the now infamous moment, at the height of the in-house furor over the serial fabulist Jayson Blair, when Arthur tried to break the ice before a large audience of restive reporters and editors by pulling a toy stuffed moose out of a bag, a favorite device of his meant to facilitate candid discussion—the moose was supposed to represent the core issues that no one dared address. Newsmen, it should be noted, are rarely shy about expressing their opinions, and on this occasion the crowd was about as reserved as a lynch mob. The moose was so silly and so unnecessary, and reflected something so tone-deaf, that Arthur has yet to live it down. One reason he hasn't is that it was of a piece with other behavior. *Times* veterans remember with pained expressions the "bonding games" Arthur forced them to play at company retreats in the late 1990s, and the time and effort he demanded they lavish on crafting "mission statements" for the newspaper and the company. "We have it written down and we carry it with us," Arthur told Charlie Rose in 2001. He handed over the mission statements on-camera with a flourish, and when asked later about his proudest achievement came back to this "defining vision of what we are and where we have to go." The mission statements are now, in the words of one former editor, "stuffed in desk drawers throughout the building."

In his eagerness to champion First Amendment rights he blundered into a losing and ultimately embarrassing fight over his old friend Judith Miller, who went to jail to protect a source, former Cheney chief of staff Lewis "Scooter" Libby, before striking a deal with prosecutors. The fight was widely regarded as a poor one to make into a First Amendment test case, but that didn't stop Arthur from charging to Miller's defense. The "Free Judy" buttons he distributed made for a ludicrous contrast to his father's storied battle over the Pentagon Papers. An explanatory *mea culpa* about the Miller case, written by the executive editor, Bill Keller, suggested that Miller had had an "entanglement" with Libby, which some read as a suggestion that she was sleeping with him. Keller, who had succeeded Raines in the wake of the Jayson Blair affair, quickly retreated from his retreat. The episode illustrated a broader perception: no adult was in charge. Where Arthur senior had been seen as stolid and serious, Arthur junior appeared callow. One of those involved in the Miller episode describes Arthur's behavior throughout as "childish." Another word you hear is "goofy."

The conventional wisdom about Arthur can be turned on its head. His goofiness might more kindly be interpreted as a winning informality, a healthy antidote to the stuffy, hidebound ways during executive editor Abe Rosenthal's long reign. So, too, his efforts to unbend and humanize the newsroom's tyrants, and get them to see the company's business managers not as enemies but as partners. No wonder they grumbled! Arthur's fixation on newsprint evidences a devotion to quality journalism amid the growing din of propaganda and digital frivolity; after all, most of the real reporting done in America is still done by newspapers. His eagerness to defend reporters' freedoms stems from noble instincts, and demonstrates that, for Arthur, the paper's mission takes priority over its profits. His enthusiastic defense of Judith Miller may have backfired, but the same impulse led Arthur to defy a strongly worded request from the Bush administration—delivered in person at the White House—not to print stories that revealed legally dubious domestic spying, stories that would win a Pulitzer Prize in 2006. Arthur's "political correctness" shows an admirable sensitivity to the rights of women and minorities in an institution where both were long held down or shut out. And might his willingness to back down and fire Raines be seen as a sign not of pusillanimity but of humility and flexibility?

"Sure, Arthur has made his share of mistakes. But they get recycled all the time, and he rarely gets the credit he deserves for what he's done right," says his longtime friend Peter Osnos, a former *Washington Post* reporter and the founder of the publishing house PublicAffairs. "You can't judge him solely on the basis of success, because no one in the business can claim success in the current situation. You do have to give him credit for good judgment in anticipating the role of the Internet and his deep commitment to the values of the institution. Arthur was talking about the impact of the Internet on newspapers earlier than anyone else in our industry, and the records show that. So you have this strange kind of thing where you have the vision and you have insight, but you don't get the business side of it right—but literally, without exception, no one has. Arthur has, however, re-invented the newspaper on several levels and positioned it for the future."

Nine years ago, in an entirely different economic climate, the industry magazine *Editor & Publisher* named Arthur Sulzberger Jr. Publisher of the Year, and he was hailed as "brilliant" and "visionary." His investments in satellite printing had pushed the national edition of the *Times* to unprecedented success, "achieving a 20 percent advertising revenue growth . . . largely due to national and help-wanted business going gangbusters." The mistakes he has made with investments and in adapting to new technology are the same mistakes made by every newspaper in America. Most journalists consider Sam Zell, the billionaire who bought the Tribune Company, to be a Neanderthal for his wholesale trashing of the once proud *Chicago Tribune* and *Los Angeles Times,* and regard Gary Pruitt, chairman of the McClatchy chain, as a well-mannered and passionate defender of journalistic excellence. Yet both are staring at bankruptcy. "Who has gotten it right?" asks one industry analyst. "Arthur has made some bad decisions, but so has everyone else in the business. Nobody has figured out what to do."

In short, you can choose whichever take on Arthur you prefer. As an old football coach once told me, "Write whatever you want: if I win, you can't hurt me, and if I lose, you can't help me." The publisher's reputation shifts with the wind, and today journalism is leaning into an exceedingly ill wind.

Arthur is still often referred to as "Young Arthur," even though he is old enough to be a grandfather, or by the despised nickname that puns on his father's, "Pinch." Even as his locks gray and he nears almost two decades as publisher, he remains the prince-in-waiting who once haunted the newsroom in his socks, his trousers held up by colorful suspenders, peering in a harmless but nevertheless insufferably proprietary way over the shoulders of hard-boiled reporters on deadline. "I have heard him many times refer back to 'when I was a reporter,'" says one former *Times* executive, theatrically cringing. "He'll just do it as a throwaway—'When I was a reporter.' I will say this to him one day: *Don't say that. You know what? You don't have to say that. Do you think it's giving you more credibility with journalists? It actually gives you less.*" On the business side, according to one former associate, he was viewed with contempt. "They saw him as insubstantial, as flighty, as glib, and as not caring about them as much as he cared about journalists."

But Arthur has one big thing going for him, particularly with the reporters and editors who are the real stars in the *Times* building. Arthur is motivated, as he himself says, not by wealth but by *value*. He believes, to be sure, that wealth follows from value, but you can see, even as he says it, that the wealth part is not what drives him. Journalism drives him. The *Times*'s reputation and influence drive him. He is not just a newspaper publisher and a chairman of the board. He is Arthur Ochs Sulzberger Jr., and the pride he feels in that name doesn't have anything to do with how much is in his bank account. No matter what moves he makes, no matter what errors he commits, Arthur will remain every journalist's dream publisher. He has long protected the newsroom from predatory managers with their bean-counting priorities, and today he represents its best hope, reporters and editors would like to believe, of weathering the crisis without the soul-killing budget cuts that turn great newspapers into little more than supermarket circulars. The same people who roll their eyes when they hear him wax nostalgic about his years in the newsroom pray for him daily, because, like them, he completely buys the myth: Journalism sells.

"This is ridiculous," says a former business-side executive at the *Times*. "It flies in the face of logic and reason, this belief that if your news product is so good and so comprehensive the normal rules of business are suspended. Think about it. Think about the inanity of saying that you survived by putting in more news and cutting ads."

Arthur repeated this belief proudly in his interview with Rose, describing how Adolph Ochs responded to the lean years after he purchased the paper by expanding its news hole—"We're going to give our readers more! That's gutsy!"—and how his grandfather Arthur Hays Sulzberger did something similar during World War II, when newsprint was being rationed: "Major decision, major gutsy decision from him there. Perhaps the critical decision of his time . . . whether to continue to print ads—revenue, money, profit—or to say, No, we're going to add more news. He went to news, the *Herald Tribune* went to ads, and the rest was just a matter of time. By the time the war ended the *Times* had taken such a huge leadership that it was just a matter of time before the *Herald Tribune* was to fold."

This story is false. It is dismissed even in *The Trust*, a mostly glowing account of the newspaper and the family written with the full cooperation of the Sulzbergers, including Arthur, and published more than a year before he spoke those words to Rose. The authors, Susan E. Tifft and Alex S. Jones, thoroughly debunked the legend.

"One of the enduring myths about *The New York Times* is that it nobly sacrificed profits from revenue-generating ads during World War II in order to print more news," wrote Tifft and Jones. "But the truth is somewhat more complicated." It seems that the *Times* actually slashed its news hole in this period "far more severely than it cut the space devoted to ads." With newsprint rationed, and with more ads and news than he could fit, Sulzberger increased space for ads and decreased space for news. In fact, he devoted the majority of the newspaper's space to ads, and earned more revenue than he had since 1931. Ad revenue "had actually increased during the period, from $13 million to $15 million, while the amount of money spent on news had slumped slightly from $3.9 million to $3.7 million," Tifft and Jones wrote.

Arthur's grandfather did make one important change during this period, but it was more of a shrewd business move than a principled stand for journalism. While the rival *Herald Tribune* sat on its swollen profits during the war, Sulzberger used his profits to print not more news but more newspapers, greatly expanding the *Times*'s reach. That strategy left the *Times* with a larger circulation than the *Herald Tribune* after the war. The *Times* was better positioned to survive. The lesson of the story is not that investing in news pays but that a clever business strategy adapts to a changing market.

Arthur likes his own version of the story better. He once told interviewers that the *Times* was his "religion": "That's what I believe in, and it's a hell of a thing to hold on to." Reason has no purchase on belief. Nor does basic business theory.

American journalism is in a period of terror. The invention of the Internet has caused a fundamental shift not just in the platform for information—screen as opposed to paper—but in the way people seek information. In evolutionary terms, it's a sudden drastic change of climate. One age passes and a new one begins. Species that survive the transition are generally not the kings of the old era. The world they fit so perfectly is no more. They are big and slow, wedded to the old ways, ripe for extinction.

When Arthur became chairman of the Times Company, in 1997, he dragged his top people to retreats in leafy locations, there to learn better cooperation and to think big thoughts. He was less worried about adapting the *Times* to a new era than about making his company and newsroom a happier place to work. The underlying assumption was that there was nothing ahead but smooth seas. Many of the newsroom's hard-bitten veterans found these events revealing.

"We were having a retreat," David Jones, a former assistant managing editor, recalls. "It was a wonderful old inn, business-meeting place, in upstate New York. They were doing games as bonding experiences. One of the games they did was fly casting. And they put three big loops out on the lawn. One was close, one was farther out, and one was farthest. And the idea was to cast your lure and hit inside the loop. The farther away you cast, the more points you got." The risky way to play was to cast for the big scores; the safest way was to steadily accrue points by hitting the nearest loop.

"So we played this game," says Jones, "and when it was all over, I talked to the guy who worked there, who ran the game, and I said, What was your impression of us from the way we played? How do we compare with other groups? And he said—and they have business groups that come—he said, 'This is the most conservative group I have ever seen.'"

Arthur himself, despite his leftist politics and social liberalism, despite the lip service he pays to the need for change, is deeply conservative where the family business is concerned. This is not to say that he resists change. His nytimes.com is the most successful newspaper Web site in the country. It can claim an ever rising number of hits and, until the general economic slump of 2008–9, recorded steady growth in ad revenue. But none of this will save him, because at the core Arthur and the *Times* remain wedded to an archaic model of journalism.

For 10 years or more, Arthur's signature phrase about this seismic change in the news business, the one he repeats to show that he *gets* it, has been platform agnostic. "I am platform agnostic," he proclaims proudly, meaning that it matters nothing to him where his customers go for *New York Times* content: the newspaper's print version, television, radio, computer, cell phone, Kindle—whatever. The phrase itself reveals limited understanding. When the motion-picture camera was invented, many early filmmakers simply recorded stage plays, as if the camera's value was just to preserve the theatrical performance and enlarge its audience. To be sure, this alone was a significant change. But the true pioneers realized that the camera was more revolutionary than that. It freed them from the confines of a theater. Audiences could be transported anywhere. To tell stories with pictures, and then with sound, directors developed a whole new language, using lighting and camera angles, close-ups and panoramas, to heighten drama and suspense. They could make an audience laugh by speeding up the action, or make it cry or quake by slowing it down. In short, the motion-picture camera was an entirely new tool for storytelling. To be platform agnostic is the equivalent of recording stage plays.

"When I first heard Arthur talk about being platform agnostic, I knew he was trying to suggest that he was not stuck in a newspaper mind-set," says Tom Rosenstiel, director of the Pew Research Center's Project for Excellence in Journalism. "But I thought there were two problems with that language. One is, agnostics are people who don't—who aren't sure what they believe in. That's the first problem. And the second problem is, in practice, there is no such thing as being platform agnostic. You actually have to choose which platform you work on first, which one comes first. At the time that he was talking about this, what he really meant was: *Everything we put in the newspaper, we'll put online.* If you really want to move to the Internet in a serious way, you need to change the culture of a news organization and decide that the Internet is the primary new thing. Platform agnostic means that all the online companies are going to zoom past you, because they're going to exploit that technology while you're sitting there thinking, Well, we don't care which platform we put it on. You need to exploit the technology of each platform. You need to be, in fact, not platform agnostic but platform *orthodox.* So that expression, platform agnostic, always struck me as something he heard someplace, rather than something that he really grasps and understands."

Arthur's idea is to continue producing *The New York Times* the way it has always been produced, and then to offer a digital edition of the product, with video, images, interactive graphics, blogs, and so on. That's what nytimes.com does superbly. According to Nielsen, it attracts more than 20 million unique visitors a month. Imagine a newspaper that was picked up by 20 million readers every month! If only a tiny fraction of that number came back and became subscribers, circulation would explode. But those users are not "picking up" the newspaper; many of them are just picking up individual stories. Nearly half of those who access nytimes.com to read a story come in, as it were, through a side door. They begin by plugging search terms into an engine such as Google, which spits out a long list of links to related sites. And in any case, they're not spending a lot of time with the newspaper: the average amount, says Nielsen, is 35 minutes per month. (The news is worse for other sites—only about 16 minutes per month for washingtonpost.com.) One of Arthur's hopes is that, once on the site, readers will linger, sampling the *Times*'s other superb offerings, but usage patterns suggest that this isn't happening.

Those who grew up using the Internet, which now includes a full generation of Americans, are expert browsers. It's not that they have short attention spans. If anything, many of them are more sophisticated and better informed than their parents. They are certainly more independent. Instead of absorbing the news and opinion packaged expertly by professional journalists, they search out only the information they want, and are less and less likely to devote themselves to one primary site, in part because it is less efficient, and in part because not doing so is liberating. The Internet has disaggregated the news. It eliminates the middleman—that is, it eliminates editors. At a newspaper, top editors meet several times a day to review the stories and photographs gathered from their own staff and wire services. They decide which are the most important or compelling, and then they prioritize and package them. When you buy a newspaper you are buying a carefully prepared meal. Inevitably stories and artwork are left off the plate for a great variety of reasons, all of them subjective—they are deemed less significant, less credible, less tasteful, less useful. Or maybe there just isn't enough room. The Internet replaces editors with an algorithm. Google is a search engine. It makes no value judgment about information unless you instruct it to. All of the stories and photos in the world are there, including billions of items that the reader never imagined wanting to see. It is unmediated. There is no adult supervision. And the kicker is: it's free.

Much more is at work here than a change of platform. Whether you think more is lost or gained depends upon which side of this evolutionary divide you fall on. For me, someone who spent most of his adult life working in a newsroom, someone who reads three newspapers every day, including the *Times*, the loss will be far greater. Newspapers enable serious journalism. They provide for the care and feeding of career reporters and editors. They strive to be fair, accurate, and objective. They are independent sources of credible, well-researched information. They are watchdogs for the public interest, an important part of the communal mind and memory of the nation. When an editor is replaced by an algorithm, all information is equal. Propaganda shares the platform with honest reporting, and the slickest, most attractive Web sites and blogs will be those sponsored by corporations, the government, or special interests, which can afford to pay for professional work.

Arthur's argument, or his hope, is that the quality of the *Times*'s brand will prevail, that quality independent journalism is so obviously valuable that serious readers will continue to seek it out. He has been offering the *Times* content for free because experience has shown that subscriber-only stories leak—they are copied and e-mailed and rapidly proliferate for free anyway—and because Internet users, accustomed to getting information for free, are loath to pay for it. Do you remove yourself from the global conversation if you wall yourself off? Can you make enough money on subscriptions to survive? *The Wall Street Journal* has gone in this direction online, while offering some free content. The jury is still out. Arthur has continued to provide *Times* content for free, but is considering reversing direction. His brand remains the best in the business, but that hasn't solved his revenue problems. *Journalism costs.* The revenue from Internet advertising is still only about a tenth of total revenue. Even if those millions of brief hits on nytimes.com continue to swell, the *Times* itself may be in bankruptcy court long before the Web site generates enough revenue to replace what Arthur has lost.

In fairness, no one has the answer for newspapers. Some, such as former *Time* managing editor Walter Isaacson, Alan D. Mutter, a former newspaperman and Silicon Valley C.E.O., and Peter Osnos, of Public-Affairs, all of whom have experience as executives, are pushing some form of micro-payment. If the *Times*, in partnership with the big search-engine companies, got paid a few pennies for every person who clicks on a link to its content, it might replace the old business model for advertising. The price of accessing a single item would be so small that it would hardly be worth the trouble to hunt up a pirated version. Some have suggested that all of the major news providers should band together and withhold their content from the Internet until such a pricing agreement can be put in place. It seems clear that drastic action is required. One top editor at another newspaper put it this way: "Ask yourself this—if the Internet existed and newspapers didn't, would there be any reason to invent newspapers? No. That tells you all you need to know."

Some at the *Times* anticipated this tectonic shift years ago, but Arthur wasn't listening. Despite lip service about change, he presides over a slow-moving beast. Diane Baker, who was regarded as an energetic and forceful outsider, ran up against this in her years as C.F.O. When she took the job, in 1995, she was shocked to discover that the company was still doing all its accounting by hand. "They literally did not have the ability to produce spreadsheets," she says. "They had not invested in the software you need to analyze data. It is a company run by journalists. The Sulzbergers are journalists at their core, not businessmen."

Her biggest disappointment came when she crafted a potentially lucrative partnership with Amazon.com, already the biggest bookseller on the Internet. The *Times* would link all the titles reviewed in the paper's prestigious Sunday Book Review section, ordinarily a money drain, to the online bookseller and receive a percentage on every book sold. "We could have made the Book Review into a big source of revenue," she recalls. Baker knew that Amazon.com planned to eventually sell everything under the sun, to become the first digital supermarket. Not only would the deal have produced revenue from book sales, it would also have cemented a partnership with a tremendous future. She envisioned the newspaper as a virtual merchandising machine. Instead of the old carpet-bombing model of advertising, it would in effect target ads to readers of specific stories. "You know what they said?," Baker recalls. "They said, We can't do it, because Barnes & Noble is a big advertiser."

Toward the end of his tenure as executive editor, Max Frankel was asked to think about the impact of computers on the news business. This was back in the mid-1990s, when the *Times*'s national edition was taking off and most Americans were embarking on their first hesitant drives on the "information superhighway." For the *Times* there was money to maneuver with, and to invest, and a chance to adapt to the new age. Frankel wrote two memos, which he no longer has, but whose content he remembers clearly. In the first memo he argued that, because computers were so good at generating lists, and cross-referencing them, classified ads in newspapers were doomed. He suggested that the *Times* set up a computer system to allow buyers and sellers to deal with each other directly online— "It was essentially Craigslist," Frankel jokes. "I should have started it up!" Craigslist was created in 1995 and today averages billions of page hits per month, with reported annual revenues in excess of $80 million. It is a major factor in the decline of newspaper ad revenue.

"The second idea was much more important, and came a little later," Frankel says. "I wrote that one big coming threat posed by the computer was disaggregation: the Internet disaggregates the hunt for information. The need for information would survive the advent of the digital era, but the package offered by *The New York Times* might not. So how do you protect the package? What was so great about *The New York Times* was not that we offered the best coverage in any particular field but that we were very good in so many. It was the totality of the newspaper that was a marvel, not any of its particulars. The Web threatened to break that up. One way to weather this, which I suggested, was that we needed to pick the fields in which to be pre-eminent. If you want to have the best sports package, then start hiring the staff and make yourself the best go-to place for sports information. If it is business, or politics—whatever—pick one and make yourself the best, or make a strategic alliance." This is the approach taken by ESPN.com, by Bloomberg.com, IMDB.com, Weather.com, and a multitude of others. Any one of dozens of sites specializing in, say, politics or the arts could have been taken over and built up around the *Times*'s expert staff. It could still happen. *The Washington Post* is increasingly staking out the national government as its field, but an even more immediate threat to the *Times* is coming from downtown. Rupert Murdoch's *Wall Street Journal* already has a larger national circulation than the *Times*, and its rapacious new owner is vigorously competing on new fronts. Both newspapers are losing revenue in the current downturn, but the *Journal* may be in a better position for the long term. It has a smaller staff, and a clearly specialized arena with deep importance and broad appeal—business and finance. It has clearly dominated coverage of the ongoing economic crisis, with perceptive stories that are more knowingly reported, more analytical, and consistently better written. Online, the *Journal*'s editorial matter is largely password-protected, which means its readers are already paying for content, and it has been steadily improving its coverage of culture, sports, and lifestyle, and in its weekend edition featuring original essays by acclaimed writers and thinkers. And while the *Times* is busy throwing assets overboard to stay afloat, the *Journal* is attached to Murdoch's international empire, News Corp. Arthur aspires to be the patron saint of journalism, but the smart money may be on the pirate. The kind of specialization Frankel forecast is also driving most smaller newspapers, which are aggressively focusing coverage on their own communities, where they have exclusive content. Many see this as the only strategy that will enable them to survive.

The retired executive editor says that he sent both of his memos up the chain of command—as he puts it, "off into the ether." He did not hear a word from Arthur or anyone else about them.

Arthur Sulzberger can be a loyal and thoughtful friend, someone who will surprise a distant or old acquaintance with a small note of congratulation or commiseration, a gesture out of the blue that is felt and remembered. He is sincere and determined. He is, by all accounts, a doting and involved father. He did not have to work at all, yet he has always worked hard. "He is kind, decent, and good," says his longtime friend Steve Rattner. "In everything he does, he means well." His convictions about journalism are above reproach, and he cultivates his journalistic values in the ever expanding Sulzberger clan. In speaking with many who know him well, I discovered a near-universal desire to *protect* Arthur. "It's funny. There's something about him that makes you want to—it's almost like this maternal instinct kicks in," says Vivian Schiller, who was an executive at the *Times* before becoming president of NPR. Part of the desire to protect Arthur stems from his role at the head of a great newspaper in hard times. Part of it is loyalty to the Sulzberger family. But beyond all of this is fear—not just that Arthur will be hurt but that he will *fail*.

It is sometimes true that a man's greatest strength is also his greatest weakness. Soon after Robert J. Rosenthal was named managing editor of the *San Francisco Chronicle,* in 2002, he ran into Arthur at a conference on the West Coast. Arthur congratulated Rosenthal, who had started his career as a copyboy at the *Times,* and when they shared a car ride Arthur talked about how different their challenges were. "Yours is to turn the ship around," he said. "Mine is to keep the *Times* on course."

He still might—though in fact staying on course *means* turning the ship around. If he makes the right moves in the next few years, he may yet be able to ride his inheritance into the digital age. If he pulls that off, the achievement will outstrip those of his revered ancestors. It would be something more akin to the feats attributed to the original Arthur, the one who pulled Excalibur from the stone. But precisely because he is who he is, Arthur may be the last person in the world with the answers. The more likely outcome is that he will lose the *Times* to someone with deep enough pockets to carry the enterprise at a loss until circumstances sort themselves out—a rich individual, or a rich corporation, or some rich philanthropic institution. In recent years there have been persistent reports of Rupert Murdoch's interest in the *Times,* if only because he has historically lusted after prestige broadsheets. Michael Wolff, who wrote a biography of the Australian billionaire, reported in these pages last year that Murdoch had entertained the idea of a merger with his *Wall Street Journal*'s backroom operations and "fantasize[d] about the staff's quitting en masse as soon as he entered the sacred temple." (Given the recent layoffs at the *Journal,* and reports of the newspaper unit's drag on News Corp's bottom line, the acquisition of another sagging national newspaper might seem to be an irrational act—but that may be beside the point.) A business model to sustain a professional staff of reporters and editors could yet emerge in this new era, most likely a model devised by entrepreneurs with everything to gain and little to lose. This is a course that would save the institution, but would mean the end of the Sulzberger dynasty.

Arthur keeps a framed quotation by Winston Churchill in his office, a passage from a speech Churchill delivered during Britain's darkest hours: "Never never never give up." What Churchill actually said was "Never give in, never give in, never, never, never, never—in nothing, great or small, large or petty—never give in," and he added an important qualifier: "—except to convictions of honour and good sense." The bulldog approach worked for Churchill. But, for Arthur, as the prospect of success dims, good sense may dictate the very terms he resists. Serving the institution at some point may require selling it. Many of the newspaper's superb journalists have already left. Many others are actively eyeing second careers. It is hard to imagine what a second career would be for Arthur.

The inheritance has shaped Arthur Sulzberger's life, but as he turns 58 the age of the newspaper may be ending. For *The New York Times,* the greatest of them, it would mean the collapse of a dynasty and a national treasure. No one would feel the loss more than Arthur. For him, more than anyone, everything is at stake.

"What would he do?" asks Penny Abernathy. "What would he do? That's who he is."

· 15 ·

Marc Dreier's Crime of Destiny

By BRYAN BURROUGH

November 2009

The sun-drenched apartment, perched high in a Midtown Manhattan building looking down on the famed restaurant Le Cirque, is as luxurious as one would expect for space that cost $10.4 million. Lined with floor-to-ceiling glass, the living room features low divans wrapped in rich golden fabric. On the vast outdoor deck, as big as many apartments, the views stretch north and east, all the way across Long Island Sound toward Connecticut.

Yet even a casual visitor would notice that something is amiss. Dozens of bare hooks line the white walls; all the paintings are gone. Boxes of paperwork litter the floors. In the kitchen, the knives are missing. Bags of trash overflow. The dining-room table is strewn with containers of half-eaten Chinese food. In an adjacent nook, an older man slumps on a sofa watching CNN on a wall-mounted flat-screen television. Unpaid bills are piling up. As nice as this apartment once was, it now feels like a $10 million dorm room.

That's because it's a jail. Sort of. On the orders of a federal judge, its owner is living here under house arrest. That man watching CNN? He's a retired F.B.I. agent, one of several who rotate through all week long. One morning I arrive after 11. The owner, the man the security guards are watching, is just getting out of bed.

His name is Marc Dreier, he is 59 years old, and his life is over. A smallish, tightly wound man with red, stubbled cheeks and a silvery pompadour, Dreier was once a hotshot New York litigator with multi-millionaire clients. Then he stole $380 million from a bunch of hedge funds, got caught, and was arrested in Toronto under bizarre circumstances, having attempted to impersonate a Canadian pension-fund lawyer as part of a scheme to sell bogus securities to the big American hedge fund Fortress Investment Group. Now, as he wanders into the living room rubbing sleep from his eyes, Dreier is waiting for the judge to tell him just how many years he will spend in prison.

As he takes a seat across from me, he is wearing a loose-fitting black sweater and black jeans. And then, in the lifeless monotone of a death-row inmate, Marc Dreier begins to tell his story.

Maybe you remember the Dreier case. Or maybe you don't, given that just five days after Dreier's arrest, last December, federal authorities announced the discovery of the largest Ponzi scheme in U.S. history and the detention of its mastermind, Bernard Madoff; ironically, you can just glimpse a corner of Madoff's 53rd Street headquarters from Dreier's kitchen windows. Once the Madoff scandal hit, Dreier all but vanished from the headlines. If he's remembered today, it's probably for the details of his arrest, the sheer audacity of impersonating that Toronto attorney inside the man's own offices.

The Canadian incident turned out to be the tip of one very dirty iceberg. Re-arrested upon his return to La Guardia Airport, Dreier was revealed to have defrauded more than a dozen hedge funds, not counting the $45 million or so he stole from his own clients' escrow accounts. His 270-lawyer Park Avenue firm, Dreier L.L.P., imploded practically overnight. He was indicted, thrown in a jail cell, then allowed to spend several months under house arrest at his 58th Street apartment. In June, after our interviews, he pleaded guilty to all charges. A judge sentenced him to 20 years in prison. As of this writing, he is in the Metropolitan Correctional Center Chicago.

Dreier's downfall left half the New York bar scratching their heads.

Here was a lawyer who seemingly had every toy a middle-aged American man could want: not one but two waterfront homes in the Hamptons, condominiums in the Caribbean, a 120-foot yacht moored in St. Martin, a $200,000 Aston Martin, an oceanside condominium in Santa Monica, plus his own Los Angeles sushi restaurant, not to mention a collection of modern art that included works by Warhol, Hockney, Picasso, Matisse, and Lichtenstein.

There were all kinds of theories, though, most assuming that Dreier had resorted to theft to cover losses at his firm, or perhaps to support his outsize lifestyle. Some veteran trial attorneys, however, noting how addictive the adrenaline of courtroom combat can be, came up with a novel notion: Dreier, they speculated, did it out of boredom. "People caught in these situations—Madoff, whoever—they all share a similar profile," muses David Keyko, a partner at the Manhattan law firm Pillsbury Winthrop Shaw Pittman. "At some point this stops being about the money. They've got enough money. At some point this becomes about the thrill of getting away with it."

There was at least one other theory you heard, mostly from those who grappled with Dreier in court. "You know everyone's theory about Dreier is that this guy went bad because he overreached financially, that he got in over his head," says Jerome Katz, a Ropes & Gray attorney, who had clashed with Dreier in the past. "I'm sorry, but I don't buy that. I think this guy has always been bad."

They were all wrong. What no one understood is something that Dreier, the first of the Madoff-era criminals to tell his story publicly, explains here for the first time. This wasn't the case of a man who had everything going bad, Dreier makes clear. What no one understood is that everything Dreier owned—the cars, the mansions, the yacht, the sushi restaurant, even the law firm itself—was made possible by his crimes. This was a man who went bad to have everything.

B ack in April, two months before his sentencing, Dreier consented to a wide-ranging set of interviews with *Vanity Fair* and *60 Minutes*. (The only condition was that publication be held until after his sentencing.) Talking with Dreier was like talking with a dying man. During our conversations in that sunny living room above Le Cirque, he was all but a zombie, breaking a smile exactly once during five hours of discussion, a wry chuckle as he described what it was like occupying a darkened prison cell with a urine-covered floor and a triple murderer. Dreier's blue eyes, dull and lifeless, seldom made contact with mine. His speech, marred by a slight lisp, was formal and repetitive, almost stilted, as if he had rehearsed exactly what he wanted to say.

"Obviously, people who knew me are puzzled by what I did," Dreier says, "and I hope talking to you helps begin to explain it. I obviously am sincerely, deeply remorseful and sorry about what I did, and hopefully an interview can convey to people I hurt how remorseful I am. That's the truth. I am deeply sorry. And the frustrating thing is not to be able to say that." He wants the world to see he is not some comic-book villain, he says, that he was once a decent man who found himself swept up in a culture that rewards material gains. All he ever wanted, Dreier says, was to be viewed as a success, and when he wasn't, he began to steal to get the things he craved.

"Even a good person can lose their way," he goes on. "This is not just a story about someone who engaged in a significant crime, but the less dramatic point, you know, is people who are following a certain path, who go to the right schools, who do the right things. . . . You can still lose your way. In a terrible way. As I did."

Marc Stuart Dreier was born in 1950 and grew up in Lawrence, Long Island, one of the fabled, affluent "Five Towns." His father was a captain in the Polish Army who, assigned to the New York World's Fair in 1939, found himself marooned in America by the start of war. He stayed, married, and went on to found a string of movie theaters in Manhattan and on Long Island. The elder Dreier retired to Florida in the 1970s, but restless there, he started a second string of theaters that Marc's brother, Mitchel, runs today. Dreier describes the family as close and loving, which sounds right; they paid the $70,000 a month it cost for private-security men during his house arrest.

From childhood, Dreier was a golden boy. At Lawrence High he was head of the student council and voted "Most Likely to Succeed." He was very smart, a good talker, and from an early age, perhaps unsurprisingly, he wanted to become a courtroom attorney. Talk to those who have known him the longest and the one fault some cite was Dreier's mercenary streak. Marc Dreier was in it for Marc Dreier. He was charming, ambitious, hard-working, and determined to excel. Everyone who knew him, especially his parents, predicted great things.

"I [grew] up experiencing a lot of success, even in elementary school," Dreier says. "I had always been a leader. Things just came easy to me. People expected I would achieve real success in my life."

He got into Yale, earned a degree in 1972, and went on to Harvard Law School, where he graduated in the middle of his class in 1975. He was hired as a litigation associate at the white-shoe Manhattan firm of Rosenman & Colin, where he fell under the supervision of its litigation chief, Max Freund, who was also the firm's co-chairman. Dreier started out carrying Freund's briefcase, then graduated to "third chair" in Freund's trials, then moved up to second chair. His baptism by fire came during years of work alongside Freund in the so-called Betamax case, in which the plaintiffs, Disney and Universal Studios, sued Sony, Rosenman's client, makers of the Betamax videocassette player, for copyright infringement. By the time the trial finally wrapped up, in 1979, Dreier was known within the firm as "Max's boy." As they had since he was a child, people predicted great things.

Into the 1980s, Dreier lived alone in a sadly neglected Upper East Side apartment, grinding through 100-hour weeks working for Freund. A fervid fan of the New York Mets, he pitched on the Rosenman softball team—one of his few outside pursuits. In 1985, to no one's surprise, he made partner. At the same time, he began dating an attractive Rosenman associate named Elisa Peters. They married in 1987, honeymooned in Italy and France, and later had two children, a boy and a girl, both now in their teens.

But if Dreier's career was thriving, Rosenman wasn't. The old-line firm had lost its most important client, CBS, on the day Dreier joined, in 1975, and some said it never recovered. Older lawyers jealously guarded their clients, frustrating their younger colleagues, many of whom, especially the litigators, began to grow restless. Some attorneys began to leave. (Rosenman eventually merged with a larger firm in 2002.)

Dreier, for one, found making partner didn't bring him the money or the responsibility he felt he deserved. "Life didn't change as much as I would've wanted it to change," he says. "I was disappointed the position didn't mean everything I had hoped for. I guess you would say I didn't get either the financial success or the recognition I would've liked."

Just as Dreier's eye began to roam, he received a job offer from Fulbright & Jaworski, the massive Houston firm, which was opening a New York office. Dreier leapt at the chance to head Fulbright's New York litigation section. The move meant more money and more recognition, and Dreier hoped he would be representing Fulbright's big Texas clients in their courtroom battles. Instead, as at Rosenman, he found older lawyers not willing to let go of their clients. For the most part, Dreier and his group were obliged to find their own clients, which was difficult.

Dreier did manage to snag one large fish, a medium-size Wall Street firm named Wertheim Schroder & Company, which hired him in 1991 to sue Avon, the consumer-products giant. It was a complex securities case involving the disputed redemption price of some Avon preferred stock, and Dreier plunged into it with zeal, eventually persuading a New York judge to make it a class action, meaning Dreier was named to represent all the preferred holders. If he could win the suit, Dreier thought, the damages might run into the hundreds of millions of dollars. His own payday could easily run into the tens of millions.

But it was not to be. Dreier's frustrations with Fulbright management had been building for several years when, in 1994, Wertheim was purchased by a British investment bank, Schroders P.L.C. To Dreier's dismay, executives at Schroders had no interest in pursuing the Avon litigation. Fulbright's management committee in Houston, hoping to keep the British bank as a client, agreed and told Dreier to drop the lawsuit. Dreier, unwilling to surrender a case he felt could make him very rich, angrily refused. When Fulbright insisted, Dreier asked the case judge to replace him, thus embarrassing both Fulbright and Schroders, which quickly backed off. Instead, his bosses ordered Dreier to settle the case for a nominal sum. A settlement was reached, but Dreier opposed it in court, at which point Fulbright tried to push him aside and named another attorney to help run the case.

It was the final straw. In March 1995, Dreier pulled a Jerry Maguire, sending a long resignation memo to Houston and taking his one piece of major litigation, the Avon lawsuit, with him. He joined a tiny law firm,

Duker & Barrett, to pursue the case. The three lawyers didn't get along, however, and Dreier left within a year, determined now to go it alone. "I saw a small firm wasn't that hard to run," Dreier says. "I thought I could do it myself." (Ironically, Duker's founding partner, William Duker, would later plead guilty to fraud for overbilling the U.S. government $1.4 million; he received 33 months in prison.)

Striking out on his own, Dreier rented a small office suite in Rockefeller Center and hired a few associates. Shortly after, in 1996, he agreed to partner with a friend of his brother-in-law's, Neil Baritz, who practiced in Boca Raton, Florida. Their new firm, Dreier & Baritz, muddled along for several years with little distinction; Dreier argued a string of cases for various small businesses, and for a time he felt content. "I was much happier," Dreier says. "I loved being my own boss. For the first time I felt like I was doing something meaningful."

Running his own firm, however, presented a host of new challenges, chiefly the pressure of luring clients. That meant entertaining, and Dreier quickly realized that prospective clients judged him in large part not on his legal talent but on the trappings of his success. He moved his family into a duplex on 76th Street, then into a far larger apartment on 58th Street, which he rented because he couldn't afford to buy it. He spent nearly $1 million on renovations, then thousands more buying art and furnishings. In 1998 he moved his offices to 499 Park Avenue, designed by I. M. Pei.

"I needed to give people the idea I was doing very well," he says. "That was the first step in a pattern toward living above my means."

His new surroundings, in fact, soon drove Dreier into debt. The only way to get out, he realized, was to expand his firm and its revenues. Neil Baritz had a friend in Oklahoma City named William Federman, and Dreier, impressed with Federman's practice, lured him into their partnership. The new firm, Dreier, Baritz & Federman, had 20 lawyers in New York, Boca Raton, and Oklahoma, and Dreier, as lead partner, used it to launch a series of new class-action securities lawsuits, similar to the strategy he was employing in the Avon case, which was still dragging on.

By 2000, after two full years, the expanded firm was having "modest success," Dreier says. "We were paying the bills." Dreier turned 50 that year, a point when many men assess their lives. As he took stock, Dreier began to realize he hadn't fulfilled the potential so many had seen in him.

Friends from Harvard were heading giant firms and bringing in multi-million-dollar judgments. It was depressing that, after all those years as a golden boy, Dreier was still mired in a small firm, still hustling to pay his bills. It was then that 9/11 hit, bringing on the dark days when Dreier's world began to collapse.

Dreier watched the towers fall from his Park Avenue office. He doesn't blame any of what happened on the events of that day, but he does trace the source of almost all his ensuing difficulties to the months after 9/11. "I had a very emotional response to that," he says. "I remember feeling an emptiness I couldn't shake in the last quarter of '01, feeling emotionally drained and looking to find myself."

Dreier won't say it, but in some inescapable way he found the fiery fall of the Twin Towers a metaphor for his career, for his entire life. Part of it was the conclusion of his 10-year fight against Avon, which finally ended in November 2001; only later would a judge rule against Dreier, sending the biggest case of his life spiraling down the drain. But it was more than that. He and Elisa had been growing apart. They began to argue more. Dreier won't explain what happened, only that he was to blame, saying, "I wasn't attentive enough to my family." Elisa filed for divorce in January 2002. This, in turn, exacerbated simmering tensions with Dreier's Florida partner, Neil Baritz; the wives were close. Dreier and Baritz agreed to split up. William Federman left as well, after objecting not only to Dreier's penchant for secrecy—he says he never received the monthly financial statements he was promised—but also to the exorbitant sums Dreier had spent on their Park Avenue offices.

All this sent Dreier into an emotional tailspin. "I was very distraught," he says. "I was very disappointed in my life. I felt my career and my marriage were over. I was 52 and [I felt] maybe life was passing me by. . . . I felt like I was a failure." His feelings of despair were deepened by his keen, life-long sense of entitlement, a hard-core belief that he was destined to achieve great things.

And now, suddenly, he realized he hadn't. Worse, for the first time since early adulthood he was alone. "I didn't go into therapy," Dreier says, "though I should have. It might have helped to have someone to talk to, to make me stay grounded." He pauses for a long moment. "I thought I was too smart, I was too confident," he says finally. "You can lose your way a little bit. It was all my fault. I didn't have a therapist, a wife, or a friend. I didn't have anyone I could talk to. I don't do that. I kept everything inside."

There have been rumors that Dreier engaged in a man's typical divorce-era vices—alcohol, women, even recreational drugs—but he waves it all away. His only vice, he insists, was work, but it couldn't lift the gloom. For months he brooded over the wreckage of his life. His epiphany, Dreier remembers, came in the summer of 2003, during a long walk he took on the beach near his vacation home, in Westhampton Beach, New York. He experienced a moment of clarity, he says, in which he saw the path he needed to take; unfortunately, it was a path that would lead to his downfall.

It happened one day when he found himself staring at a palatial beach-front home. His own house was inland. He had always wanted one right on the beach. It was at that moment, Dreier says, that he came to two conclusions. He would buy himself a big house on the beach. And he would get the money by dramatically expanding his firm, now renamed Dreier L.L.P. Dreier knows how ridiculous this sounds, that his criminal behavior can be traced to his yearning for a better beach house.

"I wanted to just, well, appease myself," he says. "Well, not appease myself. Gratify myself . . . I was very, very caught up in seeing the criteria of success in terms of professional and financial achievement, which I think was a big part of the problem. But I thought it would make me happy. And I wanted to be happy again."

He returned to his Park Avenue office that fall determined to lure teams of all-star lawyers to Dreier L.L.P. Each would get a guaranteed salary, plus a bonus based on performance. But unlike other major U.S. firms, Dreier L.L.P. would not be a partnership. Dreier himself would own it all.

The plan looked promising on paper, but in practice there was one major problem. "It required a lot of cash," Dreier admits. Each lawyer had to be paid up front, and as more came on board Dreier was obliged to lease an entire new floor of offices, complete with furniture and computers. Every penny had to come from his own pocket—money, needless to say, that he simply didn't have. In fact, given the support he was required to pay his wife, he was already living far beyond his means. He had tried borrowing from banks, but "the banks all turned me down," he says. "I had no assets.

No credit history." To begin his expansion, he had resorted to borrowing money from factors, firms willing to lend against his receivables—but at steep interest rates. "The factors," Dreier says today, "were just killing me."

Still, within a year, Dreier managed to bring almost 40 new attorneys into his firm, including an entire group or two, such as the four-lawyer wealth-advisory practice he snagged from Kaye Scholer. An essential part of the recruiting process, at least in Dreier's mind, remained draping his life in the trappings of success. He had moved into a large rental on 57th Street after the separation and, as before, plowed nearly $1 million into a renovation. "Lawyers are very risk-averse," he says. "They want to see someone who is very successful already. That was key. The problem was, I had to succeed immediately, or at least present the appearance I was succeeding."

It was during this period, in the first half of 2004, that he began considering, as he puts it, "crossing the line" into illegal behavior, into fraud. "I was [still] very unhappy," he says. "I was really desperate for a solution. I wanted to have more success in my life. There was that desperate component for me that made it easier to cross the line. The second part of it was an irrational overconfidence in myself. I had always been able to will myself through problems."

Dreier says he can't remember the moment he actually began considering fraud. But he acknowledges the decision was made easier by a long track record of what he calls "cutting corners." As he acknowledges, "Yeah, I took advantage of expense accounts, statements on tax returns, that kind of thing. You know, I discovered once you cross a gray line it's much easier to cross a black line." And once he did begin thinking about fraud, he rationalized it as a onetime event that was necessary to fuel his expansion plans. "I thought I could do what I had to do, and get out of it relatively quickly," he explains. "How much did I struggle with the ethical issue? I'd like to say I have a clear recollection of going through some great ethical analysis and agonizing over it. But I don't believe I did. I should have. I just don't remember that kind of angst. I don't."

If he was to become a thief, Dreier reasoned, his target was obvious: hedge funds. It was 2004, and every dinner party he attended seemed to be thronged with young hedge-fund billionaires eager to throw around investment money. "I had to come up with some quote-unquote great idea for a hedge fund," Dreier remembers. "I couldn't sell anything tangible. It had to be a financial instrument at some level to sell to a hedge fund. So I came up with the idea of selling debt."

He would sell an IOU, a one-year note with an interest rate of 8 or 9 percent. But it would need to come from a bogus issuer. No hedge fund would invest in Dreier L.L.P. itself. The issuer needed to be an attractive firm, something to excite a hedge fund. In a perfect world, the issuer should be exceedingly private, someone it would be difficult to ask questions of, the better to conceal his scheme. The more Dreier thought it over, the more obvious it was who the putative issuer of his fake debt had to be: his best client, Sheldon Solow.

Well known for building 9 West 57th Street, the office tower where Henry Kravis and Ross Johnson squabbled throughout *Barbarians at the Gate*, Solow is a cantankerous, 81-year-old Brooklyn-born developer renowned in Manhattan real-estate circles for all manner of legal wrangling. And he has plenty of money to wrangle with: in 2008, *Forbes* named him the world's 605th-richest man, with a net worth estimated at $2 billion. Dreier met Solow in the mid-1990s through a family friend, and argued his first case for him several years later.

Solow became Dreier's dream client, a deep-pocketed billionaire whose appetite for corporate combat meant a string of big-money assignments. Wherever Solow went into battle, Dreier led the charge. In 1998, when Solow became embroiled in a nasty tussle with Hard Rock Cafe chain co-founder Peter Morton over a Hamptons mansion they both sought to buy, Dreier sued Morton in state court, lost, appealed the verdict, and lost, then filed two federal lawsuits, losing both. When Dreier filed a third federal lawsuit, a judge named Loretta Preska dismissed it, saying that Solow "had so many bites at the apple, [he] has swallowed the core." Dreier and Solow appealed, but at that point the upper court lost all patience, fining both men for filing a frivolous action.

Then there was the time in 2005 when Solow had Dreier sue the owners of 380 Madison Avenue, alleging a conspiracy to inflate the rent Solow was paying to them. During oral arguments, the defendants' attorney, Jerome Katz, then of Chadbourne & Park, marveled at Dreier's ability to make his implausible conspiracy theory sound coherent and reasonable.

"This guy is a combination of great intellect and complete sleaze; he is very clever, very smooth, very agile, a high-I.Q. guy," Katz says. "He is a guy who, in my case, drafted a complaint that was extremely clever but based on a pure fantasy, where he concocted this alleged conspiracy that just didn't exist. He would speak in these sentences that were silky smooth, but his argument made absolutely no sense."

The judge agreed wholeheartedly, throwing out the case. Katz then asked the court to impose the maximum sanction against both Dreier and Solow, forcing them to pay the defendants' legal fees. "I don't believe in my entire career I had ever made a motion for legal fees, and I've been practicing law for 34 years," Katz says. The judge consented to the unusual order. Four years later, thanks to a blizzard of legal protests from Dreier, Katz is still trying to collect. (Sheldon Solow did not respond to requests for comment.)

A third case involving Dreier and Solow suggests behavior even more questionable. Its pivot was a long-running feud between Solow and another prominent Manhattan developer, Peter Kalikow. The incident began in February 2004, when Kalikow opened both the *New York Post* and *The New York Times* and, to his dismay, found large, bogus legal notices listing more than 400 creditors from a bankruptcy he had endured more than a decade earlier, in 1991. The ads suggested that the bankruptcy was somehow ongoing and, worse, that Kalikow had understated his assets. It concluded, "You may have additional rights of recovery based upon a failure by the debtors to make truthful disclosure."

Kalikow was incensed; the ads were utterly untrue. He was convinced that someone had placed them to humiliate him personally. Seeking to find out who, he turned to Stanley Arkin, a crafty New York attorney who specializes in ferreting out corporate espionage and all kinds of international intrigues; it was Arkin who famously built the case that American Express had hired private detectives to plant articles defaming the late international banker Edmond Safra, a story I told in a 1992 book. In the intervening years Arkin has become his own mini-conglomerate, forming an intelligence agency, Arkin Group, run by a former top official at the Central Intelligence Agency.

It took Arkin and his men barely a week to identify the secret hand behind the strange ads. At the bottom of the ads was a company name,

Evergence Capital Advisors; a check of Florida records indicated Evergence was a dissolved corporation formerly headed by someone named Kosta Kovachev. A cross-check of records revealed that Kovachev was the target of an S.E.C. lawsuit involving some kind of time-share scam; his attorney was listed as Marc Dreier. Even more telling, a telephone number on the ads was answered at Dreier's office.

Kalikow wasn't surprised; he and Solow had been squabbling for years, ever since Kalikow had repaid a loan from Solow earlier than Solow had hoped, leaving Solow irked at the lost income. Once Dreier was linked to the ads, Kalikow sued, drawing both Solow and Dreier into a series of court pleadings and depositions in which Dreier was forced to admit the entire scheme. The presiding judge, Burton R. Lifland, ruled firmly in Kalikow's favor, declaring Dreier's actions "somewhat sleazy," then reached for a thesaurus to add a few more choice adjectives, including "tacky, shabby, base, low, malicious, petty, nasty [and] unsavory." Judge Lifland ordered Solow to once again pay his opponent's court costs, then went a step further, suggesting that Kalikow explore filing some sort of action against Dreier before "professional or legal tribunals that govern professional conduct."

His work for Solow, including the sanctions and the embarrassing Kalikow case, damaged Dreier's reputation and left him deeply resentful. Though he won't go into details, it's clear the relationship with Solow was irrevocably damaged. During our talks, Dreier's face reddens as he discusses formulating his revenge on Solow.

"You rationalize your behavior," he says. "Mr. Solow is a difficult client whom I had served with enormous hours, with enormous stress and sacrifice. I felt, for good reason, underappreciated. I felt a little victimized. I had gone out on a limb for him, and I felt like he cut off the limb." For a moment it appears Dreier will lose his composure. "That's childish [to say]; it doesn't justify anything," he goes on. "But at the time, I didn't believe I was being treated fairly." He takes a deep breath. "I had a good relationship with Mr. Solow. I had a lot of affection for Mr. Solow. Obviously, I exploited that. I betrayed Mr. Solow. . . . That is a terrible thing to do."

The scam, once it began, wasn't that hard to pull off. Alone at his office computer, Dreier opened an Excel spreadsheet and began constructing a fake Solow Realty financial statement he could show to a hedge fund.

"It wasn't easy," he says. "I don't have a financial background. I would find financial statements of similar firms and extrapolate from them." He knew Solow's auditor and placed the fake financial statements under its letterhead. In another file, he drafted the note he would sell. He decided it would be in the amount of $20 million. Through a friend, Dreier offered to sell the note to a big Connecticut hedge fund named Amaranth, run by a trader named Nicholas Maounis. (The fund later failed spectacularly after a bad bet on natural-gas futures in 2006.) Dreier explained that Solow Realty needed the $20 million to expand. To his mild surprise, the transaction went off without a hitch.

"I don't recall how I identified the first fund, but it was common knowledge they had a very big appetite," Dreier says with a sigh. "I mean, it was easier than you might think. I had the impression the hedge funds were under a mandate: they had money, they had to invest it. I said I was representing Mr. Solow. All the meetings [with Amaranth] were either in their office or mine."

And like that Dreier walked off with $20 million. He used it to hire more lawyers, build out more office space, and buy the beachfront home he had dreamed of, a sprawling mansion in the Hamptons town of Quogue. The problem was, once Dreier got a taste of the good life, he wanted more. The law firm's growth, in particular, he found intoxicating. For years he had supervised barely a dozen lawyers. By the end of 2004 he had close to 50, and with their healthy new salaries, these new attorneys all but worshipped him. "Meeting him at his office, it was like seeing the Wizard of Oz," marvels one Dreier client. "Everyone was so deferential, just kowtowing to him like he was God—he could do no wrong. Because, I guess, he was making them all rich."

After that first $20 million, Dreier quickly sold a series of additional phony notes in amounts ranging from $40 million to $60 million, eventually totaling roughly $200 million. He kept track of the sales in a series of small black notebooks. "The initial misappropriation proved to be inadequate to make the firm what I wanted," Dreier notes dryly. "So I did it again. I had one leg into building this law firm, you know, and I couldn't bring myself to take that leg out. It was a little like quicksand. So I kept doing it."

Dreier pauses in his retelling, his eyes searching the skyline outside his apartment windows. "Each time I always thought it was the last one," he says. "I never thought I'd have to do it again."

Practically overnight, the new money created the life of Dreier's dreams. He added a second waterfront home in Quogue. He drove an Aston-Martin for fun, while a chauffeur ferried him around Manhattan in a Mercedes 500 for work. He laid out $10.4 million for the apartment overlooking Le Cirque. The *pièce de résistance* was *Seascape*, the $18 million yacht he kept docked in St. Martin; it came with a crew of 10 and a Jacuzzi. But the lion's share of the illegal cash went into the law firm. By the end of 2006, Dreier L.L.P. had again doubled in size, to more than 100 lawyers. By the end of 2007 there were 175. His offices expanded in tandem, eventually taking up 11 floors at 499 Park Avenue. Dreier went on an art-buying spree, shelling out $40 million to fill the firm's walls with Hockneys, Warhols, and Picassos. Some clients were impressed; others weren't. "These were major pieces of art," recalls one client. "You had to ask yourself, 'Who would spend $10 million on a piece of art and hang it in the receptionist area?' That's always a bad sign, when they spend the money glorifying themselves."

In Southern California, beginning in 2006, Dreier hired two large groups of attorneys, more than 50 individuals in all. Mostly entertainment lawyers and litigators, they brought with them a string of celebrity clients, including Jay Leno, the Olsen twins, Rob Lowe, Andy Pettitte of the New York Yankees, singer Diana Krall, and the band Wilco. Dreier's start-up costs were enormous: a number of lawyers worked with guaranteed salaries of $1 million or more. To house them, Dreier rented and renovated office space in the Century City skyscraper featured in the movie *Die Hard*—the lease alone cost him an estimated $300,000 a month.

Dreier began spending a week every month in Los Angeles, where, as in New York, he spent heavily to impress prospective clients. He paid $180,000 to play golf as a member at the Brentwood Country Club, rented a condominium on Ocean Drive in Santa Monica, then opened a branch of a sushi restaurant called Tengu nearby. When in L.A., Dreier could be found most nights there, surrounded by attractive young women and potential clients.

Within the legal community, Dreier was viewed as a rising star. He told anyone who would listen that Dreier L.L.P. was a new kind of law firm, one where lawyers could work with freedom, unburdened by old-school bureaucracy and administration, all of which Dreier handled himself. In a 2007 article for *The National Law Journal*, Dreier argued that the "Dreier Model," as he christened it, freed attorneys from petty bickering over profits and allowed them to operate as true legal entrepreneurs. It certainly appeared to work. Dreier L.L.P.'s functions were glittering. In 2007, he and Michael Strahan, of the New York Giants, co-hosted a charity golf tournament for which William Shatner served as M.C. and Diana Ross was the entertainment. Alicia Keys sang the next year. One of the firm's Christmas parties was held at the Waldorf-Astoria, where Dreier danced wildly to the song "Shout," from *Animal House*. At a firm party at his Quogue beach house a plane flew overhead trailing a banner that said, DREIER LAWYERS ROCK.

Through it all, Dreier kept quietly selling bogus notes. During the first three years of his scheme, in fact, from 2004 until the summer of 2007, he found it simple to keep going. Almost every time a note came due, the hedge fund in question would simply renew it for another year, usually with a slightly higher interest rate. No one ever asked to meet Solow or any of his executives; they simply accepted that Dreier was operating on their behalf.

The trouble began in mid-2006, when the housing market started to weaken. By the fall there were rumblings that Wall Street firms would begin taking losses. Those worries blossomed into something like panic the following June, when two massive Bear Stearns hedge funds imploded, nearly bankrupting Bear. At first, Dreier's hedge funds only began rethinking their decisions to renew his notes. With several, Dreier secured renewals by offering better interest rates, as high as 11 or 12 percent. But by early 2008, even that wasn't enough. For the first time, several funds refused to renew and demanded their money back. Dreier managed to repay a few by selling more notes to other funds, the classic Ponzi tactic. He kept still others on board by selling new notes at a steep discount; these new notes not only offered 12 percent interest but cost 30 percent less.

Wall Street's "credit crunch," however, deepened all that winter, eventually leading to the collapse of Bear Stearns, in March 2008. After that, almost every hedge fund refused to renew; all they wanted was their money back. For the first time, Dreier began to sweat. By that summer, he was facing a full-blown crisis. Almost all his outstanding notes were coming due that fall. During walks on the beach at Quogue, he confronted the unthinkable: $48 million of notes due in September, another $15 million in November, a whopping $100 million in December, plus $60 million in January 2009. All told, he would need almost $225 million to cover these redemptions.

"Obviously," Dreier observes without a hint of irony, "I had put myself in a ridiculous predicament."

For the first time, he began to think he might not, as he puts it, "pull out of this." Still, he clung to hope. After all, he had raised this much before. He had a line on some Persian Gulf investors who might inject awesome sums. And Dreier L.L.P. was expecting a good year in 2009; its profits might yet make a dent in what he owed.

Dreier began his sales push after Labor Day. It was rough going. No one wanted to buy anything, only sell. In desperation, Dreier resorted to offering notes due in less than a year, in some cases as little as eight months. He was digging himself quite a hole: a 12 percent note, sold at a steeply discounted price, to be repaid the following May. He managed to sell a small note, for $13.5 million, to a hedge fund named Verition, but the big catch was the $100 million note he sold to a fund named Elliott Associates, a $10 billion fund run by a lawyer turned money manager named Paul Singer. All told, the two sales raised half the money Dreier needed.

As it became harder to market his notes, Dreier found himself relying increasingly on the same hedge funds. By October, in fact, four held almost all his debt, roughly $100 million apiece: Fortress, one of America's largest hedge funds; the new buyer, Elliott Associates; Eton Park Capital Management, run by 31-year-old wunderkind Eric Mindich, once the youngest partner in the history of Goldman Sachs; and GSO Capital Partners, a $25 billion hedge fund owned by the Blackstone Group. By October, GSO was the biggest headache. The firm had $115 million of notes, and it wanted its money back—right away.

Dreier, citing market conditions, pleaded for an extension until year-end. GSO executives reluctantly consented to a few weeks, but there was a catch. To grant the extension, they demanded to meet with top executives at Solow Realty. Unable to wriggle out of it, Dreier scheduled a meeting at Solow headquarters at 9 West 57th Street for October 15. It was at that point that, desperate to extend the note, he staged his most elaborate charade to date. To pull it off, he brought in the odd little man who had helped him before: Kosta Kovachev.

The son of Serb-born doctors, Kovachev, 57, was a Wall Street refugee who had graduated from Harvard Business School and begun his career at firms such as Morgan Stanley, but, during the 1990s, for whatever reason, he spiraled downward through a series of increasingly obscure companies, eventually ending up selling time-shares in an alleged Missouri-based real-estate scam. He was sued by the S.E.C. and surrendered his broker's license in 2003 while admitting no wrongdoing. Kovachev was a shadowy figure in Dreier's life, a onetime client—Dreier says only that they met through a friend—with two ex-wives in Florida, six children, and a cell-phone number that rang at the Harvard Club. He wasn't quite the Igor to Dreier's Dr. Frankenstein, more a financial flunky. He had an electronic pass to Dreier L.L.P. and court papers indicate he was paid as much as $100,000 for his role in Dreier's plan.

Dreier is maddeningly vague about Kovachev, who was also arrested last December; presumably he doesn't want to undermine Kovachev's defense. Kovachev did not respond to requests for comment, but from legal papers filed in the case, it appears he had carried out impersonations for Dreier before, at least once during a conference call with one of Dreier's hedge funds. That day in the Solow conference room, however, Kovachev delivered his performance in person, easily convincing a team from GSO that he worked for Solow; afterward, Dreier got his brief extension. A top Solow executive, Steven M. Cherniak, has said he actually noticed the meeting going on—the conference room has glass walls—and later told associates he wondered what Dreier was doing. Dreier, however, visited Solow's offices often enough that his unexplained appearance was shrugged off.

By the first week of November, it appeared Dreier had created some breathing space. That's when things really began to fall apart.

As Dreier pieced it together for me, this is how it started. The small fund to which he had sold a $13.5 million note, Verition, was looking for ways to reduce its exposure. Verition executives reached out to another fund, Whippoorwill Associates, based in suburban Westchester County, to see if it might be interested in buying half the note. Whippoorwill, in turn, contacted Solow Realty's auditor, Berdon L.L.P., to obtain financial data. Berdon executives were confused; they didn't know anything about any Solow Realty notes. They called Sheldon Solow himself, who didn't either. A Berdon attorney named Thomas Manisero began investigating. One of the hedge funds turned over a Solow financial statement Dreier had supplied. It was clearly forged.

By the first week of November, Manisero and several Solow executives, including Solow himself, all suspected Dreier had committed fraud—a single act, but fraud nonetheless. Solow and Manisero telephoned Dreier and confronted him. "I tried to double-talk my way out of it, but I knew that would not work," Dreier recalls. "They accused me. I didn't acknowledge the extent of my wrongdoing. I acknowledged that what appeared to have happened had only happened once, with one small fund, and it had been rectified." Dreier said he was deeply "ashamed," and swore it would never happen again.

Neither Manisero nor Solow was satisfied, however. Manisero told Dreier that unless he could fully explain himself he was going to the authorities; Dreier assumed he would anyway. In fact, within days the U.S. Attorney's Office in New York became involved.

"I knew in that first week of November that unless I got extremely lucky I was going to get caught," Dreier says. He decided to do the only things he could: deny, delay, and obfuscate.

Just days later came a second shot across his bow. In concluding the Elliott deal, Dreier had given an Elliott executive a bogus e-mail address for Solow Realty—the address actually delivered any e-mail to Dreier's computer. When the Elliott executive attempted to use the address, he apparently made a typing error and was obliged to phone Solow Realty directly, as Dreier learned, to his horror, when he found himself c.c.'d on the man's e-mail exchanges with a Solow executive.

"From that point on, I knew I wouldn't get out of it," Dreier recalls. "I knew I couldn't talk my way out of that second one."

The clock was ticking. That same week Dreier flew to Dubai and Qatar, where he met with a group of Arab investors who he hoped might buy notes worth enough to bail him out. One evening, standing in the desert air, he finally began pondering what had once been unthinkable. Here he was, out of the country, with $100 million in cash. Why not run? Why not spend the rest of his days on some balmy Indian Ocean beach? For the moment, though, he just couldn't. He returned to New York for a day, then jetted to St. Martin, where he sat on his yacht, brooding. If he wanted, he could simply have his captain sail for Venezuela. He might be safe there.

But he couldn't do it. "I thought I would never see my kids," Dreier recalls. "I thought that, even if I did, they would be in danger. I guess I thought that, even more humiliating than coming home to face the music, would be a long life as a fugitive. I thought that, at 58 years old, what was the point of living as a fugitive?"

For two more weeks Tom Manisero peppered Dreier with calls, demanding to know more about what he had done. Dreier says he assumed the authorities were recording Manisero's calls. They were. On the Friday after Thanksgiving, he asked Manisero if there was some kind of settlement he could offer to make Solow whole. Prosecutors would later characterize this as an attempt to bribe Manisero, a contention Dreier firmly denies.

That same Friday, Dreier received more worrisome news. One of his attorneys, Norman Kinel, needed to retrieve $38.5 million from one of Dreier L.L.P.'s escrow accounts; the money belonged to a bankrupt client who needed it to repay creditors. But to Kinel's surprise, less than half the money remained in the account. Dreier couldn't tell him the truth, that he had stolen it. He promised to get back to Kinel on Monday. Suddenly Dreier was consumed with replacing that money. He phoned Elliott Associates, which agreed to buy a new $40 million note. For a few hours, Dreier thought he was safe. Then, later that same day, an Elliott executive called to say the firm was backing out of the deal; he didn't say why, but Dreier thought they had become suspicious.

A ll that weekend Dreier frantically sought ways to replace the missing escrow funds. On Monday, December 1, he secured a commitment from Fortress for a new, $50 million note, this one to be "issued" by a firm whose name he had begun using, the Ontario Teachers' Pension Plan, a massive, $100 billion fund based in Toronto that had once been a Dreier client. The new agreement, however, was struck with a different group inside Fortress, and this one insisted on signing the legal papers in a face-to-face meeting with an Ontario Teachers' executive.

Dreier knew what this meant: he would need to impersonate the executive, at the fund's offices in Toronto. That night Dreier telephoned Toronto and set up a meeting for the next day, Tuesday, with an Ontario Teachers' attorney, a man I'll call "Tom." He told Fortress to have one of its people come to the pension fund's offices to sign the papers. When the Fortress executive arrived, Dreier would need to be there, somehow masquerading as "Tom."

It was a dicey proposition at best, but as Dreier's private jet descended toward an Ontario commuter airport the next morning, he thought he could pull it off. Then, at the last moment, "Tom" telephoned and canceled their meeting. Dreier, fighting off panic, quickly set up a new meeting, this one with an Ontario Teachers' attorney named Michael Padfield, whom he did not know. He took a limousine downtown to the shimmering glass Xerox Tower. Inside, he boarded an elevator to the Ontario Teachers' third-floor offices, where he and Padfield held a quick meeting, ostensibly to discuss the sale of another bogus note; at one point, the two exchanged cards. Then Dreier asked if he might kill some time in a spare conference room. His jet back to New York was running late, he explained.

For the next hour or so, a receptionist watched as Dreier paced the pension fund's lobby, obviously waiting for someone. This is where things got strange. At one point, a man emerged from the elevators and moved toward the receptionist's desk. Before he could reach it, however, Dreier cut him off. The man was Howard Steinberg, the Fortress executive who had come to sign the note. He was to meet with Michael Padfield, the same attorney Dreier had just seen. Dreier introduced himself as Padfield, handed him Padfield's business card, and guided Steinberg into the same conference room where he had been waiting.

Everything appeared to be going smoothly until Steinberg suddenly asked if Dreier knew "Tom" 's extension—apparently the two men were acquainted. Dreier reluctantly read off the number, at which point Steinberg rose, asked for a moment, and stepped outside. Dreier realized he was about to call "Tom," who of course knew nothing about the meeting or the note; if the two men spoke, it was all over. Dreier watched as Steinberg began dialing a phone in the lobby. As he did, Dreier yanked up a conference-room phone and, in a bid to somehow prevent the two from speaking, dialed "Tom" as well.

"He called the guy, I called the guy," Dreier recalls with a sigh. "He beat me to it."

He cut off his call, knowing the end was near. When Steinberg returned to the conference room, Dreier says, "I could see he was suspicious. It was the questions he asked me and the look he gave me. He asked several questions about personnel at Ontario Teachers', which indicated he was suspicious." Sensing the worst, Dreier hurriedly signed the legal papers, then excused himself for a moment. But instead of returning, he headed for the elevator and left the building.

After a few minutes, Steinberg emerged from the conference room.

"Was that Michael Padfield?" he asked the receptionist.

"No," she said.

Dreier's plane was waiting. He had just boarded when his phone rang. It was a Fortress executive, informing him there had been "some kind of problem" at Ontario Teachers'. The Fortress man, not knowing Dreier was in Canada, much less that he was behind the "problem," explained what little he knew. Dreier feigned astonishment. Moments later, his phone rang a second time. This time it was Peter Briger Jr., Fortress's co-chairman of the board. "We don't know what's going on," Briger told Dreier. "But we think there's some kind of impersonation going on."

"I played dumb," says Dreier, "and said I would look into it." When Dreier concluded the call, his mind raced. At that point, 9 out of 10 men would have simply fled back to New York. For some reason, Dreier returned to his limo and had the driver take him back to the pension fund's offices.

"I was 90 percent sure I would be caught when I went back," he says. "I was not thinking clearly. I was desperate. Clearly, there was a part of me that just wanted this to be over. I knew I was defeated. I went back knowing I would probably never leave that building [a free man]."

Once he was back in the Ontario Teachers' offices, an attorney asked him to wait in the conference room. By and by, security guards appeared and told him to wait for the police, who appeared not long after and arrested him. Dreier went without resistance.

It was over. Canadian authorities held Dreier for four days, then put him on a plane back to New York's La Guardia Airport, where U.S. marshals took him into custody, just as Dreier suspected they would. He didn't bother with denials for long. He would admit everything: four long years of fraud, 80 or more bogus notes, 13 hedge funds and four private investors, $380 million— everything. His glorious new life, the firm, the "Dreier Model"— it had all been built on lies. Within days, attorneys began resigning from Dreier L.L.P. At one point, Dreier's 19-year-old son, Spencer, barged into a meeting there and attempted to rally the assembled lawyers to his father's defense; he was hooted out of the room. Ten days after Dreier's New York arrest the firm declared bankruptcy. By that point almost every attorney had left. Dreier L.L.P. simply imploded.

Dreier was tossed into a dark cell on the ninth floor of the Metropolitan Correctional Center New York, a federal holding pen in downtown Manhattan. It was the shock of his life: Dreier, in fact, has quite a lot to say about the "M.C.C.," as it's known. He and his cellmate, the triple murderer, had no electric light, no reading materials, no heat, and a broken toilet, which left the floor covered in urine. Each night Dreier shivered beneath a thin blanket while other inmates yelled and screamed "like it was an insane asylum," he claims. He was allowed out of the cell for rooftop exercise once a day, at five A.M., for an hour. Meals were shoved through a slot. He showered twice a week, in cold water. "This was like *Midnight Express*," Dreier says in dismay. "I mean, it's beyond what people can imagine." (An M.C.C. New York spokesman disputes Dreier's account of his time there.)

It was certainly beyond anything Marc Dreier of Yale College and Harvard Law School had ever imagined. Finally, after eight days, he was released into the general population. Two months after that, following his indictment, a judge allowed him to return to his apartment under house arrest. During the period when we spoke, in April, Dreier was sleeping a lot, spending every available hour with his children, briefing lawyers tasked with sorting through the wreckage of Dreier L.L.P., and trying to come to grips with the end of life as he knew it.

"I expect to spend most of the rest of my life in prison," he tells me. "I hope I don't die there. I've been blessed with good genes, you know. My father died at 91. So I think I have a few years left. I will try to have a meaningful life in prison. It won't be the life I anticipated. I won't attend my daughter's wedding. I will miss all the moments in life I assumed would be part of my life."

526 The Great Hangover

"This is a particularly sad case," Dreier's lawyer, Gerald Shargel, says. "Marc Dreier had everything going for him and essentially threw it away. To his credit, he realized early on that it was no one's fault but his own. When he went to prison, he was in many ways in a state of grace."

During 25 years of writing about financiers, I have spoken to several on their way to prison. Dreier was by far the most philosophical, and while his critique of America's material culture is no doubt self-serving, some of his final words were instructive.

"Many people," he observed, "are caught up in the notion that success in life is measured in professional and financial achievements and material acquisitions, and it's hard to step back from that and see the fallacy. You have to try and measure your life by the moments in your day. I see people my children's age first coming into finance, the working world, as having to make basic choices about how to define happiness and success. Obviously, I made the wrong choices.

"But they don't have to."

· 16 ·

Wall Street's Toxic Message

Global Consequences of the Meltdown

By JOSEPH E. STIGLITZ

July 2009

Every crisis comes to an end—and, bleak as things seem now, the current economic crisis too shall pass. But no crisis, especially one of this severity, recedes without leaving a legacy. And among this one's legacies will be a worldwide battle over ideas—over what kind of economic system is likely to deliver the greatest benefit to the most people. Nowhere is that battle raging more hotly than in the Third World, among the 80 percent of the world's population that lives in Asia, Latin America, and Africa, 1.4 billion of whom subsist on less than $1.25 a day. In America, calling someone a socialist may be nothing more than a cheap shot. In much of the world, however, the battle between capitalism and socialism—or at least something that many Americans would label as socialism—still rages. While there may be no winners in the current economic crisis, there are losers, and among the big losers is support for American-style capitalism. This has consequences we'll be living with for a long time to come.

The fall of the Berlin Wall, in 1989, marked the end of Communism as a viable idea. Yes, the problems with Communism had been manifest for decades. But after 1989 it was hard for anyone to say a word in its defense. For a while, it seemed that the defeat of Communism meant the sure victory of capitalism, particularly in its American form. Francis Fukuyama went as far as to proclaim "the end of history," defining democratic market capitalism as the final stage of social development, and declaring that all humanity was now heading in this direction. In truth, historians will mark the 20 years since 1989 as the short period of American triumphalism. With the collapse of great banks and financial houses, and the ensuing economic turmoil and chaotic attempts at rescue, that period is over. So, too, is the debate over "market fundamentalism," the notion that unfettered markets, all by themselves, can ensure economic prosperity and growth. Today only the deluded would argue that markets are self-correcting or that we can rely on the self-interested behavior of market participants to guarantee that everything works honestly and properly.

The economic debate takes on particular potency in the developing world. Although we in the West tend to forget, 190 years ago one-third of the world's gross domestic product was in China. But then, rather suddenly, colonial exploitation and unfair trade agreements, combined with a technological revolution in Europe and America, left the developing countries far behind, to the point where, by 1950, China's economy constituted less than 5 percent of the world's G.D.P. In the mid–19th century the United Kingdom and France actually waged a war to open China to global trade. This was the Second Opium War, so named because the West had little of value to sell to China other than drugs, which it had been dumping into Chinese markets, with the collateral effect of causing widespread addiction. It was an early attempt by the West to correct a balance-of-payments problem.

Colonialism left a mixed legacy in the developing world—but one clear result was the view among people there that they had been cruelly exploited. Among many emerging leaders, Marxist theory provided an interpretation of their experience; it suggested that exploitation was in fact the underpinning of the capitalist system. The political independence that came to scores of colonies after World War II did not put an end to economic colonialism. In some regions, such as Africa, the exploitation—the extraction of natural resources and the rape of the environment, all in return for a pittance—was obvious. Elsewhere it was more subtle. In many parts of the world, global institutions such as the International Monetary Fund and the World Bank came to be seen as instruments of post-colonial control. These institutions pushed market fundamentalism ("neoliberalism," it was often called), a notion idealized by Americans as "free and unfettered markets." They pressed for financial-sector deregulation, privatization, and trade liberalization.

The World Bank and the I.M.F. said they were doing all this for the benefit of the developing world. They were backed up by teams of free-market economists, many from that cathedral of free-market economics, the University of Chicago. In the end, the programs of "the Chicago boys" didn't bring the promised results. Incomes stagnated. Where there was growth, the wealth went to those at the top. Economic crises in individual countries became ever more frequent—there have been more than a hundred severe ones in the past 30 years alone.

Not surprisingly, people in developing countries became less and less convinced that Western help was motivated by altruism. They suspected that the free-market rhetoric—"the Washington consensus," as it is known in shorthand—was just a cover for the old commercial interests. Suspicions were reinforced by the West's own hypocrisy. Europe and America didn't open up their own markets to the agricultural produce of the Third World, which was often all these poor countries had to offer. They forced developing countries to eliminate subsidies aimed at creating new industries, even as they provided massive subsidies to their own farmers.

Free-market ideology turned out to be an excuse for new forms of exploitation. "Privatization" meant that foreigners could buy mines and oil fields in developing countries at low prices. It meant they could reap large profits from monopolies and quasi-monopolies, such as in telecommunications. "Liberalization" meant that they could get high returns on their loans—and when loans went bad, the I.M.F. forced the socialization of the losses, meaning that the screws were put on entire populations to pay the banks back. It meant, too, that foreign firms could wipe out nascent industries, suppressing the development of entrepreneurial talent. While capital flowed freely, labor did not—except in the case of the most talented individuals, who found good jobs in a global marketplace.

This picture is, obviously, painted with too broad a brush. There were always those in Asia who resisted the Washington consensus. They put restrictions on capital flows. The giants of Asia—China and India—managed their economies their own way, producing unprecedented growth. But elsewhere, and especially in the countries where the World Bank and the I.M.F. held sway, things did not go well.

And everywhere, the debate over ideas continued. Even in countries that have done very well, there is a conviction among the educated and influential that the rules of the game have not been fair. They believe that they have done well *despite* the unfair rules, and they sympathize with their weaker friends in the developing world who have not done well at all.

Among critics of American-style capitalism in the Third World, the way that America has responded to the current economic crisis has been the last straw. During the East Asia crisis, just a decade ago, America and the I.M.F. demanded that the affected countries cut their deficits by cutting back expenditures—even if, as in Thailand, this contributed to a resurgence of the AIDS epidemic, or even if, as in Indonesia, this meant curtailing food subsidies for the starving. America and the I.M.F. forced countries to raise interest rates, in some cases to more than 50 percent. They lectured Indonesia about being tough on its banks—and demanded that the government not bail them out. What a terrible precedent this would set, they said, and what a terrible intervention in the Swiss-clock mechanisms of the free market.

The contrast between the handling of the East Asia crisis and the American crisis is stark and has not gone unnoticed. To pull America out of the hole, we are now witnessing massive increases in spending and massive deficits, even as interest rates have been brought down to zero. Banks are being bailed out right and left. Some of the same officials in Washington who dealt with the East Asia crisis are now managing the response to the American crisis. Why, people in the Third World ask, is the United States administering different medicine to itself?

Many in the developing world still smart from the hectoring they received for so many years: they should adopt American institutions, follow our policies, engage in deregulation, open up their markets to American banks so they could learn "good" banking practices, and (not coincidentally) sell their firms and banks to Americans, especially at fire-sale prices during crises. Yes, Washington said, it will be painful, but in the end you will be better for it. America sent its Treasury secretaries (from both parties) around the planet to spread the word. In the eyes of many throughout the developing world, the revolving door, which allows American financial leaders to move seamlessly from Wall Street to Washington and back to Wall Street, gave them even more credibility; these men seemed to combine the power of money and the power of politics. American financial leaders were correct in believing that what was good for America or the world was good for financial markets, but they were incorrect in thinking the converse, that what was good for Wall Street was good for America and the world.

It is not so much Schadenfreude that motivates the intense scrutiny by developing countries of America's economic failure as it is a real need to discover what kind of economic system can work for them in the future. Indeed, these countries have every interest in seeing a quick American recovery. What they know is that they themselves cannot afford to do what America has done to attempt to revive its economy. They know that even this amount of spending isn't working very fast. They know that the fallout from America's downturn has moved 200 million additional people into poverty in the span of just a few years. And they are increasingly convinced that any economic ideals America may espouse are ideals to run from rather than embrace.

Why should we care that the world has become disillusioned with the American model of capitalism? The ideology that we promoted has been tarnished, but perhaps it is a good thing that it may be tarnished beyond repair. Can't we survive—even do just as well—if not everyone adheres to the American way?

To be sure, our influence will diminish, as we are less likely to be held up as a role model, but that was happening in any case. America used to play a pivotal role in global capital, because others believed that we had a special talent for managing risk and allocating financial resources. No one thinks that now, and Asia—where much of the world's saving occurs today—is already developing its own financial centers. We are no longer the chief source of capital. The world's top three banks are now Chinese. America's largest bank is down at the No. 5 spot.

The dollar has long been the reserve currency—countries held the dollar in order to back up confidence in their own currencies and governments. But it has gradually dawned on central banks around the world that the dollar may not be a good store of value. Its value has been volatile, and declining. The massive increase in America's indebtedness during the current crisis, combined with the Federal Reserve Board's massive lending, has heightened anxieties about the future of the dollar. The Chinese have openly floated the idea of inventing some new reserve currency to replace it.

Meanwhile, the cost of dealing with the crisis is crowding out other needs. We have never been generous in our assistance to poor countries. But matters are getting worse. In recent years, China's infrastructure investment in Africa has been greater than that of the World Bank and the African Development Bank combined, and it dwarfs America's. African countries are running to Beijing for assistance in this crisis, not to Washington.

But my concern here is more with the realm of ideas. I worry that, as they see more clearly the flaws in America's economic and social system, many in the developing world will draw the wrong conclusions. A few countries—and maybe America itself—will learn the right lessons. They will realize that what is required for success is a regime where the roles of market and government are in balance, and where a strong state administers effective regulations. They will realize that the power of special interests must be curbed.

But, for many other countries, the consequences will be messier, and profoundly tragic. The former Communist countries generally turned, after the dismal failure of their postwar system, to market capitalism, replacing Karl Marx with Milton Friedman as their god. The new religion has not served them well. Many countries may conclude not simply that unfettered capitalism, American-style, has failed but that the very concept of a market economy has failed, and is indeed unworkable under any circumstances. Old-style Communism won't be back, but a variety of forms of excessive market intervention will return. And these will fail. The poor suffered under market fundamentalism—we had trickle-up economics, not trickle-down economics. But the poor will suffer again under these new regimes, which will not deliver growth. Without growth there cannot be sustainable poverty reduction. There has been no successful economy that has not relied heavily on markets. Poverty feeds disaffection. The inevitable downturns, hard to manage in any case, but especially so by governments brought to power on the basis of rage against American-style capitalism, will lead to more poverty. The consequences for global stability and American security are obvious.

There used to be a sense of shared values between America and the American-educated elites around the world. The economic crisis has now undermined the credibility of those elites. We have given critics who opposed America's licentious form of capitalism ample ammunition to preach a broader anti-market philosophy. And we keep giving them more and more ammunition. While we committed ourselves at a recent G-20 meeting not to engage in protectionism, we put a "buy American" provision into our own stimulus package. And then, to soften the opposition from our European allies, we modified that provision, in effect discriminating against only poor countries. Globalization has made us more interdependent; what happens in one part of the world affects those in another—a fact made manifest by the contagion of our economic difficulties. To solve global problems, there must be a sense of cooperation and trust, including a sense of shared values. That trust was never strong, and it is weakening by the hour.

Faith in democracy is another victim. In the developing world, people look at Washington and see a system of government that allowed Wall Street to write self-serving rules which put at risk the entire global economy—and then, when the day of reckoning came, turned to Wall Street to manage the recovery. They see continued re-distributions of wealth to the top of the pyramid, transparently at the expense of ordinary citizens. They see, in short, a fundamental problem of political accountability in the American system of democracy. After they have seen all this, it is but a short step to conclude that something is fatally wrong, and inevitably so, with democracy itself.

The American economy will eventually recover, and so, too, up to a point, will our standing abroad. America was for a long time the most admired country in the world, and we are still the richest. Like it or not, our actions are subject to minute examination. Our successes are emulated. But our failures are looked upon with scorn. Which brings me back to Francis Fukuyama. He was wrong to think that the forces of liberal democracy and the market economy would inevitably triumph, and that there could be no turning back. But he was not wrong to believe that democracy and market forces are essential to a just and prosperous world. The economic crisis, created largely by America's behavior, has done more damage to these fundamental values than any totalitarian regime ever could have. Perhaps it is true that the world is heading toward the end of history, but it is now sailing against the wind, on a course we set ourselves.

PART FOUR

THE MADOFF CHRONICLES

· 17 ·

Part I:
Madoff's World

By MARK SEAL

April 2009

Over dinner in New York one night in January, I was airing my frustration concerning Bernard Madoff. Everybody had read about the losses he had inflicted on foundations associated with Steven Spielberg, Elie Wiesel, and Mort Zuckerman, I told my dinner companions, but after having interviewed nearly 40 of his other financial victims, I still couldn't get a picture of what the man was like. "If you want to know about Bernie Madoff," said Mary T. Browne, the renowned psychic and author, who counsels many heavy hitters on Wall Street, "you need to talk to my friend Carmen Dell'Orefice." She was referring to one of the original supermodels, the platinum-blonde beauty who had posed for Richard Avedon, Irving Penn, Francesco Scavullo, and Norman Parkinson, and who had been a muse to Salvador Dalí. She had first appeared on the cover of *Vogue* in 1946, when she was 15. "Nobody can give you better insights into the Madoffs than Carmen," Browne told me. "I'll see if she'll talk to you."

Two days later, when I arrived at her Upper East Side apartment, Dell'Orefice was ready for me. Still gorgeous at 77, she led me to her bedroom, where she had laid out on her king-size coverlet piles of intimate photographs, canceled checks, and reams of investment statements spelling out her relationship with Madoff. Mary T. Browne was right. She had quite a story to tell.

It began in the fall of 1993. Six years after the death of her fiancé, the legendary television impresario and talk-show host David Susskind, a neighbor introduced Carmen to Norman F. Levy, a giant of mid-century New York City real estate, who, along with such titans as Harry Helmsley and Samuel LeFrak, had helped shape the city by filling its skyscrapers with blue-chip tenants. Then 80 and a widower, Levy had retired to a good life of travel, philanthropy, and passive investing, most notably with his best friend, Bernie Madoff.

On Valentine's Day 1994, after four months of dating, Levy made what Carmen called his "grandstand play" for her affection. He instructed her to meet him at the office of Bernard L. Madoff Investment Securities, in the Lipstick Building, the oval red-granite monolith at 53rd Street and Third Avenue designed by Philip Johnson and John Burgee. "Bring your checkbook," he said.

Carmen arrived early, she remembered. "And there was a little man sitting behind a very big desk. 'Are you Mr. Madoff?,' I asked."

"Yes, and I'm expecting you," he said, his mouth pursed in what she would soon discover was his trademark smirk.

"In back of me, I hear this booming voice: 'Did you bring your checkbook?' I turned around and there was Norman, all six-foot-three, two-hundred-and-something pounds of him. 'Yes, Norman, I did.' "

"Then write one out for $100,000," Levy told her. Carmen couldn't write a check for anywhere near that amount; she was still in arbitration after having lost most of her money in the stock market and having been forced to auction off her early modeling photographs at Sotheby's the year before.

"Bernie Madoff chuckled and said, 'Don't worry, the money is there.' He added, 'Mr. Levy put it in your account.' "

'T his is very special, what I am doing for you," Levy told Carmen, indicating what an honor it was to be admitted into Bernie's exclusive fund, which, while usually not as high as other funds in an up market, never lost in a down market. Its 10 and 12 percent annual returns were totally dependable. Levy's grandstand play worked. "I told Norman, yes, I would take a trip with him to London, and Bernie arranged for the honeymoon suite at the Lanesborough. It was the suite Bernie usually stayed in, but he gave it up for Norman. Bernie and Ruth, his wife, had a suite upstairs."

It was the beginning of a beautiful friendship. Along with her $100,000 investment, which, with additional infusions and the fund's steady returns, grew into millions, Carmen got a new social life. She showed me pictures and told me stories of dinners, family gatherings, charity balls, and Madoff company picnics, held at Madoff's home in Montauk, on Long Island, where the investment shaman would book every hotel room in the vicinity for his employees and their families. She recalled trips on yachts and outings in New York and evenings in the Madoffs' house in Palm Beach—12 years of Norman and Carmen and Ruth and Bernie. "The intimacy of those events," she said with a sigh. "Birthdays. Hanukkahs. Building a yacht for Mr. Levy in the last years of his life . . . " She showed me a picture of Madoff on the yacht, bare-chested and wet from a dip in the sea, kissing the white-haired Levy on the cheek. "Norman said, innumerable times, 'He is my son,'" she told me, meaning that Levy considered Madoff his surrogate son, a member of his family.

'**B**ernie was quiet, not a storyteller, not a conversationalist," said Carmen. "I often thought he was perhaps bored. He was just Bernie, pleasant and polite." He always deferred to Levy, who was 26 years his senior, and whom he called "my mentor of 40 years." I asked if Madoff was ever flirtatious. "Never!," Carmen exclaimed, adding that he rarely if ever touched alcohol. Even though Madoff didn't drink, he knew that Norman loved good red wine, so he meticulously planned wine-tasting tours for him. "He knew where all the vineyards were, and he arranged for Norman to do these excursions into the countryside. . . . *Everything* was about Norman."

Showing me pictures of birthday parties and New Year's Eve celebra-tions—Madoff in a silly paper hat, his calves showing, lounging on a divan, with Ruth, as always, at his side—Carmen said, "This was their idea of fun." In other photographs, Madoff was whispering in Levy's ear or had his arm slung around the big man's shoulders. "I think of him as always smiling," said Carmen. "Bernie was poor and from Queens and made it big." She said that Bernie and Ruth both still had a Queens accent, adding playfully, "You could tell they weren't raised in Switzerland." But then, Norman Levy had come from a similarly humble background. He had attended high school in the Bronx and worked his way up from selling magazines and Fuller brushes to taking a low-level job at the Cross & Brown brokerage firm, of which he became C.E.O. in 1976. Though at one point he had an ownership stake in 70 properties, including the Seagram Building and 21 shopping centers across America, one of his proudest treasures was his friendship with Madoff.

'Listen, it may have been bravado, Norman grandstanding to me that he spotted a genius early on. He would say, 'Bernie Madoff is the most honorable, smart person,'" said Carmen. Madoff responded in kind. "He was shy, but so sure of himself. He always did so much for Norman's comfort in the smallest details." Madoff had his suits tailor-made at Kilgour, on Savile Row, in London. Soon, Levy was having his suits custom-made in London, too.

When Levy decided to build a yacht so that he could stop chartering Malcolm Forbes's each season, Madoff helped oversee the construction of a 127-foot Royal Denship. "And when we were in the South of France, he arranged for an armed bodyguard for us. Bernie knew about piracy, because he was an oceangoing person." When Levy's yacht set sail, Bernie and Ruth were on board. "Norman and Bernie never talked business, except on the telephone," Carmen told me. When the men watched television or films, the choices were Levy's; when they listened to music, Levy selected and Madoff (whose tastes leaned to the likes of Neil Diamond) went along. After dinner, the Madoffs would depart, to their suite at the Hôtel du Cap-Eden-Roc, in Antibes, or to their house in the South of France. They'd return the next morning, sometimes with provisions, particularly Norman's favorite ice cream, and whether they were in Monte Carlo or Palm Beach, the two women would go shopping. Ruth was as polite, pleasant, and inconspicuous as her husband.

The Madoffs' favorite New York restaurant, I learned, was Primola, a friendly Italian place on Second Avenue near 64th Street. The waiters there told me how Madoff and his wife would arrive, always around 6:30, ask for a quiet table at the back, order the same thing (small salad, then chicken scarpiello and Diet Coke or red wine for him, fish and white wine for her, no dessert, no coffee), and be out in 50 minutes flat, leaving a 20 percent tip on what was always a modest bill. "I know him for 30 years," said the owner, Giuliano Zuliani, who met Madoff while working as a waiter. "When I would talk to him, though, his wife would look down at the table. In all the years she knew me, she never spoke to me." Dominick, the assistant maître d', said, "Now everybody is asking for 'the Madoff table,' but I always say, 'The F.B.I. already has it.'" One night when I was there, two women walked in, and one of them announced, "This is our last dinner at Primola. My family lost all of our money to Bernie Madoff."

Once, after Levy's health began to fail, Madoff arranged for a helicopter to transport him for medical treatment. And when Levy died, in 2005, at 93, Madoff delivered a eulogy at the funeral. "Norman told me that Bernie was the executor of his will," said Carmen. "Before Norman passed away, there was the Betty and Norman F. Levy Foundation," she said, referring to the charitable institution Levy had founded with his late wife and left to his heirs, with a reported $244 million in assets in 2007, to be used for causes ranging from cancer research to Yeshiva University. "Long before he died, he had given both of his children their own money, and each had created a charitable foundation. All three foundations closed after December 11," she said—the day Madoff admitted to F.B.I. agents that his investment fund, into which approximately 13,500 individual investors and charities had put their money, was "one big lie." (Both of Levy's children, Jeanne Levy-Church and Francis Levy, declined to comment.)

A fter Levy's death, Carmen said, she went out to dinner several times with the Madoffs. But she got the news of Bernie's arrest by telephone. "At ten minutes to five, Lillian, a girlfriend, called me up. Lillian had $400,000 with him, all she had in her life, and she's 68. She said, 'Are you all right?' I said, 'Of course I'm all right. Why?' She said, 'You didn't hear yet?' I said, 'Hear what?' She said, 'They've arrested Bernie Madoff!' And I said, 'For what?' And she said, 'It's all a fraud. Turn on the television.' By five minutes to five, I had moved past the fact that everything I thought I had on paper was gone. Ten minutes past five, I called Bernie's private office number, and a secretary picked up," she continued. "I said, 'This is Carmen Dell'Orefice.'"

"We just found out less than 45 minutes ago," the secretary said.

"Then it's so?"

"It seems so. I don't know," she said.

At that point in her story, Carmen shook her head. "I am accepting that what I thought I was experiencing was a projection of a person who wasn't there. If I didn't take all the pictures I took all those years, I would say, 'Carmen, you're delusional.' I know these people did not start out doing harm. So many people have been hurt, I feel badly about trying to say anything good. But I'm starting from where I was knowing them. Because I'm hurt, too. For the second time in my life, I've lost all of my life savings."

At seven P.M. on December 11, Carmen got a call from Norman Levy's daughter, Jeanne Levy-Church, who contributed millions to good causes around the world through her JEHT Foundation. (The name stands for Justice, Equality, Human dignity, and Tolerance.) "She said, 'I just want you to know: at four o'clock today, I had to close down my foundation.' "

Sitting there in Carmen Dell'Orefice's Park Avenue bedroom, listening to this elegant, charming woman speak about the Bernie Madoff she had known before his Waterloo, I realized that her remembrance of him as a generally quiet, caring, devoted little man was the most damning testimony I had heard yet. I thought to myself, If a son could loot the fortune of his father, what would he do to a stranger?

In truth, I had been trying for months to invest money with Madoff. As the stock market fell precipitously in the fall of 2008, I would hear my friends in Aspen, Colorado, the affluent resort town where I live, gloat about the kindly Jewish uncle, the financial genius, who didn't just keep their money safe but paid dividends, while everyone else's portfolio plummeted by 40 percent. "Bernie's gone to cash," one said. "Bernie's in Treasury bills," said another. "Thank God for Bernie!" said a third.

In November, I invited a friend and longtime Madoff investor to dinner and literally begged him to get me in. He listened politely, then shook his head slowly. "Forget it," he said. Bernie was closed; Bernie had a multi-million-dollar minimum; Bernie didn't need my money. His discouraging response only made me want Bernie all the more.

A few weeks later, on December 11, I was trying my luck again. My wife and I were having dinner in another Aspen restaurant with another friend, who, thanks to investing with Madoff for 20 years, had recently retired to a life of golf and skiing. In the course of the evening, the cell phone of the investor's companion rang a number of times, but she didn't answer right away. When she finally did, she came away with unbelievable news: Bernie Madoff had been arrested and had reportedly confessed to cheating clients of nearly $65 billion in a Ponzi scheme. Within hours we knew that half a dozen of our friends had been hit, and that my dinner companion's retirement was over.

Once the cell phones started ringing on the slopes, that day and the next, a previously unknown social class emerged in the fancy resort: the newly needy. People rushed home, where the flat screen was filled with the news, and gradually came to realize that one life was gone and another had begun. "Hysterical" was how one man described to me the mood in his home, adding that the hysteria was followed by humiliation and shame. As another said, Who wants to go out in a resort town where people are celebrating if you can't pay a restaurant tab and everybody around you knows it?

A s Christmas turned to New Year's, the roster of the stricken had ballooned—too many to believe. How the Madoff pox had found its way to the Rockies and spread, however, was still unclear. Bernie had been in Aspen, people said, as had his brother, Peter, but never to solicit blatantly. Soon I knew of approximately 50 investors in Aspen who had been stung. As one of them told me, when the stock market began to slide, they had begun shifting "from the losers to the winners," until some of them had everything except their houses—which in this town can mean a $10 million asset, frequently pure equity—invested with Madoff. Then, as Madoff kept performing and the market kept going to hell, the house would also go to him. "Everybody looked at it like a money market, backed by U.S. Treasuries," one business leader said. "They kept pulling money out and putting it in. Somebody—I don't want to mention his name—refinanced his house a couple years ago, when the rates were low, and put all of the money with Madoff. Now he has no money and no house."

They called it "playing the spread." Five years ago, if someone had a mortgage-free home in Aspen worth $15 million, he could easily get a mortgage on it for $10 million at 4 percent interest. The carrying costs on that $10 million mortgage would have been $400,000 per year. By investing the $10 million proceeds of the mortgage with Madoff at a 12 percent return, the 8 percent difference between the carrying costs and the return would have given the owner $800,000 per year. One friend said, "A lot of people here own their houses free and clear, so that would be a home run."

As the suffering increased, a certain inevitable Schadenfreude set in. Those who had begged to get into Madoff's fund and couldn't were now crowing about "what geniuses they were," as one major player who had "lost a few bucks" (meaning a few million, in Aspen parlance) told me. At the same time, I overheard the vultures plotting in the Jacuzzis of the Aspen Club and Spa. One said he was waiting for the "distress to deepen" so that he could swoop in and scoop up foreclosed homes and planes.

Then the locusts descended: the lawyers. They flew in from New York, three of them to start, and stood out in their business suits among the jeans and ski sweaters, addressing a somber audience in a 10,000-square-foot house that was rumored to be going on the market. "Grown men were hugging each other," a man who had been there told me. Once word got out that I was going to write an article about the Madoff mess, my cell phone never stopped ringing. Victims I hardly knew wanted to tell their stories, vent their anger, get revenge.

One day I called the Manhattan attorney Barry Slotnick, who has represented everyone from New York "subway vigilante" Bernie Goetz to Russian mobster Vyacheslav Ivankov. He had just been in Palm Beach, he said, where he had been speaking with Madoff victims who wanted to sue. Business was booming, he said, adding, "Remember, he took money from people who knew how to make money." Listening to Slotnick, I knew I was getting only a small portion of the story. Within hours, I booked a flight to Florida.

Madoff's fall hit Palm Beach like a hurricane. In the best restaurants, diners blanched after learning by cell phone that their money was gone. Shell-shocked guests at the December 11 kickoff party for the International Red Cross Ball, at the home of Susan and Dom Telesco, the U.S. distributor of Tommy Hilfiger, looked as if they'd "just seen ghosts," said someone who was there. "People came in and said, 'Oh, my God, I lost this much, that much. How much did he hit *you* for?'" From the private clubs to the seaside mansions, "a curse of almost biblical proportions," as it came to be called, descended like an evil cloud. "It spread like wildfire," Laurence

Leamer, author of *Madness Under the Royal Palms,* told me, singling out one of his early callers, a business titan who had lost $50 million overnight. "His charity was wiped out, his foundation was wiped out, the retirement for his employees was wiped out." Leamer got a frantic call from a woman who was at the annual ball of a Jewish charity. "She said it was like the *Titanic* going down—people screaming and yelling. She had never seen such emotion," said Leamer. "Everybody was drunk—people that don't drink—like their lives were over."

It wasn't just their money that Madoff stole from the Jews of Palm Beach; it was what their money enabled them to do. "Palm Beach is a Jewish majority," Leamer said, explaining how over the years the resort had evolved from a bastion of Wasp anti-Semitism, where Jews were not allowed in many of the hotels, much less the private clubs—in some cases they're still not—into a town whose business and social arenas were dominated by Jews. "They're richer than Wasps," said Leamer. "They're basically more cultured, more generous. This is *their* island, or was—until December 11. This not only destroys them financially but also destroys a sense of superiority they had."

"What Hitler didn't finish, he did! To the community!" a doyenne of Palm Beach Jewish society who had lost double-digit millions told me in her beautiful home, surrounded by a sizable staff and priceless art.

The center of the storm was the predominantly Jewish Palm Beach Country Club. The sand-colored building, with its fine restaurants and 18-hole golf course, sits between the Atlantic Ocean and Lake Worth. Membership is based not on what you have—the $350,000 initiation fee is the least concern of the admissions committee—but on what you give away. Madoff became a member in 1996. "You won't get in unless you can demonstrate that you've been charitable in a big way," said Richard Rampell, an accountant with a number of clients who are members. "They want to see a history of many years of giving every year at least what the initiation fee is, and they ask you to prove it. . . . I have a few clients who give 10 to 20 times that much every year to charity." One member told me, "We built the hospital, we built the Kravis Center for the Performing Arts. We built it all. This is just not a come-and-have-a-party group."

With the arrival of Madoff in Palm Beach, the group renowned for giving became the group that got taken. According to some reports, as many as one-third of the 300 members invested with him. One woman told me to look at a recent issue of a local magazine, on the cover of which were three important philanthropists. "All big givers," she said. "They all got killed—their charitable trusts wiped out! They're all in their 80s, and they devoted their lives to helping others." She added, "And this bastard! Did you see him on television?" She mentioned the smirk Madoff turned on reporters. "I'd like to crack him!"

Next came an ugly wave of anti-Semitism. "It has opened up Pandora's box," said one society leader. *The Palm Beach Post* wouldn't even run most of the vitriolic posts that flooded its Web site. "When I started writing Madoff stories, the anti-Semitic messages started immediately," said *Post* columnist Jose Lambiet. "It took decades for the Jewish community to get past this thing, and now . . . " His voice trailed off. "The anti-Semites are ecstatic," said one resident. "Supposedly, there was a crack made at a local club: 'This is terrific. Now maybe we'll get our land back.' These people were not pleased at the way Jewish wealth has come into this community, but they have been very happy to get Jewish philanthropists involved in their charitable endeavors."

Shortly after Madoff's arrest, Rabbi Moshe Scheiner advised his congregation at the Palm Beach Synagogue to look beyond money, beyond financial losses, to matters of deeper importance. In New York, Rabbi Marc Gellman wrote in an open letter to Madoff in *Newsweek* about the pain he had inflicted on the Jewish community: "There must be some new word invented to describe the way you have redefined betrayal." Rabbi Mark Borovitz, a reformed scamster and alcoholic himself, whose Los Angeles foundation lost between $200,000 and $300,000 to Madoff, called Madoff's crooked style "affinity theft," in which the con man preys on the idea that you can trust your own people. "Whether it's Latino or black or Jewish or Christian, everybody wants to trust their own. Bernie Madoff took our trust and raped it," said Borovitz. "He took advantage of every vulnerability, because he knew our vulnerable spots."

When asked to describe Madoff's personality, most of the people I interviewed in Palm Beach could come up with very little. "Pleasant, charming, but reclusive," said one. "I go out nine nights out of seven, and I never saw him out once," said another. "We'd never heard of him before December 11," said Jeff Ostrowski, of *The Palm Beach Post*. Madoff's barber, who had cut his hair and given him manicures and pedicures at least once a month for 17 years, couldn't recall Madoff saying anything other than greetings and small talk.

"The one thing we could all agree on is that we should curse the Madoff bloodline," Roger Madoff, Bernie's nephew, wrote in *Leukemia for Chickens*, a memoir about his fight with the disease, which was published in 2007, a year after his death. Cancer runs in the Madoff family, but Roger's words have recently acquired much larger implications.

Bernard Madoff must have been a split personality, "pure Jekyll and Hyde," according to Stephen Raven, the head of Madoff's London office, which he explains was involved exclusively in proprietary trading with Madoff family money. Raven, who has known Madoff for more than 30 years, told me, "I haven't spoken to anybody in America since that tragic night when I saw he was arrested on television. I was shivering, shaking. I still find it hard to believe. I don't know the person they're talking about, and I know Bernie Madoff very well." Other people assured me, however, that when Madoff was away from the mob groveling for entry into his fund he was the opposite of the quiet, kindly, smiling Uncle Bernie he presented to the world. According to some close observers, he ruled his family by fear.

The Madoffs could often be found in a cabana at the Breakers hotel, in Palm Beach, where, according to a family friend, they considered themselves royalty: "There was a lot of arrogance in that family. Bernie would talk to people who were as rich as he was, but he didn't want to be bothered with the little people." Bernie and Ruth had come a long way from Laurelton, Queens, where they had started going steady in junior high. "Laurelton was a middle-class, substantially Jewish suburb, and everybody in Laurelton knew everybody," said a close friend from those days. Bernie's parents, Ralph Z. and Sylvia "Susie" Muntner Madoff, were both children of immigrants (his from Poland, hers from Romania and Austria). They had married in 1932, at the height of the Great Depression. On the marriage license, Ralph's occupation was listed as "Credit" and Susie's as "None." "Heavyset, fairly dark, Bernie was Ralph's son in terms of looks," one friend remembered. Ralph "was either a stockbroker or a customer's man [an account representative]," another friend told reporters. Whatever

Ralph's business was, it apparently went sour in August 1963, when the S.E.C. began "proceedings . . . to determine whether" 48 broker-dealers, including Bernie's mother, "Sylvia R. Madoff [doing business as] Gibraltar Securities," had "failed to file reports of their financial condition . . . and if so, whether their registrations should be revoked." The address of Sylvia's broker-dealer account was the family home on 228th Street, and since in those days few mothers worked, there is now some speculation that she may have been fronting for Ralph.

Ruth's father, Saul Alpern, was a quiet, successful C.P.A. "The only time I was in debt was when I borrowed $50,000 from my wife's parents to start my own firm, and I paid that back," Madoff once boasted to Credit Suisse and other investors, according to Bloomberg News. "I can't imagine that his father-in-law would invest $50,000 in his son-in-law," one friend protested. "That was a hell of a lot of money!" She said Bernie and Ruth had been married in a "very nice Jewish wedding—sit-down dinner," on the Saturday night after Thanksgiving 1959, at the Laurelton Jewish Center, the only synagogue in town. "Their first apartment was in Bayside. I know the rent was $87 a month, so that will give you an idea of what $50,000 was like," she added. "We never thought Bernie was going to set the world on fire." Ruth, however, might have. While Bernie spent his freshman year at the University of Alabama—at that time, some say, an easier entrance portal for students who couldn't get accepted into eastern colleges—Ruth passed the entrance requirements for Queens College. "She graduated and had a job on the stock market in Manhattan. She was a very smart girl and a very good student." Once Bernie had gotten through Hofstra University and attended Brooklyn Law School for a year, the couple fled Queens and never looked back. In 1960 they began working together at Bernard L. Madoff Investment Securities, which Bernie founded with his savings of $5,000 from lifeguarding and installing sprinkler systems. From the start, Ruth's office was right next to her husband's.

Saul Alpern was an early feeder for them. After retiring, Ruth's father attracted investors through word of mouth, especially when he stayed at the Sunny Oaks, a Borscht Belt hotel in the Catskills. As David Arenson, a relative of the owner, wrote on his blog, "Way back when, our little hotel turned out to be fertile ground for investors for Bernie. Almost everyone in the family had a Madoff account. Accounts radiated out through the guest population, through our distant relatives and the distant relatives of guests. All told, I can think of a dozen people I know who are, collectively, out at least $5 million, and I am sure those people know another dozen people."

With information from a variety of reliable sources, it is possible to get a fairly clear picture of Bernard Madoff. He reportedly has a major case of obsessive-compulsive disorder and is an "anal retentive" neatness freak, Julia Fenwick, the manager of Madoff's London office, told me. The offices in New York and London were almost identical—starkly modern in shades of black and gray—and everything in them had to be perfectly in place. A messy desk, scratches or scuffs on furniture, even an undrawn window blind, could drive Madoff crazy. He installed two cameras on the trading floor of the London office so that he could monitor it from New York, and he had a videoconferencing camera ripped out of the office wall in London because he couldn't stand the circular shape of its casing. Last year Fenwick flew with the family on a golf trip to Mexico. That same week Bernie celebrated his 70th birthday. "It was a brand-new plane, and he was maniacal about keeping it pristine, to the point that his brother, Peter, told me, 'You can't put your luggage with metal edges on that seat! Bernie will kill me!'" she said. "He was very insistent that we did everything by F.S.A. [Britain's Financial Services Authority] guidelines," she continued. "Everything was by the book in the U.K. office. And he wanted to make sure—as it says in his brochures and on his Web site—that his name was on the door. His name was the most important thing."

"Bernie is not what you would call Mr. Nice Guy, not someone you would want to have a beer with," one insider volunteered. "He was imperial, above it all. If he didn't like the conversation, he would just get up and walk away. It was 'I'm Bernie Madoff and you're not.'" In view of the fact that Madoff looted so many charities, it is therefore interesting to note that his own favorite charity—the Lymphoma Research Foundation—did not invest in his fund.

'All of his family members grew up with this being our lives," the Madoffs' elder son, Mark, then director of listed trading, said in a 2000 interview. "When it is a family-operated business you don't go home at night and shut everything off, so you take things home with you, which is how all of us grew up." Mark, who is 44, and his more reserved brother, Andrew, 42, were the heirs apparent, both trying to carve out a place for themselves within their father's daunting shadow. "He loved his sons, but he never showed it," said a family friend. "Mostly tough love and fear. People were afraid of Bernie. He wielded this influence. They were afraid of his temper."

The second Madoff family is headed by Bernie's brother, Peter, a lawyer and computer whiz, who is seven years his junior. Peter became senior manager of trading and compliance director, but he and his two children—his daughter, Shana, a rules-compliance lawyer for the trading division of her uncle's firm, and his late son, Roger, a Bloomberg News business writer who joined the firm before his death, in 2006—were strictly second-tier Madoffs, working for the company but owning only a very small part of it. "Bernie's little brother, Peter, is a sweet kid," said one insider, adding what many add when describing Peter Madoff: *poor Peter.* "Peter could never live up to Bernie." But Bernie rarely made a move without his brother. "Peter would watch over Bernie's ass. Peter is much more religious, more even-keeled. Bernie is more cocky, arrogant, a showman. Shrewd like a fox." Peter's wife, Marion, a bridge player and dog-lover, could never quite make the grade in the eyes of the powerful, matriarchal Ruth. (All of the Madoffs point out that they have no involvement in the firm's asset-management business.)

"When everybody thinks your dad's a god, why shouldn't his own sons think that?," Mark Madoff once said to a friend. Mark and Andrew sat at adjacent elevated desks overlooking the trading floor. Friends described them as caring, considerate all-American guys, passionate about baseball, fly-fishing, their children, and their families. They both lived very large. Mark owns numerous properties, including a multi-million-dollar Vicente Wolf–designed apartment on East 72nd Street, in Manhattan. Until his recent separation from his wife, Deborah, Andrew lived at fashionable 10 Gracie Square. Each brother has an expansive country house in Greenwich, Connecticut.

"Mark got divorced and married a babe—hot, blonde Stephanie," said a friend. "They had a million-plus wedding on Nantucket." Meanwhile, Andrew was diagnosed with mantle-cell lymphoma in March 2003, and had to consider radical treatment, "which would quarantine him for at least half a year," as Roger Madoff wrote in his memoir. Andrew didn't want to take more time than necessary away from the family firm. He eventually survived the disease and returned to work. He became chairman of the Lymphoma Research Foundation in January 2008, but he resigned a few weeks after his father's arrest.

In November 2007, Mark and Andrew led a private investment group in acquiring Abel Automatics, a manufacturer of fly-fishing equipment, and invested in Urban Angler, a Manhattan fishing shop. Andrew also acquired a new girlfriend, Catherine Hooper, who owned Urban Angler with her previous boyfriend. Hooper was once on the cover of *Fish & Fly* magazine, her black hair in Bo Derek braids, wearing the scantiest of bikinis. There were six more pictures of her inside, holding a rod, with a tool belt slung across her hips. "Come *here* you big, shiny hunk of hard-swimming silver!" read the caption for one picture of her reeling in a bonefish. The article, which she wrote, was "the fascinating tale of how I came to be the tropical boatmate of an Israeli commando and 10 guys filled with fish-lust in the wild, wild west of the Indian Ocean—home to the biggest, brightest bonefish in the world."

Andrew's wife, Deborah, happened to file for divorce the day Bernie was arrested. "She got the house and everything in it," said L.A.-based interior designer Paul Fortune, whom Andrew flew from L.A. to New York to decorate an apartment on East 74th Street for him and Catherine. "They'd gotten basically a Crate & Barrel sofa and a bed. They wanted to get it pulled together." On December 11, however, Fortune got an e-mail from the couple: *Have you seen the paper today?* "So everything was kind of canceled," he concluded.

Despite her colorful manner, Catherine Hooper seems fairly tame compared with Bernie Madoff's niece, Shana, who is 38. She began working for Uncle Bernie when she was 26, straight out of Fordham Law School. In 1997 she married tall, handsome Scott Skoller, the manager of a men's-wear store called Tyrone, in Roslyn, on Long Island. The couple had a daughter, Rebecca, before they divorced. "She had a thirst for social climbing," said someone who knows Shana well. "It was all about image. She was proud she was a Madoff, but she wasn't getting as much juice from the economics." According to Julia Fenwick, "Her responsibility was looking over everything, the rules and regulations. She was very strict with compliance rules." Shana's job, however, did not cover the firm's private-investment division.

After her uncle was arrested, Shana's friends rushed to extol her intellect and her charitable endeavors—she had recently been honored as a Girl Scouts of America Woman of Distinction. Then an article about her that had appeared in *New York* magazine in 2004 resurfaced. In it, Shana asks her daughter, "Rebecca, what color does Mommy wear a lot of?" The child, who was then four and a half years old, exclaims, "Black!" The article included the following assessment of Shana:

> Her salespeople at Jeffrey messenger a shipment of [Narciso] Rodriguez's clothes and shoes to her at the beginning of each season and simply charge her for what she doesn't return. "If I see something I like, I call around," explains Madoff, a securities lawyer. "I just don't have time to shop. I get a little bit aggravated when I go into a store because I could be doing so many other things that are so much more productive. And the salespeople are around the clothes all day. They know them much better than I do."
>
> She can be quite determined about getting certain items. Last summer, while sitting on Georgica Beach [in East Hampton], she was thumbing through *Harper's Bazaar* when she stumbled across a tweed Prada bag she knew would go perfectly with her Rodriguez basics. She left her friends and walked down the beach saying she had "to make an important phone call." She ordered the bag on her cell phone. When it arrived two days later, she came clean to her boyfriend. "That was my important phone call!"

"Shana had a shoe fetish—like 30, 35 pair of Manolos. She was a real fashion victim, always wanted to be on the best-dressed list. She only cared about the labels," said a friend. "Her focus was on clothes and yoga. Private instructor—Ashtanga. She wore very skintight clothes."

After her divorce from Scott Skoller, Shana began dating some of the young masters of Wall Street—"bad boys living the fast life," as a friend described them. These were exciting, good-looking men, in the social pages more than the business press. That is why many people thought it out of character for Shana, in 2007, to marry a man some say is the polar opposite of her prior swains: Eric Swanson, who was a lawyer for the S.E.C. for 10 years. (Swanson resigned from the S.E.C. four months after his romance with Shana began.) "She went for these Wall Street stud muffins, some of the most eligible men in New York, but then goes to a pudgy, sort of non-sexy, mid-level S.E.C. attorney," the friend said. At a 2007 business round-table meeting, Bernie Madoff bragged about his "very close" relationship with an S.E.C. regulator, adding, "In fact, my niece even married one."

Like Shana, Ruth Madoff also appreciated the finer things, especially when it came to her husband. For one of Bernie's recent birthdays, she went to Davidoff of Geneva, the cigar boutique on Madison Avenue, and bought him a $14,500 humidor, inlaid with a buffalo motif and filled with his favorite cigars. According to one observer, Ruth allegedly did not allow her husband to travel alone for more than one day. "She didn't let Bernie out of her sight."

'**B**ernie was such an unbelievable figure that people would move into areas or join clubs just to get a chance to talk to him," said a man who had gotten his break one afternoon in 2007. It was after a round of golf, and he and his associates met Madoff in the bar, in a scene repeated at all of Madoff's clubs, from Fresh Meadow, in Lake Success, New York, to the Palm Beach Country Club, to the Boca Rio, in Boca Raton. Madoff breezed in, and the subtle groveling began. "You almost had to do a solicitation to him. It never got down to pleading and begging, but we wanted in," said the man. The minimum required to get into the fund was up to Madoff. "There was never a fixed number. It was subject to a person's individual wealth." The day they met, Madoff was his typical "sweet, never arrogant, happy self." As they spoke, the man realized that Madoff had already sized them up and calculated their net worth. He said, "Your minimum to me is $10 million." Not prepared to open with that much, they declined. "We were pissed! But there was no bargaining. It was what it was, and if you couldn't handle it, it was tough shit." He added, "We were lucky."

On a cross-country tour to speak with those who weren't lucky, I felt like the Angel of Death, knocking on the doors of the once privileged, *chosen* people who had gained admission into Bernie Madoff's amazing investment vehicle, only to be fleeced by him. They all shared the same stacks of now worthless paper (monthly statements from Bernard L. Madoff Investment Securities) and an overnight obsession with terms such as "feeder funds" (the myriad individuals and businesses that funneled money to Madoff) and "claw back" (the government's threat to make investors return money they'd taken out of Madoff's fund from as far back as six years).

Many of the victims I visited in Palm Beach were widows, including a lady of leisure with the mouth of a truckdriver, who cursed "that ganef, that thief, that nasty son of a bitch." She had lost millions, but at least she had a roof over her head. "There are widows down there who lost everything, because their husbands, when they were dying, told them, 'Honey, keep your money with Bernie,'" said Muriel Siebert, the first woman to gain a seat on the New York Stock Exchange, who is counseling many of the bereft. "Emotionally, they're totally confused. They don't know how it could happen. You're dealing with an era where husbands would say, 'Don't worry, my little darling, I'll always take care of you.' Now, that's tough. One said, 'I have to go and live with my daughter.' That's a hard thing when you were on top of the world."

Maureen Ebel, 60, was introduced to me by a real-estate agent after she put her home, on a lagoon within the grounds of the International Polo Club Palm Beach, on the market. Following the untimely death in 2000 of her physician husband, she got sucked into the Madoff fund. "All your problems are over," said an elderly relative of her late husband's. "My guy Madoff has agreed to take you as a favor to me. I pulled on his heartstrings." Feeling blessed, she eventually transferred everything she had: $7.3 million. Now she was sitting among the ruins, having returned Christmas gifts, begged back her annual $5,000 International Polo Club membership fee, persuaded the Leukemia & Lymphoma Society to return her $1,000 donation, sold valuable jewelry, put her Lexus up for sale online, and listed her home. Gone were her days of extended lunches and tennis; gone was her boyfriend, from whom she separated when she had to take a job caring for a wealthy friend's 93-year-old mother, which devolved into "basically being a maid," she said. On the day of my visit, she had just been informed by her employer, "We're interviewing a Hispanic woman to do the work. We have to do what's best for us." But she won't let this defeat her, she stressed as she sat on her porch with her dog, Scarlett (for O'Hara), on her lap. "If I have to feed myself," she said, "I can go and work as a waitress."

I dialed another widow who, I was told, had obeyed her husband's deathbed instructions and invested the whole of his estate with Madoff. I got no response, so I drove to her gated community, where the guard called the woman, who said she would receive me. It was an expensive home on a sunny street, but when the door opened, I was facing a disheveled lady in her late 60s with an odd facial tic. One minute she looked as if she was about to cry; the next minute she would break into a broad smile. She had lost everything, I had been told, but she said she couldn't talk about it now. She promised to call me back that evening but never did.

'I want justice!" screamed Joan Sinkin, who, along with her husband, Arnold, a retired contractor, had sunk every cent from 55 years of work and the proceeds from the sale of several houses into Madoff. After learning that they had lost everything, she was hospitalized with what seemed like a stroke, and her husband collapsed. "I want to be treated like G.M. and A.I.G. and Bank of America! I can't wait years! I want S.I.P.C. [Securities Investor Protection Corporation, which insures investors up to $500,000] to put people like us back on our feet!" Out of her husband's hearing, she whispered, "We had a good life, and it's gone." The night the news hit, her husband "turned old overnight," she said. "It was such a blow to him, to realize that everything he worked for all of his life, someone else just"—she snapped her fingers—"plucked."

Irwin Salbe had considered himself privileged to be able to invest with Madoff since 1984, and his parents had had the account 20 years before him. The returns were so steady that he got his kids into Madoff, then his grandchildren, then his entire family. "It's a four-generation account," he said. "I trusted him with multiple I.R.A.'s and all my other money. And all of a sudden we woke up one afternoon and we have nothing." He was sitting with his son Steven, 42, in the Fort Lauderdale restaurant they own. "I'm 72 years old and I have to worry about Social Security taking care of me?," Irwin demanded angrily. Steven said, "I have two daughters, six and seven, and they asked, 'Why is Daddy crying? Why is Grandpa crying?' We showed them the newspapers and pictures of Mr. Madoff and said, 'This man stole our money.' And they asked, 'How do we get it back?' "

"It's boring now, the poor-victims story," said Larry Leif, a Florida investment adviser who lost $8 million, and who has since become a lightning rod for victims' rights. "I'm into legislation and action for those who were fooled. I've been on CNN six times, and it looks like Fox is going to give me a one-hour show, and we're going to a town-hall victims' meeting in Boca next week." His ex-wife, Ronnie Sue Ambrosino, called me from Surprise, Arizona, where she said she's been stranded since she learned that she'd lost all she had, $1.7 million. "Everybody knows we're penniless and can't pay our mortgages," she said. "That's not what people need to hear anymore. They need to hear the next step. Write about how the government let this happen and how the government is letting the victims down. I need people to know that the S.E.C. failed miserably for at least 10 years, if not more, that they were warned, and that they didn't stop this devil from doing his deed. I need people to know that S.I.P.C. has taken more than a month to get a claim form out to help the victims. I need people to know that the I.R.S. has been collecting taxes on phantom income for at least 10 years. I need people to know that Bernard Madoff has given money to senators across the country in their campaign funds. So you tell me how our government is helping support the victims, or are they supporting themselves?" At that point her cell phone went dead, and she couldn't afford to call me back—"thanks to Mr. Madoff," she wrote in an e-mail.

'This isn't about a bunch of widows and orphans that got taken in by some huckster selling vacuum cleaners door-to-door," said one observer. "He hit smart people. The ones who are really rich have big egos, and they don't want to look stupid." Most of the big losers insisted on speaking without attribution. "It's just incredible that the man could have been such an evil sociopath that he came into this community, came to the country club, smiled at everybody, shook our hands, greeted us while he knew he was stealing our money," said a member of the Palm Beach Country Club who reportedly added to his sizable investment just 11 days before Madoff was arrested. "It's safe to say he had a very limited circle of friends in this community. He didn't participate in a lot of the local activities. He kept pretty much to himself."

New York Mets principal owner Fred Wilpon had hundreds of millions invested with Madoff, his buddy since the 1960s. "Wilpon would tell anyone he met what a terrific friend Bernie Madoff was," said a Wall Street insider. "He must feel like a total fool. Here's a nice enough guy, decent and honorable, but he tended to brag that he had deals that were better than other people's." (Wilpon didn't respond to requests for a comment.) Hit even harder was Long Island developer Edward Blumenfeld, known to many as Madoff's best friend—they had been neighbors in Roslyn in the 1970s. They shared vacations and a $24 million jet, and Mark Madoff was best friends with Blumenfeld's son David and Wilpon's son Jeff. "I assume this will affect Eddie's liquidity, and his liquidity is his business," said Bert Brodsky, an entrepreneur and Madoff investor who knows both men. "He told me he's not sure if he feels worse that he lost all of his money or that it was his friend who did it to him—his absolute best friend, who, I hear, he had dinner with on the Tuesday night before the Thursday night [when Madoff was arrested]." Blumenfeld's public-relations representative said, "Mr. Blumenfeld was a friend to a man who apparently didn't exist," adding that his client would be making no comment. On December 18, however, Blumenfeld reportedly walked into a meeting of the Association for a Better Long Island wearing a T-shirt that read, I WAS A FRIEND OF BERNIE MADOFF AND ALL I GOT WAS THIS LOUSY T-SHIRT.

Donald Trump flew into Palm Beach the week I was in town. "Madoff said to me one time, 'Why don't you invest in my fund?' Which was a little different than what I'd been hearing, in terms of his philosophy. Usually he'd tell people they *couldn't* invest," said Trump, adding that Bernie and Peter Madoff played golf at his Trump International Golf Club, where Bernie's game was as steady as his returns. "Out of hundreds and hundreds of rounds, he never shot lower than 80 or more than 89," said Trump. "Experts said he's either the most consistent golfer in the world or he's cheating." Trump said he had declined Madoff's offer to invest. "Many people gave 100 percent of their net worth to this maniac, and what do they have for it?" he continued. "They have nothing. They'll be golf pros. . . . This guy was a Svengali for rich people. He took their money like it was candy, chewed it up and spit it out."

I visited the Palm Beach branch of Circa, which specializes in buying and selling high-end jewelry, and met the manager, Tracy Sherman, who has become something of a counselor to Madoff's victims. She described one "home visit" to a Palm Beach mansion where three generations of women investors—grandmother, mother, and daughter—had lined up three generations of jewelry on their dining-room table, eager to sell it all. "Earrings and bracelets and things that went together," said Sherman. "Every decade had a different look."

Houses were the only asset remaining to many investors. I sat with six real-estate agents in the offices of Fite Shavell & Associates, in Palm Beach. "Three condos went up for sale in Breakers Row," one of the men said of the exclusive oceanfront estate where nothing *ever* opens. "All Madoff. Two houses on Via Los Incas, one on Tangier. Madoff, Madoff, Madoff. These are beautiful properties, between $3 and $5 million, and the ones in the Breakers are $7 to $17 million. But their AmEx bills are due, and they're $100,000 to $500,000 a month. Most of these guys are Marquis Jet. They charge it on AmEx for points. They need cash to pay their bills."

Naturally, there are those who now say they knew all along it was a sham. One early skeptic told me that, when he and some friends expressed doubt about Madoff's complicated strategy of puts and calls, Madoff told them bluntly, "I know what I'm doing," and insinuated that he was smarter than the men he was pitching. (They didn't invest.) Joyce Z. Greenberg, a stockbroker from Houston, had a bundle with Madoff. She had inherited an investment from her husband, but when Madoff discovered that she had resumed a part-time job at a brokerage, he called her in 1999, fuming. "I never manage money for *anyone* who works at a brokerage," he said, and demanded she choose between her account with him and her job. He gave her one week to decide. She chose her job, and Madoff immediately closed her account and wired her the money. "That's the good part," she told me. "The stupid part is that I retired in 2001 and asked to open a new account." She showed me a letter from Madoff's secretary: "Bernie says the answer is yes." She sighed and said, "And now that's gone with the wind."

The most relentless skeptic was Harry Markopolos, an accountant and private fraud investigator mostly unknown outside of Boston, who repeatedly sounded the alarm about Madoff to the S.E.C., starting in 2000. When the S.E.C. took no action, Markopolos began a crusade to prove his point. In 2005 he sent regulators a 19-page memo entitled "The World's

Largest Hedge Fund Is a Fraud." He was referred to the New York branch chief, Meaghan Cheung, who, he wrote in an e-mail to one of her colleagues last year, didn't "have the derivatives or mathematical background to understand the violations," much less prosecute them. The S.E.C. eventually opened an investigation into Madoff but closed the matter in November 2007 without bringing any claims against him. Cheung, 37, who left the S.E.C. last September, had difficulty defending her findings in the Madoff case, telling the *New York Post* after his arrest, "If someone provides you with the wrong set of books, I don't know how you find the real books." Markopolos, who lambasted the S.E.C. in a congressional hearing in February, said, "I felt like I was an army of one."

Laura Goldman, now of the Tel Aviv–based LSG Capital, told me she had met Madoff at the lunch counter of Green's Pharmacy in Palm Beach in 1992, when she was a broker with Paine Webber in Philadelphia, visiting South Florida in search of clients. "When I fortuitously bumped into Madoff, I thought I'd found my lottery ticket," she remembered. He was dressed Palm Beach casual—polo shirt and slacks—on his way to play golf. As soon as the name Bernie Madoff floated across the counter, she knew who he was—the Jewish T-bill. They talked about politics, the weather, golf—everything except business, because Madoff didn't talk business with strangers. "Finally, in 1997, I said to him, 'Isn't it time we started talking turkey?' " By then she was at a smaller firm, so Madoff got serious. "At this meeting he changed. He was still charming, but he did not tolerate my style of many questions," she said.

"He would try to change the subject by saying that I was lucky to invest with him." Look at the returns, he told her, and talk to some of his clients. But Goldman felt that she needed specifics. She knew almost everyone in the options business, she said, but she couldn't find anyone who was trading with Madoff. "I found that strange."

She asked him about custody issues, types of accounts, and Madoff came up short on everything, especially his auditing firm—two people in a 13-by-18-foot office in the sticks outside of New York. "I'm saving a few pennies on the auditors so I can give my clients more return," she said Madoff told her. Why, she asked, wasn't he set up like a typical hedge fund, which takes a 2 percent management fee and 20 percent of the profits? "He told me, 'I'm making up for the lower fees by attracting greater volume.'" He added, "Jews like a discount."

Goldman decided not to invest. In 2001, two skeptical articles appeared about Madoff, one in *Barron's* and another in a hedge-fund trade publication (articles, sources said, that upset Mark Madoff but that Bernie seemed to take in stride). "Wherever I went, I'd tell people, 'Don't invest with this guy!,'" Goldman said. She even sent the articles to members of the Palm Beach Country Club. "I was expecting a thank-you, and all I got back in return was a hostile response. Some of the Madoff investors said that I was behaving unprofessionally and was bad-mouthing a competitor. Oh, they were nasty! *Nasty!* They said all these publications were jealous of Bernie. They were being anti-Semitic. People called me an anti-Semite. I'm not only a Jew, I live in Israel!"

Her detractors said there could be no question whatsoever about Madoff's integrity, because he had been chosen by a man considered to be a god among the Jewish communities of Palm Beach and Boston: Carl J. Shapiro, a wealthy philanthropist of epic proportions.

'**B**ernie Madoff was the son Carl Shapiro never had," wrote Shannon Donnelly in the *Palm Beach Daily News* five days after Madoff was arrested. The story had a photograph of Madoff sitting at the family table at Carl Shapiro's 95th-birthday celebration, wearing a tuxedo and a Cheshire-cat grin. As with Norman F. Levy, Madoff became a surrogate son to the wealthy Shapiro, not only looking after the older man's money but also, according to Donnelly's story, traveling with him and appearing "on the short list of invitees to every family birthday, anniversary, bat mitzvah, wedding, or graduation."

Known as the cotton king of the garment industry, Shapiro had sold Kay Windsor, Inc., his women's-apparel company—which he founded in 1939 in New Bedford, Massachusetts, and built into one of the country's largest clothing manufacturers—in 1971 and devoted his life to philanthropy, moving between his lavish condominiums at the Taj hotel, in Boston, and on Breakers Row, in Palm Beach. With Ruth, his wife of 70 years, he has three daughters and three sons-in-law. Everyone I met described him as a devoted father, husband, and giver—hundreds of millions to Brandeis University, the Dana-Farber Cancer Institute, Brigham and Women's Hospital, in Boston (where the Carl J. and Ruth Shapiro Cardiovascular Center recently opened), the Museum of Fine Arts, the Boston Symphony Orchestra, and the Beth Israel Deaconess Medical Center, to name a few—until he lost more than half a billion dollars in Madoff's Ponzi scheme, more than any other individual investor.

Shapiro met Madoff in 1960. Back then Madoff was involved in arbitrage: buying stocks, commodities, and currencies low and selling them high. "He was 22 years old, a smart young guy," Shapiro told the *Palm Beach Daily News* in his only interview. "A friend asked me to meet him and maybe throw him a little business. I had plenty of irons in the fire so I declined. But my friend insisted. In those days it took three weeks to complete a sale," Shapiro continued. "This kid stood up in front of me and said, 'I can do it in three days,' and he did." Shapiro gave him $100,000 to invest. "And he did very well with it. That was the beginning."

Shapiro insisted that he had never steered his friends to Madoff. "In fact, we agreed when our friendship began that I would not introduce him to potential clients. I wanted to avoid putting him in the awkward position of saying 'no' to a friend of mine." No introductions were needed. Everyone at the Palm Beach Country Club *knew* that Madoff had made Shapiro rich. "It was like *Fiddler on the Roof*," said the accountant Richard Rampell, breaking into "If I Were a Rich Man," Tevye's song about the wisdom conferred upon the wealthy: "When you're rich, they think you really *know!*" According to Rampell, "Everyone had long whispered that Carl Shapiro went from rich to big rich because of investing early with Madoff." Shapiro's wealth and ostentatious philanthropy provided an irresistible siren call for potential Madoff investors, and eventually Shapiro's son-in-law Robert Jaffe took a job at a company founded by Madoff. "Bernie would not solicit business," Jaffe said after Madoff's arrest. "People went to him." They found him through feeders such as Jaffe, the son of a middle-class construction executive, who had worked in a Boston clothing store to put himself through Suffolk University. In 1969 he married Shapiro's daughter Ellen, and he was immediately admitted into the family's rarefied world. "The clothing I wear is more—dare I say—cutting edge," Jaffe told a men's-wear publication in 1998, explaining that his wardrobe included Kiton, Brioni, and Zegna. "Once you've had filet mignon, you don't want to go back."

He spent 11 years working for E. F. Hutton and 9 years at another investment firm, and in 1989 he joined Cohmad Securities—founded by Madoff and his friend and former neighbor Maurice "Sonny" Cohn—whose offices are on the same floor in the Lipstick Building as Bernard Madoff Investment Securities. Eventually Jaffe moved to Palm Beach, where he now lives in a $17 million, 11,800-square-foot home two houses over from Madoff's $9.4 million house, on the property that once belonged to newspaper heir Peter Pulitzer. Jaffe and his wife, Ellen, were among the top charitable figures of Palm Beach. With his slicked-back hair and bespoke clothing, behind the wheel of his antique roadster, whose top was *always* down, Jaffe seems to have become an unwitting show pony for Madoff's scam. "He never has a hair out of place, he almost marches when he walks, and he's a classic, dashing presence straight out of an F. Scott Fitzgerald novel," said Richard Rampell. An excellent golfer, Jaffe would tee off at his clubs—the Palm Beach Country Club and Pine Brook, near Boston—and prospective investors would clamor for his attention. For those he deemed worthy, Jaffe would receive a 1-or-2-percentage-point commission on their first trade. Thus, Jaffe became another front man for what Rampell calls "country-club investing, where, once one person who everybody thinks is smart gets in on something, everybody wants in on it, too. It's a herd instinct."

It was brilliant. With the most revered Jewish philanthropist in Palm Beach as his surrogate father, and the philanthropist's glamorous son-in-law as his local feeder, Madoff could remain aloof and say no while Jaffe—who many insist was duped along with his father-in-law—attracted investors. (A spokesperson for Robert Jaffe and Carl Shapiro says, "Both men are victims and had no knowledge of Madoff's fraudulent scheme.") As late as Thanksgiving of last year, two weeks before Madoff's arrest, Jaffe was reportedly considering new clients in Palm Beach. While Jaffe and other middlemen were pulling in money, however, Ruth Madoff was withdrawing: $5.5 million on November 25 from Cohmad Securities, the investment entity co-owned by Madoff, of which Jaffe is vice president.

By late 2008, as the market continued its slide, Madoff needed more and more money, more grist for the mill, and he apparently didn't care where it came from. The deaths of friends and family were reduced to dollars and cents, as seen in a case that played out in Madoff's offices six weeks prior to December 11. One of the Madoffs' close friends had died, leaving behind a widow who was at a total loss as to how to handle her husband's sizable estate. "You've got to talk to Bernie!" she told her son.

"I made an appointment and went up to see him," the son told me. He had joined Bernie and Ruth and their family on countless occasions, and that afternoon Madoff was the gracious, caring, immaculately dressed gentleman he'd always been, consoling the young man for half an hour in his conference room. "He said, 'How's Mom? Your dad was such a great guy. How are *you* doing?' " the son remembered. "He was Uncle Bernie, making you feel that you're special, that we were getting favors. Finally, he said, 'Don't worry, we'll take care of Mom.' And he got this guy on the intercom and said, 'Take care of him. He's family.' "

They stood up, and Madoff gave his visitor "a hug, a warm embrace." A week later the young man returned to Madoff's office, this time with his mother. "He gave my mom a hug, and soon after we consolidated everything and sent the money in. Looking back on it, it was an amazingly chilling thing."

By Thanksgiving, Madoff was creating a new investment fund for "special friends"—five investors for a total of $500 million. "I wouldn't want to be sitting at a poker table with him. He would clean my clock," Home Depot co-founder Ken Langone, who got pitched by Madoff about the new fund on November 24 but declined to invest, later told CNBC. "You wouldn't think this guy had a problem in the world." By the first week of December, however, Madoff's façade was crumbling. He told one of his sons that there had been requests from clients—believed to include his main feeder fund, the Fairfield Greenwich Group—for $7 billion, and that he was "struggling to obtain the liquidity necessary to meet those obligations." On or around December 1, Madoff asked Carl Shapiro to wire him $250 million, ostensibly to put in Treasury bills, which Shapiro did. "[Bernie] seemed a little anxious this time," Ruth Shapiro would later reflect. "He kept calling, saying, 'I didn't get it. It hasn't come yet. Are you sure you sent it?' " It came, and now Carl Shapiro had about $400 million personally invested, along with $145 million of his family foundation's charitable funds.

During the week of December 8, Madoff hosted his annual holiday party for the employees in the New York office. "I was told by American staff that he was all happy, saying, 'Happy holidays to everyone! We're going to have a great year!'" remembered Julia Fenwick. "It has to be some psychopathic mind. How you can tell your staff, people who rely on you for their income, that we're going to have a great year and then within 48 hours admit to the feds that you've committed this enormous fraud?"

Although many people have doubted, considering the closeness of the family in the Madoff business, that the whole charade was known to Bernie alone, here is what the Madoffs have told authorities:

On December 9, a Tuesday, Bernie advised Mark that he wanted to pay employee bonuses in December, instead of February, as he normally would, and he wrote out $173 million in checks, explaining that it represented "profits through the business operations." Mark—"a little bit of a scaredy-cat, whose nerves got the best of him," according to one source— was alarmed and reportedly expressed his concerns to Andrew. The sons were already worried about their father's increasingly apparent levels of stress; now here was this strange explanation about the $173 million. On December 10, Mark and Andrew went into their father's glass-enclosed office to challenge him about the payments. "I'm not sure I will be able to hold it together," Madoff told them, meaning he'd break down if they continued the discussion in the office, and he insisted that they go to his penthouse, nearby. When they got there, Bernie did break down, telling his sons what he said he'd already told his brother, Peter: that he was "finished," that he had "absolutely nothing," that "it's all just one big lie," his esteemed investment fund "basically a giant Ponzi scheme" involving $65 billion. He would surrender to authorities in one week, as soon as he disbursed the $200 to $300 million he had left to certain selected employees and friends. The sons said they then called a lawyer, who advised them to call the Department of Justice and the S.E.C. That same day Ruth Madoff withdrew yet more money—this time $10 million—from Cohmad.

At 8:30 A.M. on December 11, Special Agent Theodore Cacioppi and another agent went to Madoff's apartment building, at 133 East 64th Street, which has two units per floor starting at $5 million. Madoff opened the door to his $7.4 million penthouse.

"We are here to find out if there's an innocent explanation," Cacioppi said.

"There is no innocent explanation," said Madoff, adding that he "paid investors with money that wasn't there." He was "broke," he said. "It could not go on," he added, saying he fully expected to go to jail.

"If you work on a trading desk, stop what you're doing for a second · before you walk out the door and clean out your desk for the day," aspiring Money Honey Michelle Caruso-Cabrera said on CNBC late on the afternoon of December 11. "Bernie Madoff has been arrested."

That afternoon the telephone rang in Carl Shapiro's home beside the Atlantic, and the nonagenarian picked up. His son-in-law Robert Jaffe was on the other end. "Turn on CNN," Jaffe said, and Shapiro saw his friend Bernie and heard the unimaginable news of his arrest. It wasn't just the money, it was the betrayal, the betrayal, Shapiro kept repeating. "It was," he would later say, "like a knife to the heart."

Carl Shapiro lost more than half a billion dollars to Madoff, but far worse was the fact that Madoff had tarnished irreparably what was more important to Shapiro, second only to his family: his good name, which is engraved on buildings from Palm Beach to Boston (three on the Brandeis University campus alone, and two more under construction). "He had to pick out all the furniture and the curtains, and you would have to put his name on the napkins and on the this and that—you know, he wanted to see his name everywhere," said one Bostonian. "He owes about a hundred million in pledges around Boston, so this has created a huge ripple effect." Shapiro insists that he will honor all existing obligations, but that he will make no new ones. His sunset years will most likely be consumed with fighting the aftershocks of Bernie Madoff. As for Robert Jaffe, he has reportedly been physically threatened, and he and his wife have resigned as chairs of the $90 million Palm Healthcare Foundation and abruptly canceled the December engagement party they were planning for their son at the Palm Beach Country Club.

"I've found that whenever there is one cockroach in plain sight, many more are lurking behind the corner out of plain view," wrote Harry Markopolos in his 19-page 2005 report warning the S.E.C. about Madoff. After the lid blew off Madoff's operation, an underworld of dubious middlemen came to light, notably Frank Avellino and Michael Bienes, who had gotten their start as junior accountants in Ruth Madoff's father's accounting firm in the 1950s. Avellino had been investigated for possibly running a Ponzi scheme back in 1992, when he was promising his 3,200 clients a 13.5

to 20 percent return. (All their money was invested with Madoff.) "We did not know who Bernie Madoff was," said Nancie Taylor, who, along with her California-real-estate-developer husband, Jack Daley, became acquainted with Avellino in the early 90s after he purchased Taylor's 10,000-square-foot house on Nantucket. In 2001 they invested a combined $1.1 million with him. "We first heard Madoff's name on December 11, and when I called Avellino, he didn't get on the phone, but his wife did. She said, 'Things are grim!'" Daley added, "I am wiped out." Avellino is now fighting a number of lawsuits, including one by his Bulgarian housekeeper, who alleges that she and her husband were told to write their $124,000 check to "a fictitious entity," only to be told by Avellino 10 days before Madoff's arrest that all was lost. A number of those who had only recently upped their investment with Madoff, including the daughter of an extremely wealthy couple I met in Palm Beach, rushed to the Lipstick Building in panic mode. When they got to the lobby they found a flock of fellow fatalities, but they were all brusquely turned away. Since Madoff's surrender to the authorities, he has been under house arrest in his Manhattan penthouse, awaiting indictment.

The most brutal indignity befell the debonair Palm Beach feeder Robert Jaffe on the evening after Madoff's arrest, in the most public of places: Mar-a-Lago, the private club owned by Donald Trump in the former home of Marjorie Merriweather Post, who built the estate when she was Mrs. E. F. Hutton. The cream of the Palm Beach Jewish community had gathered at a seated dinner in the little ballroom to celebrate carpet king Jerry Stark's 60th birthday. Jerome Fisher, the co-founder of Nine West shoes, walked in with his wife, Anne. Fisher had "a few bucks"—reportedly $150 million—invested with Madoff through his friend Jaffe. When Fisher spotted Jaffe that night at the party, he exploded. "I was sitting at the next table, and I will tell you Jerome Fisher went wild," said one guest. "I mean this guy Jaffe got him into the deal to start off with, and on top of it he got a commission. And Fisher didn't know about the commission. Fisher was screaming, 'What the hell are *you* doing here! And you got a fucking commission—a point and a half—on me!' And he let out a roar at this guy that was unbelievable."

That roar echoed though homes, offices, and institutions worldwide. But it was too late. By then Bernie Madoff and $65 billion were gone.

· 18 ·

Part II:
"Hello, Madoff!"
What the Secretary Saw

By MARK SEAL and ELEANOR SQUILLARI

June 2009

From 1942 to 1945, Adolf Hitler employed a young secretary named Traudl Junge. She took dictation from him, handled his correspondence, even typed his last will and testament, and was inside the bunker in Berlin the day he shot and killed himself. Yet despite their close proximity, Junge later claimed that she had rarely heard Hitler utter the word "Jew" and had learned about the Holocaust only after her boss was dead and the war was over. She suffered enormous guilt, she said, over having once actually liked "the greatest criminal ever to have lived."

In writing about Bernard Madoff for *Vanity Fair*'s April issue, I frequently heard his victims refer to him as another Hitler, who decimated his largely Jewish clientele by stealing their money in the biggest Ponzi scheme in history. The night the magazine shipped to the printer, my cell phone rang. "This is Eleanor Squillari," the caller said in a heavy New York accent. "You left me a message a couple of weeks ago. As you can imagine, I've been pretty busy." She paused, then added, "I was Bernie Madoff's secretary."

· A few days later, in an apartment on the Upper East Side of Manhattan, I met this smart, attractive, gutsy Italian-American, who for 25 years had sat right outside Madoff's office. Like Traudl Junge, Squillari insisted that in all that time she had had no idea what lay beneath her boss's affable, if frequently peculiar, façade, or what transpired on the 17th floor of the Lipstick Building—two floors below *her* office—where $65 billion in investors' funds disappeared. Unlike Hitler's secretary, who spent years trying to distance herself from the Nazi war crimes, Eleanor has spent nearly every moment since her boss's arrest, on December 11 of last year, trying to help bring about justice.

She was still working with the F.B.I. in the emptied-out offices of Bernard L. Madoff Investment Securities L.L.C. when she decided to write this story with me. Exposing the truth was the least Eleanor felt compelled to do for the thousands of individuals Madoff had robbed of their money and their future. Since the story is all Eleanor's, we have cast it in her voice.

Bernie staged the whole thing, the way he did everything. Bernie was never careless. He always had to be in control. He set up *exactly* how he wanted to go down. The feds—along with the public and his 13,500 investors—got wind of his scam exactly the way he wanted them to get it.

December 11, 2008, the day Bernie chose to get arrested, was the culmination of several very strange months at Bernard L. Madoff Investment Securities. But then, Bernie was always strange—never in a bad or weird way, just different. He liked to find your weak spot and poke at you with his sarcastic humor. He had to take everything way too far. "You know, you remind me a lot of the Larry David character," I once told him, referring to the obsessive-compulsive but lovable guy on *Curb Your Enthusiasm*. "So I've been told," he said, "but I'm a lot better-looking."

In late 2008, things suddenly got out of control for Bernie. For two decades I had sat within shouting distance of him as his number-one assistant while his investment business exploded and he became, as he liked to remind me constantly, "one of the most powerful men on Wall Street." Now he started to become somebody I didn't know. His habits and behavior changed in the weeks just before his arrest. He would walk into the office looking tired. His voice, always so strong, had become weak, almost inaudible. Instead of stopping at my desk to review the day ahead, he would rush straight past me, distracted, without even saying hello. I had always been able to get his attention from my desk with just a wave, but now he never even looked up. If he wasn't staring off into space, he was looking down, working on figures. "He seems to be in a coma," I would tell employees who came looking for him.

I assumed it was the market downturn, but I didn't ask. Bernie and I got along well because I knew when *not* to bother him, and this was definitely one of those times. One day, though, I pointed out that his hands were discolored. "It's a side effect from the blood-pressure medicine I'm taking," he said. He bought a blood-pressure-measuring gadget and began taking his blood pressure every 15 minutes. Then his back problems began. He complained of back pain and would just lie on the floor with his arms outstretched and close his eyes. People passing by would ask, "Is Bernie all right?"

"No," I would respond, "but he's not dead," and they would just shake their heads and walk away. Nobody was ever shocked at anything Bernie Madoff did. Up to then.

December 10, the day before Bernie's arrest, was the day of our office Christmas party, at the Rosa Mexicano restaurant on First Avenue. Everybody had been looking forward to it. Business couldn't have been better, and we all felt so fortunate to have secure jobs in light of the depressing economy. After all, Bernie Madoff had never had a down year.

That day, however, turned out to be quite unusual. For one thing, I realized that Bernie hadn't scheduled a single phone call or meeting for the entire day, which was a first for him. Then I noticed that Ruth Madoff, Bernie's wife and partner of nearly 50 years, seemed to be trying to sneak past my desk. Ordinarily, she would let me know when she was in the office, in case anybody was looking for her. But that morning she was not at all her usual calm, composed, perfectly put-together self. When I caught her eye, she laughed nervously and said, "Oh, hi. Don't worry, I didn't forget you."

Every year, on the day of the Christmas party, Ruth and Bernie would have gifts for the women who worked in the office, and Ruth was letting me know that mine was on the way. Only later would we discover the real reason for her visit that day: she was withdrawing $10 million from her personal account.

A few hours later, Bernie and his younger brother, Peter, who was senior manager of trading and compliance director, had what I believe was their last meeting together before Bernie's arrest. They met in Bernie's office, with Bernie's two sons, Mark and Andy, whom I've known since they were teenagers. I called them "the boys." The only reason I took notice of the meeting was because of Peter. He seemed relaxed, sitting beside Bernie's desk with his legs crossed, and Peter was *never* relaxed in a meeting with Bernie. We called him the Energizer Bunny. But that day it looked as if the air had been sucked out of him. When I walked over to drop off some mail, Bernie and his sons stood up, startled, and stared at me. I had no idea that Bernie was about to confess to them—and had already confessed to Peter—that he had committed the worst securities fraud in history.

I also noticed how anxious the boys looked that day. I watched them get their father's coat and help him into it. Then the three of them abruptly started to leave. "And where are *you* going?," I asked Bernie, because he never went anywhere without telling me. His collar was pulled up so high I couldn't see his face. "I'm going out," he said without looking at me. Mark leaned over and whispered, "We're going Christmas shopping."

I knew something was wrong, but I thought it was a problem in the family. I couldn't reach Bernie for the rest of that afternoon. I tried his cell phone several times, but all I got was his voice mail: "Hi, you've reached Bernie Madoff. I'm unavailable right now. If you need me, you can call my office at 212-230-2424. Or just leave a message and I'll get back to you."

Before I left for the Christmas party, however, I realized that he *was* using his cell phone. One of his drivers said he had overheard Bernie on it, telling Frank DiPascali Jr., the go-to guy for the investment-advisory business, "Andy was so nervous he almost pissed his pants." Clearly, Andy had just found out what I was about to discover the next day: his father was a crook.

Mark and Andy didn't show up at the party; I later learned that they had gone to the Justice Department instead. But Bernie and Ruth were there, and you wouldn't have thought they had a care in the world. I was so put off with Bernie for his behavior that day and for not checking in with me all afternoon that I didn't even say hello. But I could see him and Ruth across the restaurant, exchanging stories about children and grandchildren with some of their longtime friends, who so trusted Bernie that they had invested their life savings with him.

They were hours away from discovering that everything they had worked all of their lives for was gone. I will always wonder why Ruth and Bernie attended the party, looking so calm. Did they want to see us all one last time? Or was it part of Bernie's plan?

Bernard L. Madoff Investment Securities occupied three floors in the 34-story Lipstick Building, on Third Avenue in Manhattan. All the interior walls were made of glass, so there was no privacy. Bernie, Peter, Mark, Andy, and I worked on 19, the administrative floor. Four-fifths of the floor was occupied by the trading room for our market-making business. Mark and Andy sat on a raised platform in the trading room, surrounded by about 50 traders, but they also had private offices on the floor. Bernie had the largest office, and I sat about 10 feet in front of his door. Peter's office was directly across from Bernie's, on the other side of the floor. Between their offices was a big conference room.

There was a circular staircase down to the 18th floor. At the foot of the stairs was a reception area behind which Ruth kept a large office. A few years ago, she stopped coming in full-time, but she would still show up once or twice a week. Nearby was a second conference room. Shana Madoff, Peter's daughter, who was the rules-compliance lawyer for the trading division, and Rick Sobel, our in-house attorney, also had offices on 18. "Systems," the computer area for everything on 18 and 19, was situated directly beneath the trading room. Also on 18 was the office of Cohmad Securities, an investment entity Bernie had co-founded with his friend Maurice "Sonny" Cohn, which had a core staff of six.

On the 17th floor was the investment-advisory business (later better known as the Ponzi scheme). At the other end of 17 was the "cage," the stock-loan department, where wire transfers came in and went out.

December 11 started like any other day, except that instead of taking the ferry from Staten Island, where I live, I rode in with my friend Debbie, who headed the legitimate Madoff auto-execution, or computerized-trading, department. By seven A.M., I was at my desk. Ordinarily, Bernie didn't get in until nine, and I would spend the two hours before his arrival going through the calendars and getting ready for the day.

Around 7:30, Ruth called. Usually she was upbeat, bubbly, but that day her voice sounded dead. "Are the boys in yet?" she asked. "I haven't seen them. Hold on, let me check," I said, and went into the trading room, where Mark and Andy were always at their desks by 7:30 or 8. There was no sign of them. "No," I told Ruth, and I heard her say, obviously to Bernie, "They're not there." Now I felt something *had* to be wrong.

A little later I went to say good morning to our receptionist, Jean, who worked on 18. As I walked down the circular staircase, I could see the glass-walled conference room on that floor, where Peter Madoff, his face pale and blank, was surrounded by serious-looking men in suits. "Lawyers," Jean told me. It was now nine, and still no sign of Bernie. A big guy in a trench coat tried to rush past me into the conference room. "Excuse me, can I help you?," I asked.

He flashed a badge in my face and barked, "F.B.I." It was Ted Cacioppi, who, along with another agent, was about to go to Bernie's apartment and place him under arrest. I put out my arm and barked back, "Wait right here!" He turned beet red, and I thought the veins in his neck were going to burst. But he stopped. I went into my protective mode, because we never let anyone into the office unless we knew the reason for their visit. I poked my head into the conference room, but Peter seemed oblivious. "There's a—" was all I got out. One of the lawyers said, "Send him in. We're expecting him."

I guess I watch too many crime shows, because I immediately thought, A family member has been kidnapped, and this is an extortion attempt. By now it was after nine, and people were looking for Bernie. I kept calling his cell phone. No answer. Later Peter's secretary, Elaine, who's British, walked over to me, looking stunned. I'd never seen her like that. "They're saying," she said, "that Bernie was arrested for securities fraud."

"*Who's* saying that?," I asked.

"It's what Peter is telling the traders," she said.

Just then Peter walked by and we stopped him in his tracks. "Bernie has been arrested for securities fraud, and that's all I know," he blurted as he rushed off. Then the S.E.C. arrived, and soon everyone in the office knew that Bernie had been arrested. Once the news hit television, our phones began ringing. I told the frantic callers, "I know as much as you do. All I can do at this point is take your name and number." One elderly woman called four times from Florida, crying hysterically; I was worried that she might have a heart attack. A very agitated gentleman also called several times, telling me that all of his money was invested with us, that the bank was calling the note on his mortgage, and that he was going to lose his house—was there *anything* I could do? Another longtime client called, said he had lost a huge amount, and whispered, "Eleanor, did you *know?*"

It wasn't just the question; it was the way he said it, like it was a secret between us. I was crushed that he could have thought I was in on the scam. But this man had just lost a fortune. He had the right to ask whatever he wanted. If I had sat outside Bernie's office for so many years, why *wouldn't* he think I knew? The calls went on all day. That night when I went home, all I could do was go to bed, but I couldn't sleep. "It can't be true," I kept saying to myself. "There must be some innocent explanation. It's got to be a mistake."

By the next morning, a Friday, the news was everywhere. I rode to work again with Debbie. We were both very nervous. "You know there are going to be TV cameras outside," she said. "I wouldn't be surprised if there's somebody with a gun," I said. We walked through the mob of reporters with our heads down and rode the elevator up to the office. It was filled with investigators, whose first act was to cut the wires to the paper shredders. The phones were ringing off the hook, the fax machines were spitting out reams of paper from clients demanding redemptions, and a group of at least 25 angry investors down in the lobby were screaming for someone to come and speak with them. I finally found Peter and asked him, "What am I supposed to be telling all these people?" He just threw up his hands and walked away.

That's when I realized we were all on our own, and whenever bad things happen to me, I take charge and hit them straight on. I told the women I worked with, "Let's just start taking messages." As the calls multiplied until they spun out of control, I decided I needed help from the people on 17. Surely they knew these investors and could give them some sense of what was going on. I went down to 17 and put my card key up to the box on the wall next to the door. There was a click, and when I opened the door I was taken aback: the place was empty. The day before there had been a full staff down there. Now there was only Frank DiPascali, who handled the investment accounts. A cocky Italian-American in his early 50s, he was dressed in jeans and Top-Siders and had a cell phone glued to his ear. "Frank, the phones won't stop ringing!," I said. "What should I say to them?" He stared at me without taking the phone away from his ear. "Tell them nobody's available," he snapped, and went back to his conversation. (DiPascali has not been charged with any wrongdoing.)

That afternoon, concerned that the phones were probably bugged by the feds, I took my cell phone into Mark Madoff's office and punched in Bernie again. This time I called his home number, since I knew it was the only place he could be. His answering machine came on, and I said, "Bernie, you know that I love you and I'm thinking about you, and I'm trying my very best to handle the phones. If you need anything, please call me." Twenty minutes later the private line on my desk rang, and it was Bernie. "Hi, sweetie," he said. He had never called me "sweetie" before.

"Are you all right? Is Ruth all right?," I asked.

"Sure, we're all right," he said.

Then his tone changed. "Is anyone in my office?" he asked.

"Yes," I said. "The F.B.I.'s already been in there, and now there's a woman from the S.E.C."

"Did they go in my briefcase?"

"Yes."

"Did they look in my appointment book?"

"Yes."

"O.K.," he said.

"Call me if you need anything," I told him, and we said good-bye.

It was at that moment that all the pieces began to come together. I realized that Bernie had staged the whole thing, and I suspected that he was planning to take the fall alone. I felt sick. Suddenly I knew why he had written in his appointment book the week of the arrest, "Remember to pay employees," which was totally out of character for him, because he *never* paid employees himself. And now it made sense why he had left his appointment book out on his desk for the last couple of days. Normally, he never went anywhere without it. I figured he had left it behind for the F.B.I., so when his sons told them their father had suddenly started paying employees for no apparent reason, the agents would find proof of it in the appointment book. It also now made sense why he had written the name Ike in his book for meetings on two different days that week. Ike was Ira Sorkin, Bernie's lawyer and longtime associate. Bernie was planning to be arrested, but he wasn't sure which day it should be arranged to happen.

The only thing that didn't make sense, if he had planned everything so carefully, was why Ruth would come into the office for the $10 million withdrawal from her Cohmad account on the day before his arrest. Did Bernie tell her to do it? Or did she do it on her own, without Bernie's knowledge, because she was panicked and wanted to make sure she would have enough cash after her husband was hauled off to jail?

In any case, the phone call from Bernie made me lose it. On Saturday, I couldn't even get out of bed. I was sobbing, trying to comprehend the enormity of what my boss had done. My home phone kept ringing—employees and ex-employees who had invested money with Madoff and lost everything. By the time I went to work on Monday, my shock had turned to anger. I started looking through my drawers and calendars for possible evidence. Most of the 150 people on our New York staff would be terminated in the weeks to come. Several of us were kept on to help the investigators and the bankruptcy trustees sort out the mess. However, in the beginning nobody talked to us. They'd never experienced anything of this magnitude, and they were trying to figure out where to start.

I kept going through my files from previous years, hoping to be helpful. The team of investigators quickly grew, swarming over everything, but they kept to themselves. By Tuesday, I could hardly take it anymore. The office was a mess, and I had always kept everything so neat and organized. There were papers strewn everywhere, and the antique trunk in Bernie's office, where he kept his important financial documents, had been opened and torn apart. I could see his prized four-foot-tall black rubber sculpture of a screw behind his desk, and somehow it took on new meaning that day. I suddenly had the sinking feeling as I looked at it that we were all screwed.

That was the last straw for me. I knew that I had to help the agents find out what the hell had been going on in that company. I stood up and shouted above the noise, "Hey, guys! *Hello?* I'm the secretary! I have the calendars. I must *know* things! *Doesn't anybody want to talk to me?*"

In 1984, I was a 34-year-old single mom with two young children, living in Bensonhurst, in Brooklyn, and working as a part-time bank teller. One day that March, a friend told me, "Somebody I know is looking for a receptionist at a brokerage firm on Wall Street. Are you interested?" I took the subway into Manhattan, nervous about the interview, because by then I'd heard that this guy Madoff and his brother were a sharp team, so this could be a great opportunity. Their offices were on a floor and a half at 110 Wall Street, and there were about 40 people on their staff. They were market-makers, involved in volume trading of stocks with other institutions. (Madoff claims that his fraud began in the early 1990s; the government believes that it began in the 1980s.)

"He's very particular and very conservative, and the phone is his lifeline," Bernie's secretary, Barbara, told me. Then she walked me into his big corner office, where Bernie sat at his desk. He was in his mid-40s, with long, wavy, European-cut hair. His shirtsleeves were rolled up, and he was on the phone. He motioned for me to sit down. Through open sliding doors, I could see the trading room, all sleek and modern, in shades of gray and black.

"Sorry to have kept you waiting," Bernie said. "My firm is built on reputation, and I liked the way you sounded on the phone. How someone sounds on the phone is very important to me, because it's the first impression people get." He looked me up and down. I was wearing a black skirt, tweed blazer, and black pumps. "Appearances are very important, and the way you're dressed is perfect."

The interview lasted 15 minutes. The only recommendation he needed was the fact that the bank I worked for had rehired me after I had my children and re-entered the workforce. "I'd like you to take the job," he said. "Can I get back to you about it?," I asked. "Sure," he said. "I have something to do, but I'll be back in 10 minutes. You can give me your answer then." In other words, it was take it or leave it. When he came back 10 minutes later, I said, "I'll take it."

A younger man walked into the office. "This is my brother, Peter," Bernie said. "He's the one who will keep you busy. I'm the easy one. Peter's the one who generates all the paperwork." As I shook Peter's hand, I was struck by his good looks. He reminded me of Lee Majors, the star of the

series *The Six Million Dollar Man.* Bernie told me, "If you're loyal and dedicated, you'll go far here. And if you're good to us, we'll take care of you."

My salary was $160 a week. My duties included answering the phones,
opening the mail, and, as I got to know the traders, helping them tally up
their tickets. We weren't fully automated back then, so at the end of each
day I would total the trades—what was bought, what was sold—on an
adding machine.

Everyone in that office adored Bernie, especially Barbara, his secretary.
When she talked about him, she had love in her eyes. "He's accomplished so much, and he's such an incredible man," she told me more than
once. We went out one night after work and found ourselves in front of
Bernie and Ruth's apartment building, at 133 East 64th Street. "You see
that penthouse up there? That's Bernie's! Look how far he's come," Barbara
gushed.

I soon learned that Bernie was prone to mood swings, and Barbara
couldn't take criticism from him. At times, if he criticized her, she would
just walk out and go home. One day, she left for good. (Barbara declined
to comment.) By then we had moved into the Lipstick Building, at 885
Third Avenue, which was partly owned by Bernie's longtime friend Fred
Wilpon, who was also part owner of the New York Mets. (Wilpon would
later become a victim in the Madoff scam.) I asked Bernie if I could have
Barbara's job. "O.K.," he said, "we'll try it."

It was a family business. Bernie and Peter were opposites who made a
whole. Peter was very bright technology-wise, able to do 10 things at once.
Bernie was the boss, but was more laid-back. He didn't have Peter's capacity
for multi-tasking, and, despite his reputation as an electronic-trading pioneer, he didn't seem able to use a computer. When his Ponzi scheme came
to light, however, I discovered that nobody could multi-task better. The
Bernie I knew wasn't tech-savvy at all. I never saw him touch a computer or
a BlackBerry; he didn't even know how to go on the Internet. If he needed
something online, he would have me search for it. It was another Bernie I
saw in a picture taken through his penthouse window after his arrest. To
my surprise, there he was, working away on a computer.

Peter ran the legitimate trading room and pulled everything together,
but Bernie made all the decisions. It was obvious that Bernie loved his

brother, but he clearly felt that he was more important than Peter. Once, after flying back from Washington together, they both called me from the airport to see if there were any phone messages. The first call I got was from Bernie, and then my other line rang. I said, "Hold on," and punched the other line. It was Peter. I told him, "Let me tell Bernie you're on the phone," and put him on hold. I said to Bernie, "Do you mind holding, because I have Peter on the other end." I could hear Bernie call to Peter, "Hang up the fucking phone. She's *my* secretary!" Peter got his own secretary soon after that.

Ruth Madoff didn't take to me at first. She was guarded around new people; it took her time to warm up to them. As I got to know her, I learned that she would spare no expense for her appearance—clothes, designer handbags, expensive haircuts, cosmetic surgeries (over the years there were several). Ruth did the office bookkeeping. She paid the bills. I don't know what else she was doing, but she definitely handled all the invoices that came in.

There was never any doubt that Bernie's sons would work for their dad. Mark came in first. He was handsome, sweet, and outgoing. Andy, his younger brother, was friendly but more reserved. Mark started learning the business while he was still in college. He liked to sit and answer the phones with me, but Bernie wanted him in the trading room. At first Mark didn't want to go, possibly because Bernie expected perfection, and the responsibility of going into the trading room had to seem enormous to Mark. Peter's daughter, Shana, began coming in to the office when she was 13 or 14. Peter wanted her to get accustomed to the office at an early age.

When I started, Annette Bongiorno had the office next to my reception area, and her staff had an office in the back. I often typed letters for Annette, and I would give her title as "administrative assistant." Everyone called her department "bookkeeping." In fact, she headed Bernie's investment-advisory business, where individuals would invest money and receive dividends. It would later become the vehicle for his Ponzi scheme. It was completely separate from his market-making business, which traded with institutions, not individuals.

A couple of years into the job, I asked Bernie if he thought I should go back to school to learn about finance. "No, you don't need to do that," he said. "You've got two kids to raise. If you have to take a class, take an art class, and I'll pay for it. But not a business class." Now I realize that he didn't want me to know too much.

Back then, Bernie's and Peter's phones never stopped—brokers, investors, friends. I thought there was only one business, the market-making business, and that Bernie dealt exclusively with institutional clients. It wasn't until 1993 that I became fully aware that there was a second business, in which Bernie invested money as a favor to a limited number of individuals.

I learned about this advisory business by means of two controversial moneymen: Frank Avellino and Michael Bienes. They were certified public accountants who had gotten their start in the early 1960s working for the accounting firm of Ruth Madoff's father, Saul Alpern. After Bernie started his own firm, in 1960, Avellino and Bienes began raising money from clients to invest with him. I met them both in the office.

In a 1992 lawsuit, the S.E.C. claimed that from 1962 to 1992 Avellino and Bienes illegally issued unregistered securities (meaning not registered with the S.E.C.), which promised annual returns of between 13.5 and 20 percent. They entrusted more than $441 million from 3,200 investors with Bernie. When the S.E.C. got wind of this, in 1992, and shut them down, Avellino and Bienes had to return the money to their clients. Soon the clients were calling Bernie Madoff to open new accounts directly with him— most of them were unaware that their money had been invested with Bernie in the first place.

One day Bernie told me, "We're going to be busy for a while. We'll be getting a lot of phone calls for new accounts."

"What's going on?," I asked.

"The S.E.C. shut down Avellino and Bienes, and all of their clients are now coming to us."

"Why were they shut down?"

"Oh, it was something stupid, an accounting glitch." He made it all sound totally insignificant. "But listen," he added, "I don't want the whole world knowing about this, so don't repeat what goes on in here." It was so Bernie to think the whole world gave a damn about what went on in our office.

"So who cares?," I said.

"I just don't want you talking about it," he said, exasperated that I would question him. "I don't want to be associated with a firm that was shut down by the S.E.C., because my reputation is my business." He was so insistent about it that he wouldn't even allow me to utter the names Avellino and Bienes in the office. "Just refer to them as A and B," he said.

A and B's investors contacted us in droves. They didn't call *asking* to open accounts; they called *expecting* accounts to be opened for them. Most of them were elderly retirees, many of them widows. They had been accustomed to living off the double-digit dividends they'd been promised by Avellino and Bienes. Now they put their money in Bernie's hands. (Bienes has said that he was scammed as well and didn't suspect that Madoff was running a Ponzi scheme.)

Bernie was irresistible to women. There was a mystique about him— the money, the power, the legend. Women were very flirtatious around him, and he was comfortable with that, even if Ruth wasn't. There were two Ruth Madoffs: one was very sure of herself and very committed to her family, always finding time for friends and relatives. Being a workout junkie kept her in perfect shape—she weighed barely 100 pounds—and gave her the energy to get through busy days that would have exhausted most people. Many mornings, Ruth would call me first thing with a list of reminders for Bernie—thank-you notes to be written, travel to be booked, dinner reservations to be made. She was always on top of everything.

Then there was the other Ruth: the aging blonde who seemed to wish she were taller, younger, prettier. On a bad day, I would see this other Ruth, frazzled, moody, and temperamental. She could speak very harshly to people, including her family. If Bernie said something to Ruth that annoyed her, she'd say, "Go fuck yourself," or "I don't give a shit." That's the way they talked to each other. I remember one time Mark asked Ruth, "You want to know what I had for lunch, Mom?" She said, "To tell you the truth, I really don't give a shit." She was never that way with outsiders, however, because image meant everything to Ruth. Her apparent insecurity was surprising, but it was there, especially when it came to Bernie. She wanted to be perfect for him. She would never allow herself to gain weight or have a hair out of place, and she always kept an eagle eye on him, especially when he was around young, attractive women.

One day Bernie told me that he and Ruth were having dinner with Arpad "Arki" Busson, of the hedge-fund firm EIM SA, who had money invested in our company, and his girlfriend, the actress Uma Thurman. "Ruth doesn't want to go," he said. "She's intimidated, because Uma Thurman is so beautiful and so tall."

"Well, it's probably your fault," I said. "You made her that way."

"You're probably right," he said with a sigh.

Like the Larry David character, Bernie got a kick out of making suggestive sexual remarks, but he did it in such a way that you had to laugh. "Oh, you know you're crazy about me," he would say to me. Sometimes when he came out of his bathroom, which was diagonal to my desk, he would still be zipping up his pants. If he saw me shaking my head disapprovingly, he would say, "Oh, you know it excites you." If a pretty young woman came in, he'd say, "Do you remember when you used to look like that?" I'd tell him, "Knock it off, Bernie," and he'd go, "Ah, you still look good." Then he'd try to pat me on the ass. I never considered it sexual harassment; it was just his way of being affectionate. Once, he gave me a picture of him taken by Karsh, the famous Canadian photographer, saying, "Here, hang this over your bed."

Bernie had a roving eye, and I knew he had a habit of getting frequent massages. One day I caught him scouting the escort pages that run alongside pictures of scantily clad women in the back of a magazine. He was slunk down so low in his chair that he was practically under the desk. He didn't know I was watching him. "Keep it up and it's going to fall off," I told him.

He straightened up in his chair, startled, and said, "I'm just looking!"

"Right," I said, and laughed.

Once, I looked in his address book and found, under *M*, about a dozen phone numbers for his masseuses. "If you ever lose your address book and somebody finds it, they're going to think you're a pervert," I said.

He would sometimes schedule a massage in the middle of the trading hours. "I'm going out for a while," he would say. "Where are you going?," I'd ask. "Just taking a walk," he'd lie. He'd return an hour or so later, always in a much better mood.

In 2002, cancer spread through the Madoff family. It began when Bernie and Peter's beautiful seven-year-old grandniece, Ariel, was diagnosed with leukemia. She was in treatment for two years. I recall how distressed we all felt, especially Peter. This heartbreaking event must have saddened Bernie too, but he never showed any sign of emotion at work. Today, Ariel is cancer-free.

That same year, Peter and Marion Madoff's only son, Roger, learned that he also had leukemia. In his late 20s, Roger was all you could ask for in a son—good-looking, gifted, with an upbeat personality. Roger had made his mark as a writer for Bloomberg News before coming to work with us. His passing, in 2006, was a major blow to the family. Peter began going to synagogue every morning before work in order to deal with it. While Bernie cared, he didn't allow the tragedy to interfere with business. I don't think I ever saw him react over illness, or even death.

In 2003, Bernie's son Andy was diagnosed with lymphoma, and I thought for once Bernie's steely façade might crack. I remember seeing Andy talking to his father in Bernie's office. Bernie just had a blank look on his face. Later I realized that Andy was telling his father what the doctor had found. The next morning, Mark and I got into a little debate about something, and we raised our voices. It wasn't an argument; Mark and I just went back and forth with each other at times. Bernie came out and shouted, "Stop it!" He glared at me and said, "You're an idiot."

"Don't talk to me like that," I said, "or you're going to feel sorry."

That's how Bernie handled stress, by saying something nasty: *You look terrible. You're gaining weight. You're stupid.* I never took anything he said to me personally, because I knew it wasn't about me, it was about him. Nine times out of 10, he would end up apologizing.

After Andy's diagnosis, Bernie developed the habit of sitting next to his sons in the trading room at some point every day. I noticed how he would stare at Andy, as if he was trying to absorb every expression that came across his face. I believe he cared very much about his sons, but he never got emotional. He stayed in full control. After aggressive treatment, Andy is doing well today.

Several other Madoff employees who got cancer are still battling it. A number of people died of the disease: Marty Joel, a trader who had been with Bernie from day one and entrusted him with his sizable estate (now all gone); David Berkowitz, our soft-spoken attorney; and Liz Weintraub Caro, the head of systems. After Bernie's arrest, some of us joked that he would blame everything on Marty, David, and Liz, because they couldn't defend themselves.

The 17th floor was a different world from where we worked. Whereas the upper two floors were modern, with everything state-of-the-art, on 17 the corporate image didn't seem to matter. The desks were close together, the computers were antiquated, and the printers were old ink-jet jobs, not the laser printers we had in our offices. Bernie insisted that everything on 18 and 19 be absolutely pristine—picture frames had to be exclusively silver or black, employees had to clear off their desks before they left for the day—but on 17 those rules didn't apply.

The two people who ran the floor, Frank DiPascali and Annette Bongiorno, had once lived next door to each other, in Queens. Annette handled Bernie's seasoned clients and managed her staff on 17. Short, tough, and overweight, she was rigid and guarded at work. She and Frank had come a long way, considering that neither of them graduated from college. Frank, who handled Bernie's newer clients, including the hedge funds, or feeders, had a 61-foot boat with a crew and a seven-acre estate in Bridgewater, New Jersey. Annette had a $2.6 million house on Long Island and a $1.25 million vacation home in Boca Raton, Florida, which she called Casa di Bongiorno. She drove two Mercedeses and a Bentley, and much of her wealth had to have come from Bernie, whom she had worked for since he started his business, in the 1960s.

Frank, Annette, and a few other key employees had company American Express cards, which they used for dinners and nights on the town. I saw their receipts, and they were high. One evening I ran into Frank at a restaurant in Montauk, on Long Island. I was with four people, and when we went to pay the bill the waiter said, "Mr. DiPascali has taken care of it." I thought, How generous, but now I suspect our meal was paid for by Madoff investors. Through the years, clients would frequently complain about the lack of customer service on 17. Please don't tell Bernie I said so, they would say to me, but whenever I call, they make me feel like I'm bothering them. If I mentioned this to Bernie, he would wave me off. "They're doing a good job down there. Most of these customers are a pain in the ass." He would never reprimand anyone on 17—they were untouchable.

Annette's staff of six were mostly low-level, clerical women, many of them working mothers, who probably made no more than $40,000 a year. They were young and naïve, with no background in finance, so they weren't able to connect the dots. Annette allegedly instructed them to generate tickets showing trades that had never been made, at least two of them have reportedly told prosecutors, and they simply did as they were told. (Bongiorno has not been charged with any wrongdoing.)

I knew these women. Two of them, Winnie Jackson and Semone Anderson, would come up to 19 every day to deliver figures. Whenever I went downstairs, they were always busy doing paperwork while Annette watched them like a hawk. Once, I remember, Annette had the phones removed from her employees' desks after she became concerned that they were making personal calls. She treated them like children.

A t the end of each month, the investors' statements were generated and printed by a big computer encased in glass in the middle of the 17th floor. Annette would bring up statements to people in our offices who had accounts, including Peter, Shana, and the boys. I never saw her bring one to Bernie. The rest of the statements were sent out in a mass mailing on 17.

In Frank DiPascali's area was a staff of four. In Annette Bongiorno's area, located across the floor from Frank, were Winnie and Semone and four other women. Every day I would receive a report with all of the figures from Winnie or Semone and another report of wire transfers from the cage. I would immediately take them to Bernie, and if he was out of the office I would read or fax them to him.

When Bernie was traveling, he would often call me about specific files. "Go to my desk and put me on speaker," he would say. Then he would instruct me to go to a certain drawer and a certain file. "It will be three folders back," he would say. "O.K., now go 10 pages in and read me that page." What he needed was always exactly where he said it would be, and he would always call me back minutes later to make sure I had put the page back exactly where I found it.

In the last few years, Bernie had a suitcase on wheels to take with him whenever he traveled. When I questioned him about it, he said it contained files he might need for reference. Now I believe that that suitcase held the papers of all the feeders he dealt with in his fraudulent advisory business. After the F.B.I. took over the office, I told them about this suitcase. They asked me if it was the one they had found empty in his office, and I said no. Though it looked similar, I don't think it was the same one.

We never once got wind about Harry Markopolos, the now famous fraud investigator who warned the S.E.C. for eight years that Bernie was operating a Ponzi scheme. "We were idiots," I told one of the few people left after Bernie's arrest. Bernie didn't even register with the S.E.C. as an investment adviser until 2006, but nobody noticed or raised any questions. That's how slick he was.

B ernie could be incredibly generous and absolutely horrible. When my kids were teenagers, I needed $4,000 fast to put them on my car-insurance policy. I had been working for Bernie for some time, so I asked him if I could take an advance on my bonus. When I got my weekly pay-check, there was an extra $4,000 on it. "Bernie, what is this?," I asked him. "I don't know. Peter must've done it," he said. When I asked Peter, he said, "Bernie must've done it." They just gave me the money and never asked for it back. I was so touched that I stood between their two offices and yelled, "Thank you, guys!"

In 1988 my father died and left me $150,000. I told Bernie and said, "I don't know what to do with it."

"How much?" he asked. I told him, and he just said, "O.K."

At the time I thought he was doing me a favor, letting me participate. But now all I can see is what so many of his other victims see. My father worked his whole life as a detective in the New York City Police Department. He took extra jobs to achieve his lifelong dream of leaving something behind for his children. Bernie would have taken that dream away had I not withdrawn the money in the early 1990s, when I needed to supplement my salary in order to raise my children.

We all trusted Bernie, confident that he would take care of us. If you got sick, your job would be waiting for you when you came back. After one employee was killed in an accident, Bernie opened an educational fund for her grandchildren. If you were a longtime employee and had children in college, they could come in and work in the summer, and when they graduated they could get a job at Madoff. If you got married, Bernie would pay the airfare for your honeymoon, and in some instances he'd pay for the whole honeymoon.

Bernie rarely showed his dark side, but I saw it several times. When we changed insurance carriers a few years ago, I said to him, "Why don't you put this new insurance card in your wallet, in case you have to go to the doctor." He said, "Do I look like a peon to you?" I was embarrassed for him when he said that. His temper erupted most memorably one time in the 1990s, when a co-worker named Laura spent months putting together the Interbourse Ski Week in Colorado, where all of the stock exchanges would get together for a week of sports and parties. That year it was Madoff's turn to organize it, and Laura did such an incredible job that Bernie gave her a $25,000 bonus. Shortly after that, Laura decided to move to San Francisco. When she told Bernie, he flew into such a rage that it was scary. He said he felt betrayed that someone he had just rewarded would up and leave him. He fumed not only at Laura but also at me, for not warning him, and brought us both to tears. He claimed that I was disloyal and called me a traitor. There was no reasoning with him, and he stayed incensed for days. That's when I learned that Bernie always thought he was right. Ruth was the same way. It was always your fault, never theirs. After that, whenever they told me I'd done something wrong, I would just say, "You're right. You know what, I'm sorry. And it'll never happen again."

Looking through Bernie's calendars for 2005 and 2006, I can see how his circle of friends and scope of operations widened. "Milan to London and same day London to Teterboro," reads a typical entry of the travel schedules I arranged. I set up appointments with senators, ambassadors, billionaires, and international business leaders. I made daily reminders for Bernie to attend lunches, dinners, board meetings, and benefits. By 2005, Bernie and Ruth were on top of the world and had begun spending money at a rate they never had before. They had four grand residences—the Manhattan penthouse, the Montauk beach house, a $9.4 million home in Palm Beach, and a three-bedroom apartment in a gated community in Cap d'Antibes, in the South of France. Always fanatical about staying connected, Bernie had a videoconferencing system set up in the Cap d'Antibes apartment so that he could communicate with the New York and London offices. When we used it the first time and I watched his face come into focus, the first words out of his mouth were "Eleanor, this video thing adds 10 pounds to you." I said, "Thank you very much, Bernie." He kept needling me until I finally put him on mute.

Bernie and Ruth's most prized possession was a $7 million yacht, which they kept docked near Cap d'Antibes and named *Bull*—the same as his other three boats. The Madoffs never seemed happier than when they were on the yacht enjoying their jet-set lifestyle. This extravagance usually didn't extend to gifts: they never seemed to give expensive things to each other. One day, however, Bernie came out of his office beaming. "I want to show you what I bought Ruth," he told me, and held up a gorgeous platinum Art Deco chain covered in diamonds. It must have been 60 inches long. "It cost me $250,000," he whispered. "I've never spent that kind of money on a piece of jewelry before, but I wanted her to have it." I said I wished *I* was married to him, and laughed.

At the time I thought his gesture was great. Now I know that the necklace was on the clients, as was Bernie's $24 million Embraer Legacy jet, which had "BM" on its tail and which he shared with his best friend, the Long Island developer Eddie Blumenfeld. (Blumenfeld would turn out to be one of Madoff's victims.)

B ernie's clients would have been only too happy to see him living well. They would have felt he deserved it, because he not only kept their money safe but also made it grow. An appointment with him was considered a privilege. While most of our major clients, from titans of industry to the heads of major charities, knew they had to call for an appointment, some took it for granted. The late Hannah Tavlin, for example, would stroll in whenever she wanted. An Israeli Jew with big red hair who wore designer jeans and glitter sneakers, Hannah had millions invested with Bernie, so she felt she had a right to keep an eye on the place. She would drop by at least once a week and ask, "What's Bernie doing? Who's he talking to? How's his mood?" Whether or not she got to see him, she would usually stay a couple of hours talking to me. One day I asked her how she had made her fortune. "Exotic chocolates," she said. "If you keep being friendly with her, she's going to be here all the time," Bernie would complain every time he saw her sitting by my desk.

If Bernie considered Hannah a nuisance, he viewed the S.E.C. as the enemy. Every year we were audited, and Bernie would always go into his audit mode. The auditors would be put in an office where he could keep a constant eye on them, and they were allowed in only that office and the bathroom. He made sure we got them whatever they needed so that they didn't have an opportunity to wander around. If they asked to use our Xerox machine, Bernie would tell me in a low voice, "Offer to make the copies for them, and tell me what they're copying." He would never travel when an audit was scheduled. If he had to be out of the office, he would want to know where the auditors were every minute. "What time did they go to lunch?" he would ask me. "What time did they get back?"

One year an audit occurred in July, the month Bernie and Ruth always had the employees out to Long Island for our annual Montauk weekend, a couple of days of fishing and fun. Bernie used the Montauk weekend as an excuse to get the auditors to leave early, telling them that the annual company party was starting that Thursday, so they would have to finish by then. Actually, the weekend was scheduled for a week or two later, but Bernie's ruse worked. The auditors were out of the office by Thursday. He was paranoid, however, that they would discover that he had lied. When one auditor went to the men's room, Bernie jumped up and told me, "Get one of the guys to go into the bathroom and make sure nobody tells him that this isn't the weekend!"

Bernie would probably have exerted total control until the day he died if the stock market hadn't tanked in the fall of 2008 and big investors hadn't demanded large redemptions—later revealed to be $7 billion—which he couldn't meet. I could never figure out why Bernie was suddenly spending so much time with Frank DiPascali. They would have long conversations in Bernie's office, which seemed odd to me, because Frank usually spent all of his time on the 17th floor. If Bernie wanted to see him, ordinarily he would go down there.

The $7 billion in redemption requests must have been weighing heavily on them both, and they were probably trying to find a way out of the mess. Bernie desperately needed money to keep afloat, and he tried to get it the way he always had, through his feeders, who were paid excessive fees by their clients while allegedly failing to provide the due diligence that would have surely raised multiple red flags. That fall, those feeders and hedge-fund managers began flocking to our office more than ever before. When Bernie wasn't meeting with people who could bring him more money, he was meeting with Frank.

September turned to October and then November, and the stream of important visitors grew. I noted in my diary that Sonja Kohn came over from Europe. A kindly Jewish grandmother in her 60s, with puffed-out hair and eclectic outfits, she funneled about $3.2 billion of her clients' money to Bernie through Bank Medici, which she ran in Austria. She was always thrilled to meet with Bernie, and always sent in staggering quarterly in-voices—never less than $800,000—for her commissions. After Bernie's arrest, I heard rumors that Sonja had gone into hiding to avoid some of the furious Russian investors whose money she had lost.

I remember Bernie met about that time with the distinguished French financier René-Thierry Magon de la Villehuchet, who had invested $1.4 bil-lion with him, from clients including Liliane Bettencourt, the daughter of the founder of L'Oréal cosmetics, who is the world's wealthiest woman. Eleven days after Bernie's arrest, Villehuchet swallowed sleeping pills and slashed his arm with a box cutter. He wrote in a suicide note, "If you ruin your friends, your clients, you have to face the consequences."

Walter Noel and Jeffrey Tucker, of Fairfield Greenwich Group, which had a total of $7.5 billion invested with Bernie, also visited the office during the fall of 2008, sometimes bringing select clients with them. They were suave, stately, seemingly seasoned financiers whom you felt you could trust implicitly. Tucker had formerly been a lawyer for the S.E.C. Fairfield's prospectuses declared that the group employed a significantly higher level of due diligence than most funds of funds, but now you have to wonder how deeply they dug into Bernie. At that time statements showed investors that they had money in the Fidelity Spartan U.S. Treasury Money Market Fund, which hadn't existed since 2005.

I was less impressed with J. Ezra Merkin, a big, bearded bear of a man who was the former chairman of GMAC Financial Services and one of our top feeders. Merkin funneled $2.4 billion to Bernie, reaping a sizable com-mission on every dollar. He and Bernie talked regularly throughout the fall of 2008, either by phone or in person. I never once saw Merkin smile or say hello; when he visited Bernie, he wouldn't even look my way. The numerous client lawsuits filed against him indicate that he was equally dismissive about due diligence. This was especially damnable in his case because of the millions entrusted to him by institutions such as Yeshiva University, which he invested exclusively with Bernie. It's interesting to note that the infamous fugitive financier Marc Rich lost approximately $15 million to Bernie through Ezra Merkin. As I told the F.B.I. before the news of Rich's investment came to light, I had been informed by a reputable source that Bernie and Ruth had had lunch with him recently in the South of France. It's also interesting that one of the advisers to Merkin's Ariel fund, which had $300 million with Bernie, was a felon convicted of insider trading. Barred from the licensed securities industry, Victor Teicher had once advised Merkin from federal prison, and he warned him that Bernie's returns were impossible to achieve.

How could we all have been so blind? Keith, one of the F.B.I. agents, summed everything up very simply. "I've never seen a place like this," he told me. "You were all living in Disneyland!"

In the fall of 2008, Bernie's nervous tic, a facial twitch I had noticed occasionally over the years, would flare up when he was talking to major clients and feeders. More and more I would see him staring off into space. He told me he didn't want to be disturbed, and he spent more and more time with Frank DiPascali. A few days before his arrest, he threw the stack of morning mail I'd brought him back on my desk. "I don't want this anymore," he said.

On the Monday before his arrest, Bernie chaired a board meeting in our offices for the Gift of Life foundation, which matched donors to recipients in bone-marrow transplants. The people on the board were a veritable Who's Who, including Ezra Merkin; Fred Wilpon; Charles R. Bronfman, the billionaire Canadian co-chairman of Birthright Israel International; Warren Eisenberg, a founder and co-chairman of Bed Bath & Beyond; Richard Joel, president of Yeshiva University; Michael Minikes, former C.E.O. of Bear Stearns; Barbara Picower, head of the Picower Foundation; and Robert Jaffe, Bernie's longtime feeder from Boston and Palm Beach.

When Jaffe arrived for the meeting in his perfectly tailored suit, he gave me a quick kiss and said, as he always did, "So good to see you, sweetheart." He slipped a stack of envelopes into my hand, as he did each December, containing gift certificates in varying amounts to the New York wine-and-liquor store Sherry-Lehmann. The largest ones always went to the people who ran the investment-advisory business. "Give them out to everybody next Monday," said Jaffe. Three days later, when Bernie was arrested and Jaffe learned how much he had lost of his and his clients' money, he angrily dispatched his son to pick up the gift certificates designated for the staff on 17. Jaffe clearly did not want to share any goodwill with people who may have participated in a scheme that had cost him millions of dollars.

That day, a client called saying she'd known Bernie for so long that he was like part of her family. She had heard that he had some checks written for friends and family members and, please, could I find out if one of them was for her? The checks she mentioned—100 of them, totaling $173 million, left in Bernie's desk drawer—were later cited by prosecutors as evidence that Bernie was trying to give away his ill-gotten assets, and that his bail should be revoked. But I believe he never intended to send them out. Bernie was so meticulous and organized that there could have been only one reason for the checks: he wanted his sons to find out about them and think that he'd lost it. Then they would confront him, and he could confess. I remembered the Tuesday before his arrest, when a woman from 17 brought up the stack of checks that Bernie had requested. "Where are you going with those?," I asked her, because I couldn't remember the last time Bernie had signed a check. He was much too busy to do that. And checks would *never* be left overnight. They were always signed and sent out on the same day.

Who was Bernie trying to protect? Quite a few people had to have been involved in the Ponzi scheme. The scam was too massive and went on too long for one person to manage it. How did he do it? Did Bernie manipulate the whole thing through the ignorance of most of his staff and the intelligence of a few?

On the day of Bernie's arrest, I remembered a recent thank-you note an investor had sent him: "At a time when so much seems to be falling apart and so many people hurt, it is simply amazing to see how your discipline, instincts, your talents have kept it all together. It is truly an astonishing performance, and we are very grateful for it."

Performance. The perfect word. As the calls from now destitute investors mushroomed, I felt sick, manipulated, and abused by the boss I had so long admired. I got up from my desk, went into the bathroom, and threw up.

The days following Bernie's arrest were surreal. Most of the employees showed up for work, but not Bernie, Ruth, Mark, or Andy. I never saw them again. Peter and Shana came in, but she left later on that week. Peter stayed on, trying to help, but he was visibly overwhelmed. One day a co-worker and I looked into his office and saw him sitting at his desk with his head in his hands, sobbing. "*Now* I hate Bernie," said the co-worker, who had lost her life savings. A couple of days later, the F.B.I. asked Peter to leave and escorted him out of the building.

Amid all the confusion I spotted Noel Levine, a thin gentleman in his 80s who owns a real-estate company called Troon Management and who shared office space with us. He had just lost double-digit millions to Bernie and was walking around in a daze. I thought back a few years, to the time when Levine's secretary had been caught embezzling $6 million of his money. She was sent to prison, and I asked Bernie what he thought about it. "You know, Noel has to take some responsibility for this," he said. "He should have been keeping an eye on his personal finances. That's why I've always had Ruth watching the books. *Nothing* gets by Ruth." I was surprised when he added, "Well, you know what happens is, it starts out with you taking a little bit, maybe a few hundred, a few thousand. You get comfortable with that, and before you know it, it snowballs into something big."

I think that may have been the way it happened with Bernie.

The Monday after Bernie's arrest, the private line that only the Madoff family called me on rang: "Eleanor, it's Ruth."

"How are you?"

"I'm all right," she said. "Eleanor, I'm sorry about what happened."

"I'll be all right," I said.

"I'm worried about Bernie losing his cell-phone number," she said, and I knew immediately what she meant. Bernie was fanatical about his phone, and the bankruptcy trustees were freezing everything. It was just a matter of time before all of the phones, including Bernie's, would be shut off and people wouldn't be able to contact him. Ruth told me she had tried to change the billing herself, but the service provider had told her she needed the personal identification number, and she didn't have it.

"I'll see what I can do," I said. After I hung up, I decided to drop the matter, because the bankruptcy trustees had told us we couldn't give out any information without notifying them first. I didn't call Ruth back, therefore, and an hour later the private line rang again.

"Did you get the PIN?," Ruth demanded.

"Ruth, I don't know what to tell you. The trustees are telling us we can't do anything," I said. To myself I thought, Isn't it sinking in that this isn't her and Bernie's office anymore, that it's now a crime scene?

Ruth asked to be put through to another person in the office, who also told her that nothing could be done without the permission of the bankruptcy trustees. I heard that Ruth yelled, "You will do what I tell you to do!" After a brief exchange, she hung up.

Then Ruth called me again, asking me to find a certain invoice regarding their yacht. "I'll look for it and get back to you," I said, knowing I wouldn't. She said with a nervous laugh, "And you don't have to mention this to the trustees."

I never picked up the private line again. Instead, I told the F.B.I. what had just happened. I was working for them now, not for Ruth and Bernie Madoff.

People ask me if I think Ruth knew that her husband was running a Ponzi scheme. I always say only that her behavior after Bernie's arrest seemed strange: she didn't leave him and go straight to her sons, who were obviously devastated. As a mother, if my husband were arrested for a massive fraud, I would leave him immediately—if I didn't kill him first—and go to my children. Ruth not only stood by Bernie but also fought to keep $62 million that the government says was clearly not hers. The money belonged to the clients. In the days following Bernie's arrest, the F.B.I. caught the Madoffs mailing more than $1 million worth of watches and antique jewelry to relatives and friends.

After I approached the F.B.I. and said I wanted to speak to them, two agents asked me to go into Bernie's office with them. One of them sat down in Bernie's chair. "I apologize for sitting in your boss's chair," he said.

"That's fine with me," I said. "I'm not talking to him anymore."

He asked me how much I had been making at Madoff. "Just under $100,000 a year," I said. I thought he was going to fall off the chair. "That's *it?*" he asked. They had to know from my salary that I wasn't involved in the Ponzi scheme. The people at Madoff who had been highly compensated were the ones they were looking at. In the end, most of those people "lawyered up" or fled. Annette Bongiorno walked out the day Bernie was arrested and never came back. Frank DiPascali came back the next morning, then vanished. Some others on 17 came in, but they had been advised not to talk to the F.B.I. without legal counsel. "Most of the people downstairs are claiming to be stupid," one agent told me, "but we have a couple who are trying to convince us that they're *retarded.*"

My anger sustained me, and I did everything I could to help in the investigation. I explained how all the people involved—Madoff family members, executives, employees, clients—were connected and how everything worked. My help had to end, however, when I decided to co-author this story. I felt compelled to tell the investigators that I was doing it. They thanked me for my help and wished me good luck. "You need to take care of yourself," one of them said, "because nobody else will."

I still find myself reflexively answering my phone, "Hello, Madoff." But I'm trying my best to put it all behind me. I'm haunted by the people Bernie fleeced, ranging from Holocaust survivor and Nobel Peace Prize recipient Elie Wiesel to Yair Green, the trustee attorney for the Yeshaya Horowitz Foundation, to all the widows and retirees, and their children and grandchildren, that I've been honored to know. I worry about not only the clients but also the employees. Bernie stole our trust. Most of us were honest, hardworking people with families. We thought we were living the American Dream and felt privileged to work for such a brilliant, wonderful, generous man who was doing such good and charitable things. Now we feel like fools.

A few days before Bernie's arrest, he came out of his office and said something I'll never forget. "Eleanor, I'm sorry I've been so hard on you lately." He took a deep breath and threw up his hands, and he seemed so sincere that I felt total sympathy for him. "I've been under a lot of pressure, and I just feel so sorry for everybody."

"Don't worry about it," I said, adding facetiously, "you've been a pleasure." For once in his life, Bernie didn't have a sassy comeback line.

· 19 ·

Part III:
Did the Sons
Know?

By DAVID MARGOLICK

July 2009

One night in late January, a newly out-of-work trader named Reed Abend spotted Andrew Madoff inside East Side Poultry, a take-out chicken joint on First Avenue and 79th Street in Manhattan. It was the first and only time Abend had seen Andrew since their employer, Bernard L. Madoff Investment Securities, had imploded six weeks earlier; this, Abend realized, was his big chance to exact some justice, or at least to blow off some steam. He removed his hat and gloves and waited patiently for Bernard Madoff's younger son, a handsome man of 42, to emerge from the store. And when he did, Abend pounced.

"Where's my money?" he demanded, referring to the $450,000 year-end bonus to which he thought he was entitled. Lots of other traders were owed a lot of money, too, he noted. The Madoffs had always boasted that their employees were like family to them, so why had they left them all high and dry?

"What about *me?*" Andrew replied.

"What about the charities, your employees, and your investors?"

Abend, undeterred and unpersuaded, went on, referring to the thousands of people and organizations Bernie Madoff had bilked in a $65 billion Ponzi scheme, history's largest. "We all know you stole the money! It's obvious you took it! You're a criminal!" By now Andrew had reached his car, where his fiancée, Catherine Hooper, sat in the front seat. "Is that your new whore girlfriend?" Abend demanded. With that, Andrew Madoff stopped, placed his bag of chicken down on the hood, and socked Abend on the side of the head. Then he got into his car and drove off. Abend shouted for help, to no avail. Later, he tried to file a report with the police. More remarkably, Andrew also contacted the police—to hand himself in. (Not surprisingly, they weren't interested.)

The punch may be the climax of the story, but other aspects of it matter more. One is Abend's conviction that Andrew Madoff and by extension his brother, Mark, two years his senior—both of whom had spent their entire careers working with and for their father—were in on the scheme. In that, Abend represents not just the majority but, it seems, the super-majority view. "Hundreds of people would have had to be involved in something this gigantic, and Madoff would have needed people to manage it," said Gaytri Kachroo, a partner at McCarter & English, in Boston, and counsel for Harry Markopolos, the financial wizard who tried blowing the whistle on Madoff for a decade. "For such management roles, he would have had to go with the folks he trusted the most. And would he have trusted anyone more than his own children?"

It matters little that Bernie Madoff has repeatedly said his two children had nothing to do with it; if anything, that insistence has only fueled suspicions that he's taking the fall for them—that his well-publicized confession to them last December was both a con man's finishing touch and a father's final act of love—and that his sons were in on *that* too. And their subsequent estrangement—they've not talked to him since, they say—is but one more chapter of the charade. "Dad was 70 years old," said one seasoned former prosecutor who's following the case closely. "Surely he told them what the family recipe was. *Surely they asked.*" But the sons say they were shocked by what he told them, I remonstrated. "That's a good story," he replied. "You can go with the Easter Bunny or the tooth fairy too."

Another notable aspect of the encounter is something Andrew said: the "What about *me?*" (Or, as Andrew has insisted he declared, "I'm as much a victim as you are.") For Andrew and Mark Madoff not only maintain their innocence, adamantly, but insist that they, too, were stung by Bernard Madoff. Through spokesmen and surrogates—they've given no on-the-record interviews—they claim they really knew nothing about their father's crimes. To friends, Andrew has called what his father did to him and his brother "a father-son betrayal of biblical proportions." To say he was blind-sided by it all, he has also said, would be the understatement of the century. Their names, too, appear on the list of Bernie Madoff's more than 8,000 victimized investors; between them, in deferred compensation and direct investments, they are said to be out more than $15 million, along with their jobs, their reputations, their prospects, their property (probably), and their peace of mind.

Actually, there's a third intriguing aspect to the story: Andrew Madoff's attempting to blow the whistle on himself, even though, he maintains, it was Abend who threw the first punch. Up to now, he's been a straight arrow. So has his brother. Nothing either has ever done thus far suggests an inclination to aid and abet a colossal crime, or, for that matter, the clever-ness required to devise a cover-up or the acting skills to pull it off.

Except for a six-year span when they were off at their respective colleges, Mark and Andrew Madoff have always either lived or worked together. Both joined their father directly out of school, taking positions in Madoff Securities' legitimate trading arm, which involved either market-making (handling over the counter trades for others) or proprietary trading (making bets with the company's own money). By all accounts, they spent most of their time on the 19th floor of Madoff's offices in the Lipstick Building, in Midtown Manhattan, two flights above the notorious (and largely empty) epicenter of the Ponzi scheme.

To all but those who watched them up close, they're almost inter-changeable. Both are good-looking. Both grew up in Roslyn, New York, and went to public schools there. Both graduated from good undergraduate colleges (Mark, from the University of Michigan in 1986; Andrew, from the Wharton School at the University of Pennsylvania two years later). Both married pretty Jewish girls from suburban New York. Both upgraded to the Ralph Lauren–like countrified life of Greenwich, Connecticut, and had a pair of children. Both saw their marriages disintegrate. Both recouped;

Mark remarried in 2003, and Andrew was poised to when the family debacle put things on hold. Both were well compensated, making as much as $4 to $5 million some years. Though each lived well—Mark had lovingly restored an old farmhouse in Greenwich and owned expensive homes in Manhattan and Nantucket, while Andrew lived in the luxurious East Side building where Gloria Vanderbilt once owned the penthouse—both were generally unpretentious.

And before becoming fodder for the paparazzi, neither was particularly well known. Michael Bloomberg wrote a letter recommending Andrew for membership in the Century Country Club, the exclusive hangout of establishment "Our Crowd" Jews in Purchase, New York, but says he doesn't remember Andrew at all, let alone vouching for him. A prominent official at the Palm Beach Country Club—a Bernie Madoff hangout and feeding ground—says that, in several years running the place, he never saw either Madoff son. A fellow resident of Mark's Mercer Street building, in Manhattan's SoHo section, said he never even knew Mark lived there.

B ut there are differences too. Mark is more gregarious, outgoing, charming. That has meant he is either more likable or more glib and superficial, depending on your point of view. Around the office of Madoff's legitimate operations, Mark was more a salesman and front man than an active trader or administrator. He was a nervous sort: he had stomach problems, for which he was always trying out some new remedy—yoga or blood-type diets or protein shakes—that he talked about endlessly. He was the hip one, living downstairs from Jon Bon Jovi and André Balazs.

Andrew, by contrast, was more quiet and cerebral and staid. He was more technologically savvy and involved with trading. People thought him the more genuine of the two, but he struck some as arrogant, snooty. Over time he grew more detached from the business, more restless, more eager to strike out on his own.

Their different temperaments and trajectories may account for their varying responses to their predicament. Mark is said to be obsessed with the scandal, huddled over his computer, hyper-scrutinizing every story and blog posting he can find, and, when it suits him, answering his e-mail instantaneously. Andrew, meanwhile, has shut down, or maybe even partly moved on. He may also have managed to put his outsize father behind him a bit. "He discusses him—'casually' is not the right word—unemotionally, devoid of feeling, which I take to be a way of protecting himself from this monster," said Alexandra Lebenthal, head of Lebenthal & Co., who has visited Andrew several times since the wheels came off his life. "I do think he's still in some form of shock. He's gotta be."

It's difficult to capture just how toxic the name "Madoff" has become. At the Securities Traders Association of New York, known as STANY, which Mark headed for a time, no one will discuss him. Evidently fearful of assassins crouching in vestibules, parents of classmates of Andrew's daughters at a prestigious Manhattan private school worry about letting their children attend parties at the Madoff home on East 74th Street. At the Lymphoma Foundation, which Andrew headed following his own brush with the disease—it's now in remission—he's as much a nonperson as Mark is at STANY. Their children have to cope with hate calls to their homes. When Andrew's estranged wife orders groceries from FreshDirect, she uses her maiden name. Investors, co-workers, friends, frat brothers, former wives, all recoil and lapse into paranoid or belligerent silence when asked about them.

A spokesman for the sons said they have not spoken to their father since his dramatic confession to them on December 10, nor to their mother, Ruth—not because they think she was involved (they don't) but because they believe that her tendency to side with him, no matter what, when they complained to her about him, enabled his dirty deeds. When Bernard pleaded guilty and was carted off in handcuffs to the Metropolitan Correctional Center, in Manhattan, in March—he'll stay there until sentencing on June 29—Andrew told friends he couldn't find it in his heart to pity him. The closest either son has come to their father's cell is when each was on jury duty, a few hundred yards away.

Many expect that Mark and Andrew will be indicted: the pressure to go after them, to implicate them in *something*, will simply be too great. Should their cases ever get to a jury, one former prosecutor predicted, their trouble will really begin. "Madoff? These days? They would be convicted of murder in the death of Judge Crater 50 years before they were born," he said. "The father was a gimme, and they're the most conspicuous targets in the case," said Daniel Richman, another former prosecutor, who now teaches at Columbia Law School. That will be all the more true if their cover story turns out to be a ruse; even more than most people, prosecutors don't like to be had.

Come what may criminally for Mark and Andrew Madoff, their futures appear bleak. The federal bankruptcy trustee will likely argue that virtually everything they own was purchased with their father's tainted funds, including $31 million he lent them. (The *real* question may be whether the trustee will take everything away from them or leave them with at least a few kernels of seed corn.) There will be a million lawsuits, in which frustrated investors will try to pick them clean; already Fairfield, Connecticut, seeking to recoup $15 million in lost pension funds, has attached the sons' homes in Greenwich. If their money is not their own, how can they afford lawyers? And when it's all over, who will hire either of them?

Whether or not Mark and Andrew in fact knew what their father was up to, it's pretty clear they should have known something was seriously amiss. Were they willful or lazy or fearful or indifferent or oblivious or adoring or in denial? Were they too intimidated or loyal to object? Too passive to care? Too addicted to their wealth to resist, or just too dumb to discern? As a father, Bernie is said to have been strict, controlling, secretive. A fading photograph from Andrew's Bar Mitzvah shows Bernie alongside his two mop-topped sons, looking proud and proprietary. Did those fatherly instincts impel him to bring them into a good thing (and protect them when it went awry) or to keep them out of a fraud?

Thus far only one person has come forward to say Mark and Andrew actually recruited investors for their father, and that claim is disputed by the brothers. The moguls who stocked Madoff's hedge fund—Ezra Merkin and Walter Noel, for example—appear not to have known the sons well, if at all. Nor did the vast majority of investors, even those in the communities where the boys grew up and lived. Investors who *did* know them, moreover, don't seem to hold them accountable. The family of Fred Wilpon, the owner of the New York Mets, lost hundreds of millions in the scam, but the Madoff spokesman said that Fred's son, Jeff, who runs the team, maintains his longtime ties to Mark (though, according to a Wilpon-family friend, Jeff has tired of Mark's excessive self-pity). The family of New York developer Edward Blumenfeld, who shared the lease on Bernie Madoff's plane, also lost a fortune, but in April he invited Mark to his Passover Seder.

Some former colleagues and subordinates, who now must cope with having "Madoff" on their résumés, especially those who were not investors, have stuck by "the boys." "They wouldn't have been able to do what Bernie did: they just didn't have that evilness in them," said Deborah, who put in 24 years at the company and asked that her last name not be used. It's a sentiment, she conceded, that many of her co-workers don't want to hear. "If I were to say that Mark and Andy are innocent, I'd get people looking at me like I'm absolutely nuts," she said. "So I just keep it to myself." Some employee-investors whom the sons have called to console have not returned their calls, she said.

When Anthony Guerra of *Wall Street & Technology* caught up with the Madoff family in 2000, they were a contented lot. "All of his family members grew up with this being our lives," Mark said about his father. "What makes it fun for all of us is to walk into the office in the morning and see the rest of your family sitting there. That's a good feeling to have."

Mark and Andrew oversaw the company's expanding trading business. Over time, Mark largely stopped trading himself, instead spending his time supervising the activities of others, along with joining organizations and selling the firm's services outside. Andrew, meanwhile, took over the NASDAQ desk and the proprietary operation. In his own trading, his success was mixed; former colleagues vividly recall his losing a million dollars on the day Palm stock went public. "The eyes of every trader in the room were on him," one remembered. "He got absolutely demolished." (Also demolished was Mark's Palm device, which he smashed against his desk in fraternal frustration and solidarity.) After that chastening experience, Andrew decided to trade less, or Bernie told him to, since, according to traders, Bernie clearly ran the show.

How did Bernie treat his sons? Eleanor Squillari, who was Bernie Madoff's secretary for 20 years, said he would "just light up when he saw them," calling them "dear" or "sweetheart." One trader recalled how, whenever Bernie would return from his increasingly frequent vacations to Montauk or Palm Beach or Cap d'Antibes, he would find them and give them each a kiss. But another painted a different picture. "He could beat them down," he said. "He was vicious. He would yell at them in the conference room, and then they'd come out and take it out on everyone else. He gave them no credit. They're talking about how good a year they'd had, and he'd look at them and dismiss them: 'You guys had nothing to do with it!' With one quick comment, everything stopped. You saw them just kind of deflate." On some level, this trader went on, Bernie considered his sons soft: after all, he was an up-by-the-bootstraps kind of guy, and he'd given them everything. "Mark and Andy had never gone against him," the trader said. "They were always trying to please him, and never could."

To one of the sons' confidants, however, such contempt cuts the other way. Bernard Madoff did not bring his sons into his schemes for the same reason, she said, he never let them stay in his home: he thought they'd somehow screw things up. ("Completely false," the sons' spokesman said about Bernie's alleged lack of hospitality.) "They saw one another all the time, but emotionally there was no intimacy," the sons' confidante went on. "The kids visited them, but it was like visiting their grandmother. Andrew saw this huge gulf between him and his dad and saw his father as being patronizing and even somewhat antagonistic."

Similarly, the sons' spokesman maintained that Bernard's taking his nonexistent trading elsewhere—to European countertraders, he told them—rather than have Mark and Andrew handle it was frustrating and humiliating for them. They had no ownership interest in Madoff Securities, he said, nor access to financial statements. Of their father's hedge fund, the spokesman said, they were completely ignorant; only rarely were they even on the 17th floor. They seldom spoke to Frank DiPascali Jr., Bernard Madoff's general manager and a major focus of the investigation, he added, and then only about fly-fishing. Squillari agrees. Part of her job, she said, was to keep track of everyone, and she never saw the boys go down to 17. Squillari believes that she knows who *was* complicit, and that Mark and Andrew neither were among them nor knew them very well.

Several former traders don't buy it. Whatever separated 19 from 17 was actually quite permeable, they say. Money sometimes moved between them, with dollars from Bernie's hedge fund used for the firm's proprietary trading, and so did people. Bernie regularly sat on the "throne"—the platform overlooking the 19th-floor trading operation—with his sons and often retreated with them to the conference room behind, whose glass walls went magically white at the flick of a switch. DiPascali was sometimes there, too. "Why would they go into the conference room to talk about fishing?" one former trader asked.

They have other questions. Wouldn't Mark and Andrew have wondered where their hefty salaries came from, particularly in years when their trading operations were less profitable? Were they not alerted, and concerned, when reporters, investigators from the S.E.C., and Harry Markopolos questioned Madoff's steady, undeviating profits? (One trader recalled how in 2001, when *Barron's* expressed doubt over Madoff's methods, Mark and Andrew laughingly attributed it all to jealousy: if anything were really wrong, the authorities would have been in there.) If Bernie made his trades in Europe, wouldn't his sons have seen the paperwork such arrangements generate, especially since they were directors of the London office? If, as Madoff has confessed, he laundered $250 million through that office, wouldn't they have known about it? If these guys didn't run things when Bernie was away, who did? After all, weren't they the heirs apparent?

Perhaps a better defense for the boys than ignorance would be indifference. Over time, traders say, Mark and Andrew became disenchanted and distracted. Mark spent his days checking out real estate or buying gear or planning his next vacation or dealing with his souring marriage. (Divorce papers reportedly show that by 1999 Mark's net worth was $8.3 million.) Andrew's marriage, too, took a wrong turn. Then, one day in 2003, the office masseuse, Brenda, felt a lump near Andrew's neck; he had mantle-cell lymphoma. After that "it became a much more you-only-live-once kind of mentality" for him, as one trader put it.

Fly-fishing, something Andrew and Mark had been doing since they were children, became an obsession, especially for Andrew. It soon became more: in 2007, for a million dollars and change, Andrew bought a piece of Urban Angler, a fly-fishing store in Manhattan's Flatiron District. Bernie rarely kvelled about his sons, but he'd go on and on about the place, evidently because of the big names associated with it: former Treasury secretary Robert Rubin and onetime Morgan Stanley president and C.O.O. Robert Scott were part owners; former Treasury secretary and Goldman Sachs C.E.O. Hank Paulson and financier Joe Perella were among its many illustrious customers. Not long after he got there, Andrew took up with Catherine Hooper, another part owner, who had won fame in fly-fishing circles for appearing scantily clad in *Fish & Fly* magazine. Hooper had been living with the store's co-founder, Jonathan Fisher, with whom she had a young daughter. (Unsurprisingly, Fisher quickly arranged for someone to buy Andrew out. "Different management styles" is how he later explained the split.) Last September, Andrew Madoff and Catherine Hooper became engaged.

Andrew also led a group of investors purchasing, for a few million dollars, Abel Automatics, a Camarillo, California–based manufacturer of high-end fly-fishing reels. And Andrew is primarily responsible for Madoff Energy, an oil-and-gas-exploration company which late last year contracted with two local firms to drill for natural gas in Pecos County, Texas.

Following his divorce, Mark went into a long funk, one trader remembered. "He went from a confident, fun-loving guy to really depressed, mopey," he said. He left Greenwich for an apartment near the office. But in 2003 he married Stephanie Mikesell, who worked in the fashion industry. After that, he got showier. "Mark loved his lifestyle, loved the fact he could fly on a private jet or walk into Dunhill and spend $200 on an umbrella," the trader recalled. Last June, Mark swapped a more modest house in the town of Nantucket for a $6.5 million McMansion, a cold and uninviting ski-chalet-type place better suited to Vail or Aspen than to quaint New England. "It feels almost like you're entering a mausoleum," one visitor said. Mark, she went on, was personable, attractive—he looked like Matt Lauer, which is what a neighbor jokingly called him—and impressive: surf casting from the beach last summer, he caught himself a shark. But there was something incomplete, unexplained about him, too—like how he got all his money—which is why the visitor to his Nantucket house Googled him as soon as she got back home. "There were all sorts of things about his dad but practically nothing about him," she recalled. "I thought it was really weird."

For four years, Mark was a trustee of Lincoln Center Theater, where he was especially active with programs involving inner-city students. He later switched allegiances to the Public Theater. Officials there were impressed by his earnestness and punctiliousness, particularly on financial matters; he agonized at great length, for instance, over whether the table he bought at the organization's annual gala should be paid for out of his personal funds or those of his foundation. But when the Madoff saga exploded, the Public suddenly went dark for him. "I thought of e-mailing him good luck, but what if he *is* guilty?" one former colleague said. "What if he *did* know?

How could he *not* know? I didn't want to be a *wuss* or something." "I just don't believe he was involved," said another, who promptly insisted on anonymity: anyone raising funds these days can't afford to praise a Madoff, since so many major donors were stung. A month after the story broke, Mark showed up at the Public Theater. "He looked like he hadn't slept for a month," someone there recalled. Shortly thereafter, he took a leave of absence.

As the end drew near, Bernard Madoff had showed some signs of stress—backaches, even more kvetching than usual—but never any panic. When he flew with his family to Palm Beach the weekend after Thanksgiving, everything seemed normal. That Friday night, Ruth made stone crabs and salad for everyone. The next day, they all went to the Breakers, where they ran into Carl Shapiro and his son-in-law Robert Jaffe, one of Madoff's largest investors and one of his prime recruiters, respectively. For Bernie, there was a round of golf, a massage, and a meeting with a South American investor. Nothing at all seemed awry, except, perhaps, when he was shown Catherine Hooper's new engagement ring. "You may have to hock it," he declared cryptically. Was he being prophetic, or just his usual wiseass self?

On December 9, according to the Madoff sons' version of events, Bernie told Mark about his inexplicable plan to pay out $173 million in bonuses two months early. Concerned, Mark told Andrew; Andrew thought Madoff Securities was going belly-up. The next morning, Mark and Andrew went into their father's office for an explanation. Fearing he could not "hold it together" there, Bernie suggested repairing to his apartment. As they left en masse, the sons looked grim: perhaps Andy's wife and girlfriend were fighting, Squillari speculated. In the kitchen, as Ruth Madoff hovered nearby, Bernie told them he was "finished," that he had "absolutely nothing" left, that his investment fund was "just one big lie" and "a giant Ponzi scheme." Mark was angry; Andrew was on the floor, sobbing.

Bernie told his sons that within a week, once he'd paid out $200 to $300 million to some employees and friends, he'd hand himself in. Walking, still stunned, along Lexington Avenue afterward, Mark and Andrew decided not to wait that long. They went to see Mark's wife's stepfather, Martin London, a retired partner at the New York law firm of Paul, Weiss,

Rifkind, Wharton & Garrison, and told him what they'd just learned. London knew all about their father, or thought he did; at Mark's suggestion, London too had invested money with Madoff. London promptly contacted another Paul, Weiss litigator, Martin Flumenbaum, who met with Mark and Andrew later in the afternoon. Flumenbaum then called the offices of the United States Attorney and the Securities and Exchange Commission, arranging for Mark and Andrew to go there the next morning.

The night of Bernie Madoff's confession to his sons, Madoff Securities held its annual Christmas dinner, at Rosa Mexicano on Manhattan's East Side. Bernie was standing in a corner of the restaurant—"a look of death on his face," one trader said—but his sons were nowhere to be seen. "Something is majorly fucked up," the trader told his wife: maybe Andrew's cancer had reappeared, he theorized, or his impending divorce case had grown nastier. In fact, Andrew had returned to his glass-walled apartment and plopped down on his bed, where, for the next four hours, without taking off his tan Burberry overcoat or his suit or even his shoes, he lay, perfectly inert.

The next day, Bernie Madoff was arrested. Andrew soon began preparing for his new life. For one thing, his apartment would now need curtains, to provide some privacy from the press that might soon be camping outside. He listened to a recording of a talk, made at a TED Conference, about finding happiness in adversity. At first it simply didn't dawn on him that people would actually think him complicit. But a wire service identified him and Mark as possible accomplices, and the paparazzi soon appeared. BERNIE'S BOY, WIFE SHOP AS INVESTORS GO BROKE, declared the *New York Post* on December 22. "What, me worry?" the story went on to say. "Andrew Madoff and wife Deborah saunter around SoHo yesterday loaded with holiday goodies to pack into their BMW, which Andrew can still afford." (The woman was in fact Hooper, who, at that point, could much more easily pay for the gifts; though Andrew and Deborah had been separated around a year, Deborah had for some reason filed for divorce only on the day of Bernie's arrest—the very moment that her marital assets were vaporizing.)

A few days later each of the sons received in the mail packages containing watches, jewelry, and some Hanukkah presents. They were from their father, who was under penthouse arrest. One of the packages—a vintage "Paul Newman" Rolex Daytona, a Piaget, and a Cartier Tank watch were among the dozen timepieces it contained—came with a handwritten note, on "Bernard L. Madoff" letterhead. "Dear Mark + Andy," it began. "If you can bear to keep these watches, they are given with my love," their father wrote. "If not, give them to someone who might." "Love, Dad," he signed it. The sons brought the gifts, which violated a freeze placed on the elder Madoff's assets, to the attention of prosecutors. Again, it was either a gesture of uprightness and independence or the latest instance of stagecraft.

In Eleanor Squillari's view, Bernie scrupulously insulated his sons from his crimes. "I don't think he wanted that for them," she said. "As horrible as Bernie was, he was so family-oriented. . . . These boys just woke up one day and everything that was wasn't." She's baffled, though, by Ruth's decision to stick with her husband. "For a mother to not just say, 'Your life is over, I gotta go to the kids,' it just blows my mind," she said.

Mark Madoff has largely disappeared since that time. He has additional distractions; in February, his wife gave birth to another Madoff, a boy. Andrew has been more visible. On Christmas Eve, for instance, he had a visit from Alexandra Lebenthal. Lebenthal, whose father, James, was a television fixture for decades selling municipal bonds, had met Andrew only a few weeks earlier, and had quickly identified with him over the burden of having well-known fathers. Lebenthal's husband likened the excursion to a shivah call—the visit Jews make to the recently bereaved—but she confessed to a bit of voyeuristic curiosity too. "It was as if we were at a car accident and we wanted to know where all the skid marks came from," she said.

In her subsequent visits with Andrew, Lebenthal said, his mood has brightened a bit: "After Bernie went to jail, that was meaningful for him in terms of getting to the next level." His principal concern remained his daughters—to make them feel loved and convince them that, as she put it, "just because their grandfather turns out to be one of the worst criminals ever doesn't mean they're bad people." Is it possible, I asked her, that all the shock and outrage Andrew has displayed is an act, like the Mob boss Vincent Gigante wandering around Greenwich Village all those years in a bathrobe and house slippers, feigning dementia? "Yes, of course," she replied. "We may never know or find out."

Andrew's apartment renovations are on hold: no sense fixing up a place you might soon have to vacate. His wedding, too, has been put off indefinitely; with all his assets under siege, why throw his fiancée's in the pot? They make their restaurant reservations in Hooper's name now. His birthday—April 8—was the first time he missed his parents. Still, there was room for some gallows humor. "Hope you have a fun day doing all the things people in prison wish they could do," the card Catherine bought for him declared. "I wish I had my parents back," he told her. "Yeah," she is said to have replied. "They were a really nice idea."

Andrew is lucky to have his own companies, at least for now; that way, he doesn't have to be hired. ("I'm unemployed, I don't have any money, and I'm just trying to stay out of jail—my name is mud," he lamented to an African-American friend. "Well, now you're just like every black man in America," the friend replied.) But money is short—too short, apparently, for him to hire guides for any therapeutic fishing trips. If he gets really strapped for cash, there are always his business cards. When he learned that they were selling on eBay for $50 apiece, he noted sardonically that he still had a box of 500 of them.

The boys' fates will be determined by people like DiPascali—who, according to *Fortune* magazine, has said the sons weren't involved—and various other employees on the 17th floor who may be in the prosecution's crosshairs. Or by their former or soon-to-be-former wives, who could theoretically implicate them simply by recalling something their husbands once told them. Or by some actual or would-be investors whom Mark and Andrew may have approached to go in with their father. In late March, Dalton Givens, formerly an executive at Wachovia Securities, told Mike McAndrew and Charley Hannagan of the Syracuse *Post-Standard* how, over steaks in Charlotte, North Carolina, Mark and Andrew had tried to sell him on their father's hedge fund. The sons' spokesman said Givens is mistaken, and that it was market-making (for which Wachovia was already using the firm) the sons were hawking.

One trader recalled for me that Mark had taken great pride in Bernie's successes as a hedge-fund manager, comparing his wizardry to that of George Soros. But when it came to getting friends into the fund, it's unclear how much clout the sons had. When Beau Doherty of Special Olympics

Connecticut, with which Mark had long been active, wanted to invest $1 million, for instance, Mark couldn't help. "He said, 'I'll talk to my father about it,'" recalled Doherty, who continues to stand by Mark. "He called me back the next day to say, 'Beau, you know what, the answer's no. We really do much larger amounts of money than that.'"

That no one has come forward to finger the two for involvement in their father's scheme, the sons' spokesman says, is powerful proof they weren't involved. Of course, few talk about the Madoff case these days unless compelled. According to Dan Richman of Columbia Law School, even were Mark and Andrew technically unaware of any Ponzi scheme, they could still be charged in much the same way the wives and girlfriends of drug dealers often are—that is, for receiving funds they should reasonably have known were tainted. At some point, though, dumb *can* be a defense: as the retiring district attorney of Manhattan, Robert Morgenthau, always liked to say, "Stupidity in the first degree is not a crime." If their luck holds, the brothers will enjoy the same fate as their salmon and striped bass and bluefish: after wriggling and bucking and fighting for their lives, they'll be thrown back into the water, scared and scarred but at least free to swim away.

For now, they will wait for the government to make its case. They haven't spoken to the authorities since December. If one proves more involved than the other, the case could bifurcate, but that seems unlikely—in business, the Madoff sons stuck together. That's become less true personally; according to the family confidant, the two have seen and spoken to each other little in the past few months, at least outside their lawyer's office. (The sons' spokesman called that "completely false." "They're very close and in touch, probably daily," he said.)

To one investor who knew the Madoffs, especially Mark, back in Roslyn, the truth about them lies somewhere between innocence and guilt. "I think Mark knew something was wrong but didn't know the magnitude," she said. "He was negligent to work there, but it wasn't 'Let's make up these fake trades with these dot-matrix printers.' I think he was just content to keep living his life, with his Rolex watches and his fishing trips. He was not an evil guy.

"I've often said to myself, 'Where's Mark right now?'" she went on. "'Is he with his mom? Does he visit his dad? What's he doing? Is he crying? Can he possibly enjoy himself? How can he live with himself?' I feel sorry for him, and for Andy too. However, I'm angry they led lives that weren't theirs to lead. That money belonged to me and my family and every other hardworking person who was fooled into investing with Bernie. But I do pity them. Their dad ruined their lives."

·20·

Part IV:
Ruth's World

By *Mark Seal*

September 2009

On June 29, Bernard Madoff was sentenced to 150 years in prison for operating the largest Ponzi scheme in history, and for the first time since his arrest, seven months earlier, his wife, Ruth, issued a statement. "I am breaking my silence now, because my reluctance to speak has been interpreted as indifference or lack of sympathy for the victims of my husband Bernie's crime, which is exactly the opposite of the truth," it began. That day, nine of Bernie Madoff's victims read statements of their own at his sentencing in court, telling horror stories of the overnight devastation he had brought on them, calling him the epitome of evil, and making references to the Devil, who chews up traitors in Dante's *Inferno:* "May Satan grow a fourth mouth where Bernard L. Madoff deserves to spend the rest of eternity." To compound the victims' outrage, the news was just out that Ruth Madoff, who had been her husband's closest companion and sometime bookkeeper through their 49 years of marriage, had cut a deal with prosecutors to keep $2.5 million in exchange for surrendering a potential claim to $80 million in assets, including her homes.

So her statement of contrition could not have come at a worse time.

Since the previous December, she had not shown the slightest sign of public remorse, and had routinely said that she had no comment whenever a reporter got near her. Now the 100-pound blonde who had come to embody all the ills of America's latest age of greed—who had withdrawn $15.5 million from her account in the Madoff offices in the weeks before her husband confessed his Ponzi scheme, who, with Bernie's brother, Peter, had posted her husband's $10 million bond, and who had fought to keep her houses and property—was actually claiming to be a victim herself.

The outrage was universal.

"Hey Ruth, give up the $2.5 million for your husband['s] thievery. And get your ass to work to pay all the restit[uti]on!" was just one of the vitriolic comments on the *Los Angeles Times* Web site. On the *New York Times* Web site, a reader wrote, "$2.5 million? I would leave her with $5,000 plus whatever Social Security she has coming. Would be good to see her begging with a cardboard sign on Wall Street." Another took to verse: "Ms. Madoff will never let go / Of that 2.5 million or so, / And those bank accounts hidden / Will be at her biddin' / That's the way settlements go!"

Ruth Madoff said in her statement, "From the moment I learned from my husband that he had committed an enormous fraud, I have had two thoughts—first, that so many people who trusted him would be ruined financially and emotionally, and second, that my life with the man I have known for over 50 years was over."

The comedian Andy Borowitz savagely parodied this on the Huffington Post: "Just hours after her husband Bernie Madoff was sentenced . . . Ruth Madoff expressed shock and dismay at her husband's behavior, telling reporters, 'This is not the man I owned nine homes with. When you spend hundreds of millions of dollars with someone, you think you know him. . . . I guess I was wrong.'" On the *New York Times* Web site, a furious observer said, "Wow, it was all his fault, you had nothing to do with it? Really? Is that the depth of your apology for the last 50 years of enjoying the plunder from charities and pensioners? Really? You would have done better to keep silent. This is repugnant."

"The word 'façade' kept popping into my mind," says Ronnie Sue Ambrosino, who lost $1.7 million to Madoff and whose husband read a statement in court. "This is somebody covering their own back! Let's give her the benefit of the doubt; let's say she knew nothing. On December 11, the day of Bernie's arrest, she knew everything, and she had every opportunity to show the sorrow she spoke about in her statement, but she didn't until it served her purpose. She continued to have arrogance for the victims and hide behind the façade of supposed sorrow, just as her husband had."

In the course of writing three stories on the Madoff case for *Vanity Fair*, I've spoken to close to 100 people who knew Ruth, Bernie, and their family, and the majority believe that Ruth must have known about the scheme. Otherwise, if she was embarrassed, ashamed, betrayed, and confused, as she said in her statement, why did she stay with Bernie during his three months of house arrest—apparently at the cost of losing her sons, Mark and Andrew, who say they haven't spoken to their mother since the still not fully explained day in their parents' kitchen when Bernie confessed his crime to them with Ruth standing nearby? She's still under scrutiny by investigators, as are her sons, Bernie's brother, and Frank DiPascali Jr. and Annette Bongiorno, who directed Madoff's investment-advisory business, on the 17th floor of the Lipstick Building, in Manhattan. One longtime observer of the Madoffs told me that Ruth's statement, like everything preceding it in the case, may very well be just one more example of Bernie Madoff's brilliance at deception and manipulation. He always ran the show, and probably still does, the observer believes. From the day he turned himself in and pleaded guilty, Madoff was determined to take the fall alone. He continues from behind bars to try to control every detail of his destiny, including, at least one person is willing to venture, Ruth's statement.

"Like everyone else, I feel betrayed and confused," Ruth wrote. "The man who committed this horrible fraud is not the man whom I have known for all these years."

But the life she led with Bernie—and the one she continued to share with him from his arrest onward—tells a dramatically different story.

> *It pains me so much to remember my husband getting up in the*
> *middle of the night. He was a very fine physician. He would get up in*
> *the middle of the night year after year in all kinds of weather to go*
> *to the hospital to save someone's life in rain, ice and snow. He would*

save someone's life so that Bernie Madoff could buy his wife another
Cartier watch.

—Statement read in court by
Maureen Ebel, *Madoff victim*

'I thought she was one of the Belle Harbor girls," says Millie Tirado, who attended Far Rockaway High School with Ruth and Bernie, referring to the affluent Queens community that was home to "the golden girls, the girls with money, whose parents did not have to worry about sending them to college." But Ruth was from Laurelton, a middle-class community in Queens, and her single-family house was already a major step up for her parents, Saul and Sara Alpern, who had moved there from an apartment building in Brooklyn. "Laurelton was Siberia, as far as we knew," continues Tirado. Although "Ruthie," as everyone called her, didn't live in Belle Harbor, she strove to be the Belle Harbor type. "She was very well groomed, a real blonde, plus she didn't look Jewish—she looked Waspy, Doris Day–ish." A cheerleader as well as an honors student, Ruthie was voted "Josie College," and everyone agreed that she was destined for big things.

Along came tough, cocky Bernie, who worked as a lifeguard and a part-time sprinkler-system installer, and who once said he didn't like a book because it contained "hardly any pictures." Ruth fell in love with him by 14. They were neighbors in Laurelton—she lived on 224th Street, he on 228th—and rode to school together every day. Whereas a childhood friend remembers Ruth's parents as an intelligent, politically liberal couple who played bridge, read *The New York Times*, and summered in the Catskills, nobody remembers much about Bernie's, except for the tsuris they got into with the S.E.C., in 1963, over the registration of a broker-dealer firm apparently run out of their home.

"Bernie being a lifeguard was a joke," says Tirado. "I think he was really a cabana boy. In his off time, when he wasn't tending to the cabanas, he had to watch the kiddie pool. I don't have a recollection of him as an actual lifeguard. It was a very tough exam, and I don't think he was a super athlete. He was always at the periphery with that trademark smirk. I pretty much had my pick of guys, and I wouldn't put him out if he was on fire. There was something really creepy about him."

Bernie's best friend then, according to one classmate, thought Ruth at 15 was "an airhead." Some, however, insist that she was the smarter of the two. They were married at the Laurelton Jewish Center on the weekend after Thanksgiving 1959, and from that day forward Ruth made her man her mission. "I don't play the role of courtesan very well," Carmen Dell'Orefice, the supermodel and longtime Madoff investor and friend, told me, referring to the type of woman who is always "deferring to a man's wishes against her own."

"Did Ruth?," I asked her.

"To perfection!"

Ruth soon brought her husband together with her father, an accountant, and that was the beginning of everything. "Saul and Sara Alpern were plain and simple, good people, no-nonsense. Charm was not in their vocabulary—they told it like it was," says Michael Bienes, who joined Saul Alpern's firm as a junior accountant in the 1960s and was soon feeding clients to Madoff. "Easy, easy-peasey, like a money machine" is how Bienes described on *Frontline* Madoff's strong and steady returns over the years. He tells me that Saul Alpern thought his son-in-law was "the Second Coming. Never any doubt. . . . He promoted Bernie to family, clients, and friends." In a 1990s video, bespectacled Saul dances with his beloved Sara, a wry grin on his face. He was known for his "sharp sense of humor," explains Bienes, and for living "simply and without pretense." Alpern provided the launching pad for the grandiose life his daughter and son-in-law would eventually achieve.

"I think Saul Alpern was the mastermind of Bernie Madoff's original fund-raising template: promise 20 percent, and bring in more investors," says Erin Arvedlund, who blew the whistle on Madoff in a largely unheeded story in *Barron's* in 2001, and whose book, *Too Good to Be True: The Rise and Fall of Bernie Madoff*, will be published this month. As Saul was "going around to his friends and accounting clients to get some initial money for Bernie," according to Arvedlund, "Ruth and Bernie worked together out of Ruth's father's office." It was near Grand Central Terminal, in Manhattan. Ruth wrote in a book for the 50th reunion of her Far Rockaway High School class, "After college I married Bernie Madoff, F.R.H.S. class of '55. Bernie and I worked together in the investment business he founded in 1960." Michael Bienes says, "Ruthie was *always* with Bernie. I saw her almost every time I was in his office. She looked busy." Woe to anyone who dared to besmirch her husband's name, Bienes adds. "Get this: I take Ruthie to lunch. She wears a man's watch and says, 'This is what I *only* wear—I don't like jewelry.' Huh! I made a joke about Bernie. She turned on me and said, 'My Bernie is the most honest man in the world!' "

"She wasn't this dumb blonde—she was smart with numbers," says Erin Arvedlund. "So I find it hard to believe that if Ruth's father was one of Bernie's original fund-raisers, and she was there at the inception helping keep the books, how could she not know that Bernie had an 'advisory business' and that he was not registered with the S.E.C. [until 2006]? Was it a Ponzi scheme at that point? I don't know."

From an $87-a-month apartment in Bayside, Queens, with one bedroom and a schnauzer named Muffin, the newlyweds began their rise. After sailing through Queens College while Bernie plodded through the University of Alabama and Hofstra, Ruth went from bookkeeping to mothering their two boys, Mark and Andrew. "*Nobody* was a career woman in those days," says a friend, adding, "I spoke to her every single day, and I know she was at home with the kids—no nanny." A former female Madoff trader adds, "I know it was tough for her, raising the kids. Bernie was not around a lot—traveling or just working. She was at one point crying about how hard it was to raise the boys."

They moved from an apartment in Bayside to a bigger apartment in Great Neck, on Long Island, and then to a house at 73 Dianas Trail in the suburb of Roslyn, where their neighbors were future New York Mets principal owner Fred Wilpon and his wife, Judy, and Long Island developer Edward Blumenfeld and his wife, Susan. "Eddie" became Bernie's closest friend and an investor who would suffer heavy losses in the Ponzi scheme. Susan became the Madoffs' image guru, establishing the look in their homes and offices. She also seems to have transformed Ruth from simple Ruthie Alpern from Queens into Mrs. Bernard L. Madoff of Upper East Side Manhattan, Montauk, Palm Beach, and Cap d'Antibes.

On the Web site of Susan Blumenfeld Interiors, whose clients range from Gloria Vanderbilt to Universal Music Group, Blumenfeld appears thin and flaxen-haired, wearing a crisp white T-shirt and a dark blazer. "The Madoffs did a lot of antiquing but would not buy a piece of furniture, not even the tiniest thing, without Susan's approval," says Julia Fenwick, who ran Madoff's London office. "They would take pictures of things and send them to Susan. If Susan didn't like it, they wouldn't buy it. Susan was a very independent woman, and Ruth really looked up to her, because Ruth wasn't independent. Ruth was absolutely under Bernie's thumb. If Bernie said, 'Jump,' Ruth would say, 'How high?' If her makeup was slightly off, he'd say, 'What happened to your face?' For Ruth, looking good was all for Bernie.

"I was told by Shana Madoff [Bernie's niece and a compliance lawyer in his firm] that Ruth would not buy any *clothing* without Susan's approval," Fenwick continues. "They went everywhere together, and she would wear a lot of the same clothes as Susan. They were kind of like clones—everything was very basic, straightforward. Neither would go out on a limb." With her Susan-approved wardrobe and accessories (Prada and Goyard handbags, Susan Bennis Warren Edwards crocodile-leather flats), her hair colored Soft Baby Blonde (maintained at the Pierre Michel Salon, on East 57th Street, whose owners asked her not to return after Bernie's arrest), her skinny, firm figure (toned by a trainer at Equinox), and her taut face (tucked by plastic surgeries, one of which turned out badly and left her hospitalized), Ruth emerged as the perfectly preserved and packaged society wife.

Some rough edges, however, not even Susan Blumenfeld could erase. "Ruth has a deep voice, a Queens brogue that could get loud," says Carmen Dell'Orefice. "And, boy, if she wanted to let you know something, she had good projection. Whereas Bernie had a quiet voice, Ruth would be *Oh, my God, the traffic!* or *Oh, the clothes were wonderful!*" A social leader in East Hampton, who hosted two charity benefits the Madoffs attended, told me, "I found Ruth and Bernie to be most peculiar. They said hello when they came in and good-bye when they left—otherwise, not a word. Not 'It's a nice party, thank you for having us.' Nothing. It was more than rude. It was like I didn't exist."

Sisterhood was limited for Ruth, especially when it came to Bernie's brother Peter's wife, Marion, a tall, full-figured, outgoing brunette. "Ruth treated Marion as if she was a little bit of a second-class citizen," says Julia Fenwick. Marion wasn't Susan-approved. She dared to wear color. "Marion had her own style, which was terrific, and Ruth would dress like Susan—

white pants, white shirts, white shoes. Susan and Ruth would give Marion a look that was like 'You are not the same.' "

Beneath Ruth's bluster was a mass of insecurity. "Ruth always felt her sister-in-law was more attractive, more long-legged than she was," says a friend. "I always thought Ruth was more attractive and more fun, but that was her perception of herself. She would talk about Marion's long legs, which she didn't have, and how Marion was a better golfer."

In Ruth's world, the landscape was filled with younger, taller women. "I brought my fiancé to a STANY [Securities Traders Association of New York] party, and the two of us were talking to Ruth, who kept looking over my fiancé's shoulder at Bernie talking to two women, one of whom was a blonde," says a guest.

"If they were prettier, I'd be worried," Ruth said.

"You're a beautiful woman," the guest's fiancé said. "Why would you be jealous if Bernie talked to a pretty woman?"

"Because I'm the only woman he ever dated," Ruth answered, which the guest's fiancé took to mean that she felt that the slightest temptation might open the floodgates of Bernie's natural desires. "The rules of society didn't apply to him," says the guest.

"In London we hired a very pretty receptionist last year," remembers Julia Fenwick. "And Bernie came over and said, 'Ruth would *never* let me hire somebody who looks like that in New York. She vets the women who work in the office there.' She knew he was terribly flirtatious. He would come up with really inappropriate things, and you'd think, *Jesus*, Bernie!" A female trader recalls, "We had a belly dancer at one of our Christmas parties. I remember looking at the other female traders and thinking, Did they think we would find this entertaining? It was completely insensitive to have a belly dancer at an office Christmas party. I remember saying, 'This is so inappropriate! What does Ruth think?' And someone said, 'Ruth is the one who *booked* the belly dancer!' "

Bernie depended on her, both as wife and watchdog. "*Nothing* gets by Ruth," he would say. She paid the bills at his early New York office, at 110 Wall Street. "Any kind of vendor that charged us for anything, from electricity to charge cards, any bill that came into the office went to Ruth," says Eleanor Squillari, Bernie's longtime secretary, who also assisted Ruth in the 1980s. In her little office near the trading room, Ruth would sit, checkbook out, files at the ready, a picture of perfect efficiency, while her husband tended to the trading, confident that she always had his back.

"I wanted to open an M.R.I. center, but I didn't have the money," says a physician who approached longtime Madoff investor Robert Gettinger for the financing. Gettinger told him at the last minute that he would be bringing Bernie Madoff into the deal, with each of them investing $150,000 for what would be a limited partnership. "But when I got the check, it didn't come from Bernie Madoff—it came from *Ruth* Madoff," says the physician. "I asked him, 'I thought the investor was Bernie Madoff, so why is the check from Ruth Madoff?' And he said, 'He does his investments through his wife.'" (Gettinger didn't respond to a request for comment.)

> *I have reread Madoff's March 12 statement to you. Certain quotes jumped out at me. His continuing self-serving references, and I quote, that his proprietary trading in the market-making business managed by his brother and two sons was legitimate, profitable, and successful in all respects, or that he felt "compelled to satisfy my clients' expectations at any cost." It sounds as if he is laying the blame on his clients' expectations and never admitting the truth he was stealing from these clients and the lives he ruined. If he was attempting to protect his family, he should not be given that opportunity, because we, the victims, did not have the same opportunity to protect our families. Madoff the beast has stolen our ability to protect our loved ones away from us. He should have no opportunity to protect his family.*
>
> —Sheryl Weinstein,
> *Madoff victim*

Eventually, Bernie hired a full-time financial executive to take over the billing and banking. "And Ruth eased her way out," says Squillari. But Ruth still wrote checks on her husband's behalf. Most mornings she left a to-do list for Bernie. And her name pops up frequently in the hundreds of pages of Madoff documents recently released by the bankruptcy trustee. The papers, which track the ebb and flow of billions of dollars, also show that many of Madoff's assets were in Ruth's name. "The books and records of BLMIS [Bernard L. Madoff Investment Securities] show that Madoff also used BLMIS funds to purchase assets for his personal enjoyment and that of his family," reads one affidavit. "Madoff and his family created a web of shell companies to hold these assets after purchasing same with BLMIS funds. For example, BLMIS funds were used to purchase and maintain two yachts, the first in 2003 and the second in 2007. . . . These yachts were used by Madoff and his family and served no apparent business purpose. The second yacht, named Bull, is held by Yacht Bull Corporation, a corporation in which Ruth Madoff has an interest."

Another company to which Madoff made substantial loans is Madoff Technologies, L.L.C., "owned in part by Ruth Madoff," according to the affidavit. Yet Ruth seemed like a technological neophyte. "I worked with her in her private office, teaching her how to send digital photographs," says computer tutor Lonson MacCargar. "She wasn't a computer whiz. I don't think she's capable of managing online banking. The extent of her computer knowledge is e-mail and sending photos to her children and grandchildren."

"I think she struggled, like so many wives of successful men do, to forge her own identity," says a friend. She went back to school to get a master's degree in nutrition at New York University, which included working in a health center on the Lower East Side of Manhattan. She gave her time and money to charities and educational endeavors, played golf, went to matinees on Broadway—keeping herself free for the ritual 6:30, 45-minute dinner in a restaurant with Bernie. She came to play the role of the financial icon's spouse expertly. "So controlled she was almost like a robot," says one former employee. "She was normal, normal, normal—nothing but normal," says a friend. "Her family came first," says another. Others call her "nice," "fun," "unpretentious," "a terrific friend," "a mensch," "a class act." Her landscaper of 25 years says, "The only Ruth Madoff I know is so loving, so intelligent, so respectful of my work." A friend of her son Mark's says that with the Madoff family there were "no airs, no snobbery," adding that both Ruth and Bernie were always gracious and warm. "She was a hot mom," says another. She was very proud of Mark and Andrew, and, as one friend puts it, "she *adored* her sons." Yet they almost all add, "Somebody's got to prove to me that she wasn't in on the whole thing."

She was certainly a way into Madoff's fund. One old Laurelton friend, after not seeing Ruth for 50 years but knowing she had become Mrs. Bernard L. Madoff, cold-called Bernie to try to wheedle his way into investing. Bernie said he was *beyond* closed—besides, he had a $2 million minimum. "He said, 'By the way, Ruthie's *here*. Want to talk to her?'" the friend remembers, and for 30 minutes he and Ruth reminisced. When Bernie came back on the phone, he said, "You know what? We've known each other a long time. You can come in."

On vacation at their Montauk beach house in the late 1980s, Ruth joined other well-off wives in cooking classes at the Sapore di Mare restaurant, in East Hampton. "She was this little skinny barrel of a woman, like a bull," remembers chef Mark Strausman, who taught the classes. Ruth and Idee German Schoenheimer, whose husband, Pierre, is a financier, came up with an idea for a book: *The Great Chefs of America Cook Kosher*. They asked almost 50 famous chefs, including Wolfgang Puck, Emeril Lagasse, and Alice Waters, to provide kosher recipes for their favorite dishes. Ruth and Idee enlisted an editor and then self-published the book—"They spent a fortune on it," says Strausman.

Ruth talked the chefs into donating their recipes. "This is what pissed me off: she sold the deal to me like 'You'll get so much press! It'll be so good for *you!*'" remembers Strausman. "I thought, What do you mean, good for me? This is the kind of woman she was: you did her a favor and she turned it around that she's doing *you* a favor."

Ruth took her team into the Madoff offices in the Lipstick Building, where they worked on the cookbook in a spare room. The book opened important doors, especially for Ruth. "Ruth was a fucking social climber," says an insider. "For a little lady, she clawed onto the ladder and climbed it." Idee Schoenheimer became a connection in the Hamptons. Schoenheimer also invested in Bernie's fund, as did at least one of the chefs who provided recipes, Nancy Silverton, who runs the restaurant Osteria Mozza, in Los Angeles. (Silverton invested through Beverly Hills money manager Stanley Chais. Chais has been sued by both the court-appointed Madoff bankruptcy trustee and the Securities and Exchange Commission. He has denied any wrongdoing.) "Idee got conned more than anybody," says a friend. "She was the one who invited Ruth and Bernie into her home for 20 years. Can you imagine what she must feel like? The obsessive-compulsive guy, who was so picky about his food, and the wife who facilitated him? . . . People lost money with Ivan Boesky, but it wasn't done around dining-room tables and fireplaces in people's homes. Madoff did it to friends at family affairs—weddings, Seders. People they summered with in the South of France. Now these people are walking around dazed, thinking, When we were in the South of France eating bouillabaisse, did Ruth know we were being conned?"

Once the cookbook was published, Ruth and Idee hit the media circuit, including what Strausman remembers as a torturous appearance on television. "I went on CNN with Ruth and Idee, and they were both petrified," he says. "I remember something happening and Ruth snapping at me. . . . She's a hundred pounds soaking wet, but when she opens her mouth it's like a hurricane coming out." In recent years, the hurricane roared again at Strausman, in Fred's, the restaurant he runs in Barneys New York. "She's walking out, and I say, 'How are you?' and she says, '*Not happy!*' She points to the poor maître d' and says, '*He* gave me a bad table!'" Strausman tried to smooth things over. "But Ruth was inconsolable—really, really nasty. I wanted to say to her, 'How would you expect him to know who you are? And who are you anyway? You're just another short Jewish lady on the Upper East Side, for God's sake!' But Ruth was nasty. *Red.* It was like an exorcism."

Proceeds from the cookbook were to benefit the Jewish National Fund, but a representative from the fund says it received no money. The book also spurred the threat of a copyright-infringement lawsuit, from the "Great Chefs" television shows, books, and videos, whose chairman, John Shoup, says the women brazenly lifted the name without permission. He eventually had to threaten them with a cease-and-desist order to make them stop distributing the book.

How to reconcile the red Ruth, ranting in restaurants, with the blonde Ruth, cool and collected around the country club, at the charity event, in the boardroom? "She was conflicted," says Michael Skakun, a freelance writer, who, along with another writer, Ken Libo, was summoned to the Madoff penthouse in late 2003. Ruth wanted to create a special gift for Bernie's 65th birthday, and Skakun immediately noticed the contradictions in her. "I saw a woman who was very artificially made up . . . Botoxed . . . sort of artificial and frozen—her face, her home." In an article published in the *Forward* in 2008, after the scandal broke, Skakun and Libo described the apartment as "Queens High Baroque," such a cold, austere, over-the-top interior that Ruth led them into the kitchen, saying they'd be more comfortable there. "It's *haimish* here," said Ruth, employing the Yiddish word for informal, which Skakun took to mean: I'm just a plain, outer-borough girl entombed in a stage set reflecting someone else's image of success.

For four hours she described what she wanted, "a birthday present he won't forget. . . . Maybe a surprise scrapbook, you know—pictures, photos, invitations, the works." She brought out albums of snapshots and artifacts from her life with Bernie. "Other men slow down, take it easy," she said. "Not him. He's got the world on his head." But even as she spoke, Skakun felt that she was actually talking herself out of the project. "She said he was a very secretive person," he remembers. But here she was opening up her husband's life to two strangers, whom she called the next day to say she had decided to scrap the idea. "It was a paradox, wanting to do something special, which she knew would be transgressive," says Skakun. "She felt she was treading on thin ice, and I think she was disappointed and angry, maybe at herself and maybe at her husband, that he was so secretive that she couldn't do something to please him."

Try as Ruth might to forge her own identity, it was inscrutably tied to her husband's. She kept a place for herself in the office, not as the high-level power broker or financier she is often described to be, but mainly as a wife and mother. "I go to the office," she is said to have told a friend, "to keep Bernie from killing our sons."

> *I cry every day when I see the look of pain and despair in my husband's eyes. I cry for the life we once had before that monster took it away. Our two sons and daughter-in-law have rallied with constant love and support. You, on the other hand, Mr. Madoff, have two sons that despise you. Your wife, rightfully so, has been vilified and shunned by her friends in the community. You have left your children a legacy of shame. I have a marriage made in heaven. You have a marriage made in hell, and that is where you, Mr. Madoff, are going to return. May God spare you no mercy.*
>
> —Marcia FitzMaurice,
> *Madoff victim*

'The characterization given of Ruth as being low-key, not flashy, is not correct," says an individual who served with her on the board of the Queens College Foundation. "She had a very large amount of wealth, a big diamond—and I mean *big*—and a Mercedes with a driver."

Ruth regularly gave this friend lifts to board meetings. During one ride she said, "Bernie and I are going on vacation in Cap d'Antibes. We have a boat there."

"How long you going for?" her passenger asked.

"About two months."

"Two months! How can Bernie leave the business for two months?"

"Oh, we can go away because the boys [Mark and Andrew Madoff] handle the business." The board member adds, "That stuck with me, because either the kids were in on the nuts and bolts of the business or there is no business." (The Madoff sons did not work for the fraudulent investment-advisory part of their father's company.)

Ruth was a shareholder in her husband's London business, for which "she was paid a dividend each year of less than $200,000," says someone close to the operation. She also kept an office on the 18th floor of the Lipstick Building, where she and Bernie would frequently arrive at work together. Like him, she was extremely secretive. Ruth had an account with Cohmad Securities, the brokerage firm established by Madoff and his longtime friend Maurice "Sonny" Cohn. According to the court-appointed trustee who is charged with liquidating Madoff's company and recovering funds for investors, Cohmad and what Erin Arvedlund calls its "top individual free-market fund-raisers" were paid hundreds of millions of dollars for steering high-end clients into Madoff's advisory arm. "Cohmad was like having an A.T.M. in your house, but only certain people in the firm had access to it, and one of those people was Ruth Madoff," says Arvedlund. "And all of her Cohmad money was in cash."

When former Madoff employees speak of Ruth, they invariably bring up the company Christmas party at the Rosa Mexicano restaurant on December 10, the day before Bernie's arrest. That same day, according to his sons, Bernie had confessed his crime to them with Ruth standing nearby in their penthouse, but at the party Ruth and Bernie acted as if nothing were wrong, as if Bernard L. Madoff Investment Securities were rock-solid. "Ruth was at the party, staring at these people, knowing they were penniless," says someone who knows her, adding that Ruth reportedly said at the party that she and Bernie were going to Florida for the holidays.

After Madoff was arrested, Ruth and Peter Madoff posted his $10 million bond and he returned to the two-level penthouse on East 64th Street. A week later he got into a pushing-and-shoving scene with a mob of reporters and cameramen staked out in front of the building.

Ruth promptly began dealing with the aftershocks and the finances. She called Angela Gonther, their real-estate broker in the South of France, who had sold them their town house in Cap d'Antibes, where they spent eight weeks a year. ("Her French was pretty good—his wasn't," Gonther told Janelle Lassonde, who wrote about the Madoffs in "French Lessons," her weekly blog from Cap d'Antibes.)

"Are you willing to talk to me?," Ruth asked Gonther, according to Lassonde.

"Of course," said Gonther.

"What's the town house worth?" asked Ruth.

A few months later, it was unloaded for $1.4 million to Russian buyers. The Madoffs' Peugeot was also sold, and one of their boats, which they had bought for $7 million, was put on the market. Its captain, Bruno, who calls Ruth "Madame," is reportedly staying on until the boat is sold.

Ruth believed that her husband might be allowed to stay at home with her until his case was sorted out. Even after Judge Denny Chin revoked Madoff's bail, on March 12, and ordered him to jail, Ruth still held out hope that he would be able to spend the time until his sentencing with her. But Bernie would never return to the apartment.

From then on, Ruth Madoff's very existence—and freedom—served as an insult to her husband's victims. THE LONELIEST WOMAN IN NEW YORK was the headline of an article about her in *The New York Times*, which Ruth certainly read, because she read *everything* about the case; she became so haunted by the incessant coverage that she considered a day without their name in the papers a blessing. "Everyone assumes that she knew," says an old friend of Ruth's, who lost everything to Madoff. "I hate to speak of her like she is dead," says another. But the woman Ruth Madoff once was—the seemingly perfect wife, mother, grandmother, cook, charity lady, and sportswoman—died on December 11. Her sons wouldn't, or couldn't, speak to her. Former investors wanted her head. Her fortune was gone, and until she cut the deal with prosecutors to retain $2.5 million in exchange for surrendering everything else, the former world-class shopper who would charge through Paris powered by AmEx ("Get both!" she once encouraged a shopping companion, who couldn't decide between two extravagant items) was suddenly reduced to a debit card.

Her accounts were frozen; she couldn't even get access to her Social Security checks. Deprived of funds, she subsisted on chili, chicken, and skirt steak, while petitioning the government to pay her monthly bills and the upkeep on her and her husband's properties until they could be sold off to repay investors. As soon as she got one month paid, bills for the next month would come roaring in. Bernie was the only man she had ever loved, and now he was all she had left.

Among Ruth's first concerns was the press. Reporters vultured her 24-7, so rabid they followed one neighbor down the street, thinking she was Ruth. She knew they would be waiting for her at the jail as well, but she defied them—she'd crawl through a pack of mongrel dogs to see Bernie.

She visited him every Monday at the Metropolitan Correctional Center, where she would try to buoy his spirits while hers sank. She had to wear clothing without zippers—any trace of metal would set off the detectors and cancel her visit—and nothing revealing or exposed. Always insecure about her appearance, that part was easy for Ruth. But she couldn't see Bernie with imperfect hair, so she called a nearby salon and asked them to send someone over to give her a haircut, and not to breathe a word about it, especially to the media. She sent Bernie books to get his mind off his troubles, and she collected quarters and dollar bills to take to him so that he could buy junk food from the jailhouse vending machines. This was quite a comedown for a person whose AmEx bills, released by the bankruptcy trustee—just one of an endless array of humiliating documents illustrating the ebb and flow of billions of Madoff dollars—showed charges one month alone of tens of thousands for clothing and charity donations.

She called her incarcerated spouse Doll, Darling, Baby, and Sweetie. She tried not to be dull or depressing; she wanted to be at her best for him. The visits were always over way too quickly, and she would take a taxi back home. The television gave her little comfort. "I don't care how dumb you are. There is no way that you can . . . think that they're not going to take this money from you. Ruth, you might as well just give it up, honey!" exclaimed Whoopi Goldberg one day on *The View,* chuckling with her co-hosts about the desperate housewife trying to hang on to her ill-gotten assets. Those assets were all evidence now, spoils of the crime, which she had to catalogue and report to government investigators and bankruptcy trustees, who were selling off what she and Bernie had spent a lifetime painstakingly collecting. With many of her friends transformed into victims, the notion that she was allowed to remain free and unfettered while her husband sat in jail before his sentencing must have seemed like a ludicrous joke to Ruth. To compound the pain and punishment, she believed she would be left broke and alone, and without any foreseeable future.

So she sat in her penthouse with the shades drawn and—to save money—the air-conditioning off. Only a handful of her bravest friends and closest relatives came to visit, as they might visit a patient with a terminal disease, bringing her fish, videos, and her favorite candy, Peanut Chews. She tried not to dwell on the $65 billion her husband had defrauded from investors and institutions. To Ruth this may have been a situation, a predicament, in which Bernie had gotten himself entrapped— something that *happened* to him, not some diabolical scheme he had devised and orchestrated. She believed that somehow time would return to her what she treasured most: her family. She managed to have quick meetings with her grandchildren, but always without their fathers present. Her sister, Joan, came to see her. But how often could Joan and her husband make the trip from Boca Raton? (Joan's name was also on Bernie's victims list—stung for $2.7 million, while her husband got hit for $8.7 million.)

Other visitors arrived hungry, which meant Ruth had to spend money she didn't have for food and drink. Whereas before she had dined at the best restaurants, with no thought of the tariff, now she fretted over the tiniest expenditure. When the guests were gone, the woman who had once sailed the world on private yachts, her every whim tended to by a captain and crew, would dust and mop her apartment.

*Six months have passed. I manage on food stamps. At the end of
the month I sometimes scavenge in Dumpsters. I cannot afford new
eyeglasses. I long to go to a concert, but I never do. Sometimes my heart
beats erratically for lack of medication when I cannot pay for it. I shine
my shoes each night, afraid they will wear out. My laundry is done by
hand in the kitchen sink. I have collected empty cans and dragged them
to redemption centers. . . . By self-admission, this thief among us knew
his victims were facing a kind of death at his hands, yet he continued to
play with us as a cat would with a mouse.*

—Miriam Siegman,
Madoff victim

The items so carefully selected—the $39,000 Steinway, the $35,000
Lavar Kerman Persian rug, the $20,000 Chippendale-style tea
table—only reminded Ruth of what had once been. As the walls closed in,
she *had* to get out, but she dreaded it. Her first public appearance had left
her in a constant state of panic. On March 19, six days after Bernie went to
jail, she had barreled out into the chilly New York night, trailed by a bodyguard and her building's superintendent, hurrying past two photographers,
headed toward Third Avenue to go grocery shopping at the Food Emporium.

The cameras caught a woman who bore no trace of the blonde in a much-
reproduced May 2008 photograph of her and Bernie in Mexico, drinking
white wine and eating white fish. Immaculately tanned, toned, and perfectly
preserved, looking at least a decade younger than her 67 years, Ruth wore a
crisp white jacket and a Mona Lisa smile. Now, 10 months later, with a ski
cap pulled down low, she wore a bulky coat over a hooded orange sweat-
shirt with a white polo shirt underneath. She looked tired and pale, and a
smear of lipstick defined her pout. "I had trouble believing it was her," says
Joe Marino, who took a photo of Ruth for the New York *Daily News.* "She
looked haggard and extremely distressed, like she'd aged 15 years." When
the photographers chased her into the grocery, Ruth pushed her shopping
cart into a shelf and snapped, "Forget this—this is *crazy!*" Then she walked
out of the store and back to her apartment.

Later outings were equally frustrating, each episode pushing her deeper into Leona Helmsley territory in the public's eye. May 11: "Ruth Madoff, in sunglasses, schlepping a roller bag (filled with jewelry?) north on Lexington Avenue at 60th," read the *Post.* June 25: when photographed by the *Post* while riding the subway, sitting under an ad for a 99-cent cell-phone deal, she said, "Are you having fun embarrassing me and ruining my life?" ("Ruth Madoff Takes F Train to Schadenfreude Station," snickered Gothamist.com.)

Actually, she went out undetected more often than not. A guard in her building would alert her when the coast was clear of paparazzi, and she would escape to a movie or occasionally a play, always looking over her shoulder for fear of running into one of her husband's former investors. She loves the theater. As time went on, she felt she couldn't afford taxis, so she would walk to theaters, where she could be invisible for a couple of hours. But when the lights went up, she was a pariah again. Hours on end she sat beside a phone that didn't ring, in her lonely apartment, reading books, waiting for sleep to rescue her.

The bad press was relentless. In Ruth's eyes, *Vanity Fair* was the lowest of the low. She considered the stories written by me—especially my collaboration with Bernie's longtime secretary, Eleanor Squillari—the worst of them all. (Meanwhile, her son Andrew has told friends that Eleanor's story was terrific.) The New York *Daily News* was doubtless second on Ruth's media shitlist, for reporting that Bernie had had an affair with an executive assistant at a major media company a decade or so ago.

In June, things seemed to look up for Ruth as some reports raised doubts about her complicity. Court documents indicated that Ruth and her sister, Joan, were co-trustees of trusts created by their parents, and that assets from these trusts had been invested in Madoff's fraudulent business. Why would Ruth deliberately place family money in a Ponzi scheme? Attorney Jerry Reisman, who represents 16 Madoff victims, with claims in excess of $150 million, says the fact that Ruth invested the money in her husband's fund lowers her possible complicity in the deception—which he'd previously ranked at 100 percent—to around 95 percent. "No wife who inherits money from a parent gives that money to a husband who she believes or knows is conducting an investor fraud," he says. "That investment dates back to 1999. At least up until that period, to my knowledge, she had no knowledge of the fraud." In midsummer, *The Wall Street Journal* reported that, according to two sources, "federal investigators have concluded for now there is no physical evidence that Ruth Madoff, the wife of convicted swindler Bernard Madoff, actively participated in or concealed her husband's fraud."

On June 26, some financial relief came when Ruth cut her deal with U.S. prosecutors, forfeiting the right to assets valued at $80 million in exchange for $2.5 million, money that may be tied to older real-estate holdings. "In compromise of claims RUTH MADOFF would have pursued, the Office [of the U.S. attorney] will not contest RUTH MADOFF's claim to a sum of money equal to $2,500,000 . . . which sum the Office shall cause to be tendered to RUTH MADOFF promptly after she vacates the real property and surrenders all personal property," the court order reads. (Ruth may still be liable to civil claims.)

At noon on July 2, six U.S. marshals arrived to take possession of the 133 East 64th Street penthouse, which was in Ruth's name, and where she and Bernie had lived since 1984. The marshals had a court order to seize the $7 million property and all of its contents as restitution to the victims. It was yet another public-relations nightmare for Ruth, with the Associated Press reporting that she argued with the marshals and asked to keep a fur, which the marshals made her leave behind. (I was informed that she knew about the eviction well in advance and told the marshals she would need the coat for the coming winter. Ruth's attorney said that she had forfeited the fur days earlier in accordance with an agreement with the court.) She looked grim as she exited, with nothing but a straw beach bag, while a small crowd jeered. "What goes around comes around," one bystander told the *New York Post.* "Go get a job now like the rest of us slobs!" screamed another. "Show us the money!"

For Bernie's 70th birthday, on April 29, 2008, Ruth planned a party on a starlit beach in Cabo San Lucas, Mexico. A dozen of the Madoffs' best friends, some of whom were investors, gathered to celebrate the great man of the markets, and Ruth had commissioned orange sweatshirts embroidered with "BLM EST. 1938" over the heart. The polite, pleasant, perfectly put-together Ruth, consummate wife and hostess, presided over cocktails and dinner, serenaded by the crashing waves and kissed by the ocean breezes off the Sea of Cortez. But soon after people began making toasts, the red Ruth came roaring out. "Bernie's brother, Peter, got up and said how much he loved his brother, and Ed Blumenfeld talked about how Bernie was such a great guy," says Julia Fenwick, who attended the event.

Next, one of Bernie's longtime friends and associates stood up. He raised his glass and praised Madoff for his brilliance and accomplishments. Then, in what was supposed to be a funny aside, he added, "And, Bernie, you know you're a complete shyster."

"Everybody laughed," Fenwick remembers. "But Ruth went nuts. She screamed at the guest, 'You're a complete *shit!* How dare you say that to Bernie? All the things he's done for you, and you treat him like this? You're out of order!' And he said, 'Ruth, I was just roasting him!' But Ruth went absolutely crazy, at the table, in front of everybody, saying 'fuck' and 'shit,' and wouldn't let the matter drop. The party was kind of over after that."

Seven months later, the party was really over for the Madoffs and those who had given them their money, trust, and friendship. Some say the Madoff family went down on December 10, when Bernie confessed to the boys. One friend says they probably chose up sides, like players in a baseball game: *Bernie, you get Ruthie, and, Mark and Andy, you get each other, and we'll be the Madoff family once again once the heat dies down.* But others, including Mark and Andrew, insist that Ruth chose Bernie at the expense of everything and everyone else. In mid-July, Ruth learned that Bernie might be able to serve his sentence at Otisville, a medium-security prison 70 miles northwest of New York City. "I'm so glad! It's just what we wanted," she reportedly told a friend at a pizza parlor, where she had tried to use expired coupons to get a discount. But then word came down that Bernie had been shipped to the Butner Federal Correctional Complex, near Durham, North Carolina.

Days after that, Ruth was believed to be visiting Mark's first wife, Susan, on Nantucket, and was sighted having her hair done at an RJ Miller salon. She was there under an assumed name.

In her prepared statement, Ruth seemed to be distancing herself from her husband, saying that the life they had shared was over. Many insist that merely one chapter is over and that a new one has begun, and that

Ruth will continue to stand by her man. "I had to sell my home because of Bernie," says one investor, who had considered herself a close friend of Ruth's. "Quite frankly, I don't know whether she knew or not—and I don't know which is worse. Either way, it's a tragedy for her. He's ruined a lot of families, but none worse than his own."

Twice while writing previous stories on the Madoff case for this magazine, I contacted Ruth Madoff's attorney, Peter Chavkin, for a statement from her, only to be told, essentially, no comment. On May 20, 2009, I sent an overnight letter directly to Ruth Madoff, advising her of the story I was researching about her. "I am hoping to humanize a woman who, I sense, is more than the person portrayed in the media," I wrote, asking her for a meeting, a phone call, anything. She never responded. On July 9, I again e-mailed Chavkin, who suggested I send a list of questions, which I did at nine A.M. on July 14. I requested a reply by the end of the next business day. Here, unedited, is his answer in full:

> Mark, the following is our statement in response; it should be kept intact and portions not picked out of context. This statement is intended as an on-the-record comment *only* in its totality.
>
> The proposed statements sent to us by *Vanity Fair* for comment are filled with factual falsities and reflect a clear bias. With *Vanity Fair* imposing essentially a 24 hour turnaround time to respond, we do not intend to rebut each of the over 30 statements Vanity Fair sent. Characteristic of the flat out falsehoods in those statements is *Vanity Fair*'s allegation that Ruth Madoff abandoned her sons. That is a lie. She loves her sons dearly and because of restrictions on communication with them imposed by the sons' counsel—restrictions we respected—she was not in contact for several months. She never stopped loving them and it pained her deeply that she could not see them. Similarly false is the notion that Bernie Madoff was not around to help with the family. He took off a good deal of time to be with Ruth, Mark and Andrew throughout their lives. Ruth also never ordered a belly dancer, never envied her sister in law or anyone else, never

screamed at a maitre d' or chef, never screamed at someone at a party for Bernie, and focused on her family, not social status. Moreover, she did not know of or participate in her husband's wrongdoing and all financial decisions, including Cohmad, the running of all Madoff companies, and investments in vehicles like Madoff Technology were made by Bernie for Ruth without Ruth's participation. Notable among *Vanity Fair*'s very few accuracies are the statements that Ruth and a colleague published a cookbook at their expense—which they did to benefit the well respected charity Jewish National Fund—and that she lived with her husband after his arrest when he was confined, by the conditions of his court ordered bail, to the co-op that she owned.

·21·

Part V: Greenwich Mean Time

The Noel Family

By *Vicky Ward*

April 2009

December 11, 2008, began much like any other day for Walter Noel: the tall, silver-haired, 78-year-old businessman strolled into the headquarters of his Fairfield Greenwich Group, on Manhattan's East 52nd Street. Then employing around 140 people, the company was a (supposedly) diversified alternative investment fund with $14.1 billion under management. Despite the recent turmoil of markets and the massive global demand for redemptions by investors terrified by the credit crisis, Noel was calm and collected, as usual. He had semi-retired two and a half years previously, worked on his golf game, and handed over day-to-day operations to the younger people at his firm, but he still went in to the office most days.

That morning F.G.G. salesman Andrew Douglass was on the phone with a potential investor, pitching a new fund that would invest with top Wall Street broker Bernie Madoff. The fund was named Emerald, and Douglass told the investor that F.G.G. had already raised at least $50 million to put into it. Suddenly a news bulletin came over the Bloomberg wire:

Madoff had reportedly confessed to his sons the night before that he'd been running a giant, [$65 billion] Ponzi scheme for years. "It [his investment strategy] was all a big lie," he'd apparently told them.

Because their firm had 48 percent of its capital tied up with Madoff, F.G.G. executives watched on their office TV screens with particularly acute horror as Madoff, dressed like a courtly grandfather, was handcuffed by F.B.I. agents outside his New York apartment building. Noel went into F.G.G. co-principal Jeffrey Tucker's office to consult on the situation. Tucker tried to reach Madoff by phone, but he was no longer talking to anyone other than his wife, his attorney, and federal and criminal investigators.

Noel called his wife, Monica, now 67, and told her to sit down while he explained what had happened.

Tucker and the Fairfield team were all in shock. According to one source, F.G.G. had recently received a highly unusual call from Madoff, demanding that the company halt its customers' redemptions. (A spokesperson for F.G.G. says that, over the life of the funds, redemption requests were honored by Madoff without complaint or delay.) Madoff, usually self-contained, was not known to get irate. Now it was clear why he had behaved so uncharacteristically.

Noel and Tucker are said even to have wired Madoff cash—a family member calls the amount "substantial"—from their personal accounts. (They deny having done so.) They realized now, as someone close to them says, that "they should have just burned the dollar bills on the F.D.R."

But Walter Noel was only beginning to realize that it wasn't just his investors' money that was gone. So too was his business and his reputation, as well as his family's.

Russell S. Reynolds Jr., an executive-recruitment consultant and an old friend, saw him the next day having lunch with Monica at Greenwich's Round Hill Club. "Walter was shaking, he was so upset," Reynolds recalls.

Noel had started F.G.G. in 1983 as a tiny operation, with just a few clients. Originally from Nashville, he had been a private-banking executive for Chemical Bank and Citibank in such diverse locations as Lagos, Switzerland, and Brazil. Tucker, who came on six years later, was the son of an accountant from Brooklyn and was a former lawyer for the Securities and Exchange Commission. Friends say Noel always described Tucker as "a prince of a guy."

In 1974, the Noels had purchased for $225,000 ($936,000 in today's dollars)—borrowed from both of their families—a modest house on prestigious Round Hill Road in Greenwich, Connecticut. Even though the house had five bedrooms, the couple made room for their five daughters. According to a friend, the family was popular with its neighbors. Attractive, dark-haired Monica "worked her tail off," the friend says, "building a small children's clothing line named 'Monica Noel.' " She did it for what she called "my shrimp money."

As they grew up, her daughters helped her with it. The eldest four—Corina, Lisina, Ariane, and Alix—went to public and private schools. They spent summers at Monica's parents' home in Brazil and skied in Klosters, Switzerland, in winter. Like their mother, they spoke several languages; all were athletic and strikingly beautiful.

In the early years the Noels were well off but not rich by Greenwich standards. Only Marisa, now 31, the youngest daughter by 10 years, got a fancy car—a BMW—to drive as a teenager. This was because by then F.G.G. had brought Noel and Tucker unexpected riches. Quite suddenly, in his 60s, Noel found he had the money for a truly lavish lifestyle that included vacation houses in Palm Beach and Southampton and on the Caribbean island of Mustique.

F.G.G. was sometimes steered to clients by Monica Noel's cousins. Half Swiss, half Brazilian, she was a member of the prominent Haegler family. Her cousin Jorge Paulo Lemann is Brazil's richest financier and co-owns InBev, Budweiser's parent company. But it was Tucker's wife, Melanie, "a dedicated tennis player" from Scarsdale, who had the connection that made them all rich. Her family knew Bernie Madoff, whose firm, Bernard L. Madoff Investment Securities, begun in 1960, was a legend on Wall Street for the volume of its over-the-counter (as in off-the-exchange) trades and the clockwork-like returns of 10 to 12 percent a year from its private-investment arm. Tucker introduced Noel to Madoff, although Noel now tells people he never got to know Madoff particularly well socially—in fact, Monica seems eager to emphasize to friends that in 20 years her family and the Madoffs socialized together perhaps three times.

By the time F.G.G. really got going, its primary product was Fairfield Sentry, a feeder fund into Madoff Securities. In 2006, the S.E.C. concluded that Fairfield had not properly revealed how heavily the fund depended on

Madoff, but thereafter the firm bragged about the connection and used it as a selling point.

As Tucker would tell Noel, the difficulty with Madoff was gaining access to the whiz trader. Providing that access was what would justify Fairfield's management fees of 1 percent to its clients as well as 20 percent of the returns—twice the normal rate for a typical "fund of funds." Madoff supposedly was picky. He often turned investors down. He was reserved. He was a workaholic. He didn't want clients who peppered him with questions about his investment strategy and how he guaranteed such regular returns. But if you were happy to trust him, then each month you'd get your 1 percent.

What F.G.G. offered Madoff was new markets. Initially only a small circle of individuals, almost all members of country clubs in Westchester and Palm Beach, invested with him. What Madoff did not have much of—and what F.G.G. could help provide—was an international clientele. Accordingly, F.G.G. sold Fairfield Sentry internationally until the fund's total exposure to Madoff reached $6.9 billion, almost half the company's assets under management by December 2008.

As Fairfield Greenwich expanded, the most prominent of its salesmen came to be Noel's own sons-in-law, whose European and South American backgrounds were invaluable to the firm. As things stand, Walter Noel owns 17 percent of F.G.G.'s business, as does Tucker, who like Noel semi-retired two years ago. F.G.G.'s chief shareholder is Andrés Piedrahita, who owns 22 percent. Piedrahita, 50, is a short, brash Colombian married to Noel's eldest daughter, Corina, 45. The Piedrahitas have four daughters. In 2003, they moved from a mansion in London's Chester Square to a house in Madrid's swanky Puerta di Hierro, and they own a vacation home on Majorca as well as an apartment in the Sherry-Netherland hotel, in New York. They also lease time on a Gulfstream 200 and own a 150-foot yacht, which is being decorated and is due for delivery shortly.

The other Noel sons-in-law have also reaped riches from F.G.G.—and all but one of them worked for the firm. Yanko Della Schiava, 44, an Italian married to Noel's second daughter, Lisina, 44, sold F.G.G. in Northern Italy and southern Switzerland. The couple live in Milan with their three children.

Noel's fourth daughter, Alix, 41, often called the "earthiest" of the sisters, is married to Swiss-born Philip Toub, 43. Noel put him to work selling Fairfield Greenwich mostly in Brazil, where the Toubs moved before returning recently to Greenwich with their four children.

The family's "baby," as she is often called, Marisa, married a dashing New York hedge-fund manager, Matt Brown, 39, in 2002. In 2005 his company merged into F.G.G., where his job was to bring in new business. The Browns, who have three children, recently bought a $13.5 million town house on New York's Upper East Side and are renovating it.

Only the third Noel daughter, Ariane, 42, chose a husband who decided not to work for F.G.G. Marco Sodi, 50, is a partner of the media investment bank Veronis Suhler Stevenson. The couple live in London and have five children. The terrible irony is that Sodi invested his personal wealth in Fairfield Greenwich.

Several people have observed that, after the Noels got really rich, they began to be perceived as irritating people who were not so welcome in the places where they bought new houses—in Southampton, Palm Beach, and Mustique: the world's richest and snootiest communities, widely known to be minefields for the socially ambitious.

The Noels' vast house on Mustique, named Yemanjá, was featured—along with the Noel women—in a cover story in *Town & Country* in 2005. Coming after a 2002 feature in this magazine, headlined "Golden in Greenwich," it gave ammunition to people who believed that the Noels were shameless self-promoters. (Monica has told people that she agreed to the *Town & Country* feature only because she believed that it would increase the value of the house.)

One friend from Greenwich was astonished by the stories she heard about them in Southampton, where they bought a $10 million house in 2001. They grated on local society by taking out an entire page in the "Blue Book"—the local social register of the Hamptons. "You don't have to put every single cell phone, and every single child, and every single number. They live in Europe, they live in South America; it wasn't necessary to put down 43 names," says an observer.

They wasted no time in applying to join the beach club officially known as the Bathing Corporation of Southampton, where Philip Toub's father,

Said Toub, is a member. But older members, who expect young women to appear in Lilly Pulitzer dresses, say they were put off when the Noel women showed up in "thongs and sarongs."

Also, they table-hopped—which offended members. Some people said Walter Noel networked on the beach. "What I heard is he was actually selling the Fairfield Greenwich fund, or trying to encourage other members of the beach club to buy it, because it was an incredible thing, and he was almost using that as currency, if you will, to garner a favor," says a man in that world.

Another person who spends time in Southampton recalls, "They really did things that seemed outlandish. The first summer they were here, I won't forget seeing two of the daughters blocking traffic on Jobs Lane, leaning out of their convertibles, talking to each other and making what sounded like idle plans and blowing kisses, as if they owned the street—literally for five full minutes while a line of too-polite-to-honk Southampton matrons sat in silence."

This person also complained, "They lit up their house like a Vegas casino, which shocked some of their neighbors on the pond [Lake Agawam]," who called police several times to complain about noise and music coming from the house at night. "It is not a quality that endeared them to their neighbors, including [investor] Ezra Zilkha, [NBC New York news anchor] Chuck Scarborough, [writer] Tom Wolfe, and [financier] George McFadden [who died last year], who all cherished their quiet summer weekends."

Walter and Monica's membership application to the Bathing Corporation was blackballed, but they kept showing up on Philip Toub's guest docket for lunch anyway, until someone pointed out to them it was bad form.

Walter also tried to get into the Shinnecock Hills Golf Club, "but that died fast once Monica had a personal assistant call around to Shinnecock members inviting them to their house," says this person. "It's just not friendly to have your personal assistant call around to old club members inviting them over for a meal. . . . It smacked both of new money and being almost purposefully rude. Joining a club like Shinnecock is like joining a family. It's not expensive, but the waiting list is very long because it's very selective in inviting people to join who would fit in, in as gemütlich a way as Wasps can get. None of the members, even if they had personal assistants—which most of them are too poor to have—would use them to make a personal social call."

"If they'd just been a bit quieter for a year, it would have been better," notes a friend from Greenwich.

But the Noels—at least most of them—are not quiet. After all, Monica is half Brazilian. She effervesces, and she does things her way—even when advised not to.

So, when a friend told Monica to come to Palm Beach "very quietly" and to rent a house, not buy one, she bought. And she kept embracing everyone she saw at the local Bath and Racquet Club, because, as one friend puts it, she knows them, she likes them—why wouldn't she hug them?

On Mustique, where the family bought Yemanjá, in 2000, the story repeated itself. The Noels alienated people, especially the old-fashioned Brits who form the core of the society on this privately owned island, in the Grenadines. Mustique's unofficial ruler, Baron Glenconner, also known as Colin Tenant, says that, uninvited, they brought a houseful of guests to look around the house he was staying in, which belonged to Prince and Princess Rupert of Loewenstein. He was appalled. "They just turned up inside the house," he recalls. "I went to a cocktail party early on—they never stop having cocktail parties at Mustique—and he [Walter] drove me along the balcony into a corner. I couldn't get out. And I didn't want to be aggressed in that kind of way. I was there for purely decorative and social purposes, not to be pestered. So I said, 'You're pests! You're worms!' "

This year the Noels rented out Yemanjá for the holidays, and the *New York Post* ran a gossip item suggesting that Mustique regulars were delighted by their absence. "The No. 1 comment this winter was how much nicer it is on the island without the Noels," the piece claimed. It continued, quoting one neighbor, "If you were playing tennis, they would all come onto the side of the courts and talk so loudly you had to stop your game because you couldn't concentrate. . . . We were all so relieved that they [wouldn't] come to the main island courts anymore."

A family friend thinks the Noels' reputation for brashness is not really deserved—except, perhaps, by Piedrahita, who seemingly likes to talk about his plane and boat—and stems in part from Monica's high energy and constant motion: one moment she's planning a tennis game, the next an aerobic walk, the next a dinner for 70. However well intentioned, she can "overwhelm" people, says a friend. "She had the same qualities in Greenwich that people thought were charming, and then when it got upped by all the money and the grander lifestyle, people got jealous."

A close friend of the family's, who works in finance, says of Monica, "We've had dinner with them when we were down there [in Mustique]. The tennis pro and his girlfriend were having dinner the same night at their house. And so was the guy who worked on the house and did the wiring. . . . She's that type of person. She invites everybody on the beach." The downside of this, he explains, is that she expects others to be as hospitable. But not everyone wants to have 20 people to lunch.

Wealthy and aristocratic clients around the world, including the King of Spain, are said to be livid with Walter and his sons-in-law—in particular Piedrahita, who was the most aggressive salesman of all and who courted wealthy and titled Europeans. "The marketing of F.G.G. was very much done as a team effort," Piedrahita explains. "So I, along with others at the firm, were successful in penetrating European markets." Many of Piedrahita's closest friends in Latin America and some in Europe lost massive amounts of money with F.G.G. and Madoff.

Piedrahita is the son of a Colombian commodities trader. He attended Boston University and after graduation pursued a career as a trader. In the early 1980s he got a job at Balfour Maclaine, a Wall Street commodity-futures trading company, to sell rich individuals, such as Fernando Botero (son of the famous painter), two highly leveraged futures funds. Says a source, "He arrived at Balfour Maclaine fresh from school—he had absolutely no trading skills at all and no financial background. He was hired to sell Tapman One and Tapman Two to his rich friends in South America. The funds were disastrously highly leveraged, and he sold and sold and sold to all his family, all his friends. . . . He was a star at that. Until of course both funds went bust—and the family friends like the Boteros appeared in the office, literally fuming. The rest of us refused to sell the funds. . . . I find it hard to believe the Noels didn't know about this—it was widely, widely known, and the South American community in New York is a small world." (Piedrahita's stints at Balfour Maclaine and another firm, at which he started his career, Emanuel & Company, were left out of his official F.G.G. bio.)

Still, Piedrahita survived jobs at Merrill Lynch, Prudential Bache, and Shearson Lehman to found his own firm, Littlestone Associates. He joined F.G.G. as an equal partner with Tucker and Noel in 1997 and, according to one person, "put the strategy on steroids." No longer wanting to focus on individual investors, Piedrahita told a friend over lunch at the Club 55, in St. Tropez, "I want to take F.G.G. to a whole new level. You can never make enough fees from rich individuals—I want to get institutions."

In the wake of the successful public flotations of such financial companies as Blackstone, Fortress, and GLG, Piedrahita wanted to either sell F.G.G. or take it public. The company hired banker Charles Murphy (an alumnus of Deutsche Bank, Morgan Stanley, and Credit Suisse) and was searching for an investment bank to manage the process. A close family friend who works at a big bank held a meeting with Piedrahita, Murphy, and others at the end of 2007. Ironically, according to the friend, the difficulty for F.G.G. was that Madoff had made it clear he wanted no part of the scrutiny he'd have to undergo to be part of any sale of F.G.G. or public offering. "People [potential buyers and bankers] said, 'What a shame. The valuations are going to stink because Madoff won't be participating in it,'" recalls the friend.

One investor is furious that this didn't set off alarm bells: "These guys had a financial responsibility. . . . If Bernie tells you, O.K., you cannot come here [and do due diligence], and they don't do something drastic, like trying to find out what the hell's going on . . . that's outrageous."

Other investment firms and professionals had had doubts about Madoff for years. Goldman Sachs and Credit Suisse told their private clients that he was not on their approved list of broker dealers. Around 2003, Société Générale issued a letter advising its clients to steer well clear of him. From 1992 to 2008 the S.E.C. was called on eight times to investigate Madoff. But each time, as we now know, the agency came away with nothing. It even infamously ignored the detailed letter it received in 2005 from Boston-based investor Harry Markopolos titled "The World's Biggest Hedge Fund Is a Fraud."

It has been reported that in 2005 the S.E.C. spoke to F.G.G. about its concerns over Madoff. A person close to F.G.G. confirms that Tucker talked to the S.E.C. then. When asked if anyone at the firm had thought it should do some extra due diligence on Madoff's strategy as a result, someone close to the company says that in fact F.G.G. felt greater comfort than ever about Madoff's operation because the S.E.C. had found nothing wrong. "If the S.E.C. had cleared him, this was actually a reason to sell Madoff more, not less," says this person.

Sources close to F.G.G. have said that the Noels will argue in court that, if the S.E.C. didn't spot Madoff's fraud, why should they have? But, unlike F.G.G., the S.E.C. was not taking investors' money and charging 1 percent in fees and 20 percent of profits for looking after it. Fairfield's prospectuses bragged that "FGG's due diligence process is deeper and broader than a typical fund of funds, resembling that of an asset management company acquiring another asset manager, rather than a passive investor entering a disposable investment." The lawsuits against F.G.G. for its role in the Madoff scandal, which now number at least three, including a class-action suit, re-state a litany of other reassurances Fairfield gave to its investors about its commitment to due diligence, risk management, and "rigorous" vetting of the fund managers it invested with. Today, many people find F.G.G.'s trust in Madoff astonishing.

Eric Weinstein, the managing director in charge of hedge funds at Neuberger Berman, formerly the money-management arm of investment bank Lehman Brothers, says basic checks on all investments should include the following: audited financial statements from a recognized accountant; independent confirmation that securities were traded at the prices claimed; and an independent custodian who holds the assets of a company to prove they actually exist. Madoff, whose auditors were a three-man team in New City, New York, few had ever heard of, met none of these standard Wall Street requirements.

Ross Intelisano, whose law firm, Rich & Intelisano, is representing clients suing Fairfield, says, "I do know that historically if you're really an adviser, and you're going to put half of your business's assets under management with one firm, then you had better have done the most unbelievable amount of due diligence before you do that. And that means stress-testing the trading strategy and talking to the auditors. F.G.G. obviously didn't do that—especially when Bernie's business is self-clearing. So there's no one to talk to except the auditors."

Adds Richard Nye, managing partner of Baker Nye, "I can understand an individual investor being vulnerable to a pitch by a 'trusted' and apparently successful friend. But for a fiduciary not to take the first baby steps in performing proper due diligence is unacceptable."

Another well-known investor says, "These [F.G.G.] guys were just a marketing machine. . . . Walter was just really a customers' man. . . . They didn't even know what questions to ask. It's malpractice. It's gross negligence. It's not criminal behavior, in my view. Nobody would do this. I mean, Walter wouldn't ruin himself. Nobody would do this. . . . You can't put amateurs in a world of grownups. . . . That's really what this is. They are amateurs." ("Fairfield Greenwich performed extensive due diligence, including regular monitoring of Madoff's trading activity," says an F.G.G. spokesman. "F.G.G. also used data to perform risk-monitoring analysis, and met and spoke with Madoff frequently. Fairfield Greenwich was also aware of due diligence performed by others, and was informed of multiple on-site visits by the National Association of Securities Dealers and the S.E.C.")

The anger toward the Noels is widespread and runs deep, but the family does not appear to understand it. Monica tells people that Walter is still her prince and that he is a victim of Madoff's, just like everyone else. "He did sales—he relied on others for due diligence," she has told friends. "He accepted Madoff's statements when they came in each month."

In an effort to keep her husband's spirits up, she's been accepting invitations to dinners in Greenwich and New York, hoping that he will be buoyed to see how many friends he has.

But this strategy has gotten a mixed reception. In the weeks after Madoff's arrest, guests at a holiday party given by the financier Wilbur Ross and his wife, Hillary, were aghast to see the Noels there. "The first guy I see is Walter Noel, and he's wearing a red velvet smoking jacket!" said one guest. "There were a lot of people there who were very, very successful investors, but none of them were saying hello to him, I can tell you."

The Noels subsequently appeared at a party at the Metropolitan Club, in Manhattan, at which former New York City mayor Rudolph Giuliani was present. (Walter donated to Giuliani's presidential campaign as well as to those of John McCain and Mitt Romney, to whom Monica also gave money.) Again, many people were shocked to see them. "They were seated very carefully . . . among friends," observes one guest. But in various publications and online outlets, including *New York* magazine's Daily Intel, their social outings were criticized as being tone-deaf—especially when juxtaposed with the tragic suicide on December 23 of Thierry de la Villehuchet. Like the Noels, de la Villehuchet was a well-connected money manager who had brought his friends—mostly wealthy Europeans, including France's Liliane Bettencourt, principal owner of L'Oréal—into Madoff's web.

Those who visit the Noels, either in Connecticut or at their Park Avenue pied-à-terre, get shown a folder of supportive letters from friends, while Monica works the phone with the energy of a woman 40 years her junior. The only time she ever slows down, some have noticed, is when she speaks to her husband. She is always solicitous of him and keeps her tone bright and cheerful.

Indications of stress are rare. One was at a dinner, when an old friend of the Noels' came over to hug them. "He looked wonderful," says this friend. But as for Monica, "she looked like a train wreck. She looked beaten. . . . She's always been a most attractive woman, but she looked awful this night. I really felt for her."

Lawyers for aggrieved clients are hell-bent on finding and seizing whatever's left of the Noels' fortune. "I've been poor before. I can be poor again," Marisa said to a friend.

In January, Andrés Piedrahita was rumored to have been kidnapped for four days and held hostage by a group of angry investors, possibly from the Russian Mob. The rumor was not true. Monica has insisted to people that F.G.G. did not have any Russian investors, and, in fact, Piedrahita was at home in Madrid. But despite his outwardly normal life, he has no doubt heard that many of his former friends and clients want nothing more to do with him.

A lavish celebration on Majorca was planned for February for Piedrahita's 50th birthday, but a cancellation notice was sent out:

> Dear Family and Friends,
>
> It is with great regret and sadness that because of recent events that you are aware of, my 50th birthday

celebration in Majorca has been cancelled. As you can
imagine, I am neither in the mood to celebrate nor
would it be appropriate to do so.

What this monster [Madoff] has done to so many
people including us is known in the bible as "an
abomination." It means an act so alien to our values
and our natures that it cannot be understood or
explained. . . . And God bless you.

Love,
Andrés

Ariane Sodi, pregnant with her fifth child, found a photographer
camped outside her door in London and was horrified. Reportedly, Matt
and Marisa Brown have considered putting their Upper East Side town
house on the market, although neighbors continue to be irritated by the
noise of renovations.

Alix Toub wondered whether it would be O.K. to celebrate her 41st
birthday quietly in Connecticut at the end of January. Her friends forced
her hand. They'd be bringing the hors d'oeuvres and the music. Monica, as
ever unstoppable, would be cooking the main course—for 60.

In February, however, New York socialites were astonished to receive
an invitation on stiff paper to a surprise party for socialite Kalliope Karella
at the 740 Park Avenue apartment of Blackstone chief executive Steve
Schwarzman and his wife, Christine. The invitation proclaimed the party
had two hostesses: Christine and Marisa Noel Brown. Since Schwarzman
had been criticized for his over-the-top 60th-birthday party, some invitees
muttered that Marisa was clueless about the backlash her participation
would almost certainly engender. Once she got wind of a problem, however,
she blamed Christine, who she claimed had put her name on the invitation
without telling her. (Christine Schwarzman declined to comment.)

Monica's chief concern remains her husband. She worries he might
suffer a stroke or a heart attack from the stress of the scandal. "He's 78
and a gentleman. How will he cope with the wolves in court?" she's asked
people. She's upset that her brother, Alex Haegler, would not go skiing in

Europe, because he feared negative coverage in the Brazilian press—because so many Brazilians had lost money with F.G.G.

And she's really upset at the trashing the Noel family has received in the press.

While Walter and her daughters turned to professionals to handle their public relations, Monica remained fearful that unless she took control the real story of who the Noels were would not be told.

Her women friends admire her courage and say you won't find a stauncher ally when you are in trouble. Now it's Monica Noel who needs her friends. As usual, she's coping by keeping frenetically busy: visiting her daughters, cheering up her husband, arranging dinners for him, and pretending for everyone's sake that everything is going to be all right.

But she let slip once to a friend, "There are times when I lie awake and think, Oh my God, what does the future hold?"—and then quickly said, "Oh, don't let anyone know I said that."

The Blame

The 100 People, Companies, Institutions, and Vices to Blame for Getting Us into This Mess

By BRUCE FEIRSTEIN

October 2009

To read about all 100–in devastating detail–please visit
vanityfair.com/online/politics/100-to-blame.

EVIL INCARNATE
Bernie Madoff

THE GRAND WIZARDS OF THE FINANCIAL APOCALYPSE
Former Fed chief Alan Greenspan
Former Treasury secretary Henry Paulson

THE GOLDMAN SACHS CABAL
There was a reason the company was nicknamed
Government Sachs. Goldman alumni:
Henry Paulson

Robert Rubin (ex–Treasury secretary)
Joshua Bolten (ex–Bush chief of staff)
Stephen Friedman (ex-head of New York Fed)
Neel Kashkari (ex-head of TARP)
And on and on

The Dark Knights of Banking
Kerry Killinger (Washington Mutual)
Dick Fuld (Lehman Brothers)
Stan O'Neal (Merrill Lynch)
Jimmy Cayne (Bear Stearns)
Sandy Weill (Citigroup)
John Thain (Merrill Lynch)
Hank Greenberg (A.I.G.)

The Weapons of Financial Destruction
Collateralized debt obligations
Credit-default swaps
Subprime mortgages
Pay-option negative-amortization adjustable-rate
    mortgages
Predatory lending schemes
Feeder funds
Arbitrage
Naked short-sellers
The invisible hand

The Lawmakers
Senator Phil Gramm (Republican; Enron)
Senator Chris Dodd (Democrat; A.I.G.)
Representative Barney Frank (Democrat; Fannie Mae)

The Eyes-Wide-Shut Regulators
William Donaldson, Chris Cox, and Linda Thomsen
    (S.E.C.)
John Reich and Darrel W. Dochow (Office of Thrift
    Supervision)

The Laws
The Taxpayer Relief Act of 1997
The Commodity Futures Modernization Act of 2000
The Community Reinvestment Act
Gramm-Leach-Bliley (repealing Glass-Steagall)

The Presidents Who Signed the Laws
Bill Clinton
George W. Bush

THE FANNIE MAE AND FREDDIE MAC GANG
Jim Johnson (former Fannie C.E.O., Obama-campaign adviser)
Franklin Raines (former Fannie C.E.O., ex–Clinton budget director)
Leland Brendsel (former Freddie C.E.O.)
Jamie Gorelick (former Fannie vice-chairman, ex–Clinton Justice Department number two)
Daniel Mudd (former Fannie C.E.O.)

THE PREDATORY LENDERS
Countrywide Financial
Ameriquest
New Century Financial
Crestline Funding
Encore
Ownit
Quick Loan Funding
No income? No job? No problem! (Bonus points to Countrywide for targeting so many government officials with its reduced-rate V.I.P. mortgage programs.)

MASTERS OF THE DARK ARTS
Blythe Masters and the Morgan Mafia (invented credit-default swaps)
Lewis Ranieri (securitized mortgages)
Quants (thought they could predict the future by looking back at the past)

THE RUBBER-STAMPERS
The discredited ratings agencies:
Moody's
Fitch
Standard & Poor's

THE MANIPULATORS
Joseph Cassano (A.I.G.)
Ralph Cioffi and Matthew Tannin (Bear Stearns)
Mark Walsh (Lehman Brothers)

THE CHEERLEADERS
Jim Cramer
Maria Bartiromo
Most of the financial press

MISCELLANEOUS MALFEASANCE
House flippers
"Fix your FICO credit score" outfits

Retention bonuses
"Maximizing shareholder value"
Detroit's Big Three

THE ENABLERS
Bloomberg terminals
CrackBerries
China
Ruth Madoff

MORAL HAZARDS
Carriers of the affluenza virus:
Russian oligarchs
30,000-square-foot Greenwich mansions
Goody bags at charity events
Corporate skyboxes
After-parties
V.I.P. rooms
Bottle service
Jacob the Jeweler
Dubai
Viagra
Lifestyle porn
Botox
Tramp stamps
Prosperity theology
Sex and the City (the shoes!)
Davos (the self-importance!)

THE GREATER FOOLS
Infantile American consumers, who bought all those
luxury S.U.V.s and wide-screen TVs they didn't need,
signed all those mortgages they didn't read, lost their
retirement accounts and jobs, and, in the end, paid for
all the bailouts.

Author Biographies

GRAYDON CARTER has been the editor of *Vanity Fair* since 1992. He edited *Vanity Fair's Hollywood* (Viking Studio, 2000), *Oscar Night* (Knopf, 2004), *Vanity Fair: The Portraits* (Abrams, 2008), *Vanity Fair's Proust Questionnaire* (Rodale, 2009), and *Vanity Fair's Presidential Profiles* (Abrams, 2010), and wrote *What We've Lost: How the Bush Administration Has Curtailed Our Freedoms, Mortgaged Our Economy, Ravaged Our Environment, and Damaged Our Standing in the World* (Farrar, Straus and Giroux, 2004). Carter served as a producer of the films *The Kid Stays in the Picture, Chicago 10, Surfwise,* and *Gonzo* and won Emmy and Peabody Awards for his work as executive producer of the CBS documentary *9/11,* which has aired in 140 countries. A former writer at *Time* and *Life,* Carter co-founded *Spy* magazine and served as the editor of *The New York Observer.* He is also an owner of the New York City restaurants the Waverly Inn, in Greenwich Village, and the Monkey Bar, on East 54th Street.

DONALD L. BARLETT and JAMES·B. STEELE joined *Vanity Fair* as contributing editors in August 2006. Regarded by many as the best investigative team in journalism, Barlett and Steele have been working together since 1971 and have won two Pulitzer Prizes and two National Magazine Awards—the only reporting team to have achieved such a feat. After spending 27 years at *The Philadelphia Inquirer,* they served for 9 years as editors-at-large at Time Inc., writing primarily for *Time* magazine. They are the authors of seven books. *America: What Went Wrong* (Andrews McMeel, 1992) became a *New York Times* best-seller, remaining on the list for eight months, and was adapted for television by Bill Moyers. *Critical Condition: How Health Care in America Became Big Business and Bad Medicine* (Doubleday, 2004) received widespread acclaim.

MARK BOWDEN, a *Vanity Fair* contributing editor, is an author, a journalist, a screenwriter, and a teacher. His book *Black Hawk Down: A Story of Modern War* (Atlantic Monthly Press, 1999), which spent more than a year on the *New York Times* best-seller list, was a finalist for the National Book Award. Bowden worked on the screenplay for *Black Hawk Down,* a film adaptation directed by Ridley Scott. Besides writing the international best-seller *Killing Pablo: The Hunt for the World's Greatest Outlaw* (Atlantic Monthly Press, 2001), which tells the story of the hunt for Colombian cocaine billionaire Pablo Escobar, Bowden is the author of *Doctor Dealer* (Warner, 1987), *Bringing the Heat* (Knopf, 1994), *Our Finest Day* (Chronicle, 2002), *Finders Keepers* (Atlantic Monthly Press, 2002), *Road Work* (Grove/Atlantic, 2004), *Guests of the Ayatollah* (Atlantic Monthly Press, 2006), and *The Best Game Ever* (Atlantic Monthly Press, 2008). He is an adjunct professor at Loyola College of Maryland and lives in Oxford, Pennsylvania.

BRYAN BURROUGH has been with *Vanity Fair* since 1992, becoming a special correspondent for the magazine in 1995. He has reported on a wide range of topics, from the events that led to the war in Iraq to the battle for LVMH. His profile subjects have included Sumner Redstone, Larry Ellison, Michael Ovitz, and Ivan Boesky. Prior to joining *Vanity Fair,* Burrough was an investigative reporter at *The Wall Street Journal.* In 1990, with *Journal* colleague John Helyar, he co-authored *Barbarians at the Gate* (HarperCollins), which was No. 1 on the *New York Times* nonfiction best-seller list for 39 weeks. Burrough's other books include *Vendetta: American Express and the Smearing of Edmund Safra* (HarperCollins, 1992), *Dragonfly: NASA and the Crisis Aboard Mir* (HarperCollins, 1998), and *The Big Rich: The Rise and Fall of the Greatest Texas Oil Fortunes* (Penguin, 2009). He is also the author of *Public Enemies: America's Greatest Crime Wave and the Birth of the FBI, 1933–34* (Penguin Press, 2004), which was made into a film directed by Michael Mann and starring Johnny Depp as John Dillinger.

BRUCE FEIRSTEIN is a journalist and screenwriter who has been a contributing editor at *Vanity Fair* since 1994. Best known for the three James Bond movies he wrote or co-wrote, *GoldenEye, Tomorrow Never Dies,* and *The World Is Not Enough,* he is also the author of several books, including *Real Men Don't Eat Quiche* (Pocket Books, 1982). He was a contributing editor at *Spy* magazine, has written editorials for *The New York Times,* and has been published in *New York* magazine, *The New Yorker, The New Republic, The Washington Post,* the *Los Angeles Times,* and *The New York Observer,* where he was a "Diary" columnist for 14 years. He has also written video games, and began his career writing political advertising.

NIALL FERGUSON is Laurence A. Tisch Professor of History at Harvard University and William Ziegler Professor of Business Administration at Harvard Business School. He is also a senior research fellow at Jesus College, Oxford University, and a senior fellow at the Hoover Institution, Stanford University. A prolific commentator on contemporary politics and economics, Ferguson writes and reviews regularly for the British and American press and is the author of eight books, including, most recently, *The Ascent of Money* (Penguin Press, 2008). He is a contributing editor for the *Financial Times.* In 2004 *Time* magazine named him one of the world's hundred most influential people.

MICHAEL LEWIS became a *Vanity Fair* contributing editor in February 2009. He has published nine books, all but one of them *New York Times* best-sellers, including *Home Game: An Accidental Guide to Fatherhood* (Norton, 2009); *The Blind Side* (Norton, 2006); *Moneyball* (Norton, 2003), an examination of baseball that focuses on the way markets value people; *The New New Thing* (Norton, 1999), about Silicon Valley during the Internet boom; and *Liar's Poker* (Norton, 1989), based in part on Lewis's experience as an investment banker on Wall Street. He writes often for *The New York Times Magazine,* and his articles have also appeared in *The New Yorker, Gourmet, Sports Illustrated, Foreign Affairs,* and *Poetry* magazine. He has served as an editor and a columnist at the British weekly *The Spectator* and as a senior editor and campaign correspondent at *The New Republic.* For the BBC, he made a four-part documentary on the social consequences of the Internet, and he has filmed and narrated short pieces for ABC's *Nightline.*

DAVID MARGOLICK is a contributing editor at both *Vanity Fair* and *Newsweek.* From 1981 to 1996, Margolick was a law reporter for the metropolitan section of *The New York Times* and then the newspaper's national legal-affairs correspondent. In that capacity he covered the trials of William Kennedy Smith, Lorena Bobbitt, and O. J. Simpson. From 1988 to 1995 he also wrote the *Times's* "At the Bar" column. His books include *Beyond Glory: Joe Louis vs. Max Schmeling, and a World on the Brink* (Knopf, 2005); *Strange Fruit: The Biography of a Song* (HarperCollins, 2001); *At the Bar: The Passions and Peccadilloes of American Lawyers* (Simon & Schuster, 1995), a compilation of his essays; and *Undue Influence: The Epic Battle for the Johnson & Johnson Fortune* (Morrow, 1993).

BETHANY McLEAN came aboard at *Vanity Fair* in 2008. Previously, she had been an editor-at-large at *Fortune*, where she covered an array of subjects, from Goldman Sachs to Barry Diller and his company, InterActiveCorp, to the strange world of the Masters of Wine. In early 2001, she wrote a skeptical story about Enron, which was then a high-flying company with a stock price of around $80 a share. Her article asked the simple question "How Does Enron Make Money?," and it is widely viewed as the first critical, in-depth piece about the company to run in a national publication. Along with Peter Elkind, she wrote the definitive book on the firm, *The Smartest Guys in the Room: The Amazing Rise and Scandalous Fall of Enron* (Penguin, 2003).

NINA MUNK has been a contributing editor at *Vanity Fair* since 2001, reporting on the world of business and finance. Her work has appeared not only in *Vanity Fair* but also in *The New York Times, The New York Times Magazine, The New Yorker, Fortune,* and *Forbes.* Before joining *Vanity Fair,* Munk was a senior writer at *Fortune* and a senior editor at *Forbes.* She has published two books, *Fools Rush In: Steve Case, Jerry Levin, and the Unmaking of AOL Time Warner* (HarperCollins, 2004) and *The Art of Clairtone: The Making of a Design Icon* (McClelland & Stewart, 2008). She is currently working on a book for Doubleday about the crusade to end extreme poverty in Africa.

CULLEN MURPHY joined *Vanity Fair* as its editor-at-large in 2006. He spent more than two decades at *The Atlantic Monthly,* serving as managing editor, after stints at *Change* magazine and *The Wilson Quarterly.* He has also written a number of books, among them *Rubbish! The Archaeology of Garbage* (HarperCollins, 1992), with co-author William L. Rathje; *The Word According to Eve: Women and the Bible in Ancient Times and Our Own* (Houghton Mifflin, 1998); and *Are We Rome? The Fall of an Empire and the Fate of America* (Houghton Mifflin, 2007). For many years he wrote the "Prince Valiant" comic strip with his father, the illustrator John Cullen Murphy.

TODD S. PURDUM was named *Vanity Fair'*s national editor in 2006, after 23 years at *The New York Times,* where he started as a copyboy in 1982. His last *Times* assignment was as a correspondent in the Washington bureau, covering topics from politics to policy to pop culture, and he also served as a diplomatic and White House correspondent. From 1997 until 2001, Purdum was the paper's Los Angeles bureau chief. He also held the positions of metropolitan reporter and City Hall bureau chief in New York. Along with the staff of the *Times,* he is the author of *A Time of Our Choosing: America's War in Iraq* (Times Books, 2003), and his work has appeared in *Vanity Fair's Presidential Profiles* (Abrams, 2010) and in successive volumes of *The Best American Political Writing* (PublicAffairs).

MARK SEAL joined *Vanity Fair* as a contributing editor in 2003. Since then he has written about high life (the incredible world of con man Clark Rockefeller) and low (the heist of the 2001 Oscar statuettes), the making of *The Godfather*, the feuding kings of reality TV, and the Agnelli dynasty of Italy and has collaborated with gonzo journalist Hunter S. Thompson on a piece that helped secure the release of a young woman imprisoned for a murder she didn't commit. Seal's most recent book, *Wildflower: An Extraordinary Life and Untimely Death in Africa* (Random House, 2009), about Joan Root, the slain wildlife filmmaker and naturalist, has been optioned by Working Title Films and Julia Roberts's production company, with Roberts set to star as Root. Prior to joining *Vanity Fair*, Seal wrote for a variety of magazines and newspapers and served as a collaborator on almost 20 nonfiction books for major publishers.

MICHAEL SHNAYERSON became a contributing editor at *Vanity Fair* in 1986 and has since written more than 75 stories for the magazine, investigating politicians and business leaders, environmental hazards and government corruption, real-estate scandals and life in his own neighborhood—the Hamptons. He began his career in 1976 as a reporter at the *Santa Fe Reporter* and moved to *Time* as a staff writer in 1978. In 1980 he became editor in chief of *Avenue*. He has been a consulting editor at *Condé Nast Traveler* since its inception in 1987. Shnayerson is the author of *Irwin Shaw: A Biography* (Putnam, 1989), *The Car That Could: The Inside Story of GM's Revolutionary Electric Vehicle* (Random House, 1996), and *Coal River* (Farrar, Straus and Giroux, 2008), and he is the co-author, with Mark J. Plotkin, of *The Killers Within: The Deadly Rise of Drug-Resistant Bacteria* (Little, Brown, 2002).

ELEANOR SQUILLARI served as Bernie Madoff's secretary for more than 20 years and co-authored a 9,000-word article about her former boss in *Vanity Fair's* June 2009 issue. After spending three months helping the F.B.I. gather evidence against Madoff, Squillari, a 59-year-old mother of two from Staten Island, returned a call from *V.F.*'s Mark Seal. Together, Seal and Squillari ended up collaborating on a first-person account of Squillari's time with Madoff, whom she knew as well as anyone outside his family.

JOSEPH E. STIGLITZ is University Professor at Columbia University. Stiglitz served on President Bill Clinton's economic team as a member and then chairman of the U.S. Council of Economic Advisers in the mid-1990s before joining the World Bank as chief economist and senior vice president. In 2001, Stiglitz accepted a joint chaired professorship at Columbia Business School, the Graduate School of Arts and Sciences, and the School of International and Public Affairs. That same year he was awarded the Nobel Prize for Economics. Stiglitz has been a fellow of the Econometric Society since the age of 29 and is a member of the National Academy of Sciences, the American Academy of Arts and Sciences, and the American Philosophical Association, and a foreign member of the British Academy and the Royal Society. A recipient of the prestigious John Bates Clark Medal, he was a Fulbright scholar at Cambridge University, held the Drummond Professorship at All Souls College, Oxford, and has taught at M.I.T., Yale, Stanford, and Princeton. His most recent book is *Freefall: America, Free Markets, and the Sinking of the World Economy* (Norton, 2010).

VICKY WARD joined *Vanity Fair* as a contributing editor in August 2001. Prior to that, she had been the executive editor of *Talk* magazine and features editor and news-features editor of the *New York Post*. She began her career in the U.K. as the editor of *The Independent*'s gossip column and was a runner-up for the Catherine Pakenham Award for feature writing, England's most prestigious honor for young women journalists. Her work has appeared in *The Spectator, The New York Times, New York Press, Harpers & Queen, Marie Claire,* British *GQ, The Sunday Times Magazine, The Daily Telegraph,* the London *Times,* and the *Daily Mail.* Ward, who has been an on-air contributor to CNBC since 2008 and an op-ed columnist for the London *Evening Standard*, is the author of *The Great Mistake: The Fall of Lehman Brothers and the Weekend That Changed the World* (Wiley, 2010).

Acknowledgments

Editor	**Graydon Carter**
V.F. Books Editor	David Friend
Managing Editor	Chris Garrett
Design Director	David Harris
Production Director	Martha Hurley
Editorial Advisers	Cullen Murphy, Peter Newcomb
Designers	Angela Panichi, Piper Vitale
Assistant Editor	Feifei Sun

We are indebted to our colleagues at HarperCollins and Harper Perennial: David Hirshey, George Quraishi, Carrie Kania, Cal Morgan, Dori Carlson, and Amy Vreeland, with special thanks to Rupert Murdoch.

We commend *Vanity Fair*'s Dori Amarito, Dina Amarito-DeShan, John Banta, Aimée Bell, Dana Brown, Peter Devine, David Foxley, Anne Fulenwider, SunHee C. Grinnell, Heather Halberstadt, Bruce Handy, Michael Hogan, Claire Howorth, Punch Hutton, Jonathan Kelly, Ellen Kiell, Beth Kseniak, Wayne Lawson, Anjali Lewis, Sara Marks, Amanda Meigher, Edward J. Menicheschi, Austin Merrill, Brenda Oliveri, Elise O'Shaughnessy, Henry Porter, Jeannie Rhodes, Michael Roberts, Anthony Rotunno, Jane Sarkin, Krista Smith, Doug Stumpf, Robert Walsh, Julie Weiss, and Susan White, along with everyone on the magazine's art, copy, research, special-projects, photography, production, public-relations, and Web staffs.

For their impeccable production work, our gratitude goes to *Vanity*

Fair's Beth Bartholomew, Laura Bell, Valerie Bitici, Kate Brindisi, Marsha Cottrell, Pat Craven, Chris George, Sumana Ghosh, Leslie Hertzog, Michael Hipwell, H. Scott Jolley, Joel Katz, Theresa Lee, Timothy Mislock, Susan Rasco, Nancy Sampson, Anderson Tepper, and Julia Wachtel.

We wish to thank the *Vanity Fair* research department, including Mary Flynn, David Gendelman, Brendan Barr, Kathryn Belgiorno, Simon Brennan, Michelle Ciarrocca, Alison Forbes, Brian Gallagher, David Georgi, Laura Griffin, Marnie Hanel, Ben Kalin, Matt Kapp, Mike Sacks, Helen Vera, and Callie Wright, as well as the copy department's David Fenner, Adam Nadler, John Branch, James Cholakis, Scott Ferguson, Florence Fletcher, Diane Hodges, Mary Lyn Maiscott, Sophie Miodownik, Robert Morrow, S. P. Nix, and Sylvia Topp.

And we are also grateful to our friends and colleagues at Sabin, Bermant & Gould; the Wylie Agency; and the Rights and Permissions Department of Condé Nast Publications.